W9-CHP-030

Civic Myths

Cultural Studies of the United States

Alan Trachtenberg, editor

☆

Editorial Advisory Board

Michele Bogart

Karen Halttunen

Mae Henderson

James Livingston

Eric Lott

Miles Orvell

Jeffrey Stewart

The

University

of North

Carolina

Press

☆

Chapel

Hill

BROOK THOMAS

Civic Myths

A Law-and-
Literature
Approach
to Citizenship

© 2007
The University of North Carolina Press
All rights reserved
Designed and typeset in Quadraat and Filosofia
by Eric M. Brooks
Manufactured in the United States of America

The paper in this book meets the guidelines
for permanence and durability of the Committee
on Production Guidelines for Book Longevity
of the Council on Library Resources.

Library of Congress Cataloging-in-Publication Data
Thomas, Brook.
Civic myths: a law-and-literature approach to
citizenship / by Brook Thomas.
    p. cm. — (Cultural studies of the United States)
Includes bibliographical references and index.
ISBN 978-0-8078-3153-3 (cloth: alk. paper)
ISBN 978-0-8078-5846-2 (pbk.: alk. paper)
1. American fiction — 19th century — History
and criticism. 2. Citizenship in literature.
3. Citizenship — United States — History. I. Title.
PS374.C49T48   2007
813.009 — dc22   2007011062

Parts of Chapter 2 appeared previously in somewhat
different form in "Citizen Hester: *The Scarlet Letter* as
Civic Myth," *American Literary History* 13 (2001): 181–211,
published by Oxford University Press. Parts of Chapter
6 appeared previously in somewhat different form
in "*China Men, United States v. Wong Kim Ark*, and the
Question of Citizenship," *American Quarterly* 50 (1998):
689–717, published by Johns Hopkins University Press.
They are reprinted here with permission.

cloth   11 10 09 08 07   5 4 3 2 1
paper   11 10 09 08 07   5 4 3 2 1

To Peter Ramsay Thomas

Contents

Illustrations

Preface

This is my third book cross-examining documents of U.S. literary and legal history. As I wrote twenty years ago, in performing those cross-examinations I am not claiming that law is the key that will unlock all of the mysteries of works of literature or that literature is the key that will open up a full understanding of the law. I am certainly not claiming to uncover a hidden "logic" of an age.[1] I am, however, trying to provide a perspective on literary and legal history as well as aspects of U.S. culture and society that is not available when these relatively autonomous disciplines are studied alone. In this book, I hope to provide a fresh perspective on issues of citizenship.

I have been working on the book for over a decade. History did not take a pause while I researched and wrote. Some of the issues I touch on, such as the complicated relation between legal and illegal immigration in the chapter on *China Men*, were hot-button items when I began and remain so today. But I had no idea that my discussion of different types of ballots in the chapter on *Huckleberry Finn* would take on added significance because of disputed Florida returns in the 2000 presidential election. Nor did I know that the conflict between civil liberties and national security treated in the chapters on "The Man without a Country" and *Ex parte Milligan* would be so relevant to post-9/11 debates. For the most part, I have felt no need to call attention to such connections. Readers are capable of making them for themselves. Nonetheless, they and others—including ones I cannot now predict—give me hope that the passage of time will not make all I have to say irrelevant.

F. O. Matthiessen ends his preliminary discussion of "Method and Scope" for *American Renaissance* by quoting Louis Sullivan: "In a democracy there can be one fundamental test of citizenship, namely: Are you using such gifts as you possess for or against the people?"[2] In writing, I have been guided by those words at the same time that the works I write about have alerted me to dangers in even the most democratic appeals to "the people."

Acknowledgments

Without support from various friends and family members, I never would have found the time and effort to write this book. A fellowship from the National Endowment for the Humanities combined with sabbatical credit gave me a year to finish it. The School of Humanities at the University of California, Irvine, provided additional financial support. I tried out arguments on audiences at the University of California, Davis, the University of Constance, the University of Kansas, the Kennedy Institute for North American Studies at the Free University of Berlin, the University of Oregon, Stanford University, and the University of Washington. I benefited from the exchange of ideas those occasions generated. Robert Ferguson and Robert Levine supported fellowship applications. Many people commented on various drafts of parts of the book. They include Roy Blount, Louis Budd, Wai Chee Dimock, Myra Jehlen, Jayne Lewis, Lucy Maddox, Steve Mailloux, Robert Milder, Richard Millington, Frederick Newberry, and Henry Wonham. Werner Sollors gave some helpful tips as I worked on the conclusion. At UCI, I have learned much from Julia Lupton's and Étienne Balibar's shared interest in the literature of citizenship as well as from Richard Kroll's and Vicky Silver's historical perspective on the literature of political dissent. Students, some in the process of procuring citizenship, have been engaged listeners, discussants, and critics. The instructional staff of Humanities Core Course helped shape ideas. Gail Hart and Vivian Folkenflik deserve special mention. John Seckinger and Drew Newman wrote seminar papers that led to new research. John Barton wrote a dissertation that did the same. Two reviewers for the University of North Carolina Press provided very helpful comments, as did Sian Hunter. It has been a pleasure working with the entire production crew at the press.

Civic Myths

1   Introduction

Working on/with Civic Myths

The last decade and a half has witnessed a "return of the citizen."[1] There are a number of reasons for this renewed interest. One is globalization. Globalization places pressure on the relative autonomy of the nation-state, which has defined citizenship since the demise of the medieval city-state. National boundaries are still in place, but they seem to play less of a role in many important transactions that affect people's daily lives. For instance, Arjun Appadurai identifies five alternative "landscapes" that characterize contemporary global configurations: ethnoscapes, mediascapes, technoscapes, finanscapes, and ideoscapes. For Appadurai, these flows of people, images, technologies, capital, and ideas render the territorial boundaries of nation-states obsolete.[2] Even if talk of the nation-state's demise is premature, the increased fluidity of national boundaries does affect citizenship.[3]

For instance, by some estimates, soon 25 percent of people living in countries with modern industrial economies will not be citizens of those countries.[4] That condition has led some to advocate returning to the city as a more logical unit for citizenship. Indeed, some cities have extended municipal "citizenship" rights to residents who are not citizens of the nation, recognizing their vested interest in the community by allowing them to vote in local elections.[5]

The increased flow of people across national boundaries has also challenged the idea of a unified national culture. Countries that once prided themselves on their homogeneity now recognize their multicultural makeup. The result is arguments for "multicultural" and "cultural" citizenship. Both defend the right of groups to have full citizenship while maintaining their cultural practices. For instance, in *Multicultural Citizenship* Will Kymlicka offers a sophisticated argument for group rights.[6] Similarly, Renato Rosaldo calls "cultural citizenship" the "right to be different (in terms of race, ethnicity, or native language) . . . without compromising one's right to belong, in the sense of participating in the nation-state's democratic processes."[7]

In a different context, however, cultural citizenship reaffirms the older notion of cultural homogeneity. With the move toward economic and even political unity in Western Europe, some have turned to culture as the primary realm to distinguish national identity. Concerned about the xenophobic sentiments that such arguments can foster, major thinkers, like Jürgen Habermas and Étienne Balibar, have theorized about citizenship with the prospect of European citizenship in mind. Habermas, for instance, argues that a "political culture," not a shared language or "ethnic and cultural origins," "must serve as the common denominator for a constitutional patriotism which simultaneously sharpens an awareness of the multiplicity and integrity of the different forms of life which coexist in a multicultural society."[8]

There is even a third way of conceiving of cultural citizenship, one that has more to do with Appadurai's mediascapes than with his ethnoscapes, with culture as an aesthetic category more than as an anthropological one. In a world of changing media, possibilities of citizenship, some have argued, will be affected as much or more in the realm of culture rather than in the realm of politics or economics.[9]

Other developments can be traced to events of 1989. For one, by eliminating the most obvious barrier to the worldwide flows of economic capitalism, the demise of the Soviet empire helped to generate the present obsession with globalization. Also, once the West was no longer pressured to wage an ideological battle with the Soviets, flaws in the practice of citizenship in Western, liberal democracies were much more readily acknowledged. One result has been a reconsideration of the work of T. H. Marshall, the most influential theorist of citizenship in the 1950s and 1960s. Marshall's model grew out of the modern, democratic social welfare state that emerged in Europe from the ruins of World War II. He argued that citizenship had developed by guaranteeing three rights in chronological order: civil rights, political rights, and social rights. Civil rights gave all citizens equality before the law. Political rights allowed them to participate in the politics of rule. Social rights gave them basic economic and social security.[10]

If, on one hand, today's arguments for cultural rights simply extend Marshall's model by adding another right, on the other, his focus on rights and entitlements rendered his model incapable of accounting for the decline in citizenly participation in liberal democracies, signaled most poignantly by poor voter participation. If for conservatives that focus is itself a major cause of citizenly apathy, even leftist advocates of "radical democracy," like Chantal Mouffe, have acknowledged problems with Marshall's model and have sought new models of "active citizenship."[11] Indeed, for many, the "velvet" revolutions of 1989 inspired hope in the ability of citizens to effect important political change through grassroots, participatory democracy, even in the face of the modern bureaucratic state.

This renewed interest in citizenship is prevalent in the United States. Mark Weiner reports that "in The New York Times, the phrase 'American identity' appeared 14 times from 1980–84; 17 from 1985–89; 47 from 1990–94; 104 from 1995–99." There was an even more dramatic increase in the Lexis database for "Major Papers" that includes the Los Angeles Times, Washington Post, and others.[12] And that period of time precedes the events of 9/11, which further reinforced the importance of citizenship. On one hand, they led to a resurgence of patriotic feeling that increased many people's sense of national belonging. On the other, the "war on terrorism" has drawn renewed attention to the importance of civil liberties for U.S. citizens. It has also demonstrated how important citizenship is, since suspected terrorists who are citizens have significantly more rights under U.S. law than aliens.[13] At the same time, the fear of alien attacks has mobilized those concerned with protecting the nation's borders at the same time that it has highlighted how porous those borders are.

Initially ignited by social scientists, the "explosion of interest in citizenship"[14] has had an impact on studies of American literature. In the 1990s "citizenship" began to appear with great frequency in the titles of scholarly books and essays. In 2005 the American Literature section of the Modern Language Association chose citizenship as the topic to unite a discussion of its various divisions. The issues of concern for literary critics overlap with those of social scientists. Advocates of global and "postnational" American studies relish the opportunity to explore globalization's effect on traditional notions of citizenship, and more and more of them are exploring possibilities of transnational citizenship.[15] Similarly, disciplinary training makes various versions of cultural and multicultural citizenship especially popular topics.

Glenn Hendler identifies two trends in literary studies. One conceives of citizenship as "interior and cultural"; the other, in relation to "exterior forces." Indicated by terms such as "imagined community, affective identity, or national symbolic," the former thinks of citizenship as a "subjective process, as an affective dynamic," described by Lauren Berlant as "a relation among strangers who learn to feel [citizenship] as a common identity . . . a sense of community or mass intimacy." Exploring issues of migration, immigration, diaspora, and empire, the latter thinks of citizenship in political and economic terms. Generally, literary critics have paid more attention to affective notions of citizenship, often using the term much more broadly than political scientists and historians do. Even so, in one way or another, most try to combine Hendler's two trends as they use citizenship as a category to chart the simultaneous formation of psychological and political subjects.[16]

I too am interested in how citizenship affects and is affected by interior states of subjectivity, although as I will make clear, I take issue with the theoretical model many literary critics use to explore that relationship. One of my chapters will also deal with the challenge transnational migration poses to existing determinations of citizenship. Nonetheless, my primary focus remains on national citizenship. This is not because imagining alternatives to it lacks importance. On the contrary, I learn from and encourage work that does so. Nonetheless, as Balibar, one of the most sophisticated advocates of transnational citizenship, acknowledges, even though we are more than simply a "national being, . . . we cannot of our own accord escape this determination."[17] Work on transnational citizenship by no means rules out continued work on national citizenship.

My approach is indicated by my title. *Civic Myths* plays off the title of the most important recent work on the history of citizenship in the United States: political scientist Rogers Smith's *Civic Ideals*. Using a database of legislation and judicial decisions through the Progressive Era, Smith convincingly demonstrates that U.S. citizenship has been defined by conflicting traditions: liberalism, republicanism, and what he calls "inegalitarian, ascriptive traditions of Americanism."[18] I both endorse that argument and, more than most literary critics, share Smith's interest in the role of the legal system. But I also focus on literary analysis.

The bulk of my book is four fairly long chapters that, drawing on legal analysis, relate different kinds of citizenship to literary works: the good citizen and Nathaniel Hawthorne's *The Scarlet Letter*, the patriotic citizen and Edward Everett Hale's "The Man without a Country," the independent citizen and Mark Twain's *Adventures of Huckleberry Finn*, and the immigrant citizen and Maxine Hong Kingston's *China Men*.[19] I also look at the "cult of Lincoln" from multiple perspectives.[20] The concern with Lincoln generates a separate chapter on the 1866 Supreme Court case of *Ex parte Milligan*. Although each chapter examines a different, if sometimes overlapping, model of citizenship and related legal issues, these chapters are case studies that make no claim to provide an exhaustive account of U.S. citizenship or even how all works of literature relate to citizenship. They do, however, engage issues raised about U.S. citizenship by political scientists, legal historians, and others, such as Smith, Weiner, Judith Shklar, Linda Bosniak, T. Alexander Aleinikoff, James Kettner, Michael Schudson, and Kenneth Karst.[21]

The book has three goals. First, and most important, it tries to add to our understanding of both the country's dynamic sense of citizenship and the complexity of these four literary works by showing how they work on/ with various civic myths. Second, it speculates on how a work's engagement with civic myths can, in some instances, help account for that work's accrual of cultural capital. Third, it tries to make a case for the role of selected works of literature in civic education.

"Myth," of course, can have many meanings. The notion of civic myths draws on one articulated by René Wellek and Austin Warren, who state that "in a wider sense, myth comes to mean any anonymously composed story telling of origins and destinies: the explanations a society offers its young of why the world is and why we do as we do, its pedagogic images of the nature and destiny of man."[22] Smith, for instance, defines a civic myth as "a myth used to explain why persons form a people, usually indicating how a political community originated, who is eligible for membership, who is not and why, and what the community's values and aims are."[23] The term, however, does not originate with him. In "The Myth of Citizenship," Michael Ignatieff refers to the "civic myth" of Cincinnatus that was so important for the Roman republic.[24] Indeed, it proved important for the United States as well, with George Washington becoming the American Cincinnatus.[25]

Civic myths in the United States are numerous and varied.[26] Some exemplify broad themes such as the "virgin land," "the land of opportunity," or "manifest destiny." They can also be about individuals, such as the numerous stories about the "founding fathers." Or they can give meaning to various national symbols, such as the story of Betsy Ross and the flag. Many fit into Robert Michels's categories of der Mythos der Woher, the myth of national origin, and der Mythos der Wohin, the myth of national destiny.[27] "In America," Max Lerner wrote years ago, "the two converged in the myth of a democratic revolution and a revolutionary democracy."[28] Even if Lerner's "revolutionary" is a bit too strong, the myth of a perpetually renewing democracy that remains true to its founding ideals persists in the United States.

Smith describes the "great, perhaps indispensable value" of civic myths, which enable "a people to live together fruitfully and stably."[29] Their ability to do so is illuminated by Claude Lévi-Strauss's understanding of myth. For Lévi-Strauss, myth serves as cultural "glue," binding a community or a people together through imagined stories that respond to real social contraditions or tensions.[30] In the *Poetics* Aristotle opposes *mythos*, as narrative and story, to *logos*, as dialectical discourse. Dialectical contradictions incapable of logical resolution, it seems, generate stories. So long as those contradictions persist, stories responding to them will persist.

Resulting from such contradictions, civic myths are a particular version of what elsewhere I have called cultural narratives. Stories without specific authors, cultural narratives help give meaning to social practices that cannot necessarily find a basis in rational logic. Despite claims to the contrary, the law, Robert Cover has argued, is such a practice. "No set of legal institutions or prescriptions," he claims, "exists apart from the narratives that locate it and give it meaning." To try, as Cover proposes, to understand law "in the context of the narratives that give it meaning" requires engaging those narratives as well as the logical claims of the law.[31]

A basic premise of this study is that the concept of citizenship itself is inhabited by contradictions that generate civic myths, which, in turn, help give meaning to the practices of citizenship within particular cultures. Those contradictions can arise out of tensions between different models of citizenship. J. G. A. Pocock, for instance, identifies two basic concepts of citizenship: Greek and Roman. The Greek is political; the Roman, legal. The Greek is concerned with citizens' participation in government; the Roman, with rights and duties.[32] As important as Pocock's distinction is, there are differences within his differences, and this book treats some of them. It will also examine contradictions that develop out of tensions between (1) citizens' relations to noncitizens, (2) citizens' relations to one another, and (3) citizens' relations to the state.

Etymologically, "citizen" originally designated the resident of a city, especially one with civic rights and privileges that were linked to the protection a city provided against outsiders.[33] It implied, in another words, a special status, different from that of a "denizen," to which it is also linked. But it has also implied more. According to Peter Riesenberg the concept of citizenship has proved so durable "because it has been viewed not only as an instrument useful in controlling the passions and attenuating private concerns, but also as a means well suited to draw out the best in people." Even so, Riesenberg also notes that one of the "principal functions" of citizenship "has been as an agent or principle of exclusion. . . . It has encompassed and defined privilege and constituted the means to discriminate against non-citizens."[34]

One notion of citizenship that would seem to avoid this tension is the cosmopolitan one of a "citizen of the world," or what Cicero called *civem totius mundi*. But precisely because everyone is potentially a citizen of the world, for the concept to have meaning, it has to denote more than simply an inhabitant of earth. Thus, whether the citizen is defined, as the *Oxford English Dictionary* does, as "one who is at home, and claims his rights, everywhere" or, as Francis Bacon defined him, as someone "Gracious and Courteous to strangers," a citizen of the world is differentiated from those who lack these cosmopolitan qualities.[35] This is not to say that the concept is, therefore, discredited. On the contrary, the ability of citizenship to evoke qualities such as courteousness, graciousness, and a sense of feeling at home shows why it seems capable of drawing out the best in people. But for similar reasons, the concept of citizenship itself should not necessarily be abandoned because it involves exclusions. It is, instead, an apt reminder that, as poststructuralists used to insist, full representation is impossible. Because creation of any sense of community necessarily involves some sort of exclusion, the pressing question is not whether or not exclusions take place, but on what basis they are made.

A case in point is the frequently evoked distinction between civic (or contractual) nations and ethnic (or cultural) nations. The most common way of illustrating this opposition is to compare France and Germany. A civic nation, modern France was constituted when the people agreed, as in a contract, to adhere to various liberal, universal civic ideals articulated in the Declaration of the Rights of Man and the Citizen. An ethnic nation, Germany first developed a sense of shared cultural identity and only later was unified politically through the efforts of Bismarck. The United States, constituted through an act of rebellion and by political documents professing universal political rights, is, like France, considered a prime example of a civic nation.[36] The distinction stems from the difference between an ethnological and a political definition of the nation. Ethnologically, a nation, as its etymology implies, is a people united by common birth or descent; politically, a nation is a people united by one government.

Almost all Western theorists of citizenship who accept this distinction strongly favor civic over ethnic nations. For instance, Ignatieff argues that ethnic nationalism assumes "that an individual's deepest attachments are inherited, not chosen."[37] If ethnic nations are based on descent, civic nations—which are supposedly their opposite—must, therefore, be based on consent. David Hollinger, relying on Werner Sollors's writings on ethnicity, proclaims that civic nationalism "is based on the principle of consent and is ostensibly open to persons of a variety of ethno-racial affiliations. A civic nation is built and sustained by people who honor a common future more than a common past."[38] And yet, as Bernard Yack and Anthony Smith have shown, the idea of a nation based solely on the principle of consent is itself a myth growing out of the desire to eliminate—or at least minimize—the contradictions that arise from the need of citizens to define themselves against noncitizens.[39]

Insofar as people choose to be citizens of a nation, in theory no one who subscribes to its cosmopolitan civic ideals is excluded. But most citizens in civic nations, like most in so-called ethnic nations, are citizens because of an accident of birth. Their contingent birth does not make them disloyal citizens. But their loyalty is as likely to come from belief in myths of the past as from belief in myths of the future. Indeed, Hollinger's effort to separate *der Mythos der Woher* from *der Mythos der Wohin*, assigning the former to ethnic nations and the latter to civic nations, is flawed, as if ethnic nations do not have myths of the future and civic nations do not have myths of national origin.

To be sure, myths of origin and purpose based on political principles usually have consequences very different from those based on a common racial descent, and I certainly side with those who prefer a political over an ethnological definition. But far from eliminating the contradiction caused by the necessity to define citizens against noncitizens, a political definition heightens it. Indeed, as Rogers Smith persuasively documents, "The failure of liberal democratic civic ideologies to indicate why any group of human beings should think of themselves as a distinct or special people is a great political liability."[40]

A second dilemma inherent to the notion of citizenship has to do with the relations of citizens among themselves. The very notion of citizenship implies that all citizens are equal before the law; yet equality before the law does not necessarily eliminate other forms of inequality. Marx made this point in terms of class in "On the Jewish Question" (1843), and Anatole France gave it its most poignant expression when he has a character in *Le Lys Rouge* (1894) ironically illustrate why he is proud to be a "citizen" by noting how "the law, in its majestic equality, forbids the rich as well as the poor to sleep under bridges, to beg in the streets, and to steal bread."[41] Since then a similar point has been made in terms of race, gender, and sexuality.[42]

In addition to tensions growing out of the citizen's relation to the noncitizen and citizens' relations to one another, there is the relation of citizens to the state. In one respect, citizens have special status because they receive the privileges and immunities of citizenship. As former chief justice Earl Warren put it, "Citizenship is man's basic right for it is nothing less than the right to have rights."[43] I will spend considerable time exploring how important some of those rights are for U.S. citizenship. But a citizen's rights are also accompanied by duties and responsibilities, such as paying taxes, military service, and most important, loyalty. Those duties do not disappear in countries, like the United States, that stress the importance of the individual. For instance, in the first of an early-twentieth-century series of Yale Lectures on the Responsibilities of Citizenship, Supreme Court Justice David J. Brewer claimed that, if traditionally "the individual lives for the nation," in the United States "the nation exists for the individual." Nonetheless, because it is so important to preserve such a nation, "the responsibilities of citizenship are nowhere greater."[44]

Brewer recognizes that, even though the word "citizen" resonates with thoughts of self-governance and freedom from subjection, citizens remain subjects of the state. Indeed, as U.S. law has long recognized, even if all subjects are not citizens, all citizens are subjects. The citizenship clause of the Fourteenth Amendment, for instance, makes citizenship dependent on subjection to the jurisdiction of the United States. Or, as Chancellor Kent wrote, "Subjects and citizens are, in a degree, convertible terms as applied to natives; and though the term *citizen* seems appropriate to republican freemen, yet we are, equally with the inhabitants of all other countries, *subjects*, for we are equally bound by allegiance and subjection to the government and law of the land."[45]

The fact that all citizens are subjects is important to stress, because a number of literary critics assume that advocates of citizenship deny it. Thus they delight in exposing the "liberal ideology" of citizenship by establishing links between subjects and citizens, seemingly unaware that the law has recognized them for years. More often than not, these acts of "demystification" draw on Louis Althusser's description of how "ideology hails or interpellates individuals as subjects."[46] Playing on two different meanings of the word "subject," Althusser insists that not only citizens but all individuals are subjects. A provocative attempt to link the formation of psychological and political subjects, Althusser's argument suggests why psychological studies of subject formation are important for political analysis and why cultural and political analysis is necessary if we hope to understand how psychological subjects are constituted. Nonetheless, intent on showing how all subjects are constructed within ideology, Althusser ignores how citizens differ from other types of subjects. For instance, he pays no attention to what Simon Schama claims is the one indisputable story of the French Revolution: the creation of the juridical entity of the citizen.[47]

Silently addressing that omission by his former collaborator, Balibar has turned his attention to citizenship, answering the question "What comes after the subject?" with "the citizen." Dating that succession at 1789, he insists that any history of the relationship between political and psychological subjects take into account the historical importance of citizenship since the French Revolution. This citizenship, he claims, "is not one among other attributes of subjectivity; on the contrary: it is subjectivity, that form of subjectivity that would no longer be identical with subjection for anyone."[48] Even if Balibar knows that this dream of pure emancipation is impossible, he also knows that it opens up new possibilities for subjectivity.

Rather than point out—once again—that citizens are ideological subjects, those writing on citizenship would be better served exploring what kinds of subjectivity specific notions of citizenship make possible. For instance, citizens and slaves may both be subjects, but their conditions generate very different possibilities for subjectivity. Similarly, the federal system of the United States generates potential conflicts between national and state citizenship, a relation that was transformed by the Fourteenth Amendment.[49] That amendment also added to the Constitution the equal protection clause. How, if at all, we need to ask, has that clause altered possibilities of subject formation within the United States? Generated by France's highly centralized system, Althusser's model has special difficulty dealing with such complications of citizenship in the U.S. federal system.

Althusser's limitations in answering such questions help explain why this book is called Civic Myths, not Civic Ideologies. My title does not mean that I am naively returning to the "myth and symbol" school that existed before the political turn in criticism caused so many to refer to "ideology" rather than to "myth." An early participant in the move to ideological criticism of American literature—a reader of one of my first essays wanted to send it to the Gorki Institute—I very much understand its importance. Nonetheless, its relentless reliance on a negative hermeneutic of "unmasking" has limited its range, as evidenced by the recent turns to both aesthetics and religion. Even critically skeptical citizens need something to believe in, some stories that serve as "equipment for living."[50] My way of engaging the tradition of ideological criticism is to explore the role of "civic myths." Although they often become civic ideologies, they cannot be completely contained by the category of the ideological.[51]

To be sure, a problem with acknowledging the inevitability of civic myths is their potential to do harm as well as good. They have, for instance, contributed to and even generated xenophobic nativism. How are we to guard against those dangerous effects? The answer to that question is neither easy nor reassuring.

Rogers Smith links the dangers of civic myths to their lack of truth. Granting that myths "may contain factual elements," he, nonetheless, wants "to highlight the unpalatable fact that stories buttressing civic loyalties virtually always contain elements that are not literally true."[52] "Civic myths may be 'noble lies,'" but they may also be "ugly ignoble lies. And they are often likely to be so."[53] Thus, when Smith defines "the political task of American citizenship," civic myths are a prime target. For instance, he urges "teachers, scholars, and opinion-shapers" to "debunk both ascriptive and liberal myths about America's past and present" and to replace them "not with rival myths but, in so far as they can, with complex truths."[54] The task for political leaders promises to be "in many ways harder." They have to learn how to get elected, rule, and "foster a sense of common allegiance in ways that are consonant with liberal democratic values, without resorting to winning support via ascriptive mythologies that can easily become demonologies." Citizens, in turn, need "to be truer liberal democrats than most Americans have ever hoped to be. They must strive to be skeptical of flattering civic myths advanced by aspiring leaders. They must try to look unblinkingly at the realities of their history and their present, with all their deficiencies as well as their great achievements on view."[55]

Noble ideals, Smith's proposals have little chance of being realized. For instance, according to his own criteria, citizens would have to reject his advice to them. After all, what could be a more flattering civic myth than a story in which citizens mature enough to be capable of remaining skeptical of flattering civic myths? Similarly, if we take Smith's call for unflinching realism seriously, what are the chances that politicians will follow his advice? His program for scholars and teachers is more complicated. They should, of course, try to present complex truths. But one truth they have to wrestle with is, as Smith puts it, the (perhaps) "indispensable" value of civic myths, despite their potential dangers.

To acknowledge that truth we have to resist the temptation to oppose myths to truth. For instance, Smith distrusts myths because of their "fictional embroidery."[56] But fictions are not lies.[57] We should no more dismiss a myth because of its fictional components than we should dismiss a novel or a legal fiction because it does not conform to empirical reality. For instance, when a noted literary critic claims that the Fourteenth Amendment "intended to confer the franchise on all African-American (male) persons," her error can be corrected by reference to the Fifteenth Amendment, and her account of citizenship loses some of its credibility.[58] But pointing out that George Washington did not cut down a cherry tree does not have the same effect on the myths surrounding the "Father of His Country."

To be sure, the situation is complicated because myths frequently draw on history at the same time that some historical accounts, such as Frederick Jackson Turner's frontier thesis, partake of and have taken on the status of myth.[59] Furthermore, as Smith persuasively demonstrates, myths can affect history. The myth of Pocahontas, for instance, caused the state of Virginia to frame its antimiscegenation law to allow someone who might be an offspring of her and John Rolfe to be officially white.[60] But such interconnections support my claim that myth is not simply opposed to truth. Not opposed to truth, myth cannot be replaced by it, no matter how complex the truths we come up with turn out to be. Indeed, even if Smith's "complex truths" would gain general acceptance, which is by no means guaranteed, they would more likely spawn new civic myths than simply replace old ones.

Aware of the persistence of myth, the historian William H. McNeil sees the scholarly commitment to truth as part of the problem rather than the solution. For McNeil, myth, as "mankind's substitute for instinct," serves an important anthropological function. Convinced that believable "public myths" are necessary for "coherent public action," he worries that the academic "pursuit of truth" has destroyed myths of old without replacing them with new, more vital ones. The resulting void, he warns, will not remain empty. "Others are sure to step into the breech by offering the necessary mythical answers to human needs." Recognizing the danger if "ignorant and agitated extremists" are allowed to supply those needs, he therefore urges historians to devote their energies to mythmaking as well as mythbreaking.[61]

Attuned to the dangers of letting ignoble people control the country's mythmaking, McNeil's proposal to turn historians into a version of Plato's philosopher kings has problems of its own. First, it risks undermining the professional role of historians. Myths may not be lies, but historians have what authority they have with the public because of their perceived commitment to telling the truth. To turn them into mythmakers rather than truth tellers would jeopardize that authority. To be sure, as we have seen, some historical accounts have taken on the status of myth. But they have because they set out to tell the truth, not to create a new myth. Indeed, McNeil overestimates the ability of people intentionally to fashion new myths. The mythical status of a story depends as much on its reception as its production, and there is no way of knowing in advance if it will be accepted and repeated by numerous people. Nor is there any way to make sure that stories that become myths will serve noble rather than ignoble ends.

But even if the attempt to come up with a foolproof method to control the potential dangers of civic myths is doomed to failure, there is an alternative to Smith's and McNeil's attempts to do so, at least for scholars and teachers. It can be found in Hans Blumenberg's strategy of *Arbeit am Mythos*, "work on/with myth."[62] Blumenberg develops his strategy in response to the complicated heritage bequeathed by the Enlightenment. As Wellek and Warren note, in the Enlightenment, "myth" had "commonly a pejorative connotation"; it was, as it still is for Smith, "a fiction — scientifically or historically untrue."[63] Exposing myths to truth would, it was hoped, free people from their debilitating superstitions. Nonetheless, as Harry Levin shrewdly notes, "the denunciation of myth as falsehood" is usually undertaken "from the vantage-point of a rival myth."[64] For Blumenberg the Enlightenment's great myth was the belief that, by replacing myth with truth, it could leave myth behind. Working on/with that myth, Blumenberg recognizes that the Enlightenment's failure to find a position outside myth in general does not mean that we should abandon its project of questioning individual myths. We need to be alert to potential dangers in both civic myths and what Ernst Cassirer called "the myth of the state."[65] At the same time, we also need to resist the myth that we can somehow transcend the need for myth. Following Blumenberg's lead, scholars and teachers should continue their quest for complex truths, but they should also explore the process by which those truths can generate civic myths to rival the ones they debunk.

One way to pursue that kind of analysis is not, as McNeil urges, for scholars to become mythmakers but to turn their attention to selected works of literature. My point is not that literature is myth. On the contrary, as Julia Lupton puts it in Citizen-Saints, "literature is that which breaks from myth (as, say, writing rather than speech, as univocal rather than collective expression, or as irony rather than confirmation)."[66] It is, therefore, a form of discourse capable of working on myth, challenging and at times demystifying it. But it is also capable of working with myth, drawing on its narrative power to generate new compelling stories, with some works of literature taking on mythological status of their own.

To be sure, not all works of literature work on/with civic myths. Nonetheless, the works I write about do. In this respect, my attention to both law and literature is important. The relation of law and literature to questions of citizenship is not the same. Because of their recognized authority, laws can grant or deny someone citizenship. Works of literature cannot. Many are, however, unlike laws, structured explicitly by narrative. As a result, they can help us identify stories about national membership and national values that are only implied by citizenship laws. Selected works of literature, we might say, help us identify the civic myths implied by citizenship laws, while citizenship laws help us identify the civic aspects of various myths that literary stories work on/with.

By drawing on both law and literature, the bulk of the book will be devoted to my primary goal of showing how competing civic myths influence the country's dynamic and complicated sense of citizenship. In addition to treating a different model of citizenship, each of my main chapters focuses on how a piece of literature works on/with important civic myths. Contributing to the myth of the Puritan origins of American citizenship while working on it, *The Scarlet Letter* starts by using the term "good citizenship" to mean total obedience to the Puritan magistrates. But even as it challenges the myth of America as the place of new beginnings, it expands the notion of "good citizenship" to include actions within the nascent beginnings of an independent civil society. Indeed, in a representative democracy, where direct participation in civic life is, except for voting, confined to a few, individuals' participation in the voluntary associations of civil society is essential to the well-being of the commonwealth. In "The Man without a Country" Edward Everett Hale works with myths of patriotism, such as the story of his great uncle Nathan, the Revolutionary War hero who died regretting that he had but one life to give to his country. Nonetheless, writing in the midst of the Civil War, Hale needs to guard against the Confederates' use of the Revolution to legitimate their secession. He does so by telling a moving story in which the nation, not an individual state or section, is the primary object of one's loyalty.

In its portrayal of Huck and Jim on the river and of Huck, Jim, and Tom heading for the territory at book's end, *Huckleberry Finn* works with the pervasive myth that liberty is best achieved outside the confines of civilization. But by having Huck and Jim's journey take them deeper and deeper into the heart of slavery and by ironically undercutting the final escape west, Twain deflates the very myths that give his book much of its power. Like *Huckleberry Finn*, Kingston's *China Men* works on the myth of the United States as a "white" republic. Kingston does so by playing with the ideal of the founding fathers. Recounting the labor of her Chinese American fathers, she shows that there are ever new generations of founding fathers, perpetually making and remaking the country while redefining what it means to be an American.

In each chapter, work on/with civic myths is interwoven with legal analysis. My chapter on *The Scarlet Letter* examines legal changes that challenged the patriarchal rule of coverture in marriage and thus made possible a different role for women in civil society. It also explores how the book's narrative is generated by potential conflicts between the demands of justice and the pursuit of happiness. "The Man without a Country" responded to the most publicized civil liberties dispute during the Civil War, the case of Clement Vallandigham. A close reading of Hale's story is, therefore, juxtaposed with analysis of the legal implications of Lincoln's controversial record on civil liberties and a close look at his response to the Vallandigham affair. The legal issues raised by the Lincoln administration's crackdown on civil liberties in the name of national security leads to a transitional chapter in the middle of the book. The one chapter that does not focus on a work of literature, it uses *Ex parte Milligan*, the most famous civil liberties case to come out of the Civil War, to explore potential tensions that have arisen between the country's commitment to the civic ideals of both liberty and equality and how those tensions are related to changes in the civic mythology surrounding Lincoln. Decided a year after the war ended, *Ex parte Milligan* has been celebrated as "one of the bulwarks of American liberty," especially during wartime.[67] Nonetheless, when it was decided, it was denounced by some as a threat to the effort to provide civil rights to African Americans.

This tension between efforts to protect civil liberties and those to guarantee equal civil rights leads to the chapter on *Huckleberry Finn*. If "The Man without a Country" needs to be understood in conjunction with issues of civil liberties, Twain's poignant dramatization of Huck and Jim's failure to find a space of freedom within civil society calls attention to the importance of civil rights. Indeed, I will examine the reception of *Huckleberry Finn* in relation to the complicated history of civil rights in this country, from the book's publication soon after the 1883 Civil Rights Cases to celebrations of its attack on racism in the wake of the civil rights movement of the twentieth century. The central chapter of *China Men* is called "The Laws." That chapter is, on one hand, a reminder of how laws have shaped the lives of Chinese Americans and, on the other, a demonstration of how Chinese Americans have helped to make and remake the country's laws as well as its land. I pay special attention to *United States v. Wong Kim Ark*, the 1898 Supreme Court case that, thirty years after the Fourteenth Amendment was adopted, finally interpreted its citizenship clause to guarantee birthright citizenship for anyone born within the United States, no matter of what descent.

Although I continually interweave literary and legal analysis, my method of doing so is not always the same. In the chapters on "The Man without a Country" and *China Men*, I rely on a method of "cross-examination" that uses a close reading of legal material to illuminate a work of literature and a close reading of a work of literature to shed light on particular cases or incidents involving the law.[68] With *The Scarlet Letter* and *Huckleberry Finn* I also cross-examine legal and literary history, but I do not focus as much on close reading of particular cases or incidents. In fact, even with Hawthorne's and Twain's works, my method is somewhat different. *The Scarlet Letter* has become so tightly tied to the myth of the Puritan origins of American citizenship that some of its best critics have not been able to detect Hawthorne's contribution to that myth. Legal material can shed light on that contribution. In contrast, *Huckleberry Finn*, more than any other of my works, has become the object of controversy. Here legal material can help determine what is at stake in those controversies.

If bringing works of literature in relation to the law helps highlight their engagement with civic issues, as the titles of individual chapters indicate, I am also interested in another realm important for questions of citizenship: the civil. As George Armstrong Kelly points out, both "civic" and "civil" make reference to "citizenship, the relation of citizens, and the common public life." "Civic" is somewhat more political and affirmative, as in "civic virtue," "civic duty," "civic humanism," and "civic nation"; "civil" has more to do with the social and is somewhat more passive, as in "civilian" and "civility." Both, like the word "citizen" itself, are etymologically linked to life in cities, with "civil" implying the "culture and refinement" of civilization as opposed to "rusticity and barbarism."[69]

I stress the civil aspects of citizenship, not to deny the importance of the civic, but to show how the two are related. Works of literature are helpful in making those connections. For instance, whereas citizenship laws help to determine the conditions of civic membership, works of literature can suggest the effects that legal determinations have on citizens' everyday lives as well as how people's interactions within a community can affect what goes on in the civic realm. I make this point most self-consciously in the chapter on *The Scarlet Letter*. Indeed, by using Hawthorne's work to explore the notion of the "good citizen," I silently allude to Michael Schudson's outstanding *The Good Citizen: A History of American Civic Life*. If Schudson, quite effectively, traces changes in the notion of the "good citizen" by looking historically at "today's central act of democratic citizenship," voting on election day,[70] I point out how Hester, who could not vote, expands our notion of good citizenship to include actions within civil society.[71]

Even though Hawthorne's Jacksonian stress on the importance of actions in civil society is still very much with us, its particular manifestation in antebellum America could not avoid civil strife. Altering the terms of citizenship, the Civil War occupies a central position in this book. One result is the attention I give to Lincoln and the civic mythology surrounding him. In 1948 Richard Hofstadter wrote,

> The Lincoln legend has come to have a hold on the American imagination that defies comparison with any other political mythology. Here is a drama in which a great man shoulders the torment and moral burdens

of a blundering and sinful people, suffers for them, and redeems them with hallowed Christian virtues—"malice toward none and charity for all"—and is destroyed at the pitch of his success. The worldly-wise John Hay, who knew him about as well as he permitted himself to be known, called him "the greatest character since Christ," a comparison one cannot imagine being made of any other political figure in modern times.[72]

Given the vast amount of scholarship devoted to the man and the myth, it might seem impossible for anyone, especially someone trained in literary studies, to say anything worthwhile about him. Yet, as Roy P. Basler noted over sixty years ago, "The certainty with which this mythos will continue to live depends upon how much Lincoln is able to stand reinterpretation."[73]

Far from rendering reinterpretation impossible, the vast amount of attention given to Lincoln encourages it. Indeed, the study of the Lincoln legend has itself become an important object of study, a way of understanding changing attitudes about the nation as much as about the man. As three Lincoln experts wrote more than two decades ago, "This redefinition of Lincoln's place in American thought, his swift transcendence from history into folklore, was one of the more remarkable cultural phenomena of our history. It was the product of many influences, including religious fervor, superstition, the retrospective impact of Lincoln's own last public utterances, and popular art. Lincoln the man was swallowed by the myth, a myth neither the passage of time nor the challenge of revision has been able to tarnish."[74]

Continual work on/with Lincoln, in other words, helps to guarantee the persistence of a civic mythology associated with him. My understanding of it is indebted to the work of Peter Karsten and Barry Schwartz. Karsten argues that, as a national icon, Lincoln, more than either Washington or Jefferson, addressed issues raised by the rise of an increasingly centralized and powerful state in the twentieth century. In the nineteenth century, Jefferson was a prime symbol for local antistatism. But in the early twentieth century, "The Apostle of Liberty" was denigrated by Theodore Roosevelt as "weak and vacillating." Lincoln, in contrast, was praised for his steadiness in stormy times and for an "iron will" that got things done. The contrast with Washington is less dramatic. Praise of "The Father of His Country" has never stopped. Nonetheless, according to Karsten, Washington's celebrated traits of prudence, modesty, charity, honesty, and courage were better suited for the nineteenth century than the twentieth.[75] Today, Washington's birthday is still honored, but he shares Presidents' Day with Lincoln, who arguably gets a bit more attention.

The difference between the two Virginians and Lincoln can be seen by the fact that both were enlisted as models for Southerners during the Civil War, whereas clearly Lincoln was not. On the contrary, Lincoln's effort to save the Union helped to transform it, granting much more power to the federal government and setting a precedent for more executive power. Indeed, as both the "Savior of the Union" and the "Great Emancipator," Lincoln exhibited little hesitation in evoking—and extending—the president's powers during wartime. For Karsten, it was this Lincoln that helped to transform the "rail splitter" into the epic hero yearned for by many in the country.

As important as Karsten's argument is, Schwartz complicates it. First, he notes that the antistatist appeal to liberty Karsten associates with Jefferson and Washington remains with us today. We have national monuments to the two Virginians as well as to Lincoln. If at times complementary, the civic mythologies associated with all three create tensions that the nation has never fully reconciled. Second, Schwartz stresses a point that Karsten makes only to minimize. Lincoln was, Karsten notes, first of all a "man of the people," self-made, of frontier stock, "the mystic demi-god of the common man."[76] Nonetheless, Karsten feels that Lincoln's "iron-will" and statism, not his humbler qualities, "caused his elevation to the first rank of patriot-heroes."[77] In contrast, Schwartz argues that

> different men of the past and present, including Alexander Hamilton and Theodore Roosevelt, symbolized different aspects of America's new industrial democracy. Lincoln stood above them in the popular imagination not because his life lent itself to becoming a symbol of the majesty of the state but because it had already become a symbol of the majesty of the people. In a society where fear of expanding state power was sustained by a strong libertarian tradition, the man personifying the priority of the state and its elites would not be revered if he did not also personify the entitlements of the masses.[78]

It is Lincoln's ability to be simultaneously a man of the people and a strong, but morally righteous, executive that makes him so important for this book. The Lincoln mythos, I will argue, suggests imaginary solutions to conflicts and contradictions raised by the particular brand of representative democracy that emerged out of the Civil War. Indeed, the question of representation in general complicates the traditional political definition of citizenship. Defined politically, citizens are members of a republic, in which sovereignty resides not in an individual or in a group of individuals but in "the people," the res publica. As John A. Hayward put it in 1885, "A subject is under subjection to a monarch, and a citizen is under subjection to a government of which he is a component part."⁷⁹ According to Aristotle, citizens are, therefore, special subjects because they "share in the civic life of ruling and being ruled in turn."⁸⁰ In practice, however, in representational forms of government required by large political communities few citizens directly participate in civic life except on election day. "The people," that is, citizens, may remain sovereign, but they are represented by a state in which most do not participate. As a result, the state, in the name of the people, has the power to rule the people.

If the state's power to subject citizens is in part legitimated by the myth of popular sovereignty,⁸¹ the same myth caused Rousseau to distrust all forms of representational government and led patriots, such as Patrick Henry, to oppose ratification of the U.S. Constitution. Nonetheless, the distinction between the state and the nation, as constituted by "the people," can be helpful. Brian C. J. Singer argues that the hyphen in "nation-state" should remind us that the nation and the state are not identical. Thus, individuals and groups can appeal to the nation and its interests to protest state action, while the state—when conceived according to civic ideals of universal equality—can guard against acts of nativistic xenophobia made in the name of "the people." To be sure, the positive potential contained in the hyphenated space of the nation-state is not inevitably activated, and all too frequently the state itself has proven to be a repressive force in the name of cultural nationalism. Nonetheless, Singer feels that a healthy tension between nation and state exists in "all functioning modern democracies, though of course they differ in relative strength from one country to the next."⁸²

Lincoln's relation to these complications of representation is twofold. On one hand, he helped to increase the distance between the people and the state by greatly expanding the role of the federal government. On the other, with his famous "a government of the people, by the people, for the people," he provided a utopian image of democratic rule in which the tensions generated by that distance are overcome, a utopian image that risks effacing the representational space between the people and the state that helps to put a check on state power. Indeed, as we will see in the chapter on *Ex parte Milligan*, Lincoln's example is so powerful that it prompted a famous constitutional scholar to argue that, on the question of civil liberties in wartime, Lincoln's monumental reputation, not a Supreme Court decision, should serve as precedent. At the same time, the chapter on "The Man without a Country" will show how Hale's story helped to foster that reputation by supporting Lincoln's account of the Vallandigham affair and by dismissing Jefferson for lacking the power to govern effectively. Similarly, the chapter on *Huckleberry Finn* will demonstrate how William Dean Howells's famous comparison of Twain to Lincoln has bolstered both Twain's reputation as a political writer and Lincoln's reputation as a "wordsmith."[83] Finally, even *China Men* has Lincolnian echoes in Kingston's work on/with myths of founding fathers.

If the book's primary goal is to use works of literature to work on/with the country's competing civic myths, the persistence of Lincoln as a "national mythos" calls attention to a secondary goal.[84] I also want to understand better why some works of literature have, like Lincoln's Gettysburg Address, captured and sustained cultural prestige. That some have is well documented. For instance, Henry Steele Commager argues that in an achievement "scarcely less remarkable than that of the Founding Fathers of political nationalism," the "Founding Fathers of American literary nationalism" created a usable past for a nation that lacked one.[85] But if many captured that prestige, not all have sustained it. Of my four works, *The Scarlet Letter* and *Huckleberry Finn* have achieved almost mythical status. For instance, John Updike, author of a trilogy of novels using Hawthorne's novel the same way he uses Greek mythology in *The Centaur*, writes, "*The Scarlet Letter* is not merely a piece of fiction, it is a myth by now."[86] Similarly, the centennial anniversary of *Huckleberry Finn* sparked publication of *The Mythologization of Mark Twain*.[87] "The Man without a Country" once had mythic status but has lost it. *China Men* has never had it. I want to try to understand reasons for those differences.

To do so, my literary analysis will, as I explain in fuller detail in the chapter on *Huckleberry Finn*, look at three historical moments: a work's moment of representation, its moment of production, and its many moments of reception, from the time it was produced to today. I will not, however, emphasize each to the same extent in every chapter. My different emphases respond in part to different histories of criticism accompanying each work. Because *China Men* is so recent, I do not spend much time on its reception. I will give some attention to the reception of *The Scarlet Letter*, but my major focus will be on relating its representation of Puritan Massachusetts to its antebellum moment of production. In contrast, with "The Man without a Country," I pay close attention to all three moments, as, conducting the first extended account of its reception, I try to explain why it achieved mythic status and then lost it. With *Adventures of Huckleberry Finn*, I also look extensively at all three moments and try to show how a work of literature can affect civic mythology at the same time that its reception is affected by changing civic myths. If some works of literature heighten our understanding of civic myths, a work's engagement with civic myths can also contribute to its "staying power."

It can, but it need not. For instance, *China Men* works on/with civic myths as self-consciously as any of the other three works, yet it is not even Kingston's most popular book. That honor goes to *Woman Warrior*. Even so, *China Men* is extremely important for my argument. For one, although Commager claims that, with the exception of Twain and one or two others, the "literary task of creating a usable past was largely performed by 1865," *China Men* shows that self-conscious literary attempts to reimagine the past continue today as new waves of immigrants alter our sense of what it means to be an American.[88] It is perhaps no accident that this account by a woman that works on/with myths of the founding fathers raises questions about the crucial issue of representation. Furthermore, by mentioning *United States v. Wong Kim Ark*, Kingston invites discussion of this important, but too-often-neglected, case. Finally, precisely because *China Men* does not have the almost mythical status that Hale's work once had and that Hawthorne's and Twain's still have, it acts as a control, allowing me to speculate, as I will in Chapter 7, about qualities that help a work achieve the status of a civic myth.

If these are reasons for including *China Men*, I do not include this twentieth-century work to tell a linear story about U.S. citizenship. Civic myths about good, patriotic, independent, and immigrant citizens exist today, and an important task of this book is to show how they interact and compete with one another as well as with myths about other kinds of citizenship. Chapter 7 will call attention to those interactions and competitions by drawing comparisons between the literary works I treat. I have selected those works for a purpose, and even if my argument is not linear, each chapter should be read in relation to the book as a whole. This is especially the case with the transitional chapter on *Ex parte Milligan*. My working model, as should be clear by now, is a conflictual one. Just as there are conflicting definitions of citizenship, so civic myths grow out of conflicts within the definition of citizenship itself and between conflicting civic ideals. Insofar as the privileges and immunities of U.S. citizenship include both civil liberties and civil rights, this chapter, because it describes a potential conflict between the two, occupies, by design, a central position in the book. Expanding on points I make about civil liberties in the chapter on "The Man without a Country," the central chapter also sets the context for my discussion of *Huckleberry Finn*, which cannot be fully understood without it.

I may not offer a linear historical narrative, but I do make claims about various historical forces shaping these different notions of citizenship: for instance, how the rise of an independent civil society expanded the notion of good citizenship; how the Civil War shaped the sense of patriotism and marked a difference between civil rights and civil liberties; how an understanding of Twain's mugwumpery in relation to the partisan debates over civil rights while he was writing *Huckleberry Finn* illuminates today's celebration of the independent citizen; and how racial restrictions on birthright citizenship were lifted by a Supreme Court ruling relying on a medieval British sense of a subject's relation to the sovereign.

To end this introduction, I need to say a few words about the book's third goal. There have long been those in literary studies claiming that an interdisciplinary and historical approach to literature detracts from our appreciation of individual works. That may be true for some interdisciplinary and historical methods, but it is not, I think, true for mine. On the contrary, I hope to make a case for the renewed role of literature in civic education.

In 1909 James Bryce's *Promoting Good Citizenship* appeared in a teaching series edited by an English professor.[89] Twenty-two years later the political scientist Charles Edward Merriman published his influential *The Making of Citizens: A Comparative Study of Methods of Civic Training*, the final book in a series whose previous nine focused on individual countries.[90] Providing a comparative account of the eight countries covered by the series, Merriman paid significant attention to the role of language and literature in civic training. Similarly, in 1952 Justice Learned Hand, in a talk to over 600 educators, addressed the responsibility of preparing "citizens for their political duties" and asserted that the humanities are "an essential factor in training [the individual] to perform his duties in a democratic society, as important even as acquaintance with the persons and current events on which he is called upon to pass."[91] In the intervening half-century, however, the humanities, especially literary studies, have more and more ceded civic education to the social sciences and their classes in "civics" — so much so that a little more than a decade ago Sandra Stotsky argued that the most pressing challenge for the language arts today is to reassert their role in civic education.[92]

One way to respond to that challenge is to reestablish within the humanities a Ciceronian emphasis on the importance of rhetorical training for citizenship. As my attention to Lincoln, who himself was influenced by such an education, indicates, I fully endorse such an emphasis. But I also want to demonstrate the advantages of using individual works of literature to engage issues of citizenship and vice versa. In doing so, my book differs in method not only from that of a political scientist like Rogers Smith but also from the methods of many working in literary studies. Those differences will become apparent as the book unfolds. For now, I want to turn to one particular critic, one to whom I am as indebted as much as I am to Smith.

In the same year that *Civic Ideals* appeared, Jonathan Arac published *Huckleberry Finn as Idol and Target: The Functions of Criticism in Our Time*. Echoing Matthew Arnold's famous essay that in turn was echoed by T. S. Eliot and Northrop Frye, the book's subtitle reveals Arac's ambitions. Writing as a "citizen and as a scholar," he devotes his considerable critical acumen to engaging the reception of perhaps the most celebrated book written by someone born in the United States.[93] Very different from *Civic Ideals*, *Idol and Target* shares, nonetheless, Smith's commitment to demystification, in this case, what Arac considers idolatrous and uncritical celebrations of *Huckleberry Finn*'s attack on racism. The problem, Arac makes clear, is not Twain's novel itself; it is widespread claims made on its behalf. "*Huckleberry Finn*," he argues, "is a wonderful book that has been loaded with so much value in our culture that is has become an idol."[94] Whereas I share many of Arac's concerns and applaud his effort to link the "ethics of scholarship" with the "ethics of citizenship,"[95] my differences with him come, as they do with Smith, with his proposed solution.

Arac concludes his book by attacking the belief that "teaching *Huckleberry Finn* as a 'weapon against racism'" is "politics enough" to "purify what is still unjust in the social and economic life of the United States. To remedy such a state of affairs," he argues, "the 'Lincoln of our literature' must yield to the Lincoln of our politics. Principles and actions, and public debates over principles and actions, are more important to remember than *Huckleberry Finn* if we wish to end racism and to be citizens who can take pride in our country in a world that is not wholly 'ours.'"[96]

Arac is certainly correct to dismiss any attempt to have teaching *Huckleberry Finn* replace political debate and political action. But the opposition he sets up is a false one. How many of the book's advocates really believe that teaching it is "politics enough"? For that matter, when it comes to bringing about social justice, is there any classroom activity that is "politics enough"? Teaching should not be seen as an alternative to responsible political debate and action; it can be, and to my mind, for certain subjects, should be, a complement and supplement to them. And that includes the teaching of literature, especially works like *Huckleberry Finn* that engage civic issues and are themselves the subject of public debates, debates that raise questions of principles and actions.[97] Indeed, *Huckleberry Finn* has been linked to the country's civic mythology in part because, through its story and its deployment of language, it has come to represent a particular mode of conducting debates and following up on actions. Whereas it is extremely important to work on that mythology, as Arac does, in the end he makes a case for *not* using Twain's novel to engage civic issues. Indeed, in addition to the political cost of doing so, he lists a "literary cost," because "we cannot rightly appreciate [the book's] sublime moments of moral comedy and stylistic mastery."[98]

To get a sense of how Arac's need to deflate *Huckleberry Finn*'s cultural capital undercuts attempts to use the book in civic education, we can turn to Lionel Trilling, whom Arac blames for what he calls *Huckleberry Finn*'s hypercanonization. Trilling's importance has less to do with the sophistication of his understanding of Twain's novel, which is far less nuanced and subtle than, say, Henry Nash Smith's understanding, than with his symptomatic and influential articulation of the relation between literature and politics that convinced educators to require general education courses in literature for all students in part because of literature's importance in civic education. For Trilling, the "connection between literature and politics" is a "very immediate one"—especially if politics is understood, as Trilling understands it, in a wide sense, "for it is no longer possible to think of politics except as the politics of culture, the organization of human life toward some end or other, toward the modification of human sentiments, which is to say the quality of human life. . . . This [notion of politics] will begin to explain why a writer of literary criticism involves himself with political considerations." Noting that his essays are "not political essays, they are essays in literary criticism," Trilling adds that they, nonetheless, "assume the inevitable intimate, if not obvious, connection between literature and politics."[99]

In contrast, Arac seems to imply that the function of criticism in our time is to turn the realm of politics over to the politicians. At the same time, he is so focused on replacing the false idolatry associated with *Huckleberry Finn* with complex truths that he fails to acknowledge the role civic mythology plays in his appeal to the Great Emancipator.[100] Quoting David Potter's claim that Lincoln's views on race were "ambiguous," he asks, "Why can't we treat our literary heroes with the same critical nuance that we use for our political heroes? . . . Why have we for decades recirculated a single idealizing set of claims about Mark Twain and *Huckleberry Finn*?"[101] But if "we" really treat our political heroes more critically than our literary ones, why does David Donald claim that the "Lincoln cult" approaches an "American religion?"[102] Similarly, how nuanced is Arac's own characterization of the response to Twain and his novel? If *Huckleberry Finn* is both idol *and* target, is there really a "single set of idealizing claims?"[103]

One of Arac's biggest complaints is how people have called *Huckleberry*

Finn quintessentially "American," such as when, a year after *The Making of Citizens* appeared, Bernard DeVoto proclaimed that "Huck speaks to the national shrewdness, facing adequately what he meets, succeeding by means of native intelligence, whose roots are ours—and ours only. In a sense he exists for a delight or wonder inseparable from the American race." Twain, he claims, "more completely than any other writer, took part in the American experience. There is, remember, such an entity."[104] If Arac rightly reminds us that no one book or character can fully represent the nation, he fails to note that similar claims were being made, and continue to be made, about Lincoln. For instance, Merriman himself writes,

> Sometimes national personalities interpret better than its philosophies or institutions the inner spirit of its life. If we were to look for a personal embodiment of the typical American spirit, by whom was our national ideal more faithfully reflected than by Abraham Lincoln, with his lowly origin and his lofty words; his mingling of strength and gentleness; of caution and courage; of unpreparedness and attainment; of reconciliation of reverence for the forms of law and the vital facts of human life; of hatred of special privilege and love of practical liberty; yet with shrewd ability to discern and indomitable courage to act upon the overshadowing issue—the maintenance of the nation's life,—paramount to forms of law and privileges guaranteed under the law, and vital to democracy and liberty?[105]

Such descriptions of the "Lincoln of our politics" need to be demystified as much as the idolatry of *Huckleberry Finn*.

Someone outside the ranks of literary study might think that the case against the use of literature in civic education would be mounted by people in other fields. But, as Arac's separate but unequal treatment of the civic mythologies surrounding Lincoln and Twain indicates, some of the strongest cases against it have come from within literary studies itself. In arguing for it, I am not advocating a return to the days Merriman describes. He, for instance, warns against the "disruptive" and "revolutionary" force of "literary artistry," especially when it "coincides with an ethnic group or with a religious or economic group, out of line in the central political adjustment." In contrast, the American work he cites most favorably is "The Man without a Country."[106] A civic education informed by literary works should include "disruptive" works. But it should also include works like Hale's, although not taught by applying Trilling's strictly literary mode of analysis. On the contrary, if I am correct, the way to revitalize the role of literature for civic education is to adopt an interdisciplinary approach. As my chapter on "The Man without a Country" shows, the difference between reading Hale's story on its own and reading it in conjunction with the civil liberties dispute that provoked it is significant.[107]

Far from distracting us from our understanding of works of literature, an interdisciplinary and historical approach can enhance our appreciation of both their complications and the complications of life as a citizen in the United States. To be sure, works of literature do many things, and not all lend themselves to use in civic education. Nonetheless, some do. In the chapters that follow, I make a case for recognizing connections between four works of literature and questions of citizenship. I hope that doing so will help us understand them better while also suggesting ways to work on/with present practices of civic education.

2 *The Scarlet Letter*

The Good Citizen, Transgression, and Civil Society

Early in *The Scarlet Letter*, as Hester Prynne faces public discipline, the narrator halts to comment, "In fact, this scaffold constituted a portion of a penal machine, which now, for two or three generations past, has been merely historical and traditionary among us, but was held, in the old time, to be as effectual an agent in the promotion of good citizenship, as ever was the guillotine among the terrorists of France."[1] In a subtle reading of this passage Larry Reynolds notes the anachronistic use of "scaffold"—the normal instruments of punishment in the Massachusetts Bay Colony were the whipping post, the stocks, and the pillory—to argue that Hawthorne self-consciously alludes to public beheadings, especially the regicidal revolutions in seventeenth-century England and eighteenth-century France.[2] But none of Hawthorne's many critics has noted the anachronistic use of "good citizenship," a phrase that suggests the rich historical layering of Hawthorne's nineteenth-century romance about seventeenth-century New England Puritans.

Of course, "citizen" existed in English in the seventeenth century, but it was used primarily to designate an inhabitant of a city, as Hawthorne does when he mentions "an aged handicraftsman . . . who had been a citizen of London at the period of Sir Thomas Overbury's murder, now some thirty years agone" (127). The official political status of residents of Boston in June 1642 was not that of citizens but subjects of the king, a status suggested when Hester leaves the prison and the Beadle cries, "Make way, good people, make way, in the King's name" (54). Historically resonant itself, this cry reminds us that it was precisely in June 1642 that civil war broke out in England.[3] In fact, the book's action unfolds over the seven years in which the relation between the people and their sovereign was in doubt, the years generally acknowledged as the time when "the Englishman could develop a civic consciousness, an awareness of himself as a political actor in a public realm"—that is, as a citizen as those in the nineteenth century would have understood the term.[4] Even so, it was not until after the French and American Revolutions that "good citizenship" came into common use.

When Hawthorne inserts the nineteenth-century term "good citizenship" into a seventeenth-century setting, he subtly participates in a persistent national myth that sees U.S. citizenship as an outgrowth of citizenship developed in colonial New England. Hawthorne's participation in this myth is important to note because much of his labor is devoted to challenging its standard version. According to the standard version, conditions for democratic citizenship flourished the moment colonists made the journey to the "new world." If the people in the thirteen colonies were officially subjects of the king, the seeds of good citizenship were carried across the Atlantic, especially by freedom-loving Pilgrims, who found a more fertile soil for civic participation than in England. A recent example of this version of the story comes in the work of the noted historian Edmund S. Morgan. Describing "the first constitution of Massachusetts" in 1630 when the assistants of the Massachusetts Bay Company were "transformed from an executive council to a legislative body," Morgan writes, "the term 'freeman' was transformed from a designation for members of a commercial company, exercising legislative and judicial control over that company and its property, into a designation for the citizens of a state, with the right to vote and hold office. . . . This change presaged the admission to freemanship of a large proportion of settlers, men who could contribute to the joint stock nothing but godliness and good citizenship."[5] When Morgan designates freemen "citizens," he projects onto Puritan New England his awareness of political changes still to come, just as most studies of colonial American literature project the country's present political boundaries backward and treat only the thirteen colonies that eventually became the United States.

This tendency to read the Puritan past teleologically is a product of the antebellum period. For instance, in his multivolume *History of the United States*, which found its way into nearly a third of New England homes,[6] George Bancroft attributed the "political education" of people in Connecticut "to the happy organization of towns, which here, as indeed throughout all New England, constituted each separate settlement as a little democracy in itself. It was the natural reproduction of the system, which the instinct of humanity had imperfectly revealed to our Anglo-Saxon ancestors. In the ancient republics, citizenship had been an hereditary privilege. In Connecticut, citizenship was acquired by inhabitancy, was lost by removal. Each town-meeting was a little legislature, and all inhabitants, the affluent and the more needy, the wise and the foolish, were members with equal franchises." Quoting this passage, a reviewer for the *American Jurist and Law Magazine* enthusiastically adds that in colonial New England's "institutions lies the germ of all that distinguishes our government from others, which are more or less founded in individual freedom."[7]

Clearly, the "mild" and "humane" laws of Bancroft's Puritans are not those of Hawthorne's.[8] On the contrary, much of Hawthorne's notorious irony is directed against Bancroft's and others' idealization of their New England ancestors.[9] For instance, if Bancroft celebrates New England as the breeding ground of democratic citizenship because of the people's civic participation in town hall meetings and the like, Hawthorne's image of the scaffold reminds us that good citizenship requires obedience. If Bancroft stresses the freedom entailed in good citizenship, Hawthorne reminds us of the repressions required to produce good citizens. Hawthorne's irony reaches a peak late in the book when he calls Chillingworth, the book's villain, a "reputable" "citizen" (233). Truly good citizens, it seems, cannot be distinguished from those who simply appear respectable.

In different ways some of Hawthorne's best historically minded critics have noted his challenge to the standard version of the Puritan origins of U.S. citizenship. None, however, has noted Hawthorne's anachronistic use of the term "citizen." On the contrary, like Hawthorne, some of these same critics refer to Puritans in seventeenth-century Boston as citizens in the political sense of the term.[10] In doing so, they unconsciously participate in the very myth they think they are demystifying, a participation that makes it impossible for them to recognize Hawthorne's important contribution to it.

We can start to identify that contribution by noting that Hawthorne employs little or no irony at the end of his romance when Hester returns to Boston and devotes herself to serving the unfortunate. Having "no selfish ends," not living "in any measure for her own profit and enjoyment," counseling those bringing to her "their sorrows and perplexities" (263), Hester in her unselfish commitment to her community has by most measures earned the label "good citizen."

By most, but not by all. For instance, Judith Shklar identifies the two most important attributes of U.S. citizenship as the right to vote and the right to earn a living.[11] Although Hester earlier earned her keep with her needle, economic self-sufficiency is not a defining aspect of her citizenship. Nor is the right to vote. In fact, as a woman, Hester in the seventeenth (even in the early nineteenth) century could not fit definitions of good citizenship in either the economic or the political spheres.

Even so, rather than abandon the concept of good citizenship, Hawthorne through Hester stresses the importance of actions within what political scientists call civil society, "a sphere of social interaction between economy and the state, composed of the intimate sphere (especially the family), the sphere of associations (especially voluntary associations), social movements, and forms of public communication."[12] Acutely aware that the stress on civic participation could obscure important interior matters of the heart and spirit, Hawthorne does not, as many critics argue he does, retreat from public to private concerns but instead tells the tale of how a "fallen woman" finds redemption by helping to generate within a repressive Puritan community the beginnings of an independent civil society. In telling that tale Hawthorne provides more than a civics lesson. He participates in and helps to shape the contours of a powerful civic myth, one whose narrative, generated by a potential conflict between the classical republican ideal of justice and the liberal pursuit of happiness, focuses on an aspect of social life considered the very opposite of civility, transgression.[13]

☆ ☆ ☆ People in Hawthorne's day were quite aware of literature's potential to generate civic myths. That potential was, for instance, the topic of an 1834 speech called "The Importance of Illustrating New England History by a Series of Romances Like the Waverley Novels" in Hawthorne's hometown of Salem by the Whig lawyer Rufus Choate. Alluding to the Scottish nationalist Andrew Fletcher's often-quoted statement that "I know a very wise man . . . [who] believed if a man were permitted to make all the ballads, he need not care who should make the laws of the nation," Choate argues that a proper literary treatment of the past would mold and fix "that final, grand, complex result, — the national character." In doing so it would make the country forget its "recent and overrated diversities of interest" and "reassemble, as it were, the people of America in one vast congregation." "Reminded of our fathers," he argues, "we should remember that we are brethren."[14]

Choate understands how works of literature can serve as civic myths, but he also reveals why Will Kymlicka worries that such myths will unify only if they generate a "glorified history" based on a "very selective, even manipulative retelling of that history."[15] The stories Choate advocates would not, he admits, be a full disclosure of the past. A literary artist should remember that "it is an heroic age to whose contemplation he would turn us back; and as no man is a hero to his servant, so no age is heroic of which the whole truth is recorded. He tells the truth, to be sure, but he does not tell the whole truth, for that would be sometimes misplaced and discordant." Aware that "much of what history relates . . . chills, shames and disgusts us," producing "discordant and contradictory emotions," Choate, therefore, counsels writers to leave out accounts of the "persecution of the Quakers, the controversies with Roger Williams and Mrs. Hutchinson."[16] Literature as civic myth would seem to allow authors to avoid altogether those embarrassing national events that historians have to grapple with, even if there is, as Melville puts it, "a considerate way of historically treating them."[17]

But the Hawthorne that Melville so admired presents a more complicated case.[18] He had, for instance, already written about precisely the topics that Choate says should be avoided, evidence of a critical attitude toward the past that has caused so many critics to focus on his ironic demystifications. Even so, as we have seen, Hawthorne does more than demystify prevailing myths. As George Dekker shrewdly puts it, Hawthorne's "best hope for both short- and long-term success was to make the great American myths his own."[19] One of his greatest successes came in his representation of the Puritans, which is, we need to remember, not always historically accurate.[20] Hawthorne is neither solely a mythmaker nor a critical demystifier. Effectively working on/with the myth of the nation's relation to its Puritan past, *The Scarlet Letter* does not advocate obedience to the state or even primary loyalty to the nation. Instead, it illustrates how important it is for liberal democracies to maintain the space of an independent civil society in which alternative obediences and loyalties are allowed a chance to flourish. It should come as no surprise, then, that the novel's power comes more through its love story than through its politics, or perhaps better put, its politics reminds us of the importance love stories have for most citizens' lives.

It is in the love plot that Hawthorne works on/with the great exceptionalist myth that America offers the hope for a radical break with the past and the promise of a new start. Hawthorne's romance starts with reflections on the Puritans' attempt to establish a fresh start in the "new world" and the narrator's whimsical comment, "The founders of a new colony, whatever Utopia of human virtue and happiness they might originally project, have invariably recognized it among their earliest practical necessities to allot a portion of the virgin soil; as a cemetery, and another portion as the site of a prison" (47). It then opens the second half with "Another View of Hester" and Hester's realization that the radical reforms she imagines would require "the whole system of society to be torn down, and built up anew" (165). Hester's radical speculations are in turn linked to the book's emotional climax in the forest when Hester pleads to Dimmesdale, "Leave this wreck and ruin here where it hath happened! Meddle no more with it! Begin all anew!" (198).

Even though each of these efforts is frustrated, much of the story's emotional tension has to do with readers' hopes, secret or not, that one or the other—or all—will succeed. Of all the attempts, however, that of Hester and Dimmesdale has awakened most readers' hopes. Confronted with a book of memorable scenes, readers past and present have found the forest meeting between Dimmesdale and Hester the most memorable. Of this scene, in which Hester and Dimmesdale "recognize that, in spite of all their open and secret misery, they are still lovers, and capable of claiming for the very body of their sin a species of justification," novelist William Dean Howells writes, "There is greatness in this scene unmatched, I think, in the book, and I was almost ready to say, out of it."[21] To understand *The Scarlet Letter* we need to understand why, after marshaling all of his rhetorical force to make us sympathize with his lovers, Hawthorne does not allow them a new beginning.

Puritan authorities might have answered that question by relying on John Winthrop's distinction between natural and civil liberty. "The first is common to man with beasts and other creatures. By this, man, as he stands in relation to man simply, hath liberty to do what he lists; it is a liberty to evil as well as to good." In contrast, civil liberty has to do with the "covenant between God and man, in the moral law, and the politic covenants and constitutions, amongst men themselves. This liberty is the proper end and object of authority, and cannot subsist without it; and it is a liberty to that only which is good, just, and honest." Significant for a novel about adultery, Winthrop's analogy for political covenants is marriage. Assuming the common-law doctrine of coverture in which husband and wife become one corporate body with the husband granted sole legal authority, Winthrop compares a woman's willing subjection in marriage to an individual's subjection to the magistrates who govern the political covenant to which he or she consents. "The woman's own choice makes such a man her husband; yet being so chosen, he is her lord, and she is to be subject to him, yet in a way of liberty, not of bondage; and a true wife accounts her subjection her honor and her freedom. . . . Even so brethren, it will be between you and your magistrates." In turn both marriage and political covenants are analogous to "the covenant between God and man, in the moral law" in which a Christian can achieve true liberty only through total submission to Christ.[22] For the Puritans, the political institutions of civil society and the civil ceremony of marriage are governed by the moral law because they have God's sanction. A political covenant is not simply a contract among men; like the marriage contract between a man and woman, it needs God's witness.

To apply this doctrine of covenant theology to *The Scarlet Letter* is to see that for the Puritans Hester's greatest sin would not have been her adultery, whose visible evidence they see in the birth of Pearl, but a remark that Dimmesdale alone hears her make: her defiant cry that what the two lovers did "had a consecration of its own" (195). Resonating with so many readers, this proclamation is sinful because it implies that Hester's and Dimmesdale's love is a self-contained act, not one in need of God's sanction. As such, their love exists in the realm of natural, not civil, liberty and must be contained.

The nineteenth-century version of Winthrop's distinction between natural and civil liberty is the distinction often made in political oratory between license and liberty. *The Scarlet Letter* is about the importance of civil society, not about the glories of natural man or woman, because Hawthorne, despite the sympathy he creates for his lovers, recognizes with Winthrop the dangers of natural liberty. But he also has doubts about the patriarchal and hierarchical relations between husband and wife and ruler and subject that the Puritans used to uphold the civil order. Indeed, Hawthorne continually challenges rulers' calls for absolute loyalty. That challenge is one reason why this loyal Jacksonian Democrat was seen in the 1920s by Charles and Mary Beard in their popular and progressive history textbook as a deeply democratic writer. Describing Hawthorne's lack of "reverence for the infallibility of superior persons,"[23] they then quote "a moral" from *The House of the Seven Gables* about the Puritans and the witchcraft trials "that the influential classes, and those who take upon themselves to be leaders of the people, are fully liable to all the passionate error that has ever characterized the maddest mob."[24] Errors of this sort occur in any society ruled by fallible human beings, but they magnify in significance when "forms of authority were felt to possess the sacredness of divine institutions" (64) as they are in the Puritan theocracy of *The Scarlet Letter*.

Distrustful of granting civil authority divine sanction, Hawthorne questions the capacity of the Puritan magistrates properly to judge Hester. Their problem is not that they are evil men. "They were, doubtless, good men, just and sage" (64). Their problem is that "out of the whole human family, it would not have been easy to select the same number of wise and virtuous persons, who should be less capable of sitting in judgment on an erring woman's heart, and disentangling its mesh of good and evil" (64). Assuming the moral position of God, the magistrates lack Hester's "power to sympathize" (161).[25] That power causes a political dilemma. If, on one hand, Hawthorne appeals to sympathy to temper the rigid and authoritarian rule of a system in which "religion and law were almost identical" (50), on the other, he warns of the dangers of having that sympathy embrace natural liberty with all of its potential dangers.

That dilemma is, of course, precisely the dilemma Hawthorne's readers confront when they sympathize with his two lovers in the forest. Readers generally resolve that dilemma by taking a position between two poles. On one hand, there are those, like many students and the director of the Hollywood film starring Demi Moore, who champion the book's lovers against a repressive society. On the other, there are those, like many critics, who assume that Hawthorne takes the narrator's point of view and advocates absolute submission to the existing civil authorities. Some who take these views praise the book; others condemn it. For instance, literary critics taking the latter view sometimes condemn Hawthorne's conservatism. In contrast, an early reviewer for the *Church Review and Ecclesiastical Register* responded to Hawthorne's portrayal of a passionate adulterous couple by asking, "Is the French era actually begun in our literature?" Reading the book as advocating "sympathy for [Hawthorne's lovers'] sin," the reviewer attacks Hawthorne for implying that Hester's adultery is "a natural and necessary result of the Scriptural law of marriage, which, by holding her irrevocably to her vows, as plighted to a dried up book-worm" makes "her heart an easy victim to the adulterer." Likewise, Dimmesdale's sin seems to be "not so much the deed itself" as "his long concealment of it."[26]

Hawthorne, however, does not resolve the dilemma he poses for his readers. Instead, he builds it into the book's structure by generating two points of view in constant tension. One derives from the dramatic action itself, which in evoking our sympathies questions the prevailing measure of justice. The other is the narrator's commentary, which tries to subordinate our sympathies to justice as inscribed in the law.[27] Hawthorne's failure to resolve the dilemma he raises is not simply a case of his famous ambiguity. It is instead a recognition that there is no formula for determining whether our sympathies serve justice or not. As enacted in *The Scarlet Letter*, therefore, politics does not resolve the dilemma; it is a realm in which its competing claims are perpetually adjudicated. That adjudication is complicated further by the fact that the sympathies marshaled to question existing standards of justice frequently involve acts of transgression. Hester's transgression is extremely important to emphasize because even some of Hawthorne's best recent critics are prone to minimizing its importance.

For instance, T. Walter Herbert, one of the most sensitive readers of what he calls "the marital politics" of *The Scarlet Letter*, argues that "the Puritan community is guilty of enforcing a wrongful standard: Hester's youthful mistake could be corrected in a healthier social arrangement, where she could obtain a divorce from Roger and proceed to formalize at law the true marriage of her heart."[28] *The Scarlet Letter* certainly portrays a narrow Puritan society. But Hawthorne does not present us with a situation in which Hester could correct a "youthful mistake" if more liberal Puritans would have loosened divorce legislation.[29] If Hester made a mistake in marrying, she makes another in violating her marriage vows. Hawthorne forces her to reckon with that sin.

Hawthorne may feel that Puritan magistrates are incapable of sympathetically judging Hester, but he shares with them a recognition of the fallible and potentially sinful nature of human beings. A system that denies individuals the pursuit of happiness may appear unjust, but individuals' pursuits of happiness by no means lead inevitably to justice. Critical of harshly repressive political orders, Hawthorne, like Freud, nonetheless believes that some form of repression is necessary to maintain a just civil order. If in the 1960s Freud's view was challenged by Herbert Marcuse, who sought a nonrepressive foundation to civilization, one allowing the full flourishing of eros, *The Scarlet Letter* is in part a response to utopian movements of its day with similar aspirations.[30]

Impulses fueling the fascination with experimental utopian communities in antebellum America were various, but at least some believed that true reform had to begin by liberating the sexual energy repressed by the institution of marriage. Drawing on the tradition evoked by Winthrop that uses metaphors of marriage to describe the terms of political obligation, these early advocates of the belief that the "personal is political" felt that sexual reform would liberate society. Indeed, the reviewer for the *Church Review and Ecclesiastical Register* felt Hawthorne's stay at Brook Farm established him as a radical reformer. Of course, as *The Blithedale Romance* makes clear, Hawthorne was far from radical. Nonetheless, his response to calls for sexual reform was complicated. Mocking Zenobia's feminism, he was not unsympathetic to her concerns. For instance, Hollingsworth's hypocrisy is registered by the fact that, although he would change society by reforming criminals, he maintains a reactionary view of women. "Woman," he insists, "is a monster—and, thank Heaven, an almost impossible and hitherto imaginary monster—without man, as her acknowledged principal."[31]

Hawthorne was not, as some have accused him, afraid of sexuality. He understood why radical reformers argued that the institution of marriage needed to be more responsive to the powerful force of erotic love and the sympathies that it awakens. After all, he went to Brook Farm with marriage to Sophia on his mind. When Hollingsworth accuses the French reformer Fourier of committing "the Unpardonable Sin" for basing his reforms on "the principle of all human wrong, the very blackness of man's heart, the portion of ourselves which we shudder at, and which it is the whole aim of spiritual discipline to eradicate,"[32] he is not referring to Fourier's plans to reform the system of labor but instead to his theories about passional attractions. Skeptical as Hawthorne was about radical reform, he does not dismiss the passions, including erotic passion, as "the very blackness of man's heart." His worries are, on the contrary, twofold. On one hand, he fears that eros outside the constructive constraints of the civil institution of marriage can unleash the dangers of natural liberty. On the other, he fears that too much control by the state can stifle the productive feelings of sympathy that accompany erotic love. Thus, as much as Hawthorne shares radicals' desire for better relations between men and women, his answer is not to abolish the institution of marriage but to reform it.

The established model of marriage in Hawthorne's day was still ruled by the doctrine of coverture. Coverture guaranteed a patriarchal lineage by having the wife lose her legal standing as an individual and willingly submit to the rule of her husband. Under it, as Winthrop makes clear, a wife's loyalty and obedience were paramount. Authoritarian, patriarchal political systems on which coverture was modeled make its reform difficult to achieve. For instance, in The Marble Faun Hawthorne opposes the despotic rule that manifests itself in trying to force the character Miriam against her will into an arranged marriage "in which feeling went for nothing."[33] Similarly, whereas authoritarian Puritan rule is not solely responsible for Hester's problems, Hawthorne is certainly critical of it and links it to Hester's unhappy marriage. Indeed, if Hester and Chillingworth represent the old model of marriage, Hester and Dimmesdale suggest a new model, which substituted coverture's image of marriage as a corporate body presided over by the husband with the image of a contractual relation between husband and wife. Rather than emphasizing the obedience and loyalty of the wife, this new domestic ideal emphasized a bond held together by love and sympathy.[34]

According to Herbert, the "conflicts and psychic torment" of The Scarlet Letter result from competition in Hawthorne's day between these views of marriage.[35] Those views have political implications. For instance, Winthrop appeals to the model of coverture to bolster his claim that the primary components of political obligation should be duty and obedience. In contrast, the new model suggests a basis in love and sympathy, which because of their capacity to create bonds and establish identifications across barriers of status have great democratic potential. To be sure, the opposition between duty and obedience, on one hand, and love and sympathy, on the other, is too simple. Love and sympathy can generate duties and obedience, while obedience and adherence to one's duties can be a measure of love. For instance, the reign of Elizabeth I in England was successful in part because she exploited the image of a loving marriage between herself and the nation to solicit loyalty from her subjects.[36] Perhaps, then, the proper opposition should be between love and obedience, on one hand, and love and sympathy, on the other. But even that opposition breaks down because sympathy, as well as love, can be channeled into obedience to the state. Indeed, effective rulers know how to command support by cultivating the people's sympathetic identification with them.

Thus another factor affecting the political implications of competing models of marriage was the transformation of political subjects into citizens that corresponded with the overthrow of monarchies in both the United States and France. For instance, in England and colonial America, the killing of a husband by a wife was *petit treason*, analogous to regicide, although the killing of a wife by a husband was simply murder. The analogy did not, however, survive the Revolution. Not wanting the symbolic slaying of the king to encourage revolution in the patriarchal family, most of the new states dropped the term *petit treason*. In granting sovereignty to "the people" as citizens, who according to Aristotle, have the capacity to both rule and be ruled, the republican system of the United States challenged the hierarchical order in which sovereignty resided in a monarch — or absolute magistrates — who ruled over loving and obedient subjects.

As Linda Kerber has shown, the ideal of citizenship in the Revolutionary era undercut Winthrop's analogy between the wife under coverture and the subjects of a commonwealth. On one hand, independence generated an ideological disjunction. Founded on the principle that the terms of political obligation of British subjects could be renegotiated to create U.S. citizens, the nation was ruled, nonetheless, by men who for the most part wanted to retain a family structure in which a wife owed her husband eternal obedience.[37] On the other hand, the rhetoric of citizenship generated a new republican model of marriage that challenged the doctrine of coverture. As Merril Smith puts it, "Tyranny was not to be considered in public or private life, and marriage was now to be considered a republican contract between wives and husbands, a contract based on mutual affection."[38]

Whereas some conceived of that contract as one of absolute equality, the majority challenging coverture, Hawthorne included, felt that the duties husband and wife brought to the union should not be identical but complementary, divided along gender lines. The marital relation was, for them, balanced by adding a form of maternalism to coverture's paternalism. In the family husbands continued to have primary responsibility for relations concerning justice and authority, whereas wives presided over affairs of moral sentiment. If that division denied women direct access to the political sphere, it entrusted to them raising children.

For Hawthorne, however, bringing about the transition from the old model to the new would be as complicated as it was to move from a monarchy to a republic. In his world the breakdown of an old order risks allowing natural, rather than civil, liberty to prevail. Indeed, Hester's violation of her marriage vows is yet another example of premature efforts to begin anew. When her affair with the minister begins, she assumes, before the fact, that her husband is dead. Chillingworth appears, therefore, not only as a vengeful, cuckolded husband but also as a figure from the past prepared to block Hester and Dimmesdale from achieving the dream of starting anew. It is time to take another view of Mr. Prynne.[39]

☆ ☆ ☆ Hawthorne may elicit our sympathy for Hester and Dimmesdale while condemning their adultery, but he generates little sympathy for Hester's husband. From Chaucer's January to characters in Shakespeare to Charles Bovary to Leopold Bloom, the cuckolded husband has been treated with differing amounts of humor, pathos, sympathy, and contempt. Few, however, are as villainous as Roger Chillingworth. Hawthorne's treatment of this "reputable" "citizen" (233) starkly contrasts with the sympathetic treatment some courts gave to cuckolded husbands in the 1840s when various states began applying the so-called unwritten law by which a husband who killed his wife's lover in the act of adultery was acquitted. Arguments for those acquittals portrayed avenging husbands as "involuntary agents of God." In contrast, lovers were condemned as "children of Satan," "serpents," and "noxious reptiles" with supernatural power allowing them to invade the "paradise of blissful marriages."[40]

In *The Scarlet Letter* this imagery is reversed. It is the avenging husband who stalks his wife's lover with "other senses than [those ministers and magistrates] possess" (75) and who is associated with "Satan himself, or Satan's emissary" (128). In the meantime, we imagine Arthur, Hester, and Pearl as a possible family.[41] The narrator so writes off Chillingworth as Hester's legal husband that he calls him her "former husband" (167), causing Michael T. Gilmore to follow suit and D. H. Lawrence to designate Mr. Prynne Hester's "first" husband. A legal scholar writing on adultery goes so far as to call Hester an "unwed mother."[42]

By reversing the sympathy that courts gave to cuckolded husbands taking revenge into their own hands, Hawthorne draws attention to why nineteenth-century legal scholars insisted on the importance of seeking justice within the confines of the written law. Feminist historians have, for good reason, stressed how laws condemning adultery helped to guarantee the legitimacy of patriarchal lineage. In the nineteenth century, however, an alternative account, pointing to the law's positive function, was available.[43] Oliver Wendell Holmes Jr. summarized much writing on law's anthropological function when he wrote, "The early forms of legal procedure were grounded in vengeance."[44] Adultery is a case in point. Prior to the sixth century, revenge for adultery in England was carried out by the wronged husband and his kinship group. This reliance on vendetta resulted in long-standing blood feuds. To stop the social disruption caused by cycles of revenge, Aethelberht created his Code of Dooms that gave responsibility for punishing adultery and other crimes to the state. In his famous *Ancient Law*, published a decade after *The Scarlet Letter*, Sir Henry Maine drew on similar evidence from Roman law to argue that criminal law served the social order by taking from individuals responsibility for punishing wrongdoers. The hoped-for result was a state monopoly on violence, for if the state alone could resort to violence to mete out justice, socially disruptive cycles of violent revenge could be avoided.[45]

Dramatizing the dangers of achieving justice outside the law, Chillingworth illustrates natural liberty's potential for evil as well as for good. On one hand, it can prompt Hester to question the law in the name of a more equitable social order. On the other, it allows Chillingworth to take the law into his own hands for personal revenge. If Hester's desire to create the world "anew" suggests utopian possibilities, Chillingworth's revenge, driven by "new interests" and "a new purpose" (119), suggests the potential for a reign of terror. Hawthorne links these seeming opposites through the secret pact Hester and her husband forge on his return. Hester dreams of a new social order after having "imbibed . . . a freedom of speculation" growing out of a new way of thinking that challenges "the whole system of ancient prejudice" (164). But during her prison interview she also imbibes a draught her husband has concocted out of the "many new secrets" (72) he has learned in the wilderness from Indians. Chillingworth's "new secrets" might be associated with a more "primitive" realm that Hester's vision of an enlightened future hopes to overcome, but the "promise of secrecy" (170) that once again binds husband and wife suggests a possible connection between the two. Their secret bond in turn parallels the secret bond that Hester and Dimmesdale contemplate in their meeting in the forest.

Critics have long noted that Hawthorne does not show us Hester's violation of her marriage vows, which takes place before the book begins. But it is equally significant that Hawthorne also never presents a public ceremony of marriage. What we get instead are two parodic enactments of one: first, when Hester and her husband establish a new bond on his return from the dead; second, when Hester and Dimmesdale exchange vows in their passionate rendezvous. If the first takes place in prison and the second in the natural wilderness, they have structural similarities. For instance, just as Hester's new bond with her husband can be maintained only because he has taken on a new name, so Hester counsels her lover, "Give up this name of Arthur Dimmesdale, and make thyself another" (198). More importantly, the secrecy in which both bonds are made isolates everyone involved from the human community. As such, both are in stark contrast to the bond created by the civil ceremony of marriage whose public witness links husband and wife to the community.

Our attention is so riveted on Hester and her adulterous violation of her marriage vows that we too often forget to note that Mr. Prynne violates his as well. For instance, in prison Hester asks her husband why he will "not announce thyself openly, and cast me off at once?" His reply: "It may be . . . because I will not encounter the dishonor that besmirches the husband of a faithless woman. It may be for other reasons. Enough, it is to my purpose to live and die unknown" (76). In legal terms, this fear of dishonor makes no sense inasmuch as Hester's husband has committed no crime. But if some antebellum courts displayed great sympathy to cuckolded husbands through the unwritten law, there was a long tradition—still powerful in the seventeenth century—of popular and bawdy rituals mocking cuckolded husbands.[46] No matter what other motives Chillingworth might have, the narrator makes clear that the man "whose connection with the fallen woman had been the most intimate and sacred of them all" resolves "not to be pilloried beside her on her pedestal of shame" (118). That resolve explains "Why—since the choice was with himself—" he does not "come forward to vindicate his claim to an inheritance so little desirable" (118).

According to coverture, that undesirable inheritance was not only Hester but also her child. Aware of his husbandly rights, Chillingworth tells his wife, "Thou and thine, Hester Prynne, belong to me" (76). Nonetheless, he refuses to acknowledge his inheritance, telling Hester, "The child is yours,—she is none of mine,—neither will she recognize my voice or aspect as a father" (72). The doctrine of coverture was clearly a patriarchal institution; nonetheless, it was not solely to the advantage of the husband. It also held him responsible for the well-being of his wife and children. Chillingworth might not be Pearl's biological father, but he is her father in the eyes of the law. That legal status adds another dimension to the recognition scene that occurs when Chillingworth walks out of the forest and finds his wife on public display for having committed adultery. "Speak, woman!" he "coldly and sternly" cries from the crowd. "Speak; and give your child a father!" (68). Commanding his wife to reveal the name of her lover, the wronged husband also inadvertently reminds us that at any moment Hester could have given Pearl a legal father by identifying him. Even more important, Chillingworth could have identified himself. But the same man who knows his legal rights of possession as a husband refuses to take on his legal responsibilities as a father.

Pearl, in other words, has not one but two fathers who refuse to accept their responsibilities. Having lost his own father as a young boy and doubting his ability financially to support his children after losing his job at the Custom House, Hawthorne was acutely aware of the need for fathers to live up to their name. The failure of both of Pearl's to do so emphasizes Hester's role as a mother.

☆ ☆ ☆ The Scarlet Letter, according to Tony Tanner, is an exception to the "curiously little interest" the novel of adultery pays to the child of an illicit liaison, "even on the part of the mother (or especially on part of the mother)."[47] Indeed, Hester's relation to Pearl is a major part of Hawthorne's story. Accompanying her mother in almost every scene in which Hester appears, Pearl embodies a paradox: although there is perhaps no better symbol of hope for a new beginning than the birth of a child, Hester's daughter continually reminds her mother of her sinful past. Like the scarlet letter to which she is frequently compared, Pearl serves, therefore, as an agent of her mother's socialization. Part of Hester's socialization is, in turn, to socialize her daughter. Worried either that Pearl is of demon origin or that her mother is not doing a proper job of raising her, some of the "leading inhabitants" are rumored to be campaigning to transfer Pearl "to wiser and better guardianship than Hester Prynne's" (100–101). In response Hester concocts an excuse to go to the governor's hall, only to find Governor Bellingham and Reverend Wilson convinced of their plan when Pearl impiously responds to their interrogations. Desperately turning to Dimmesdale, Hester implores, "I will not lose the child! Speak for me! Thou knowest, — for thou hast sympathies which these men lack! — Thou knowest what is in my heart, and what are a mother's rights" (113).

As much an anachronism as Hawthorne's evocation of the concept of good citizenship, Hester's appeal to a mother's rights helps to locate Hawthorne's attitude toward motherhood. In the seventeenth century no mother threatened with losing custody of her child could have successfully evoked the idea of a mother's rights. On the contrary, as we have seen, under the doctrine of coverture the child belonged legally to the father. In fact, in custody disputes between husband and wife a common-law court did not grant custody to the mother until 1774. Even in this landmark case Chief Justice Lord Mansfield acknowledged the "father's natural right" while ruling that "the public right to superintend the education of its citizens" had more weight.[48] Mansfield's seemingly revolutionary ruling, in other words, would have confirmed the Puritan elders' sense that for her own good and that of the commonwealth, Pearl, who had no father willing to claim her, could be taken from her mother. Not until the courts were convinced that the education of children as citizens was best accomplished by their mothers could the idea of a mother's right to her child gain force.

That process began in a few highly publicized cases in the United States just before Hawthorne began writing *The Scarlet Letter*.[49] These cases in which a mother won custody from a father coincided with a challenge to coverture posed by the rise of republican rhetoric that opposed coverture's image of marriage as a corporate body presided over by the husband with the image of marriage as a contractual relation with husband and wife bringing to the union complementary, if not identical, duties and obligations. Not yet willing to grant women an active role in the political sphere of the new republic, this rhetoric gave them an important role to play, that of raising children as citizens in service of the nation. Emphasizing the nurturing role of the mother, this cult of republican motherhood bolstered a wife's claim to gain custody of her child, especially one of "tender" years. Indeed, in the D'Hauteville case, one of the most publicized custody battles, lawyers for the wife contrasted the increasingly progressive republican nature of marriage in the United States to the outmoded feudal concept of coverture maintained by her Swiss husband.

In her plea for a mother's rights, Hester echoes the antebellum rhetoric of republican motherhood, which like Hester's appeal to Dimmesdale emphasized the capacity for sympathy. A product of "paternal" and "maternal" qualities, a proper republican citizen was not simply the obedient subject produced under the patriarchal regime of both coverture and seventeenth-century Puritanism. Instead, a good citizen should also have the moral quality of sympathy nurtured through a mother's love. Appropriately, Pearl, unlike her mother, seems to find happiness in marriage. Indeed, Pearl's future is guaranteed when her two fathers finally take on their proper responsibilities. At his death Chillingworth bequeaths to his once-rejected inheritance "a considerable amount of property, both here and in England" (261). At his death Dimmesdale publicly acknowledges his paternity. Developing "all her sympathies," that acknowledgment elicits from Pearl tears that "were a pledge that she would grow up amid human joy and sorrow, nor for ever do battle with the world, but to be a woman in it" (256).

Occurring in the last of three memorable scenes on the scaffold, Dimmesdale's revelation of his paternity and Pearl's pledge culminate the book's dramatically rendered action. If in the first scaffold scene Hester, holding the infant Pearl, must face the public alone, and in the second scene, which culminates the first half of the book, Dimmesdale joins mother and child in the secrecy of night, in this final scene the three stand together in public. With that revelation civil order is restored.[50]

At the beginning of the book the scarlet letter had, we are told, "the effect of a spell" on Hester, "taking her out of the ordinary relations with humanity, and inclosing her in a sphere by herself" (54). But when Pearl consents to kiss Dimmesdale in public after refusing to do so in the forest, "A spell was broken" (256). The book's spell broken, Dimmesdale affirms the order that his and Hester's adultery had violated. Sensing the minister's impending death, Hester, still committed to their love, asks, "Shall we not meet again? . . . Shall we not spend our immortal life together? Surely, surely, we have ransomed one another, with all this woe?" Dimmesdale, however, responds, "The law we broke! — the sin here so awfully revealed! — let these alone be in thy thoughts! I fear! I fear! It may be, that, when we forgot our God, — when we violated our reverence each for the other's soul, — it was thenceforth vain to hope that we could meet hereafter, in an everlasting and pure reunion" (256).

It is tempting to read Dimmesdale's "final word" (257) as Hawthorne's own affirmation of the order his lovers violated. But he does not end with the book's last dramatically rendered scene. Instead, he presents us with a "Conclusion" that describes Chillingworth's sudden death, Hester's and Pearl's departure from the "new" world for the "old," and Hester's return to Boston. On her return Hester has a different relation to the Puritan community. On one hand, she acknowledges the importance of the civil order as she did not in her rebellious days. On the other, Hester is now accepted by the people who once spurned her. Still living on the margins of society, Hester devotes herself to counseling and comforting people with "sorrows and perplexities," especially women "in the continually recurring trials of wounded, wasted, wronged, misplaced, or erring and sinful passion, — or with the dreary burden of a heart unyielded, because unvalued and unsought" (263).

This changed relationship affords her the liberty to remove her "badge of shame" — "for not the sternest magistrate of the period would have imposed it" (261). Nonetheless, she willingly chooses to wear it as a reminder of her transgression, a choice that, ironically, allows it to take on a new significance as the community no longer sees it as a stigma. Indeed, as the narrator notes, the letter has finally done its "office," proving to be a better promoter of good citizenship than the scaffold. But just as Hester's actions change the meaning that people give to the scarlet A, so they alter the sense of good citizenship with which the book begins. What, however, does good citizenship at the end of *The Scarlet Letter* entail?

☆ ☆ ☆ We can start to answer that question by describing what good citizenship is not. Hester does not, for instance, become a good citizen according to the standards of republican motherhood. She is, to be sure, a good mother. Measured by the most important standard of success for a republican mother, however, she fails. Republican mothers were supposed to raise citizens for the nation. Pearl does not become a "citizen" even of Boston. Whereas, in typical Hawthornian fashion, we are not completely certain where Pearl ends up, circumstantial evidence indicates that she has successfully married and lives somewhere in Europe, most likely on the continent, not even in England. Rather than raise a child inculcated in proper values to serve the nation/commonwealth, Hester raises a child who finds "a home and comfort" (166) in an "unknown region" (262), just as Hawthorne ends "The Custom-House" imagining himself a "citizen of somewhere else" (44).

Hester's failure as a republican mother signals an important difference that Hawthorne has with republican citizenship in general. As the cult of republican motherhood demonstrates, the republican challenge to authoritarian forms of government involved more than exchanging the political status of subjects for that of citizens. It also tempered hierarchical rule with sympathy, which because of its capacity for identification across barriers of status is a decidedly unhierarchical emotion. Even so, much republican rhetoric continued to channel sympathy into service of the state by implying that sympathies cultivated in the family would lead to local and regional ones and then culminate in identification with all members of the nation. Within this developmental narrative, the state enforces the civil order in the name of "the people" sympathetically bound together as a nation.

Hawthorne, however, does not subscribe to that model. In contrast, he suggests an interactive, not a hierarchical, model for the relation between sympathy and the state. Also stressing the need to temper harsh, hierarchical rule with a capacity for sympathy, Hawthorne does not see sympathetic identification with members of the nation as necessarily an expansion of the moral capacity of individual citizens. Instead, a good Jacksonian Democrat, he continually stresses the importance of local attachments, which are valuable in themselves. For Hawthorne, in other words, national sympathies are not inevitably of a higher order than more local ones.[51]

Hawthorne's interactive model is compatible with a belief shared by many, if not all, Americans and indeed by many, if not all, citizens of liberal democracies. The primary goal for them is not necessarily to produce citizens who display loyalty to the state as representative of "the people" bound together as a nation. The goal instead is to produce independent citizens capable of choosing where they can best develop their capacities. In the United States of Hawthorne's day this sense of freedom of choice was officially endorsed through the government's support of a citizen's right to expatriation, whereas British subjects owed perpetual allegiance to their sovereign.[52] Even so, the notion of consensual citizenship is complicated. On one hand, as we saw in Chapter 1, many advocates of liberal democracies champion what they call civic over ethnic nations because they allow people to choose their loyalties rather than have them determined by birth.[53] On the other, critics of liberalism insist that the opposition between consent and descent has to be mediated by a third term—that of history—and that, more often than not, historical conditions make the ideal of freedom of choice an ideological illusion. Hester's decision to return to Boston at the end of the book suggests that there is a third way of understanding this issue.

Hester's decision is freely chosen in the sense that no one forces her to make it, but it is certainly not a decision made without pressure from many complicated historical and psychological factors, just as one's decision as to where to maintain or seek citizenship is not simply a rational choice about possibilities for political or economic freedom but one conditioned by numerous factors that one cannot control, such as where one was born and where one's intimate ties are located. Hester, of course, was not born in Boston, nor, when she returns, does she have any close living ties. But she is tied to the place by her personal history. That history might be made up of individual choices, if "choice" can be used when we talk about the distribution of affections. But her most significant choice—to break with the past and find a new beginning with Arthur—far from successful, leads to a tragic conclusion, giving her a new past from which, at book's end, she realizes she cannot escape. Her return to Boston acknowledges the powerful pull that past has upon her.

If that pull seems to undercut the idea that her return is freely chosen, her response tends to confirm the Hegelian notion that freedom is the recognition of necessity. Hester's freedom, limited as it is, comes from her willingness to confront that past rather than seek perpetually new beginnings. It is in confronting that past and devoting herself to the place that defined her that she finds redemption. Defined in the past by relations of status that governed the women of her time, that is, the status of lover, mother, or wife, Hester returns with her lover and husband dead and her child apparently married and in another country. Left alone, she does not, however, devote herself to individual fulfillment. Instead, she dedicates herself to helping others, especially those with histories of disappointment like her own. In the end, it is that devotion that defines her qualities as a good citizen. Through it, she offers an alternative to the idea of good citizenship as the absolute obedience that Winthrop wanted his subjects to give to their magistrates.

Noting Hester's changed attitude toward the civil law against which she once rebelled, recent critics have taken it as a sign of her submission to Puritan rule. It is important to remember, however, that she is not the only one to change. The civil order to which she submits has also changed.[54] Prior to the concluding chapter, the Puritans, as represented by Hawthorne, try to control all aspects of life. As the narrator notes regarding the concern over Pearl's upbringing, "Matters of even slighter public interest, and of far less intrinsic weight than the welfare of Hester and her child, were strangely mixed up with the deliberations of legislatures and acts of the state" (101). Likewise, Hester is allowed to live in her isolated cottage only "by the license of the magistrates, who still kept an inquisitorial watch over her" (81). When Hester returns, she reoccupies the same cottage, but she does so with a significant difference. Not perpetually watched over by suspicious magistrates, she receives their toleration of—and even admiration of—activities that are not directly under their supervision. The way in which those activities are received marks what we can call the nascent formation of an independent civil society. Operating within that sphere, Hester extends the parameters of good citizenship to an interpersonal realm of affairs of the heart that no affairs of state seem capable of remedying.

An absolutist state, as Hawthorne depicts the Puritan state to be, tries to eliminate or control all associations between it and the individual that could compete with it for loyalty. Allowing for alternative associations and loyalties, civil society helps to check state power. Not the realm of politics itself, civil society is, nonetheless, necessary for a democracy to function. As Michael Walzer puts it, "It is very risky for a democratic government when the state takes up all the available room and there are no alternative associations, no protected social space, where people can seek relief from politics, nurse wounds, find comfort, build strength for future encounters."[55] It is so risky that an important function of the state in liberal democracies is not only to protect the rights of individuals but also to guarantee a space for a relatively autonomous civil society. Indeed, an important right of the individual is the ability to participate in voluntary associations without intrusions by the state.

Theorized by figures of the Scottish Enlightenment, such as Adam Ferguson and Adam Smith, the idea of civil society modified Locke's notion of the social contract by creating a space for alternative forms of association between the individual and an undifferentiated "society." Indeed, as Alexis de Tocqueville observed, the numerous voluntary associations it allowed were a distinguishing feature of Hawthorne's Jacksonian America. Given constitutional sanction when the Supreme Court upheld the trustees of Dartmouth College in their efforts to achieve independence from the state of New Hampshire, those associations fostered a sense of communal giving that Hester, on her return, so powerfully embodies.[56] Unlike today's philanthropy, which is dominated by wealthy donors, antebellum philanthropy was a widespread phenomenon, providing a space of action for numerous middle-class women, who, in banding together to form groups in which their good works could promote the public good, found an indirect way to participate in the political process.

Because these activities coincided with religious disestablishment that moved churches into the sphere of voluntary associations, Kathleen D. McCarthy has understandably called them a new "American Creed."[57] Unfortunately, that phrase and the commonly used "American civil religion" contribute to the mistaken belief that the political system that developed in nineteenth-century America should be seen as a secularized version of a Puritan theocracy, with citizens having the same structural relation to the state as Puritan subjects had to the political representatives of God on earth.[58] In recent years no one has advanced the secularization thesis more persuasively than Sacvan Bercovitch, whose complicated argument about the Puritan origins of the American self informs his learned and brilliant reading of The Scarlet Letter. What that reading does not take into account, however, is how the rise of civil society potentially altered the relation between citizen-subjects and the state.[59] To say this is not to deny the powerful role that religion has played in American life. Nor is it to deny the unmistaken fact that frequently the nation has been guided by a sense of a sacred mission. But it is to insist on the difference between a process of secularization and a structural transformation.[60]

Secularization occurs when something nonreligious takes on the function previously fulfilled by the religious, as the term "civil religion" implies. But the entire point of civil society is that its associations and activities exist in a relation to the state different from those of a religious society in a theocracy. Indeed, if today we frequently contrast the civil with the military—as civilian rule is opposed to military rule—it is important to remember that originally civil society was opposed to the ecclesiastical. Responding to the bloody conflicts caused by the state's control of religion and religious groups' attempts to control the state, arguments for civil society and the forms of tolerant sociability on which it is based and which it promotes insisted on a space for people to develop associations not under direct supervision of the state. The result was a structural transformation in the relation between the subject and the state. If, as Lauren Berlant poignantly puts it, "in theory," Hawthorne's Puritan theocracy allows "neither a private part to which the state is not privy, nor a thought outside of the state's affairs," the rise of a civil society alters that state of affairs.[61] We can get a sense of the change by comparing Dimmesdale and Hester.

Tempted in the forest to break completely with the dictates of civil authority, Dimmesdale goes back on his resolve and seeks salvation by submitting to the existing civil order through participation in the civic activities of the election-day ceremonies. Prophetically evoking a "high and glorious destiny for the newly gathered people of the Lord" (249) in his Election Sermon, Dimmesdale eloquently blends his audience's "many voices" into "one great voice" through the image of a "universal impulse which makes likewise one vast heart out of many" (250). In doing so, he channels his listeners' sympathies into obedience to God and His earthly magistrates by appealing to "the great heart of mankind; beseeching its sympathy or forgiveness" (243). Perfectly illustrating Bercovitch's argument about how the New England Way becomes the American Way, Dimmesdale teleologically projects a utopian vision of a cohesive—and, it is important to emphasize, closed—Puritan community into the future, a future that Hawthorne's nineteenth-century audience could read as its own. Hester, however, is not a member of the crowd that submits to the message of her lover "with childlike loyalty" (250).

As Dimmesdale speaks to the crowd in the meetinghouse, "Hester Prynne was standing beside the scaffold of the pillory, with the scarlet letter still burning on her breast!" (250). Hester is, to be sure, entranced by the sermon, but, distant as she is, it "had throughout a meaning for her, entirely apart from its indistinguishable words" (243). She is captivated not by the content of the speech but by the musical sound of her lover's voice that "breathed passion and pathos, and emotions high or tender" (243). The intimacy of that voice, not the public occasion of Dimmesdale's sermon, moves her. In fact, when she sees the minister in the procession leading to the sermon, she "hardly knew him" in that "far vista of his unsympathetic thoughts" (239). Dimmesdale's sermon may unify the people, but Hester "stood, statue-like at the foot of the scaffold" because it is "the one point" that gives "unity" to "her whole orb of life" (244). Indeed, it is the scaffold, not the Election Sermon, that brings the lovers together. Even when they come together, however, they do not share common visions.

Repenting his sin, Dimmesdale asks Hester, "Is this not better . . . than what we dreamed of in the forest?" Her response, typically, turns to human relations. "I know not! I know not! . . . Better? Yea; so we both may die, and little Pearl die with us!" (254). Dimmesdale devotes his love to a higher power; Hester dedicates hers to those on earth closest to her. Granted, when Hester returns to Boston, she, like Dimmesdale, projects a utopian vision of the future, believing that "in Heaven's own time, a new truth would be revealed, in order to establish the whole relation between man and woman on surer ground of mutual happiness" (263). But what the two imagine is quite different. Dimmesdale focuses on "the relation between the Deity and the communities of mankind" (249); Hester, on "the whole relation between man and woman" (263).

Hester's good citizenship comes because of, rather than despite, her differences with Dimmesdale. If Dimmesdale confirms the idea of good citizenship as total obedience to the state, Hester's does not. All citizens may be subjects, but citizens living in a world in which the state allows a civil society to flourish have a relation to the state different from that of subjects in a theocracy.

To be sure, the Puritan society Hawthorne imagines is a nineteenth-century construction, not an accurate historical representation, and, as a number of critics have pointed out, he exaggerates the authoritarian power Puritan magistrates actually had.[62] But in doing so, he helps to emphasize the expanded possibilities for good citizenship made possible by the existence of a civil society. When Walzer argues that civil society involves "many of the associations and identities that we value outside of, prior to, or in the shadow of state and citizenship," he assumes that citizenship is confined to participation in the political sphere.[63] Hawthorne, through Hester, shows that Walzer's view is too narrow. Citizenship involves participation within civil society as well as within the realm of politics. Indeed, according to Hawthorne's account, it is in the realm of civil society that writers have their most productive role in a democracy, a role that he reflects upon in his introductory sketch of "The Custom-House."

✩ ✩ ✩ If the spell cast over the book's dramatic action is broken when Pearl kisses Dimmesdale on the scaffold, their story, Hawthorne wants us to believe, retains its capacity to cast a spell over those who come into contact with it. In "The Conclusion," for instance, we are told that "the story of the scarlet letter," now a "legend," retains "its spell," which is "still potent" (261)—so much so that, years later, when Hawthorne discovers the letter in the Custom House, it retains its power, continuing to perform its office by having Hawthorne tell its and Hester's story. In order for Hawthorne to do so, however, he had to give up his office as civil servant.

As Stephen Nissenbaum has documented, in real life Hawthorne, who was heavily involved in local partisan politics, fought extremely hard to retain his office in the Custom House.[64] Nonetheless, his fictional version of his dismissal tells a different story. If, according to Gordon Hutner, Hawthorne "introduces his novel about the public history of private lives with his private history of public lives," in both the novel and the sketch he ends by locating his protagonists in the space of civil society between the public and private.[65] And just as the novel looks ironically at various ideals of good citizenship, so does the sketch. For instance, Hawthorne's portrayal of the ex-military men working at the Custom House undercuts the ideal of the citizen-soldier, an ideal that contributed to the election as president of military hero Zachary Taylor and thus indirectly led to Hawthorne's dismissal. Taylor's election is a perfect example of the failure of a second ideal: people displaying and cultivating their virtue through participation in the political process. Far from a realm in which citizens sacrifice their own interests for the good of the nation, politics in "The Custom-House" has degenerated into a battle of self-interest. Its debilitating effects are most prominently displayed in the spoils system, which, especially in Hawthorne's hands, puts a lie to a third ideal: the good citizen as devoted civil servant.

Presided over by a flag that marks it as "a civil, and not a military post of Uncle Sam's government" (5), the Custom House is occupied by people who fail to heed the fierce look of the American eagle over its entrance, warning "all citizens, careful of their safety, against intruding on the premises which she overshadows with her wings" (5). Instead, they seek "to shelter themselves under the wing of the federal eagle" (5), not so much to serve the country as to be guaranteed a comfortable livelihood. Their expectation that the eagle's "bosom has all the softness and snugness of an eider-down pillow" (5) is the mirror image of the expectation that citizens, like the Puritan crowd, will with childlike loyalty submit to their magistrates' rule. Nonetheless, it has a similar effect in sapping their vitality. In contrast, Hawthorne chooses neither the nation's maternal protection nor its paternal authority. Instead, he would have us believe, as so many of us have, that he will best serve the country as a nonpartisan writer located in an independent civil society, not as a civil servant paid by the state. Thus he portrays himself as happily leaving the Custom House so that he can once again take up his pen.

In locating his office as a writer within civil society, Hawthorne self-consciously aligns himself with Hester in opposition to Dimmesdale. Hester performs her artistry with her needle to create the scarlet letter; Hawthorne performs his with his pen to create The Scarlet Letter. In contrast, Dimmesdale's artistry is connected with his eloquent voice, whose "inspiration," the narrator tells us, "performed its office" by delivering his Election Sermon (251). If the Election Sermon takes place within and gives religious sanction to the civic sphere, the book in which it appears performs its office within civil society, thus giving substance to the cliché that democracy is a way of life as well as a political system.

Such an "office" for a writer, as Nissenbaum has shown, is illustrated in the first work Hawthorne published after The Scarlet Letter, "The Great Stone Face." In that story people in a New England town wonder which citizen will prove worthy of matching the features of the Great Stone Face carved by nature into a nearby mountain. Disappointed when the rich man of commerce, Gathergold, and the military hero, General Blood-and-Thunder, fall short, the townspeople place their hopes in an "eminent statesman." Trained in the "trades of law and politics," "Old Stony Phiz," like Dimmesdale, has a "tongue" that is a "magic instrument." But he, too, proves inadequate, forcing people to turn their thoughts to a famous poet. As inspired as the poet is, he also turns out not to match the Great Stone Face's noble features. Even so, he has a special role, which is to identify the truly virtuous citizen, who turns out to be the simple, kindhearted townsman Ernest, who has lived a noble and admirable life in his daily and unpretentious routine.[66] Similarly, in The Scarlet Letter, Hawthorne points to Hester as the embodiment of good citizenship. In doing so, he takes us from the seventeenth-century definition of "citizen" as the inhabitant of a city to that of an obedient political subject and back again, as he associates good citizenship with the capacity to be a good neighbor.

As similar in this regard as Hawthorne's short story is to his novel, the uplifting tone of the former starkly contrasts the somber, almost tragic, tone of the latter. That difference is due in large part to the central role transgression plays in Hawthorne's most famous romance. Hester's sin has a sobering effect on what otherwise might be seen as an uplifting story about her ability to find redemption in the activities of civil society. It also complicates Hawthorne's vision of the relation between civil society and the realm of politics.

☆ ☆ ☆ Describing the dynamic interaction between a democratic state and a democratic civil society, Walzer argues that "only a democratic state can create a democratic civil society; only a democratic civil society can sustain a democratic state. The civility that makes democratic politics possible can only be learned in the associational networks; the roughly equal and widely dispersed capabilities that sustain the networks have to be fostered by the democratic state."[67] Close to Hawthorne's view of things, Walzer's synchronic description differs from his diachronic narrative in two crucial ways. First, Hawthorne, unlike Walzer, suggests an answer to the unanswerable question: Which comes first, democratic state or democratic civil society? Challenging the account of *der Mythos der Woher* that locates the seeds of a later democracy in the political institutions of seventeenth-century New England, Hawthorne suggests that the nascent formation of an independent civil society precedes and helps to generate a democratic state. Second, Hawthorne's narrative of how a civil society comes into being destabilizes Walzer's somewhat idealized and far too balanced description of how democracies work.

For Hawthorne the nascent formation of a civil society might precede a democratic state, but its origins are far from civil. On the contrary, its birth is narratively linked to transgressions. As much as we may sympathize with Hawthorne's lovers for being denied happiness by a repressive Puritan state and society, the sympathies they unleash are potentially dangerous. Capable of binding people together, sympathy, as Hawthorne knows all too well, can also be misdirected. In "Young Goodman Brown," for instance, Hawthorne speaks of "the sympathy of all that was wicked in his heart."[68] The problems multiply when sympathy combines with eros. Love in its erotic version involves more than sympathy. Sympathy may be necessary for love, and love can help breed sympathy; but love casts a much deeper spell. Love's deep absorption can lead to a self-enclosed isolation that threatens rather than promotes social cohesion. Hester's love for Dimmesdale regulates her erotic passion by giving her a purpose in life, but that purpose does not necessarily serve the needs of the community. On the contrary, whereas Dimmesdale's and Hester's "iron link of mutual crime, . . . like all other ties . . . brought along with it its obligations," it also severed the "links that united them to the rest of human kind" (159–60). Hester's and Dimmesdale's love is, as we have seen, most transgressive because it creates a self-enclosed world that recognizes no obligation beyond itself.

To be sure, the problem is not theirs alone. Hester is forced into isolation in part by unsympathetic judgments by both Puritan authorities and society. Nonetheless, from the God's-eye perspective the narrator tries to assume, the lovers' fall into sin turns out to be a happy fall. Dying, Dimmesdale claims to achieve this perspective when he exclaims, "God knows; and He is merciful! He hath proved his mercy, most of all, in my afflictions. By giving me this torture to bear on my breast! By sending yonder dark and terrible man, to keep the torture always at red-heat! By bringing me hither, to die this death of triumphant ignominy before the people! Had either of these agonies been wanting, I would have been lost for ever!" (256–57). In the "Conclusion" Hester struggles to achieve the same perspective. From that perspective, as Bercovitch has eloquently argued, progress is assured, as historical change establishes a teleological continuity between past and present.

But, as Hawthorne warns us, human efforts to assume a God's-eye perspective run the risk of presumption. Indeed, it is not the only perspective the book offers. From the human perspective of those caught within the book's action, change is hardly smooth, harmonious, and continuous. It is instead full of conflict, torment, and tragic loss. Dimmesdale's merciful God may guide human history toward the fulfillment of justice, but in the world of human history justice and mercy never perfectly coincide. Nor is the marriage of justice and sentiment ever perfectly achieved. In fact, the new sympathies helping to create an altered configuration of social cohesion come more from failed relations than from successful ones. Thus, in the book's final image, Hester and Dimmesdale share a common tombstone, but an eternal space remains between their graves.

Linked to human beings' capacity for transgression, the politics of The Scarlet Letter involves more than the positions Hawthorne took on particular issues of his day. If, understandably, few today agree with his views on slavery or his gendered account of the duties to the family and the state, to confine our judgments to them would be to ignore wrestling with other elements of his political vision important for citizens in a democracy.[69] More than a half-century ago Arthur M. Schlesinger Jr., the famous historian of Jacksonian America and a student of F. O. Matthiessen, captured one aspect of that vision when he contrasted liberal progressivism's "sentimental belief in progress" with the "tradition of Jackson and Hawthorne, the tradition of a reasonable responsibility about politics and a moderate pessimism about man." Dispensing with "the Christian myths of sin and atonement," the former believed that "man's shortcomings, such as they were, were to be redeemed . . . by the benevolent unfolding of history." But, as

Hawthorne illustrates through his portrayal of reformers, those convinced of "infallibility can sacrifice humanity without compunction on the altar of some abstract and special good." In contrast, Hawthorne's "pessimism about man, far from promoting authoritarianism, alone can inoculate the democratic faith against it. 'Man's capacity for justice makes democracy possible,' Niebuhr has written in his remarkable book on democratic theory; 'but man's inclination to injustice makes democracy necessary.'"[70]

To Schlesinger's and Niebuhr's comments we need to add that Hawthorne's limited and potentially sinful human beings search not just for justice in the political sphere but also for happiness in civil society. If in Walzer's formulation a democratic state and a democratic civil society complement and balance each other, in Hawthorne's world they also breed a potential conflict, as the pursuit of happiness in civil society is capable of generating sympathies that come into tension with the state's demands for justice, and the demands for justice may require repressions that preclude happiness.[71] Formally embodied in The Scarlet Letter as a tension between a point of view eliciting readers' sympathies and one concerned with judgments of justice, Hawthorne does not solve this dilemma within the pages of the book. What he does give us is a world in which mutual happiness between lovers does not necessarily correspond with justice and justice does not necessarily lead to happiness, although to abandon the quest for either would rule out greater possibilities for both. It is, in other words, a world made more tolerable by those developing Hester's capacities for citizenship.

In the next chapter we will look at another New Englander's story of transgression and redemption. But, concerned with the dangers of civil war, not the possibilities of civil society, its model citizen is a patriot who gives undivided loyalty to his country.

3 "The Man without a Country"
The Patriotic Citizen, Lincoln, and Civil Liberties

The same week Abraham Lincoln delivered the Gettysburg Address, the December 1863 *Atlantic Monthly* appeared. It contained a story by Edward Everett Hale called "The Man without a Country." Hale's story had an immediate impact. Writing to his wife from the front on December 5, 1863, Thomas Wentworth Higginson enthused, "How capital Edward Hale's Man without a Country in the Atlantic."[1] In 1907, the fiftieth anniversary of the *Atlantic*, a reader vividly recalled when the December 1863 issue arrived. She was so entranced by Hale's story that she refused to give it to her sister. The two finally agreed to read together. "To this day I can remember just where in 'The Man Without a Country' came some of the places where I had to wait for a leaf to be turned."[2] According to Allan Nevins, Hale's story was so effective that it "was worth a division of soldiers to Grant's army."[3]

The tale it tells is simple and memorable. When Aaron Burr hatches his plot in 1805 allegedly to establish a separate country within the newly purchased Louisiana Territory, he seduces a young U.S. Army officer named Philip Nolan stationed in the lower Mississippi River Valley. Although Burr escapes conviction for treason at his famous trial in Richmond, Nolan is tried and convicted in a court-martial conducted by the "Legion of the West." Given the opportunity to say something to prove that he had "always been faithful to the United States," Nolan "cried out, in a bit of a frenzy, — 'D—n the United States! I wish that I may never hear of the United States again!'"[4] Shocked, the presiding officer turns his wish into his punishment, and "from that moment, September 23, 1807, until the day he died, May 11, 1863, he never heard her name again" (667). Nolan is placed on a U.S. ship and transferred from one vessel to another so that he never again sees the United States. As time passes, he regrets his youthful impetuousness, and he dies the most patriotic citizen one can imagine. Buried at sea, he nonetheless requests that a stone for his memory be placed on U.S. soil with the words, "'He loved his country as no other man has loved her; but no man deserved less at her hands'" (679).

This story is told by Frederic Ingham, a naval officer who, in his first voyage after being appointed a midshipman, met Nolan six or eight years after the War of 1812. When Ingham comes across Nolan's obituary in the midst of the Civil War, he feels there can be no possible harm in telling "this poor creature's story" (665). He then proceeds to stitch together a narrative from his personal encounters, from research, and from others who knew him, such as fellow naval officer Danforth, who writes a letter describing Nolan's last living moments. Ingham's matter-of-fact rendition of Nolan's fate is crucial to the story's verisimilitude.

Hale, like Lincoln, is a master of the plain style. Indeed, the style of Lincoln's Gettysburg Address is often contrasted with the classical oratorical style of Edward Everett, who delivered the main address that day in November 1863 and who also happened to be Edward Everett Hale's uncle. As much as the nephew was trained in the uncle's rhetorical tradition, in his writing he was closer to Lincoln.[5] And like the Gettysburg Address, his most famous story has had a life long after the Civil War. Numerous editions have appeared. For many years it was required reading in schools, and it was frequently reprinted in anthologies and published as a textbook. It has been turned into an opera, four films, and a classic comic book, while inspiring an episode in the television series *King of the Hill* called "A Man without a Country Club."

Even for those who have not read it, its title has become a familiar phrase in the language. In 1908 an edition proclaimed that "with its simple, moral dignity it is a typical American masterpiece."[6] The 1918 *Cambridge History of American Literature* acknowledged that the story "has generally been accepted as an American classic" and called it "a haunting presence, never to be forgotten."[7] In his introduction to a 1936 edition Carl Van Doren claimed that with his story, Hale "found a legend."[8] In 1949 Clifton Fadiman called the story "an immortal, homespun folk possession."[9] In the 1950s Hale's biographer pronounced that, whereas the Civil War produced a "veritable cloud of oratory," most was "quickly dissipated on the winds of time." Even so, "there glowed in men's memories an elemental residue of simple and sincere prose — 'documents in the history of the war' transcending the war, symbols of the best in America's tradition, writings to be handed down reverently from generation to generation. Each school child in his turn learns what it would mean to be a 'man without a country,' and each in turn, bent over his memory work, highly resolves 'that a government of the people, by the people, for the people, shall not perish from the earth.'"[10] Introducing a 1960 edition, Van Wyck Brooks noted that Philip Nolan had become a "sort of national myth" and that the story is a "classic that almost everybody knows and that every child has read."[11]

For years, "The Man without a Country" and Lincoln's most famous speeches mutually reinforced the sense of the nation that arose out of the Civil War. Before the war many people gave priority to state citizenship; after the war national citizenship reigned supreme. Both Hale and Lincoln helped bring about this change by working on/with myths of the nation's founding that, open to differing interpretations, had justified both parties during the war. But if Lincoln's works remain a vital part of the national memory, with many schoolchildren still reciting the Gettysburg Address, today few read Hale's story. That difference is due in part to changes in civic education and in part to differences in the vision of the nation offered by Lincoln and Hale. To bring the two back into relation can, therefore, help us better understand both how national citizenship achieved the priority it has and why Lincoln's vision has sustained its power while Hale's has lost its. But it can do even more.

Hale wrote his story to support Lincoln in the midst of the most controversial civil liberties dispute of his administration, the case of Clement L. Vallandigham. To read "The Man without a Country" in conjunction with Lincoln's response to the Vallandigham incident is to highlight potential threats that Hale's and Lincoln's senses of patriotism pose to the nation's cherished history of protecting civil liberties. In fact, I will argue that, despite its limitations, Hale's seemingly simple story of patriotism has an unacknowledged complexity that calls attention to a danger lurking not only in Lincoln's stand on civil liberties but also in his most memorable expression of the nation's civic ideals. First, however, I need to show how Hale's story worked with and helped to contribute to "Honest Abe's" sense of the nation.

☆ ☆ ☆ It is commonplace to praise Lincoln for saving the nation when its very existence was threatened by civil war. It would be more accurate to say that, in interpreting the Constitution the way he did and in waging the war the way he did, he transformed a union of states into a nation. For instance, in his February 27, 1860, address at the Cooper Institute that helped to catapult him into national attention, he refers to the country as "this great Confederacy."[12] February 22, 1861, stopping in Philadelphia on his way to be inaugurated he again speaks of "this Confederacy."[13] But about a week later, in his First Inaugural, he uses that term only pejoratively to describe states trying to destroy the Union. "Why may not any portion of a new confederacy," he asks, "a year or two hence, arbitrarily secede again, precisely as portions of the present Union now claim to secede from it."[14] Once Lincoln assumes office, he no longer finds it appropriate to call the Union a confederacy. His need to preserve the Union altered his sense of the Union.

"The Man without a Country" helped to bring about that transformation in the public's mind.[15] Its major cultural work was to make the country, not the state or the section, the object of affection reserved for one's "home." If, according to the strict letter of the law, Nolan's punishment for treason should have been death, Hale makes us believe that to be without a country is a fate worse than death. In fact, the story helped to alter the very meaning of "country" in an American setting.

In the years before the Civil War, some people considered their state, not the Union, to be their country. This sentiment was shared by people fully committed to the Union. For instance, in 1844 a Pennsylvanian declared, "I love our Union as I love my Country. It was obtained by the blood of heroes and the wisdom of sages," and it "makes us one great commonwealth of nations."[16] If, according to Garry Wills, Lincoln "in his brief time before the crowd at Gettysburg . . . called up a new nation out of the blood and trauma," Hale helped people imagine the country as a singular rather than as a plural entity, so that today we say the United States *is*, not the United States *are*.[17] As Hale himself put it in 1897, "The United States *is* a nation, now. And there is not left any one, living in the Northern, Middle, Western, or Pacific States, who ever think that the United States *are* a confederacy."[18] Hale's story is, an 1885 essay in the *Century* magazine claims, "the best sermon on patriotism ever written. It was intended to create, and did create, a national sentiment. It has done much, and will do more, to foster the idea of national unity, of a united country as opposed to state autonomy or separate sectional interests."[19]

Both Hale and Lincoln created a new sense of the country by working on/ with myth(s) of its foundation. They were forced to do so because the Civil War was in part a conflict over the true legacy of the Spirit of '76. "Give me liberty or give me death," Patrick Henry had proclaimed, articulating the sense of moral mission motivating the colonials' revolt against the distant authority of George III. If Henry has been lionized as a great revolutionary patriot, he was easily claimed as a model for the seceding Southerners. From Virginia, he was a passionate, antifederalist advocate of state sovereignty. Like Henry, secessionists argued that the Declaration of Independence transferred sovereignty from the king to individual colonies that then became sovereign states. Starting from this premise, J. C. Calhoun argued that it was these sovereign states that had ratified the Constitution in 1789 and that the union they created was nothing more than a league of states.[20] For Calhoun and his followers the Declaration rested on the consent of the governed. Thus, states always had the option of leaving the union they had created. Calhoun was so opposed to a national government that, according to Francis Lieber, when asked why the country had no single name, he responded, "We have no name because we ought to have none; we are only States united, and have no country."[21]

Lincoln and Hale disagreed. For them, without the united act of the Declaration of Independence the colonies would still be colonies. Thus, the Declaration did not transfer sovereignty first from the king to states that could then in 1789 unite under the Constitution. Instead, as Lincoln put it in his First Inaugural, "The Union is much older than the Constitution. It was formed in fact, by the Articles of Association in 1774. It was matured and continued by the Declaration of Independence in 1776. It was further matured and the faith of all the then thirteen States expressly plighted and engaged that it should be perpetual, by the Articles of Confederation in 1778. And finally, in 1787, one of the objects for ordaining and establishing the Constitution, was 'to form a more perfect Union.'"[22]

Unionists even used Henry's antifederalism to bolster their argument. For instance, Charles Sumner claimed that Henry correctly understood the Constitution when he protested that it used "We, the people, instead of We, the States. . . . If States be not the agents of this compact, it must be one great consolidated National government of the people of all the states."[23] Since it was this national document that the Southern states had ratified, Calhoun's argument that the Constitution created nothing more than a league of sovereign states was unfounded. Instead, as Lincoln argued, the Union is "perpetual. Perpetuity is implied, if not expressed, in the fundamental law of all national governments. It is safe to assert that no government proper, ever had a provision in its organic law for its own termination."[24]

Most of Lincoln's constitutional arguments came indirectly from Sumner's Harvard Law School mentor Justice Joseph Story, who coached Daniel Webster for his famous 1830 "Reply to Hayne," the most celebrated refutation of Calhoun's interpretation of the Constitution. Lincoln considered Webster's speech the greatest delivered by an American. Ending it with "Liberty and Union, now and forever, one and inseparable," Webster appropriated the founders' love of liberty for his nationalist agenda. One of his strategies was to insist that Hayne's Revolutionary heroes from South

Carolina were national heroes. "I claim them," Webster made clear, "for countrymen, one and all, the Laurenses, the Rutledges, the Pickneys, the Sumters, the Marions, *Americans* all, whose fame is no more hemmed in by State lines, than their talents and patriotism were capable of being circumscribed within the same narrow limits."[25] In laying claim to these heroes, Webster implied that Southerners were, in Wills's words, "traitors to their own Revolutionary heroes if they tear apart a nation those ancestors built."[26] Webster's implication that Southerners in 1830 risked betraying the founders suggests that the battle over who were the true followers of the Spirit of '76 involved more than a difference over how to interpret the Constitution. It was also a heated battle over loyalties.

A nation founded in revolution faces what we can call an "antinomian crisis" on a national level. The antinomian threat was so acute for the Puritans because their very identity linked them to a founding moment of dissent against the institutional structures of an established religion. Thus anyone who dissented against the Puritans' own effort to establish themselves institutionally could claim to be following in the footsteps of the founders. Similarly, insofar as the founding fathers appealed to the consent of the governed to wage a war of independence against a distant sovereign power, those in later generations appealing to the consent of the governed to declare independence from a distant federal government could claim to be following in the Spirit of '76. Shrugging off charges that they were traitors to the national cause, they could proudly point to the fact that the patriots of 1776 had similar charges of disloyalty leveled against them by the British crown. Most wars are fought between people owing loyalty to two different nations, but both the Civil War and the Revolutionary War were wars in which those on one side were accused of being disloyal to the sovereign power under which they were born. For the North to be successful it needed to undermine the similarities between the founders' cause and the cause of the secessionists. If Lincoln was adroit at appealing to the myth of the foundation to counter Southerners' interpretation of the Constitution, Hale was a master at containing the "antinomian" threat present in appeals to the Spirit of '76.

"The Man without a Country" contains that threat by silently working on/with a myth of Revolutionary patriotism that Hale knew quite well: the story of his great uncle Nathan Hale. Hale, still in his twenties, was hanged by the British on September 22, 1776, after being caught on Long Island spying for Washington's Continental Army. What made Hale famous was not his spying, which was botched, but his courageous last words. "I only regret," he proclaimed on the scaffold, "that I have but one life to lose for my country." The dying patriot's words echo Joseph Addison's *Cato*, whose title character declares it a pity "that we can die but once to serve our country." Wills has shown the important role Addison's play had in forming a sense of civic virtue in the new republic.[27] Hale would have known it from his undergraduate days at Yale. In alluding to Cato's lines at his heroic death, young Nathan both evoked that sense of virtue valued by others of his day—including the British, who, legend has it, admired his grace in dying—and became an American embodiment of it. Along with the start of the Declaration and Henry's famous appeal to liberty, Hale's words are today some of the most often remembered of the Revolution. Hale is so firmly lodged in the pantheon of Revolutionary heroes that William Bennett includes him in his book of the founders' words of advice.[28]

It is important to remember, however, that for much of the antebellum period, Hale was largely forgotten, celebrated, if at all, mostly in New England. Bennett, for instance, excerpts his account of Hale's death from John Frost's *Lives of the Heroes of the American Revolution* published in Boston in 1849. In the conclusion to his description of Hale, which Bennett does not reprint, Frost laments that Hale was not given the same honor by his country that the British gave Major Andre, the handsome British soldier linked to Benedict Arnold whom Washington hung as a spy. "While almost every historian of the American revolution has celebrated the virtues, and lamented the fate of Andre, Hale has remained unnoticed, and it is scarcely known that such a character existed."[29] Similarly in 1845 C. Edwards Lester wrote, "Let us see what England has done for her great men. . . . Even Andre the Spy was brought across the Atlantic by a solemn act of Parliament, and entombed by the side of heroes and over him breathes the marble of a great sculptor. And where does Hale—the American spy—a loftier and nobler character—sleep? Nobody appears to know except a few brave women of Connecticut, who are building his monument with their needles; and I need not say that every stitch is to our Government a stitch of shame."[30]

The few brave women building Hale's monument with their needles were most likely sparked into action by James Staunton Babcock's *Memoir of Captain Hale* published in New Haven in 1844. Indeed, Hale's antebellum reputation was linked to Yale, which, like the C I A headquarters in Langley, Virginia, honors him today with the statue absent in 1845. During Hale's undergraduate days prior to independence, Yale was a hotbed of national sentiment. Noting the influence of John Trumbell and Timothy Dwight as tutors, David Potter writes, "It would be difficult to find anywhere in the thirteen colonies, such clear expressions of American nationalism as began to come from Yale in 1770." This climate produced Noah Webster, whose work as a lexicographer was motivated by a desire to "safeguard and foster national unity by promoting a national uniformity of language." It also produced Nathan Hale. "In an age when the term, 'my country,' might mean either America in the broad sense or one particular colony in the narrow sense—and when it more often meant the latter than the former," Potter continues, "Hale gave his loyalty to the American Union."[31] Ironically, in the antebellum period Hale's nationalism was one reason why his patriotism was celebrated mostly regionally, since his nationalism made it much more difficult for Southerners to appropriate him for their cause than Henry, who had also drawn on *Cato* for his famous quotation.[32]

Resurrected in the two decades before his great-nephew would write his story and turned into an unforgettable moment of the founding only after the Civil War altered the sense of the United States as a nation, Hale's story reminds us of the complications of loyalty during the Revolutionary War. After all, from the British point of view, Hale was committing not only espionage but treason. A British subject, he was participating in a war against British troops. Similarly, Southerners accused of treason by the North, like Hale, denied their loyalty to the sovereign nation under whose authority they were born. Edward Everett Hale does not directly address this similarity in his story. But he does have his protagonist negatively echo his great uncle's (now) famous dying words, an echo Hale invites us to hear by remarking that "half the officers who sat in [Nolan's court-martial] had served through the Revolution, and their lives, not to say their necks, had been risked for the very idea which he so cavalierly cursed in his madness" (667). Nolan's curse violates the patriotic spirit of Nathan Hale, who risked his neck and lost his life for his country. Nonetheless, the power of the story comes from the fact that in the end it is easy to imagine Nolan not only repeating Nathan's words but being considered worthy of doing so. He has become worthy because his only regret is that he did not understand the need to share Nathan's sentiments when he was Nathan's age.

An essential part of the ideological battle Hale waged with the South comes from associating the youthful Nolan with Revolutionary heroes gone bad. For instance, when Colonel Morgan, who presided over the court, hears Nolan's curse, he "could not have felt worse if Nolan had compared Washington to Benedict Arnold or had cried 'God save King George'" (667). Even more important is Nolan's association with Burr, who also had been a Revolutionary War hero but then allegedly tried, like Confederates, to create a new country by separating from the old. If Southerners laid claim to the Spirit of '76 because, like the founding fathers, they sought liberty by establishing a separate sovereignty, Hale counters by associating them with Burr's betrayal of that spirit. He makes that association clear by having Nolan, late in his life, reject "like a wretched night's dream a boy's idea of personal fame or of separate sovereignty" (678). Then, in his dying words to Danforth, Nolan mistakenly assumes that the thirty-four stars on the flag mean that "there has never been any successful Burr" (678). What Danforth does not have the courage to tell him is that new Burrs in the form of Confederates were indeed trying to take states away from the Union.

Earlier in the story officers had to decide, after Texas had been annexed, whether they should cut it out of Nolan's maps of the world and Mexico, just as the United States had been cut out from the start. But they "voted, rightly enough, that to do this would be virtually to reveal to him what had happened, or, as Harry Cole said, to make him think Old Burr had succeeded" (676). Then in conversation Nolan has occasion to mention the Texas where he had spent part of his youth. "Pray, what became of Texas?" he innocently asks. "After the Mexicans got their independence, I thought that province of Texas would come forward very fast. . . . But I have not heard a word of Texas for near twenty years" (676). To break the awful silence that ensued, Ingham blurts out, "Texas is out of the map, Mr. Nolan" (676), a cause of joy for Nolan, since it meant this beloved place was part of his country, but a cause of sorrow for readers who realize that present-day Burrs had succeeded in having Texas secede. Hale's story had such an effect on its original audience because it fully understood what was at stake in Nolan's later rejection of Burr's traitorous, but seductive, vision.[33]

The transformation that leads to Nolan's patriotism comes in stages. He first wavers while reading aloud Sir Walter Scott's "Lay of the Last Minstrel." When he comes upon the line "This is my own, my native land!" all who watched him "saw something was to pay" (670). Trying to go on, he falters with the description of a person "wandering on a foreign strand."

> For him no minstrel raptures swell;
> High though his titles, proud his name,
> Boundless his wealth as wish can claim,
> Despite these titles, power, and pelf,
> The wretch, concentrated all in self (670).[34]

Throwing the book into the sea, he vanishes into his stateroom. When he returns two months later, he is a changed man.

Another scene of explicit regret comes when the ship he is on intercepts a Portuguese slaver. Volunteering to translate, Nolan is forced to relate that the slaves, when freed, exclaim, "Take us home, take us to our country, take us to our own house, take us to our own pickaninnies and our

This frontispiece appeared in a 1960 edition of "The Man without a Country," illustrated by Leonard Everett Fisher. Fisher contrasts Nolan's lonely vigil at sea under a sky full of stars with three depictions of him in relation to stars on the American flag. Dramatizing the 1807 trial in which Nolan damns his country, the first has a flag with seventeen stars. The second illustrates Nolan's plea for Ingham to serve the flag, "as she bids you, though the service carry you through a thousand hells" (675) with a ship in the background and a large twenty-four-starred flag in the foreground. The final image shows Nolan's corpse draped by a flag with thirty-four stars. No longer alone with the nighttime stars, Nolan has, in death, been embraced by the symbol of the nation he so loved. (© Copyright 1960 by Franklin Watts, Inc. All rights reserved. Reprinted by permission of Franklin Watts, an imprint of Scholastic Library Publishing, Inc.)

own women."[35] He ends his translation by reporting, "And this one says
. . . that he had not heard a word from his home in six months, while he
has been locked up in an infernal barracoon" (674). The contrast between
these Africans allowed to return home and Nolan never allowed to return
to or hear of his country is too much to bear. The Africans themselves quiet
when they see "Nolan's agony" and "the almost equal agony of sympathy"
on the face of the officer accompanying him. Because Nolan's "repentance
was so clear" (676), readers are clearly intended to share that "agony of
sympathy."

Indeed, it has already been heightened by two incidents between these
two. In the first, during a celebration on a ship patrolling the Mediterra-
nean, Nolan tries to get information of "home" when he dances with a
woman he had known before she married. "'Home!! Mr. Nolan!!'" this "celebrated Southern beauty" (670) responds, "'I thought you were the man
who never wanted to hear of home again!' —and she walked directly up
the deck to her husband, and left Nolan alone, as he always was. —He did
not dance again" (671). Dramatizing that life without a country means life
without a home and a family, this domestic scene complements the scene
of battle that follows.

During the War of 1812 Nolan's ship encounters an English warship that
kills the officer of a cannon and much of its crew. Nolan, trained as an ar-
tillery officer, takes command of the gun and courageously brings about a
victory. Possessing "that way which makes men feel sure all is right and is
going to be right," Nolan keeps the sailors under his assumed command
"in spirits," even "though he was exposed all the time." After the ship's
commander took the Englishman's sword, he called to Nolan to express his
gratitude for his heroism. "And then the old man took off his own sword
of ceremony, and gave it to Nolan, and made him put it on. The man told
me this who saw it. Nolan cried like a baby, and well he might. He had not
worn a sword since that infernal day at Fort Adams. But always afterward
on occasions of ceremony, he wore that quaint old French sword of the
Commodore's" (672).

In establishing Nolan's bravery, Hale works within the established tradition of patriotic literature. In the early years of the republic it had been important for Americans to remind themselves and the world that they were
as brave as (or braver than) anyone. It is for this reason that the Battle of
Bunker Hill took on such importance, even though American troops eventually lost the hill. In *American Hero Stories*, for instance, Eva March Tappan
concludes her description of the battle, "News of the battle went through
the colonies like wildfire. All their lives the Americans had looked up to the

British regulars as the greatest of soldiers: and they, the untrained colonists who had never seen two regiments in battle, had twice driven them back! The hill was lost, but to repulse the British regulars was a mighty victory." Similarly, an essential element of Nathan Hale's story is the courageous way by which he meets his death. Thus, the early recounting of Nathan's story almost always told of how the British destroyed the letters he wrote to his mother and friends the morning of his execution in order that *"the rebels should not know they had a man in their army who could die with so much firmness."*[36] In this respect, it is worth comparing "The Man without a Country" with stories of another model of patriotism celebrated in the antebellum period, a man whose daring raid in February 1804 under the heavy fortifications of Tripoli harbor to recapture and to burn the ship the *Philadelphia* won the praise of Lord Horatio Nelson himself as "the most bold and daring act of the age": Stephen Decatur.[37]

One historian calls Decatur "America's first nineteenth-century military hero."[38] Another claims that "it is no exaggeration to say that his exploits, by helping to kindle the flames of patriotism, helped to forge a new nation out of thirteen former colonies not long united under one flag."[39] His courageous act against the Barbary pirates was repeatedly depicted and celebrated in plays, poems, illustrations, and journalistic accounts. He was also honored for avenging the death of his brother James in hand-to-hand combat. When, after this death, Decatur's father was toasted as "the gallant father of a gallant son," he solemnly responded with "Our children are our country's property."[40] Decatur himself died not in service for his country but in an 1820 duel with an offended naval officer. Even so, as a sign of Stephen's courage, it was reported that he had, as he had done in another duel, refused to take the man's life and instead intentionally wounded him in the hip, only to be struck by a fatal bullet in return. Sensing his end, Decatur calmly remarked, "I am fatally wounded, at least I believe so, and wish that I had fallen in defence of my country."[41] It is this national hero who is popularly credited with coining the phrase "Our country, right or wrong."[42]

In describing Nolan's grace under fire, Hale makes it clear that his hero shares the bravery of those like Decatur. A description of Decatur's courageous deed is even appended to *Classics Illustrated*'s 1969 version of "The Man without a Country." But, for Hale, physical courage alone is not enough to make one patriotic. After all, it is not a lack of courage that causes Nolan to curse his country. Instead, as a 1908 edition of the story points out, Hale's story has the power it does because it teaches "that patriotism is even more than heroism." In a time "when men and boys ran riot, and plunged, willing and unwitting, into bloody graves Doctor Hale tried to impress the larger lesson of loyalty, disclosing the country's altar beside the family hearth-stone and showing that true patriotism begins at home, where it means not only 'dying the death,' but *living the life*."⁴³ What makes Nolan such a sympathetic figure is that he uncomplainingly lives the life of patriotism, even though his initial act of youthful folly makes it impossible for him to live a life that all people seem entitled to—which is another reason why the battle scene is so important for the story's message.

Because of his bravery and his changed attitude, Nolan has clearly earned our forgiveness. Appropriately, after the battle, the commodore writes a special letter to the secretary of war, which most likely asks for a pardon. "But," we are told, "nothing ever came of it" (672). On the contrary, about this time "they began to ignore the whole transaction at Washington," and "Nolan's imprisonment began to carry itself on because there was nobody to stop it without any new orders from home" (672). This failure to procure a pardon brings about a complete transfer of our sympathies from the government to Nolan. Our sympathy is heightened because Nolan accepts his punishment, as harsh as it is, without complaint. Because "he repented of his folly and then, like a man, submitted to the fate he had asked for" (676), Nolan is redeemed.

Nolan's redemption turns his fall into a *felix culpa*. On one hand, he serves as a warning to those who might be tempted to commit a similar youthful indiscretion. On the other, he is a model for those who have strayed. Those willing to admit their mistake, Hale implies, will be forgiven.⁴⁴ In an 1864 *Atlantic Monthly* essay titled "Northern Invasions," he wrote, "The nation has no thought of insisting on its rights against Rebel States. It has no thunders of vengeance except for those who have led in these iniquities. For the people who have been misled it has pardon, protection, encouragement, and hope. It can afford to be generous."⁴⁵ Anticipating Lincoln's famous line in his Second Inaugural — "With malice toward none; with charity for all" — "A Man without a Country" clears the ground for a time of peace. As one editor points out, "At a time when war was the sublime passion of the people, he reversed an old maxim, making it really read: 'In time of *war* prepare for *peace*.'"⁴⁶

In preparing for peace, Hale did not extend his forgiveness to Confederate leaders. For them there will be no redemption. There is, according to Ingham, only one fate worse than Nolan's: "It is the fate reserved for those men who shall have one day to exile themselves from their country because they have attempted her ruin, and shall have at the same time to see the prosperity and honor to which she rises when she has rid herself of them and their iniquities" (676). He then goes on to imagine "every Bragg and

Beauregard who broke a soldier's oath two years ago" vegetating "through what is left of life to them in wretched Boulognes and Leicester Squares, where they are destined to upbraid each other till they die" (676).

As seemingly simple as Hale conveys his message, his story is in fact extremely sophisticated. For instance, one of Hale's most effective techniques in creating a sense of verisimilitude is to have Ingham frequently admit that he is not certain of the truth. Not an eyewitness to much of what he relates and confronted with the faultiness of memory, he often starts a sentence with "I suppose" or some other mark of tentativeness. This acknowledgment of the uncertainty of recall lends credibility to a story that on the face of it would test our willingness to suspend disbelief. It also gives Ingham an ethos of honesty. Because he is not someone to claim more knowledge than he has, we come to trust those parts of the story that he relates with authority. Trusting him we are positioned to distinguish the truths about Nolan from what Ingham calls the "lies," the "myths," and the "traditions" that have been told about "this man for forty years" (671). Told by Nolan himself, the story would have fallen flat, but Ingham's filter makes Nolan's tale believable.

Skillful in creating a sense of realism, Hale also provides moments that call attention to the story's fictional fabrication. Careful not to disturb the story's surface realism, he, nonetheless, gives attentive readers glimpses of the author's hand at work. Take, for instance, Ingham's description of the government's failure to acknowledge Nolan's existence: "It was like getting a ghost out of prison. They pretended there was no such man. They say so at the Department now! Perhaps they do not know. It will not be the first thing in the service of which the Department appears to know nothing!" (675). Because Nolan is a product of Hale's fictional imagination, not a real person, the government is, on at least one level, right: "There was no such man."

According to Hale, moments like these guard him against charges that he was intentionally deceiving his readers. For instance, he has Nolan die on a ship that had in fact disappeared in the Pacific two years earlier. He also planned to have the latitude and longitude of the ship carrying Nolan at his death correspond to somewhere in the Andes Mountains. But an attentive proofreader seems to have foiled his attempt. In the printed version, the ship is located in the middle of the Pacific Ocean. These details prompted an essay in the 1905 *National Geographic Magazine* exposing the errors. Hale's response: "It is one of the privileges of authors of fiction to make their narrative as plausible or possible as they can, if they give sufficient clues to the reader, from which he may know he is reading fiction."[47] "I took such pains as this," he wrote elsewhere, "to be provided with a defence, if any one should say, as the *New York Observer* did courteously, that I was a liar and a counterfeiter."[48]

In providing those clues, Hale distances himself morally from the "gay deceiver" (666) Burr, who leads Nolan astray with falsehoods. Even so, many readers were taken in. Hale, for instance, loved to tell how an "old Bostonian distinctly recalled Nolan's court-martial in 1807 and how the Navy Department was occasionally asked what records it had of Phil Nolan's exile."[49] There is a lesson, even if a complicated one, to be drawn from such incidents.

Hale's patriotic message might seem to imply that Nolan should have immediately rejected Burr's overtures. But Hale's ability to seduce so many readers into believing his fiction suggests that it is not all that easy to distinguish between lies, myths, traditions, and truths without a narrator, like Ingham, to sort them out for us. Indeed, all of us are vulnerable to the artful wiles of a skilled rhetorician, especially one, like Burr, who feels no obligation to reveal his intent to deceive. What distinguishes us from Nolan is not a higher sense of morality but an education in patriotism of the sort that Hale's story is designed to give. If both Hale and Burr deceive, Burr completely dashes Nolan's hopes in life, while Hale tries to save readers from his hero's fate. To do so, Hale lets Nolan directly deliver the message he wishes someone had told him as a boy.

No longer the rash young soldier, but now the voice of maturity, Nolan, after the incident with the slave ship, counsels the youthful Ingham, "'Forget you have a self.'" He goes on, "'Remember, boy, that behind all these men you have to do with, behind officers, and government, and people even, there is the Country herself, your Country, and that you belong to Her as you belong to your own mother. Stand by Her, boy, as you would stand by your mother, if those devils there had got hold of her today'" (675). Hale's story, as one editor puts it, "teaches something higher than heroism, loftier than courage, deeper than devotion, more loving than loyalty. It reveals that true patriotism is better than etiquette or sentiment—it is *religion of country*."[50]

☆ ☆ ☆ Hale was one of the most effective propagandists of the Civil War. Higginson notes that, even though "he did not actually go to the war itself as a chaplain of a regiment," he took an "active part for the Nation during the Civil War—so active that his likeness appears on the Soldiers' Monument on Boston Commons."[51] In the fall of 1862 he had met with seven or eight others, including Emerson, to discuss how to carry on ideological warfare for the Northern cause.[52] That meeting led to the formation of the New England Loyal Publication Society in March 1863. Hale was on the executive committee of the society, which was headed by Charles Eliot Norton. There were similar societies in New York and Philadelphia as well as Union Clubs across the North.[53] The goal was to publish works that would inspire loyalty and support the war. Hale wrote for the society and served for a year as associate editor of the *Army and Navy Journal* that it published. His most enduring effort was designed to sway public opinion as Lincoln faced heated criticism for abridging the civil liberties of a vocal political rival.

Difficult as it is for a number of Americans to accept, the revered president who saved the nation during civil war was denounced in his lifetime as a military dictator who violated citizens' civil liberties. Indeed, John Wilkes Booth, who assassinated Lincoln shouting the Virginia motto, *sic semper tyrannis*, was named after an eighteenth-century Englishman called "the father of civil liberty."[54] As Booth knew, various suspensions of civil liberties had gone on from the beginning of the war. In April 1861, because of interference with the movement of troops and supplies, Lincoln suspended habeas corpus along the communication line between Philadelphia and Washington. In *Ex parte Merryman* Chief Justice Roger B. Taney disagreed with the administration and granted a writ of habeas corpus to a Baltimore resident with Southern sympathies who had been arrested by military authorities. In a direct rebuke to the president, he also ruled that the Constitution authorized only Congress to suspend habeas corpus. The administration ignored Taney's decision, but the question of who had the authority to suspend habeas corpus was revisited on September 24, 1862. Worried that "the ordinary processes of law" were not adequate to deal with "disloyal persons" intent on hindering the military draft, Lincoln issued an executive order that created the new offenses of "discouraging enlistments" and "disloyal practices" while requiring such offenders and those who gave "aid and comfort to the rebels" to be subject to martial law, liable to trial and punishment by courts-martial and military commissions without possibility of writ of habeas corpus.[55]

Lincoln's crackdown did not go unchallenged. New England's Benjamin Curtis responded by writing "Executive Power," dedicated to those sworn to support the Constitution and to "all citizens who value the principles of civil liberty which that Constitution embodies."[56] Curtis made it clear that he supported the North's military effort as a "just and necessary war" until Southerners "submit themselves to their duty to obey . . . the Constitution as the 'supreme law of the land.'" "But," he asked, "with what sense of right can we subdue them by arms to obey the Constitution as the supreme law of *their* part of the land, if we have ceased to obey it, or failed to preserve it, as the supreme law of *our* part of the land?" Knowing that his protest would evoke cries of disloyalty, he reminded his audience that whenever the country's constitutional principles are in jeopardy, "every truly loyal man must interpose, according to his ability, or be an unfaithful citizen."[57]

Curtis had two major goals: to defend rule by law, not men, and to preserve the Constitution's commitment to civilian, not military, rule. The president, he insisted, "is not the military commander of the *citizens* of the United States, but of its *soldiers*." Yet his executive proclamation relied on his role as commander in chief of the military to place civilians under military control, putting a "military commission in place of a judicial court and jury required by the Constitution." Furthermore, he recalled, the role of the executive branch is to administer laws, not to make them. Yet, in defining new crimes, Lincoln assumed a legislative role. Even worse, his proclamation added to his constitutional "*rights* as commander the *powers* of an usurper; and that is military despotism."[58]

It is by no means surprising that this exchange occurred in wartime. Wars inevitably test the protection of civil liberties in liberal democracies. If in Melville's *Billy Budd*, Captain Vere argues that the Mutiny Act, with its lack of toleration for civil liberties, is "War's child" and "Takes after the father," William E. Rappard, writing in *The Crisis of Democracy* in 1938, claimed, "Democracy is a child of peace and cannot live apart from its mother."[59] As Supreme Court Justice Rutledge Wiley put it in 1944, "War is a contradiction of all that democracy implies. War is not and cannot be democratic."[60] World War I, for instance, led to some of the most famous free-speech cases in the nation's history. World War II forced the Supreme Court to decide if Japanese American citizens could be interned in the name of national security. The Vietnam War tested the limits of protest, and the so-called War against Terrorism has generated a number of controversies about civil liberties.

Even so, the Civil War raised special questions. Lincoln operated under the fiction that the Union still existed, meaning that it continued to include the very territory waging war against its troops. If so, could a country blockade its own ports? Could a part of the United States be considered occupied territory? These questions were part of a larger one about the status of the rebellious states themselves. What rights did the rebels have? A common refrain in the North was that they had no rights that the government had to respect, an obvious allusion to Justice Taney's claim in *Dred Scott* that African Americans had no rights that a white man had to respect. The more restrained response that they still had rights under the Constitution invited the not-so-restrained objection that they should, therefore, be tried for treason.

Indeed, the war saw a change in the law of treason. At the start of the conflict, treason was defined by a 1790 act. It mandated the death penalty for those convicted, and only a pardon could save them. Furthermore, it did not make a distinction between accessories and principals. All who aided and abetted, even if absent at the time of the act, were principals. Even so, according to judicial interpretation, conviction under the 1790 law required the actual levying of war. Plotting an act, assembling people, and gathering arms were not enough. It was on the basis of this interpretation that Burr was acquitted. According to it, a case could be made that Nolan should have gotten off as well, even though Ingham asserts that "there was evidence enough" (666) to bring him to trial.

In 1862, however, a new treason act was passed. It allowed imprisonment for not less than five years and a fine of not less than ten thousand dollars to serve as an alternative to the death penalty. Its second section did not even mention the death penalty. Furthermore, according to J. G. Randall, "Though the word 'treason' is not used, yet the wording of this section is so comprehensive as to cover the whole case of the Confederates and their adherents, so that the previous section, which does relate to treason, might possibly have been interpreted as inapplicable to them."[61]

The possibility that the Confederates would be considered under a category somewhat different from treason reminds us that the threat of disloyalty was not confined to those who left the Union. Numerous citizens in the North were suspected of Southern sympathy. It was the civil liberties of these citizens that most concerned Curtis. A former Whig, Curtis claimed to be a "member of no political party."[62] Yet his constitutional arguments resonated with many Northern Democrats. Most, like Curtis, supported the war, even if they frequently disagreed with Lincoln's conduct of it and his domestic policies, especially his record on civil liberties. At the same time, there were also Democrats, known as Copperheads, who opposed the war effort itself. Not themselves desiring to leave the Union, they argued for peace, claiming that a violent response to secession would create such animosity that it would be impossible ever to bring about a national reconciliation.

If, to their enemies, Copperheads were Southern sympathizers, from their point of view they were honest critics of the administration who questioned the war effort. Their biggest base of support was in the Midwest, especially Ohio, Indiana, and Illinois. They were in part motivated by economics. Lincoln's blockade of the Mississippi River led to a severe depression in the Midwest, which relied on the river for trade. That depression ignited already strong sectional loyalty. Midwesterners traditionally defined themselves against the East, not the South. Now it seemed as if Lincoln had become a tool of northeastern capitalists, furthering their interests at the expense of midwestern farmers and artisans. Many of those farmers and artisans fell prey to "Negrophobia," both because they felt that freed slaves would threaten their jobs or livelihoods and because of racial prejudice. They also resented a war that would free blacks while threatening their civil liberties.

The most notorious Copperhead was Clement L. Vallandigham, a Democratic lawyer/politician from Ohio. He was a special target of Lincoln supporters because he was both bold and articulate. An admirer of Edmund Burke, Jefferson, and Calhoun, he eloquently quoted from the Constitution and classical history to bolster his arguments. His motto was "The Constitution as it is; the Union as it was."[63] Both phrases registered his loyalty. He was a Unionist who defended the Constitution. But, combined, the two phrases also implied that the Union under Lincoln was no longer bound by the limits of the Constitution. Two of the most important aspects of the Constitution for Vallandigham were its protection of states' rights and individuals' civil liberties. His promotion of civil liberties was long-standing. For instance, campaigning for the Ohio legislature in 1845, he advocated—unsuccessfully—the abolition of capital punishment. In Congress, before the war, he sponsored a bill to suppress harsh disciplinary practices on American sailing vessels and a resolution to grant Jews the same rights as other U.S. citizens while traveling abroad. During the war, he sought—again unsuccessfully—to amend a bill so that rabbis could serve as chaplains in the army.

Nonetheless, civil liberties for him were reserved for whites. As the historian most familiar with his work puts it, Vallandigham was "the congenital champion of the underdog—except where the rights of black men were concerned."[64] But even so, it is worth remembering that in 1850 his stand on slavery was very close to Lincoln's. Like Lincoln at that time, Vallandigham considered slavery immoral but felt that it was a local institution that could be abolished within a state only by that state.

Lincoln would eventually change his view, while Vallandigham would speak less and less of slavery's immorality and more and more about states' rights. An important reason for this divide was the fact that Lincoln was a nationalist, while Vallandigham was a sectionalist. With midwestern sectional loyalty, Vallandigham did not blame the Confederate states for breaking up the union. He blamed, instead, abolitionists because their evocation of a "higher" standard of universal rights in order to impose their morality on the rest of the country violated the political, not moral, principle of the comity of sections. Vallandigham's hatred of abolitionists was closely linked to his opposition to New England in general, a section which he associated with the moral rigidity of the Puritans. If, Vallandigham argued, peace were declared and New England were not allowed to dominate U.S. politics, common economic, cultural, and racial interests would eventually lead to reunification. He even toyed with the idea of imagining a split in the country at the Hudson River, not the Mason-Dixon line.

Such arguments made Vallandigham a thorn in the side of the administration. Early during the war, he had even introduced a bill to imprison Lincoln if arrests of citizens in the loyal states persisted. His attacks on the administration were relentless and drew on the more radical oppositional rhetoric of the time. The United States, he claimed, had turned to despotic rule in which the rights of citizens were no longer protected. He compared Lincoln to George III and Louis XV as well as to Caesar, Cromwell, and Napoleon. If these comparisons seem outrageous to us today, we have to remember that they were made before the myth of Lincoln emerged. There was widespread fear that this unschooled backwoodsman would, on one hand, use the war to establish a dictatorship or, on the other, become simply the puppet of abolitionist or northeastern capitalist interests. Thus people listened carefully when Vallandigham and others described wartime arrests as the institution of a reign of terror.

Lincoln's defenders clearly disagreed, but their rhetoric was often just as extreme. The Republican press branded Vallandigham a secessionist traitor, compared him to Benedict Arnold and Aaron Burr, and accused him of championing Jefferson Davis. Vallandigham posed enough of a threat that getting him out of Congress became an important priority. Thus before the fall 1862 congressional elections, the Republican-controlled state legislature in Ohio redrew Vallandigham's election district to make his defeat more likely. The strategy was successful, and despite large Republican losses in that election, Vallandigham was not reelected, although he would have won under the old boundaries. Vallandigham's response to his ouster was to give a widely publicized speech from the halls of Congress on January 14, 1863, demanding peace.

Once the new Congress was seated, Vallandigham no longer had the Capitol as a forum to expound his ideas, but back in his home state of Ohio he soon found a new way to protest abuses to civil liberties. The chief military officer in the Ohio area was General Ambrose Burnside, who was placed there after commanding the Army of the Potomac in the disastrous Battle of Fredericksburg in December 1862. On April 13, 1863, Burnside delivered General Order No. 38, which announced that "all persons found within our lines, who commit acts for the benefit of the enemies of our country will be tried as spies or traitors, and, if convicted, will suffer death." In addition, "the habit of declaring sympathy for the enemy will not be allowed in this department. Persons committing such offenses will be at once arrested, with a view to being tried as above stated, or sent beyond our lines into the lines of their friends."[65]

The wide latitude by which declarations of sympathy could be interpreted made this order ripe for abuse. Protests ensued, and on May 1, 1863, in Mt. Vernon, Ohio, Vallandigham tested its limits with an impassioned speech. He chose Mt. Vernon for symbolic purposes. Although he harshly criticized the government, he wanted to make it clear that he did so as a patriot who honored the vision of the founding fathers. He began by alluding to the American flags that decorated the platform on which he spoke. They symbolized, he said, the Constitution of the country, made sacred by Democratic presidents. Expressing his reverence for the flag and his obedience to the Constitution, he went on to claim that, if it had not been for the Republican Party, all thirty-four states represented by the flag's stars would still be united. Turning to his rights as a freeman, he mocked Burnside's General Order No. 38, calling it a usurpation of arbitrary power, and asserted that his right to speak derived from the Constitution. "The sooner the people inform the minions of usurped power that they will not submit to such restrictions upon their liberties, the better," he was quoted as saying. After almost two hours, he moved toward his conclusion by urging that the "remedy" for all "the evils" was at the polling place through the "ballot-box." Denouncing "King Lincoln," he ended by professing his love of the Union and his desire to see it restored through compromise.[66]

An officer sent by Burnside took notes on the speech, and on the morning of May 5 soldiers forced their way into Vallandigham's home and arrested him. They took him to Cincinnati and tried him the next day in military court. Vallandigham protested that, as a civilian, he should be tried in a civil court, but he was convicted of expressing sympathy for those in arms against the government of the United States. He was sentenced to confinement in a fortress of the United States for the duration of the war. Vallandigham's counsel applied to Judge Humphrey Howe Leavitt of the U.S. Circuit Court for a writ of habeas corpus, but Leavitt denied the motion, arguing that Burnside was acting as an agent to the president, who as commander in chief had broad discretionary powers in such matters in time of war.

Vallandigham's arrest and conviction took Lincoln by surprise, and, most likely, if he had been consulted, he would not have condoned either. But he felt bound to support his general, although he did alter the sentence by directing that Vallandigham be sent behind Confederate lines. Lincoln's strategy was to keep Vallandigham from becoming a martyr, and he was partially successful, since some were convinced that Vallandigham was a friend of the South. In fact, although Vallandigham was treated courteously, he was not received as a compatriot, since he continued to advocate peace and reunion, while the South wanted independence. Thus, even though the Republican press depicted him as among friends, the Confederates encouraged him to leave. Running the blockade to Bermuda, he proceeded to Canada. Capitalizing on the publicity of his affair, Democrats nominated him to run for governor of Ohio in the fall election, and he proceeded to conduct his campaign in exile.

Vallandigham's arrest and conviction sparked protests across the nation.[67] The most important was in Albany, New York. It resulted in a May 19, 1863, letter to the president sent by a group of prominent Democrats led by Erastus Corning. Containing ten resolutions, the letter began by asserting the loyalty of those who signed it as well as their support of the war. Even so, it insisted that the administration stay true to the Constitution and recognize the "rights of the States and the liberties of the citizen."[68] Especially important was the maintenance of civil over military law, except in areas where civil courts could not operate. Vallandigham's arrest and conviction, it argued, violated this great constitutional principle. Not guilty of treason as defined by the Constitution, he had been arrested merely for speaking out "in public against the Administration and military orders of a general" (Corning 741). Strategically quoting the Whig Daniel Webster on the right to criticize "public measures and the merits of public men," it claimed that Vallandigham's arrest and conviction struck a "fatal blow at the supremacy of law, and the authority of the State and Federal constitutions" (Corning 742). It acknowledged that war might demand special measures but asserted, nonetheless, "that these safeguards of the rights of the citizen . . . were intended more especially for his protection in times of civil commotion. They were secured substantially to the English people, after years of protracted civil war, and were adopted into our Constitution at the close of the Revolution. They have stood the test of seventy-six years of trial under our republican system, under circumstances that show that, while they constitute the foundation of all free government, they are the elements of enduring stability of the Republic" (Corning 742). Concluding with a reassertion of the signers' loyalty, it insisted that the wrong done be undone.

Lincoln responded with a letter addressed to Corning, which, widely published, had as its real audience the public at large. He starts by congratulating the nation for his critics' patriotism, "despite the folly or wickedness" that they think his administration has committed (Corning 743). Without calling attention to itself, this opening shrewdly refutes a major charge leveled against him. Accused of unconstitutionally imprisoning someone who spoke out against him, Lincoln responds with generosity and self-mockery, proof in itself that he is open to criticism. Indeed, if the criticism were "merely personal," that would be the end of his response. But constitutional issues are at stake. Thus, he feels compelled to go on.

His critics, he notes, feel that the Constitution is always the same. But, he argues, "in its application," it is different "in cases of rebellion or invasion involving the public safety" from "time of profound peace and public security." Addressing the concern that his policies violate principles of free government, Lincoln compares taking "strong measures in time of rebellion" with taking a drug when one is sick. Just as one is necessary, even if it is not "good food" when one is well, so the others are necessary, even if unconstitutional in time of peace (Corning 749) — necessary because a widespread conspiracy, plotted for thirty years, had positioned Southern sympathizers in "all departments of Government and nearly all the communities of the people." Keeping "on foot among us a most efficient corps of spies, informers, suppliers, and aiders and abettors of their cause," conspirators, "under cover of 'liberty of speech,' 'liberty of press,' and 'habeas corpus,'" worked to destroy the Constitution at the same time that they appealed to it for protection (Corning 745). Civil courts, Lincoln insists, are "utterly incompetent" to deal with conspiracies of this sort. They "are organized chiefly for trials of individuals, or, at most, a few individuals acting in concert; and this in quiet times, and on charges of crimes well defined in law" (Corning 746). Only military courts, he claims, can deal with the threat of "insurgent sympathizers" in a time of national emergency. "Arrests by process of courts, and arrests in cases of rebellion, do not proceed altogether upon the same basis. The former is directed at the small percentage of ordinary and continuous perpetuation of crime; while the latter is directed at sudden and extensive uprisings against Government, which, at most, will succeed or fail in no great length of time. In the latter case, arrests are made, not so much for what has been done, as for what probably would be done" (Corning 746–47).

To support this theory of preventive arrests, Lincoln points to the many Confederate officers who at the outbreak of the war were still in the U.S. military and imagines what would have happened if they had been arrested.

"I think," he speculates, "the time not unlikely to come when I shall be blamed for having made too few arrests rather than too many." This example points to prominent rebels, but Lincoln gives a sense of how broadly he defines a sympathizer when he claims, "The man who stands by and says nothing when the peril of his Government is discussed, cannot be misunderstood. If not hindered, he is sure to help the enemy; much more, if he talks ambiguously—talks for his country with 'buts' and 'ifs' and 'ands'" (Corning 747). If Hale's Philip Nolan is sentenced for actively condemning his country, Lincoln turns silence and equivocation into disloyalty. Even so, he admits that, if Vallandigham had been arrested simply for criticizing the administration, he would have been wrongly arrested. But Vallandigham's crime was different. He was "damaging the army, upon the existence and vigor of which the life of the nation depends. He was warring upon the military, and thus gave the military constitutional jurisdiction to lay hands upon him" (Corning 748).

According to Lincoln, Vallandigham assaulted the military by criticizing the draft. "He who dissuades one man from volunteering, or induces one soldier to desert, weakens the Union cause as much as he who kills a Union soldier in battle" (Corning 746). If the logic of that analogy is a bit shaky, logic, as Lincoln well knew, does not always win political arguments. Indeed, the most memorable and effective passage in his response appeals not to logos but to pathos. "Long experience," he writes, "has shown that armies cannot be maintained unless desertions shall be punished by the severe penalty of death. The case requires, and the law and the Constitution sanction, this punishment. Must I shoot a simple-minded soldier-boy who deserts, while I must not touch the hair of a wily agitator who induces him to desert? . . . I think that in such a case to silence the agitator and save the boy is not only constitutional, but withal a great mercy" (Corning 748–49).[69]

Having transformed Vallandigham's conviction into an act of mercy, Lincoln concludes with an appeal to bipartisanship. Noting that his critics refer to themselves as "'Democrats' rather than 'American citizens,'" he implies that their criticism is linked to politics. "In this time of national peril," he implores, "I would have preferred to meet you upon a level one step higher than any party platform" (Corning 749).

I have quoted extensively from Lincoln's response in part because it is not widely known and in part because even scholars who mention it rarely call attention to the particular positions he defends. For instance, in 1899 James Ford Rhodes noted that Lincoln "went as far towards proving a bad case as the nature of things will permit" and admits that "we may wish, indeed, that the occasion which prompted these letters had not arisen." Nonetheless, he claimed, "their tone demonstrated that the great principles of liberty would suffer no permanent harm while Abraham Lincoln was in the presidential chair," as if Honest Abe's tone could overcome what Rhodes acknowledged to be an extremely dangerous constitutional precedent.[70] Similarly, a half-century later, Nevins, without quoting any examples, noted that Lincoln's position made his response "in the main a labored and unhappy document." Even so, he added, it has "touches of the simple eloquence that was seldom far from his pen."[71] In the bicentennial year of 1976, the noted Lincoln scholar Don E. Fehrenbacher gave two speeches that tried to provide a balanced view of Lincoln's position. But the only passages he quotes from the Corning letter are the one about the soldier boy and an analogy between Lincoln's measures and an "emetic" (Corning 749).[72] A decade and a half ago, Mark E. Neely called "Lincoln's broad attempt to impugn the loyalty of those who remained silent or who qualified their loyalty" the "most troubling" aspect of the letter, but he does so in the context of praising Lincoln's ability to "compete in the hearts of Americans" with his example of the "simple-minded soldier boy" as opposed to the "legalistic language and dignified tone" of his critics.[73] Lincoln's conspiracy theory and the "legalistic" issue of preventive arrests go unmentioned. More recently, Judge Frank J. Williams calls Lincoln's letter a "closely reasoned document" and, accepting Neely's argument, concludes that Lincoln "acted in the best interest of the country."[74] Similarly, law professor Daniel Farber acknowledges that the Vallandigham case was a "regrettable" error. Nonetheless, relying on former chief justice William H. Rehnquist on Copperhead conspiracies, not on the best historical work, he concludes that "given the extremity of the country's situation, Lincoln's record on civil liberties was not at all bad."[75]

This response is in large measure due to the mythologization of Lincoln. Indeed, his remark about the simple-minded soldier boy has proven so memorable in part because of its compatibility with the image of him as a merciful man. But in 1863 he still needed to mobilize support to defeat Vallandigham in the fall election, about which he was reportedly more "anxious" than his own in 1860.[76] Hale wrote "The Man without a Country" to provide that support.

☆ ☆ ☆ Hale wanted the story to appear early enough to affect the election. He also wanted it to appear anonymously so that readers would assume it was a real story. Neither plan worked. An attentive printer recognized Hale's handwriting and added his name to the table of contents; a publication delay caused the story to come out after Vallandigham had already been defeated. In the long run it did not matter. Helping the Northern cause for the rest of the war, Hale's story became a classic tale of patriotism long after the war. Nonetheless, the story took its shape in response to Hale's immediate concerns.

The most obvious similarity between the Vallandigham affair and Hale's story is the theme of exile. Hale had long been fascinated by Napoleon's fantasy that he had not surrendered to the English government but instead was the personal captive of Captain Maitland, who took him into custody. The English, Hale concludes, would have been wise to have indulged Napoleon in this fantasy. If they had, they could have avoided turning St. Helena into a "shrine for the worship of France for the next six years." Thus when Hale heard boys during the Civil War sing "We'll hang Jeff Davis to a sour apple tree," he thought it would be much better to put him in comfortable quarters on a U.S. ship to keep him from becoming a martyr.[77] Lincoln's decision to exile his political opponent clearly resonated with the Boston minister and helps account for Nolan's life sentence of exile at sea. The brilliance of the story comes, however, from the significance that Hale gives to that exile.

Those rallying behind Lincoln tended to downplay Vallandigham's punishment. For instance, another piece in the December 1863 *Atlantic Monthly* echoed Lincoln's charge that protests about free speech were hypocritical and despaired at the sympathy Vallandigham received. "Already dead to all feeling of patriotism, he is canonized for his crimes, with rites and ceremonies appropriate to such a priesthood. And, unhappily, he finds but too many followers weak enough or wicked enough to recognize his sainthood and accept his creed." Finding the Copperhead completely unworthy of this martyrdom, the author dismisses his arrest and punishment as a "mild rebuke."[78] In contrast, Hale turns Nolan's exile into the harshest punishment imaginable. He does this because, for him, Nolan is not so much a figure for Vallandigham as he is for Lincoln's misled "soldier boy."

As we have seen, Lincoln's most effective passage in that letter asked if he must hang a simple-minded soldier boy for deserting while letting the wily agitator who convinces him to desert go free. In "The Man without a Country" Hale gives narrative embodiment to the spirit of Lincoln's lines, turning Nolan into the naive soldier boy and Burr into the wily villain who seduces him into a treasonable act.

If Hale's imaginative reworking of Lincoln's memorable passage is the most important link between the story and the Vallandigham affair, there are other connections as well. For instance, the setting was also dictated by Hale's desire to influence the Ohio election. The original setting has multiple functions. Most obviously, Nolan is raised in the West to make it credible that for him "'United States' was scarcely a reality" (667). Growing up associating with a Spanish officer and a French merchant and lacking a formal education, except for one winter with an English tutor, he spends time with an older brother hunting horses in Texas, which was then not part of the United States. This setting both helps to explain Nolan's lack of patriotism and allows Hale to avoid an explicit conflict between Nolan's loyalty to a state and to the union. But the western setting is also important for the audience Hale hoped to influence. As we have seen, Copperheads had their strongest support in the Midwest, where sectional loyalty threatened to outweigh national loyalty. Hale, through Nolan, directly addresses that threat. He does so through Ingham as well.

In many of his writings Hale betrayed the New England arrogance that made Vallandigham's attacks on its self-righteous Puritan heritage strike a chord with his constituency. For instance, in a pamphlet he wrote in 1845 called *How to Conquer Texas before Texas Conquers Us*, he proposed Northern immigration to Texas, a "Mayflower company for the redemption of that region."[79] Likewise, in his introduction to Eli Thayer's *A History of the Kansas Crusade*, he quotes Theodore Parker favorably describing Thayer's plan to have the "free states send settlers to Northernize the South . . . and New Englandize Central America."[80] Advocating a mild policy of reconstruction, he, nonetheless, imagined redemption for the South only if it adopted New England ways.[81] But in "The Man without a Country" Hale constrains his sense of New England superiority. Trying to minimize sectional antagonism, especially with the West, Hale has Ingham begin the story on the Great Lakes. Even if he is reading an eastern newspaper, it is the *New York Herald*, not a New England publication. To be sure, the *Herald* was a Republican paper, and Ingham is not reading the Democratic *New York World*, which, even though it had previously disagreed with Vallandigham, denounced Burnside's "drumhead law" for convicting him. But Hale is careful not to have his narrator identified with the New England that Vallandigham's followers so mistrusted.

Despite his care in avoiding New England arrogance, Hale could not keep from getting in a few digs at the administrations of Jefferson and Madison. Today Jefferson is honored as the author of the Declaration of Independence, with a national memorial in Washington and a portrait on U.S. currency. Madison is considered the genius behind the Constitution. But in Hale's story they, along with Monroe, are subtly mocked. Referring to their twenty-four years of consecutive rule, Hale blames many of the country's past mistakes on the "House of Virginia." For instance, the lost opportunity to take insular possessions in the South Pacific is the fault of "Madison and the Virginians," who "flung all that away" (672). Hale's criticism of the Virginians—with the notable exception of Washington—is most obviously directed at Southerners for whom all three had a special importance. But it was also aimed at Jeffersonian Northerners, like Vallandigham. Hale was especially critical of the Jeffersonian distrust of a strong national government. For instance, describing Spanish rule in New Orleans in an 1897 explanation of the story, he writes, "That Government understood the knack of governing better than Mr. Jefferson and his friends, who thought at that time that the world was governed too much."[82]

If Hale's portrayal of Jefferson and Madison allows him to have some partisan fun at Democrats' expense, it also raises a dilemma of sympathies. Early in the story Ingham tells us how successive administrations have kept Nolan's punishment in "very strict secrecy, the secrecy of honor itself, among the gentlemen of the navy who have had Nolan in successive charge. And certainly it speaks well for the *esprit de corps* of the profession and the personal honor of its members, that to the press this man's story has been wholly unknown,—and, I think, to the country at large also" (665). Such comments seem to condone Lincoln's policy during the war of arbitrarily arresting people and secretly detaining them. Indeed, "The Man without a Country" would seem to support Lincoln's claim that military, not civil, courts were needed to deal with those intent on destroying the nation. After all, Burr, tried in civil courts, is acquitted, while Nolan, tried by a military tribunal, is convicted. But Nolan's connection with Lincoln's soldier boy rather than with Vallandigham complicates that seeming support.

Unaware of the consequences that might follow from keeping Nolan's imprisonment secret, we may tend, at the start, to sympathize with the government. But as we come to sympathize with Nolan, our attitude toward secrecy changes. We are, for instance, appalled to learn that the government stonewalls Ingham's efforts to procure a pardon for his friend. "Later in life when I thought I had some influence in Washington," Ingham tells us, "I moved heaven and earth to have him discharged" (675). But to Ingham's dismay, he is told that there is no record of such a person. At this point, a story intent on supporting Lincoln might seem unconsciously to serve the cause of those criticizing his administration for secretly keeping people in prison.

I will come back to this potential complication. For now, however, it is enough to remember that the "House of Virginia" is responsible for both

Nolan's initial sentence and his detention. It is Jefferson who originally approves Nolan's punishment, while governments under future Virginians refuse to respond to pleas for his pardon. If Vallandigham's supporters protested his arrest, Hale suggests that abuses to civil liberties attributed to Lincoln had precedent in Democratic administrations, just as Lincoln in his letter to Corning reminds his Democratic critics that their beloved Andrew Jackson was accused of a similar act. Indeed, as Hale likely knew, the Jefferson so prized for his love of liberty had disregarded many rules of impartial justice in trying to bring about Burr's conviction. When Burr was acquitted, Jefferson went so far as to write about the inapplicability of "forms of law to cover traitors" and the necessity in "extreme cases" to resort to a "dictator or martial law."[83]

To be sure, Virginians and Democrats were not in continuous power from 1807 until Nolan's death in 1863. Even so, Hale creates a situation in which the original order is unambiguously in effect only through 1817, the last year of Madison's term. Furthermore, by referring to the "House of Virginia," Hale counters the charges of despotism against Lincoln by implying that it was the Democrats who had set up a form of "hereditary" rule—a despotism, but not one capable of dealing with treason, as evidenced by Jefferson's failure to convict Burr, while "little Nolan" (666) is found guilty. Thus the Democratic Virginians did just the opposite of Lincoln's proposal to silence the agitator and save the boy. They spared the "gay deceiver" (666) and punished the boy.

The story of how Nolan, deceived as a young soldier, turns into a patriot as he grows old did much more than discredit Vallandigham during the war. It also influenced how generations of Americans interpreted his acts of dissent. In the years after the Civil War, more people encountered the name Vallandigham in "The Man without a Country" than in any other source—and not neutrally. Toward the end of the story, Ingham tells us that it should be a "warning to the young Nolans and Vallandighams and Tatnalls of to-day of what it is to throw away a country" (677). "Tatnall" refers to Josiah Tattnall, who served many years in the U.S. Navy. He was famous for defending his decision to aid a British ship attacked by Chinese on June 25, 1859, even though doing so violated the declared neutrality of the United States. "Blood," he proclaimed, "is thicker than water."[84] Less than two years later, he resigned his commission to join first the Georgia and then the Confederate navy. Tattnall, like Bragg and Beauregard, threw away a country. Vallandigham did not. As much as we might disagree with many of his positions, he never renounced his loyalty to the United States. Even so, by linking the Ohio politician with Tattnall, Hale created precisely the effect Lincoln wanted when he banished him to the Confederacy. Vallandigham was portrayed as having denounced his country.

Hale's introductions to various reprints reinforced that message. Relying on them, editors gave and continue to give inaccurate accounts of the Vallandigham affair. Almost all follow Hale's lead in mistakenly having Burnside, not Lincoln, exile Vallandigham to the Confederacy. More importantly, even though Lincoln admitted that Vallandigham was not arrested for treason, they accept Hale's characterization of Vallandigham's Mt. Vernon speech as "treasonable."[85] For instance, an early-twentieth-century edition provides the following gloss: "*Vallandigham*, the Southern candidate for governor of Ohio in 1863. Because he said publicly that he did not care to belong to the United States, General Burnside sent him over to the Confederacy."[86] Attributing Vallandigham's exile to Burnside, this note turns him into a "Southern" candidate whose discontent with the United States is unqualified. The introduction to the widely read Riverside edition paints an even more exaggerated portrait. Explaining the context of the story, the editor writes, "A group of States in the South had taken arms against the Government, and thousands of American citizens living in the border States between the North and the South had denied their obligation of loyalty. Everywhere people failed to appreciate the necessity of fealty to one's flag, and to understand the blessings bestowed upon them by their country. Men were becoming bolder in their expressions of disloyalty. In Ohio one Vallandigham, an ex-Congressman, made a violently incendiary speech against the Federal Government."[87] Forty years later, Van Wyck Brooks still has Burnside sending Vallandigham behind Confederate lines. A very recent edition of Hale's naval writings with a supposedly "authoritative" introduction does even worse. Despite publication of excellent historical accounts, it repeats the error about Burnside, tells us that Vallandigham did not find the Union "worth saving," and defines a Copperhead as a "northerner who supported the goals of the Confederacy."[88]

If Hale helped Lincoln win the historical spin on how to interpret the Vallandigham affair, he also helped to keep Vallandigham's name alive. I want to come back to what it means to read Hale's story in relation to the Vallandigham case today. But before I do so, it is important to try to understand why Hale's story has, for the most part, lost its popularity while the Lincoln legend continues to have such power.

☆ ☆ ☆ As much as Lincoln and Hale complemented each other in helping to produce a sense of national rather than sectional loyalty, their works have significant differences in vision. Although it risks simplification, one way to point to these differences is to note Hale's use of "country" in his title and the fact that Lincoln, in his two most widely quoted speeches, the Gettysburg Address and the Second Inaugural, refers only to a "nation," never to a "country." We often use "nation" and "country" interchangeably, but etymologically they are quite different. "Nation" is cognate with "nativity" and "native." It has connotations of shared identity by birth. In contrast, "country" comes from "contrary" and implies a spatial relation. "Country" refers more to a piece of land; "nation," more to a people. Whereas it makes perfect sense to speak of one's native country or one's native land, it would be redundant to refer to one's native nation. If the alliteration of "native nation" does not work, that of "common country" does because the phrase is not redundant. At the same time, no appropriate adjective can be constructed from "country." Thus, we need to speak of a national purpose or a national memory, and when we do, the adjective itself implies a unity. For advocates of national unity in the United States, the problem from the start was how to achieve a united purpose out of the vast expanse of the country.

In his Farewell Address, for instance, Washington felt compelled to combat "every attempt to alienate any portion of our country from the rest, or to enfeeble the sacred ties which now link together the various parts." He does so by directly addressing his fellow countrymen: "Citizens, by birth or choice, of a common country, that country has a right to concentrate your affections. This name of 'American,' which belongs to you in your national capacity, must always exalt the just pride of patriotism more than any appellation derived from local discriminations."[89] In appealing to a common country to concentrate citizens' affections, Washington is trying to create a sense of one people, that is, a nation. But in doing so, he is asking a piece of land to take on the task previously accomplished by the monarch.

It was, after all, the monarch, as sovereign, who concentrated the affections of his subjects. In a monarchy, all people born in the same land have a common allegiance because anyone born in the king's land is a subject of the king. A sovereign monarch, reigning over an empire, could even unite the affections of people in different countries. Thus, before he embraced the inevitability of independence, Benjamin Franklin referred to two different countries, one on each side of the Atlantic. The king, he asserted, was the "only Connection between the two Countries" and the only hope for a "continued Union," which "was essentially necessary to the Well-being of the whole Empire."[90] Once a monarchy was replaced by a republic and the people became sovereign, it would seem that, as was the case in France, affection would now be concentrated on the nation that the people constituted. But in the United States, where each state claimed a sovereignty of its own, the situation was much more complicated. Here the task was, as it would be in Germany throughout the nineteenth century, to unite separate sovereignties.

Hale solves the problem by making the country the common object of affection. There is, for him, no longer a need for the king because the country itself has become a being to whom one owes loyalty. "The country, to him," Carl Van Doren writes, "was not insensate territory which could be divided without hurt, but a mortal organism which would die dismembered."[91] As Nolan tells Ingham, one belongs to one's country as one belongs to one's mother. Like a mother, the country is nurturing. Indeed, since for Hale love of a country is akin to love of a mother, it is not surprising that we hear nothing of Nolan's mother.[92] Since we belong to a country in the same way that we belong to a mother, it is as if Nolan derives his life from the very country he initially rejects. Loyalty, in Hale's story, grows out of a physical bond, like the one a child has to its mother at birth, a physical bond that creates an affective one.

For Lincoln, in contrast, the people do not belong to the country; the country belongs to them. In his First Inaugural he refers to "country" but only when he describes the land. "Physically speaking, we cannot separate. We cannot remove our respective sections from each other, nor build an impassable wall between them. A husband and wife may be divorced, and go out of the presence, and beyond the reach of each other; but the different parts of our country cannot do this. They cannot but remain face to face."[93] Having introduced the notion of a common country, he goes on to make it clear that "this country, with its institutions, belongs to the people who inhabit it."[94] The nation's territory is important, but it is made sacred by people's deeds, some of the most important of which are the creation of the country's political institutions, especially a "government of the people, by the people, for the people." Opposed to Hale's maternal imagery, Lincoln uses predominantly paternal imagery. "Four score and seven years ago our fathers brought forth on this continent, a new nation, conceived in Liberty, and dedicated to the proposition that all men are created equal."[95] If the nation's conception in Liberty is maternal, the crucial work is done by fathers making the land special by dedicating it to the political proposition of equality.[96]

Whereas Lincoln imagines people's loyalty to rest in the political institutions and propositions they have imparted to the land, Hale's story barely mentions them. Hale preaches patriotism but offers no compelling reason why we should be loyal to one country rather than to another, other than the fact that it is, after all, our country. In contrast, for Lincoln, it is not so much that loyalty itself is right; it is that people should be loyal to a nation dedicated to democratic political institutions serving the right political principles. As a result, if both helped to change the object of people's loyalties from the state or section to the common country, Lincoln, much more than Hale, also helped to change what the nation stands for.

The country that Nolan so loves is a perfect example of what Benedict Anderson calls an "imagined community."[97] After all, even though at his death Nolan has become a model patriot, he has not seen or heard about the United States for fifty-six years. The object of his affection is, therefore, quite literally a product of his imagination. Likewise, his patriotism exemplifies the nationalism that, according to Anderson and others, developed in the late eighteenth and nineteenth centuries. Nations existed before that time, and people could express patriotism through an extreme love of country. Nonetheless, prior to the American and French Revolutions, loyalty was usually given to the sovereign, almost always a monarch. Only when the nation, constituted by its people, became sovereign could nationalism itself arise. Appropriately, in an introduction to a new edition of his story, Hale notes "a perfectly absurd statement by Charles Kingsley . . . in which he says that, while there can be loyalty to a king or a queen, there cannot be loyalty to one's country." Disputing that claim, Hale calls love of country a "universal" sentiment.[98]

In the Gettysburg Address the United States stands for abstract, universal values, such as liberty, equality, and democracy; in "The Man without a Country" the primary universal value is love of country, a value that allowed translations of Hale's story to rally patriotism in other countries.[99] This is not to say that "The Man without a Country" lacks a particular vision of the United States. But it is not what today would typically be called Lincolnian. It is, for instance, expansionist. According to Ingham, Nolan "was with Porter when he took possession of the Nukahiwa Islands," a reference to David Porter's failed attempt to claim what became the French Marquesas. Countering Herman Melville's criticism of Porter's imperialism in the British edition of *Typee*, Hale writes, "We should have kept the islands, and at this moment we should have one station in the Pacific Ocean" (672). Nolan's embrace of expansionism is revealed when Ingham visits his room just before his death. "'Here, you see,'" Nolan tells him, "'I have a country!'" He then points to "a great map of the United States, as he had drawn it from memory, and which he had there to look upon as he lay. Quaint, queer old names were on it in large letters: 'Indiana Territory,' 'Mississippi Territory,' and 'Louisiana Territory,' as I supposed our fathers learned such things:

but the old fellow had patched in Texas, too; he had carried his western boundary all the way to the Pacific but on that shore he had defined nothing" (677–78). Constructed from his imagination, Nolan's map is far from an accurate representation of the United States in 1863; nonetheless, it is how he imagines the country that he loves. Part of what he loves is that, like an organism, it has continued to grow and to expand. For instance, from the stars on the flag Nolan knows that the country has added new states, and one of Danforth's tasks is to name them, allowing Nolan to experience in a few minutes the growth of the country in the last half-century.[100]

Through such moments, Hale reinforces for his readers the progress the nation has undergone in the first half of the nineteenth century. That Nolan could imagine, from his 1807 perspective, the growth of the country to the Pacific makes that expansion seem predestined and inevitable, threatened only by the civil war Danforth does not have the heart to relate to Nolan. Indirectly addressing the concerns of those facing economic hardship during the war, such as Vallandigham's followers in the Midwest, Hale implies that, without the rebels' treasonous disruption of the country's natural growth, prosperity would be ensured. Indeed, the major reason he imagines Bragg and Beauregard regretting their actions is that they will not partake of the country's "prosperity and honor" (676).

The imperial status of the United States is also expressed in the symbology of other items in Nolan's room: "The stars and stripes were triced up and above and around a picture of Washington, and he had painted a majestic eagle, with lightnings blazing from his beak and his foot just clasping the whole globe, which his wings overshadowed" (677). This image is confirmed by one of the most subtle aspects of the story's endorsement of U.S. global dominance. In describing Nolan's wanderings, as he is transferred from U.S. warship to U.S. warship, we get a sense of the U.S. presence in all parts of the world. Thus, Hale's story anticipates Arthur Mahan's argument about naval power later in the century by suggesting that the United States is already on the way to sharing Britannia's rule of the waves.

This vision of expansion along with its message of patriotism made the story extremely popular at the time of the Spanish-American War and its imperialist aftermath. New editions were rushed into print, and sales surpassed those during the Civil War. In an introduction written for an abridged periodical reprint soon after war was declared and expanded for a hardback edition, Hale admitted that in 1898 the country was not threatened as it had been in 1863. Nonetheless, his story still had lessons for the country. Sounding like Lincoln responding to his critics, he wrote, "The man who, by his sneers, or by looking backward, or by revealing his country's secrets to her enemy, delays for one hour peace between Spain and this Nation, is to all purposes 'A Man Without a Country.'"[101] Likewise, checking page proof for a new edition of his story at the end of the war, he added a footnote to the 1897 introduction that edition was using: "As this sheet passes the press, after the short Spanish war, I think it may be well to say that the universal contempt of Spain, in the lower Mississippi valley, and the hatred bred in her treachery in 1801 in this Nolan transaction, have shown themselves, bitterly enough, in the determination to administer the well deserved punishment for which Jefferson was too weak. The wheels of the gods grind—when the time comes."[102]

The story's popularity during the Spanish-American War was matched during both World War I and World War II. Even so, the reasons for its popularity also made it a target of criticism. In 1892 Wendell P. Garrison wrote to Higginson, "What will last of Hale, I apprehend, will be the phrase 'A man without a country,' and perhaps the immoral doctrine taught in it which leads to Mexican and Chilean wars—'My country, right or wrong.'"[103] Ten years later, reviewing a new edition praised by President Theodore Roosevelt in the midst of the U.S. war in the Philippines, Garrison noted this "fresh certificate of beneficence" from the president and added that "there are some who look upon [the story] as the primer of Jingoism."[104]

Associated with the slogan "My country, right or wrong," while Lincoln's Gettysburg Address is associated with the civic ideal of a "government of the people, by the people, for the people," "The Man without a Country" began to disappear from the literary canon around the time of the Vietnam War, which raised, for a significant percentage of the American public, questions about unqualified love of country. This is not to say that its form of patriotism no longer exists. But it is to say that the way that patriotism was taught in the schools underwent significant changes about that time.

For one, literature began to play less of a role in civic education.[105] The Riverside edition of the story, first published in 1923 and still in wide use in schools in the 1950s, has a bibliography of "American Patriotic Literature." Listed are poems, like Emerson's "Concord Hymn," Longfellow's "Paul Revere's Ride" and "The Building of the Ship," Whittier's "Barbara Frietchie," and Riley's "The Name of Old Glory," none of which are taught with great frequency today.[106] To be sure, some of the works listed are still taught. But for the most part, they are works of nonfictional prose that do not fit the more narrow definition of literature that began to be institutionalized about this time, the same time that literature's role in civic education diminished. These are works like Henry's Liberty or Death speech, Jefferson's Declaration of Independence, and Lincoln's Gettysburg Address and

Second Inaugural, more often taught in civics classes or American history classes than in literature classes.

Continued teaching of these works makes it clear that, despite frequent complaints, patriotic education is not neglected. But the emphasis has changed. In *Patriotic American Stories*, in use from the 1930s through the 1950s, "The Man without a Country" is honored as the first story because "no other selection is so well suited" to the volume's goal of letting "young people . . . experience the patriotic sentiments and emotions upon which love of native land depends." This attempt to get children to love their native land did not result in simplistic nativism. On the contrary, the editor decries patriotic writings "that engender ill feeling toward other nations." "Children should," he writes, "learn at an early age that the American spirit is one of peacefulness, toleration, and good will; that we have never been and never should be, in spirit and social institutions, entirely independent of other nations; and that we have world-wide responsibilities and interests which must be met." Introducing a story about an immigrant called "The Citizen," he adds, "Sometimes thoughtless people sneer about 'foreigners.' They forget that everybody in America except the American Indian is a 'foreigner.' Whether our parents came last year or three hundred years ago does not make any great difference." What does make a difference is the material to which children are exposed. The editor chooses stories because they "appeal to the child's imagination and sentiment."[107]

The emphasis today is different. It is on what Gary Nash, the professor responsible for producing national history standards, calls the "central defining values of a democratic polity" that are "clearly stated" in the country's "founding documents."[108] The emphasis is, in other words, on giving a lesson in what, in a German context, Jürgen Habermas calls *Verfassungspatriotismus*, or constitutional patriotism.[109] Designed to be less an affective lesson in love of country and more a lesson in cosmopolitan constitutional principles and civic ideals that make the United States a democratic leader in the global community, it is a lesson better taught, it is felt, by reading Lincoln's best speeches than by reading Hale's best story.[110] Thus, whereas most of today's students are still required to read the Gettysburg Address, hardly any are required to read "The Man without a Country."

Nonetheless, to compare these two works to each other in the context of Lincoln's record on civil liberties complicates matters. Because Hale's story was written in support of Lincoln's crackdown on civil liberties in the Vallandigham affair, it might seem that both conflict with the democratic ideals Lincoln expressed in his most famous speech. In fact, rather than contradicting his belief in a government of the people, by the people, for the people, Lincoln's crackdown most likely resulted from him taking that belief extremely seriously. Given that possibility, the failure of Hale's story to conform to the utopian ideal of the Gettysburg Address does more than expose the limits of Hale's vision of patriotism. It can also help us see how Lincoln's identification of the government with the people, in his eyes, authorized him to curtail civil liberties in the name of the people. The point is not, therefore, to reject the sentiments Lincoln articulated in the Gettysburg Address. But it is to remind us that much of the appeal of Lincoln's image of democratic government comes from its seeming reconciliation of tensions and contradictions that inhabit the very notions of popular sovereignty and representative democracy.

☆ ☆ ☆ When Lincoln's critics attacked him as a despot and a tyrant, they evoked a long tradition that saw the battle over civil liberties as a contest between the sovereign and the people, the one for royal prerogative, the other for the rights of personal liberty.[111] This contest produced the Magna Charta, the Petition of Rights in the era of Charles I, and the Declaration of Rights and the Act of Settlement in 1688. Its terms also structure the Declaration of Independence, which proclaims the rights of the people against the despotism of the king, decrying his attempts to curtail the legislative powers of the populace.

From Lincoln's perspective, however, the terms of the conflict changed with the establishment of a republic in which the people themselves became sovereign. After all, when the people, as citizens, are sovereign, it makes little sense to speak of a contest between the sovereign and the people. Even so, a conflict remains, one recast as a conflict between competing claims of the people: the right to civil liberties, on one hand, and the need of national security, on the other.[112] What are we to do, Lincoln had to ask, when the Constitution's vow to insure "Domestic Tranquility," provide for "the common defense," and promote "the general Welfare" comes into conflict with its goal to secure "the Blessings of Liberty to ourselves and our Posterity"?

His answer was clear. In the same speech in which he calls the Civil War "essentially a People's contest," he asks, "'Is there, in all republics, this inherent and fatal weakness?' 'Must a government, of necessity, be too strong for the liberties of its own people, or too weak to maintain its own existence?'"[113] For him, maintaining the nation's existence takes priority, even if it means curtailing liberties of the people who constitute the nation. If that view seems at odds with Lincoln's ideal of popular government, it is, in fact, potentially compatible with it. In articulating his memorable image of a government made up of the people and serving the people's interests,

Lincoln may express a utopian democratic ideal, but he also risks effacing the inevitable space that exists between the people and the government in any form of representational democracy. If the people become identical with the government, the government can also become identical with the people.

We can get a sense of the potential danger lurking in Lincoln's memorable phrase by comparing the sentences "The president, as head of the government, acts for the people" and "The president, as head of the government, speaks for the people." The first tends to reinforce the democratic notion that, as servant of the people, the president acts on their behalf. The second tends to imply that the president has the power to represent their will.[114] In fact, because a president both speaks and acts for the people and because his words are some of his most important deeds, the two meanings tend, almost imperceptibly, to blend into each other. Nonetheless, if Lincoln often spoke and acted according to the spirit of the former, in his stand on civil liberties he acted and spoke according to the spirit of the latter.

For instance, in a July 4, 1861, speech to Congress, he reports, "These measures, whether strictly legal or not, were ventured upon, under what appeared to be a popular demand, and a public necessity; trusting then as now, that Congress would readily ratify them."[115] Since Congress was not in session at the outbreak of hostilities, this explanation seems to make sense. At the same time, it also reveals Lincoln's tendency to believe that he had the right to act directly in the name of the people. Indeed, although he had the authority to call a special session, he decided to act on his own.

Even as strong a nationalist as Charles Sumner felt that Congress, not the president, was the true voice of the people. Speaking to the issue of war powers, he insisted that "the government of the United States appears most completely in an Act of Congress." The president's role is simply executive; "he is only the instrument of Congress, under the Constitution."[116] Lincoln's precedent and example have gone a long way in helping to change people's perception of the president's role.[117] Lincoln's own perception of his role was, in turn, guided by a metaphor associated with him more than any other president: the captain of the ship of state.

Lincoln grew up with this trope. It became especially popular with Henry Wadsworth Longfellow's 1849 poem "The Building of the Ship." In his poem Longfellow compares the building of a ship with the building of the Union. Revising the poem's ending in the midst of the Free-Soil controversy after a dinner with Sumner, Longfellow made his ship-of-state metaphor an explicit call to preserve the Union. Lincoln was moved to tears when he heard the poem recited. Indeed, Longfellow's poem served as a literary equivalent to the nationalistic legal arguments of Story and Webster that were so important for Lincoln's understanding of the Constitution. Thus, it is no surprise that, traveling to Washington for his inaugural, he pleaded, "If all do not join now to save the good old Ship of the Union on this voyage, nobody will have a chance to pilot her on another voyage."[118] A close look at Longfellow's poem and its sources can help us see how, in Lincoln's mind, stretching constitutional authority to curtail civil liberties did not contradict his professed reverence for rule by law.[119]

The poem's nationalist message is indicated by Longfellow's sources. In constructing his ship-of-state metaphor, he drew on Francis Lieber's *Encyclopedia Americana*. A German emigrant, Lieber was a passionate nationalist who brought Germanic views of the state to bear on the U.S. Constitution. Fervently hoping that the Civil War would bring about "the nationalization of this country," he provided Lincoln with valuable legal advice. Lieber also established the code guiding the conduct of Union soldiers during the war. Although not officially binding, it had Lincoln's approval and was widely accepted as authoritative. With its "admixture of military sternness and humanitarianism," it served as the basis for almost all codes of conduct to follow. Making clear that "men who take up arms against one another in public war do not cease on this account to be moral beings, responsible to one another, and to God," it also had sections on military necessity and retaliation that were used forty years later to defend the actions of American army officers who had tortured Filipinos in the civil war raging when the United States took control after the Spanish-American War.[120]

For Longfellow in 1849, the most important entry from Lieber's *Encyclopedia Americana* was "Ship," written by Commodore Alexander Slidell Mackenzie. Mackenzie was the author of a popular 1846 biography of Decatur. Describing Decatur's "memorable" toast to his country, Mackenzie writes that it is "not the least valuable of the legacies left by Decatur to his countrymen," and he hopes it will "ever remain the rallying cry of patriotism throughout the land."[121] Patriot that he was, four years before his biography appeared, Mackenzie, as presiding officer onboard the U.S. *Somers*, hanged three sailors suspected of mutiny. A source for Melville's *Billy Budd*, the *Somers* incident caused Mackenzie to be court-martialed for his actions. Much to the relief of Longfellow and many others, he was acquitted. But in the court of public opinion he was not completely exonerated. To help win the battle for public opinion after the acquittal, Sumner was asked to write an essay for the *North American Review*.

Sumner admitted that in hanging the three sailors, Mackenzie had deviated from the strict letter of the law. Nonetheless, drawing on the work of his mentor Story, Sumner went on to claim that the law contained within itself a principle that justified his actions. "Does the law contain, within itself, any principle, which under the circumstances of the case, will justify this apparent violation of it? Our answer is, that it clearly does."[122] Since a captain has the duty to preserve his ship, it follows that he must also have the means to fulfill his duty. Necessary to save the ship, Mackenzie's actions were, Sumner argued, legally justified, even if they violated particular items in the law. Such arguments resonated with Lincoln, who saw the duty of the president as similar to the duty of a ship's captain. Accused of violating constitutional protections of civil liberties in his conduct of the war, he relied on the same logic as Sumner had in his defense of Mackenzie. "Was it possible," he wrote, "to lose the nation and yet preserve the constitution? By general law life and limb must be protected; yet often a limb must be amputated to save a life; but a life is never wisely given to save a limb. I felt that measures, otherwise unconstitutional, might become lawful, by becoming indispensable to preservation of the constitution, through the preservation of the nation."[123]

Lincoln's ability to use the law to justify potential violations of the law depended on one of his most commendable qualities. James McPherson may exaggerate when he claims that Lincoln won the war with his use of metaphor, but any understanding of his legacy must look carefully at his skill as a "wordsmith."[124] As praiseworthy as that skill is, it was not always used for praiseworthy ends. If it is too easy to call it, as Thomas J. Dilorenzo does, "rhetorical gimmickry" that brought about a "large, activist, centralized state,"[125] it did allow Lincoln to bring about change while seeming to adhere to existing principles. In preserving the union, he changed the nation. In seeming to adhere to the law, he altered the law. Wills is, without a doubt, correct to celebrate the "revolution in thought" and the "revolution in style" that helped bring into existence a "different America," but in doing so he confirms Vallandigham's charge that the Union and the Constitution under Lincoln were no longer the same.[126]

Indeed, Lincoln's logic remains with us. It is similar to Justice Robert H. Jackson's in his dissent in the 1949 free-speech case *Terminiello v. Chicago*. The majority had overturned the disorderly conduct conviction of a rightwing, anti-Semitic, pro-Nazi priest whose speech had provoked a riot. According to Justice William O. Douglas's opinion, the Chicago ordinance under which Terminiello had been convicted violated the First Amendment because it was too broadly constructed. Having recently served as prosecutor of the Nuremburg war crimes trials, Justice Jackson pointed out the danger of letting people like Terminiello exploit our protection of civil liberties in order to destroy our democratic form of government. "The choice," he argued, "is not between order and liberty. It is between liberty with order and anarchy without either. There is a danger that if the Court, does not temper its doctrinaire logic with a little practical wisdom, it will convert the constitutional Bill of Rights into a suicide pact."[127]

Justice Jackson was clearly influenced by the monumental reputation of Lincoln. Writing about the conflict between "liberty and authority," "perhaps the most delicate, difficult and shifting of all balances which the Court is expected to maintain," he claims that "President Lincoln in his famous letter to Erastus Corning and others, defended his conduct" and said "all that ever could be said and always will be said" in favor of suspending civil liberties "in time of national emergency."[128] For Jackson, it would be illogical for the Constitution to protect actions leading to the destruction of the nation it constituted.

His metaphor, however, can be and was interpreted another way. In arguments before the Court in Ex parte Milligan, the most important civil liberties case to come out of the Civil War, which we will examine in the next chapter, former attorney general Jeremiah Black proclaimed, "A violation of law on the pretense of saving such a government as ours is not self-preservation, but suicide."[129] Black's use of the metaphor was repeated in Kennedy v. Mendoza-Martinez (1963) when Justice Arthur J. Goldberg ruled that the government could not automatically take away the citizenship of someone who left the country to evade the military draft. Writing in the light of a long history of constitutional challenges to the draft, he wrote, "The powers of Congress to require military service for the common defense are broad and far-reaching, for while the Constitution protects against the invasions of individual rights, it is not a suicide pact."[130] For Justice Goldberg, the Constitution allows Congress to have the powers it has to institute a draft only because it simultaneously protects individual rights. Not leading to a potential destruction of the document, maintaining those protections is essential to its life. If Justice Jackson's understanding of the Constitution resembles Lincoln's, Black's and Justice Goldberg's resembles his critics'. As another attorney in Milligan put it, the president "can exercise no authority whatever but what the Constitution of the country gives him. Our system knows of no authority beyond or above the law. We may, therefore, dismiss from our minds every thought of the President having any prerogative, as representative of the people, or as interpreter of the popular will."[131]

Hale, of course, sided with Lincoln. Even so, his story raises unexpected possibilities for dissent that Lincoln's utopian identification of the government with the people potentially closes off. It does so by having the harshness of Nolan's fate raise questions about the propriety of the sorts of secret arrests Lincoln was accused of making. Even if, as we have seen, Hale tries to divert criticism from Lincoln by launching an attack on the "House of Virginia," frustration with the government's treatment of Nolan remains. Nolan is exiled from his country, but he is never free from governmental control, a control that more and more seems at odds with the cause of justice.[132]

In Hale's story the interests of the government and those of the country do not always coincide. Even if Hale intended to send the message "My country, right or wrong," he did not send the message "My government, right or wrong." Indeed, as he makes clear, service to one's country does not necessarily entail blind obedience to the government. For instance, when Nolan delivers his moral message to Ingham, he explicitly distinguishes his "Country" from its government. He even distinguishes it from its "people." "Behind officers, and government, and people even, there is," Nolan insists, "the Country herself, your Country" (675). If, on one hand, that distinction deprives "The Man without a Country" of the democratic civic ideal Lincoln expresses in the Gettysburg Address, on the other, it opens up the possibility that someone can honor his country while still disobeying governmental orders.

Indeed, there are a number of poignant moments in Hale's story when we are clearly supposed to identify with people who disobey orders. For instance, few readers are heartless enough to want Danforth to deny Nolan his deathbed wish to be told about his country simply because it would be breaking orders more than fifty years old. On the contrary, Hale uses the occasion to poke a bit more fun at governmental bureaucracy.[133] "After 1817," Ingham tells us, "the position of every officer who had Nolan in charge was one of the greatest delicacy." This is because the government had failed to renew the original 1807 order. What, therefore, was the officer in charge of him to do? "Should he let him go? What, then, if he were called to account by the Department for violating the order of 1807? Should he keep him? What, then, if Nolan should be liberated some day, and should bring an action for false imprisonment or kidnapping against every man who had him in charge?" The secretary of war was no help. When asked, he "always said, as they so often do at Washington, that there were no special orders to give, and that we must act on our own judgment. That means, 'If you succeed, you will be sustained; if you fail, you will be disavowed'" (677).

In the end, Danforth decides to disobey the 1807 order because, as he puts it, "I felt like a monster that I had not told him everything before. Danger or no danger, delicacy or no delicacy, who was I, that I should be acting the tyrant all this time over this dear, sainted old man, who had years ago expiated, in his whole manhood's life, the madness of a boy's treason?" (678). And Danforth is not alone in risking punishment. By the very act of publishing his story preaching love of country, Ingham worries that he might be exposing himself "to a criminal prosecution on the evidence of the very revelation I am making" (677).

Of course, Ingham and Danforth are frustrated by an unresponsive governmental bureaucracy, not a powerful president. That frustration raises one more complication that we have to consider. Toward the end of the Vietnam War, when protesters were chided to love their country or leave it and others denounced the government's "credibility gap," a 1973 film of "The Man without a Country" highlighted its criticism of governmental bureaucracy to such an extent that one viewer recalled, "Before there was Kafka and Orwell, there was 'The Man Without a Country.'" At first glance, Lincoln's image of a government of the people, by the people, for the people would seem the direct opposite of that nameless bureaucracy. But for that contrast to work, the abstract collective of "the people" has to be given a concrete embodiment. Confronted with an unresponsive government, citizens want to hold specific people responsible for its actions. Nothing serves that need more than to make one individual—the president—responsible for the government's actions. But that is only part of the answer. For the government to have the support of the people, the president has to have the appearance of being both representative of and accessible to "the people"—which is one reason why the civic mythology of Lincoln as a "man of the people" arises hand in hand with the rise of the bureaucratic state that, in large measure, began during his reign, when, confronted with the need to wage war, he both concentrated power in the federal government and extended its reach.

In Chapter 1 we saw how the Lincoln mythos helped to make that increased state power palatable by creating a utopian image of how a "government of the people, by the people, for the people" should function in the modern world.[134] The history of the reception of "The Man without a Country" provides a telling example of how that mythos works. Aware of readers' discomfort generated by the government's failure to respond to Nolan's predicament, a 1924 film of the story turns to Lincoln. In the film, Lincoln, nicknamed "Big Heart," grants Nolan a pardon that arrives just before his death—this after each president from Monroe on had refused to pardon someone with no official record. Delivering what viewers feel Nolan deserves, Lincoln, the embodiment of a man of the people, minimizes any resentment they might harbor against an unresponsive governmental bureaucracy. Drawing on the Lincoln mythos, the film eliminates a conflict at the heart of Hale's story, the conflict both Danforth and Ingham face between their feelings for Nolan and their sworn duty to obey governmental orders.[135]

"The Man without a Country" is, without a doubt, a sermon on patriotism. But it did not engage readers as long as it did simply by preaching love of country. Indeed, if we can trust the widely read and taught 1923 Riverside edition, many readers experienced some of the tensions it dramatizes. For instance, in his list of study questions the Riverside editor asks, "Why should the authorities at Washington ignore the punishment of Nolan? Do you suppose such a policy is ever practiced by our Government? Would it ever be justifiable? . . . Are there any conditions under which you might be justified in disregarding the law or the proclamation of your Government? Is your feeling that a law is unjust sufficient grounds for disobeying it?"[136]

Hale's story might fall short of Lincoln's best works in stating principles of democratic government, but in creating a conflict between our sympathy for Nolan and our sense of duty to the government, it forces us to wrestle with some of the dilemmas posed by the doctrine of popular sovereignty that Lincoln so memorably expresses. Indeed, the story's ultimate effect on policy makers is by no means clear.

For instance, *Kennedy v. Mendoza-Martinez*, the 1963 draft-evasion case already mentioned, involved a statute that took away the citizenship of those leaving the country to escape the draft, a punishment traced to an act passed one day before Lincoln's Second Inaugural in response to debates over desertion and duty to country influenced by "The Man without a Country." In his opinion, Justice Goldberg cites controversy over a 1912 extension and modification of the 1865 statute. Addressing the "barbarous punishment" of taking away the "rights of citizenship" on top of already harsh punitive measures, a representative from Hale's state of Massachusetts warned that "in the United States to-day there are thousands of men who are literally men without a country and their numbers will be constantly added to until the drastic civil-war measure which adds this heavy penalty to an already severe punishment imposed by military law, is repealed."[137] At the same time, Justice Goldberg's decision was harshly condemned by many patriotic citizens as the Vietnam War escalated, causing a retired marine corps officer to advocate a "Philip Nolan Law" that would make escaping the country to avoid the draft "a voluntary and deliberate renunciation of U.S. citizenship," requiring a penalty of permanent exile.[138] Does Hale's story of Nolan's rash act and subsequent suffering support this retired officer or those who decried the "monstrosity"[139] of a law that would add punishment to punishment by also stripping offenders of their citizenship?

☆ ☆ ☆ To acknowledge the story's subtle complexity is not to deny the ideological work it did on Lincoln's behalf. On the contrary, by adding credibility to the story, its complexity made its ideological work more effective. As we have seen, the story especially influenced how future generations would remember Vallandigham. For instance, Jean Holloway, Hale's biographer in the 1950s, uncritically accepted Hale's claim that "Mr. Vallandigham had been completely forgotten."[140] Just as Lincoln's Gettysburg Address transcended Gettysburg, Holloway writes, so Hale's "The Man without a Country" has been adopted "as a classic expression of American nationalism," while "history, or the vagaries of popular taste" have "left Vallandigham in the limbo of forgotten political squabbles."[141]

In this chapter I have tried to show that, far more than simply a "political squabble," the Vallandigham incident raises important constitutional questions about civil liberties. In bringing those issues to bear on a reading of "The Man without a Country," I have tried to work on/with the civic mythology of Lincoln, a civic mythology that continues to have great influence on the nation. So far I have not, however, dealt with one of the major reasons for Lincoln's mythologization: his role as the Great Emancipator. It is, therefore, appropriate to end this chapter by acknowledging how increased attention given to slavery as a cause of the Civil War has helped to keep Lincoln's works in the national canon while contributing to the disappearance of "The Man without a Country" from it.

Slavery never played much of a role in the reception of "The Man without a Country." There is, of course, the dramatic encounter with the slave ship. But in it Africans are returned to Africa, not freed to live in the United States. "The Man without a Country" was, in other words, better suited to a United States that identified the major cause of the Civil War as debate over loyalty to one's state verses loyalty to one's country, not as a debate over slavery. Indeed, whereas the Riverside edition lists poems by Emerson, Longfellow, and Whittier as patriotic literature, it lists none of their abolitionist works, even though it does include "The New South," Henry Grady's segregationist attempt to unite white North and South. Similarly, *Patriotic American Stories* of 1937 has a number of selections celebrating Robert E. Lee, including a poem by Julia Ward Howe, but none on slavery. Even the selections devoted to Lincoln portray him not as the Great Emancipator but as the merciful man intent on forgiving the South. In an excerpt from Winston Churchill's *The Crisis*, we glimpse Lincoln as he listens to a Southern woman pleading for her cousin, who is caught as a spy. Granting a pardon so that the cousin does not, like Nathan Hale or the simpleminded soldier boy, have to hang, he responds, "I have not suffered by the South, I have suffered *with* the South. Your sorrow has been my sorrow, and your pain has been my pain. What you have lost, I have lost. And what you have gained, . . . I have gained." With the emphasis on sectional reconciliation, the editor, the state supervisor of elementary schools for Louisiana, omits "two brief references of a sectional character" from "The Man without a Country": the paragraph imagining Bragg and Beauregard's exile and explicit mention of 1817 as the date when the government failed to renew the 1807 order.[142]

In today's world, when slavery, even more than issues about states' rights, is seen as the cause of the Civil War, Lincoln's role as the Great Emancipator helps to maintain for his works a place in the country's civic mythology that Hale's story no longer has. Indeed, even the Gettysburg Address, which has no mention of slavery, is read today as silently commenting on it. Those not "conceived in Liberty," Lincoln seems to imply, are a living reminder that the nation had not yet turned into reality its founding proposition that all men are created equal. What else, after all, could the Great Emancipator have intended?

Indeed, the image of Lincoln freeing the slaves has helped to obscure the specter of him cracking down on civil liberties. Even so, it is important to remember that, at the time, many linked the two. For instance, only two days before he issued his September 24, 1862, crackdown on civil liberties, Lincoln made a preliminary announcement of the Emancipation Proclamation. In "Executive Power" Curtis, who as a Supreme Court justice had written a powerful dissent in *Dred Scott*, attacked that announcement as vigorously as the one on civil liberties. The two were linked because both relied on the executive powers Lincoln claimed as commander in chief during wartime. In his First Inaugural he had unequivocally stated that the Constitution gave him "no lawful right" to "interfere with the institution of slavery in the States where it exists."[143] A year and a half later, he interfered with slavery after all, evoking his constitutional authority to put down an armed rebellion. Arguing that slavery's existence in rebellious states aided their military efforts, Lincoln abolished it, not universally, but only in those states where its existence posed a threat to the Northern army. As much as most today applaud Lincoln's willingness to find any way possible to free slaves and to make slavery a major issue of the war, he evoked the same authority to do so that he evoked to create new crimes of disloyalty and to suspend habeas corpus.

Wills praises the Gettysburg Address for "correcting the Constitution itself without overthrowing it."[144] It does so by supplementing the Constitution's commitment to protecting liberty with the Declaration of Independence's dedication to equality. Indeed, with the Fourteenth Amendment and various civil rights bills passed after the Civil War, the new nation to emerge out of bloodshed carried with it a legal commitment to both the liberty and the equality that Lincoln yokes together in his most famous speech. What Wills does not point out is that the attempt to create civil equality for freedmen caused many to claim that their liberties had been violated. Contained in the figure of a Lincoln who assumed what some called despotic executive power to free the slaves, this tension between America's fundamental civic ideals of liberty and equality is the topic of the next chapter.

4 *Ex parte Milligan*

Civil Liberties v. Civil Rights

Utopia and ideology exist in a complicated relation. An ideology gains much of its appeal from projecting a utopian possibility; utopian visions are almost always ideological.[1] Such a relation, I argued in the last chapter, helps to explain Lincoln's record on civil liberties. Opposed to both those who condemn him as a despot and those who see his record as a minor, if understandable, departure from his commitment to democratic ideals, I tried to show how, from his perspective, his crackdown on civil liberties was in keeping with the spirit of his utopian expression of a "government of the people, by the people, for the people." Yet, in presuming to act for "the people," he justified charges that he acted like a despot. The point is not to reject his utopian vision as simply ideological; the ideal is important to maintain as a standard of judgment. Nonetheless, we should be aware that lurking within the ideal of a government acting for the people is the danger that the government will assume it inevitably expresses the will of the people.

A different effort to embrace such complexity is Clinton Rossiter's claim that Lincoln was a "constitutional dictator." Self-consciously adopting this provocative label, Rossiter does not use it pejoratively. Instead, he argues that because constitutional democracies are designed for peace, they are "*unequal to the exigencies of a great national crisis.*"[2] Thus, during times of war, rebellion, and economic depression, the chief executive must take on greater power, even going so far as temporarily to suspend the constitutional order in order to save it. The sole purpose of a constitutional dictatorship, he makes clear, is "the complete restoration of the *status quo ante bellum.*" Lincoln is a model for him because, under his leadership, "it is remarkable how little change in the structure of government and how little abridgement of civil liberty accompanied the persecution of this bitter war." In claiming that Lincoln's crackdown on civil liberties was minimal, Rossiter joins recent champions of Lincoln, but he is at odds with them when he grants that Lincoln did indeed assume temporary dictatorial powers. He also differs from them on the changes Lincoln brought about. For Lincoln to fit into Rossiter's thesis, he has to argue that the president assumed dictatorial power in order to *"end the crisis and restore normal times."*[3] In contrast, people like Wills, McPherson, and Fletcher, celebrate a Lincoln who brought about a constitutional revolution.

There are two major reasons for these differences. First, in a post-Watergate era, any suggestion of the chief executive operating above the law—even to preserve it—is unpopular. Second, and most important, Rossiter wrote before the civil rights movement had its revolutionary effect on the country. In 1948 Rossiter was most intent on finding a model for preserving a democratic government committed to the spirit of liberty when faced with the threat of Soviet totalitarianism and crises such as the depression and World War II. He found one in Lincoln, who curtailed civil liberties in order to save a Union committed to protecting them. More recent celebrants seek a model for someone intent on making the country live up to its founding promise of equality through a second American revolution. Rossiter acknowledges Lincoln's constitutional violations but justifies them because they allowed him to preserve, not alter, the Union; Wills and others celebrate the changes in the nation Lincoln brought about but insist that he only bent, never violated, the Constitution.

The Lincoln I propose contemplating is one who helped bring about important changes in the country and also did more than simply bend the Constitution. To contemplate this Lincoln is to acknowledge that the ideal of equality that he so commendably tried to incorporate into the Constitution could not be added to it without altering its existing commitment to liberty. In this chapter I will illustrate how the tensions between liberty and equality played themselves out as a conflict between civil liberties and civil rights in the period after the Civil War. My primary object of analysis will be *Ex parte Milligan*, the most famous civil liberties decision to come out of the war. But I will start by looking at a speech by Charles Sumner that imagines the Civil War giving birth to a new nation committed to both liberty and equality.

☆ ☆ ☆ Sumner and Lincoln did not always agree. Sumner was a radical abolitionist; Lincoln was not. Also, as we saw in the preceding chapter, Sumner felt that Lincoln claimed powers in wartime that properly belonged to Congress as the voice of the people. After Lincoln's assassination, however, Sumner embraced him, especially his Gettysburg Address, which he called "the most touching speech of all history."⁴ He was especially moved by its vision of the nation. Thus, on the fourth anniversary of Lincoln's famous address, Sumner delivered a speech in New York that asked, through its title, "Are We a Nation?" With Francis Lieber in the audience and acknowledged in the speech, Sumner notes that "nation" originally had the ethnological meaning of a "race or people of common descent and language." Its modern meaning, however, is political. "Our own Webster, the lexicographer, calls it 'the body of inhabitants of a country *united under the same government.*'" The unity of a nation, for Sumner, must be political, not of "blood or language" (Nation 10–11).

Today's theorists of the nation would call Sumner's definition civic as opposed to ethnic, based on a political contract rather than on biological descent. The essential condition of a nation for him is that it have "one sovereignty" and "one citizenship" (Nation 12). Not surprisingly, much of the speech is aimed at dismissing the "propensity to local sovereignty" as a "species of egotism," "gratifying to petty pride and ambition." Careful to grant that "for purposes of local self-government and to secure its educational and political blessings, the States are of unquestioned value," he, nonetheless, insists that "*local sovereignty,* whether in the name of State or prince, is out of place and incongruous with the idea of Nation" (Nation 13). Hand in hand with the notion of one sovereignty is that of one citizenship with equal rights for all. A nation, Sumner argues, alluding to Lieber's writings, "is naturally dedicated to the maintenance of all the rights of the citizen as its practical end and object" (Nation 12). According to him, the United States can trace its national unity to a time when all of the colonies were united under the British sovereign with "common and interchangeable rights of citizenship, so that no British subject in one Colony could be made an alien in any other Colony" (Nation 53). A crucial measure of whether the United States could truly be called a nation in 1867 was whether it was prepared to provide equal political and civil rights for all of its citizens, including African Americans. It must, he felt, citing the Gettysburg Address, incorporate into the Constitution the ideal of equality put forth in the Declaration of Independence. "Liberty is won: Equality must be won also. In England there is Liberty without Equality; in France Equality without Liberty. The two together must be ours" (Nation 63).

Sumner's view of what the nation should be is clearly different from what the Union was in 1860. That difference is registered in his insistence that we call the government in Washington the national government, not the federal government. If prior to the Civil War the United States recognized two citizenships, one for individual states and one for the country, for Sumner, when it came to rights, there could be only one citizenship. "Each locality has its own way in matters peculiar to itself. But the rights of all must be placed under the protection of all; nor can there be any difference in different parts of the country. Here the rule must be uniform, and it must be sustained by the central power radiating to every part of the empire." He was not shy about acknowledging the consequences of this centralization. "Call it imperialism, if you please: it is simply the imperialism of the Declaration of Independence with all its promises fulfilled" (Nation 60). The goal of that imperialism should be securing equal civil and political rights for all citizens.

Such blatant calls for a centralized imperial power were, of course, heard with alarm by those intent on blocking attempts to give equal rights to recently freed slaves. But they were equally threatening to those attached to the traditional view that centralization of power was a threat to liberty. Both fears were increased when Sumner announced that achieving equality for all citizens would be the culmination of the recent war. "This final victory will be the greatest of the war; it will be the consummation of all other victories" (Nation 63). For Sumner to equate bringing about civil rights for African Americans with an extension of the North's war against the South would help justify those arguing that Reconstruction was the North's imperial infringement on the rights of white Southerners. The campaign for civil rights became, in their eyes, a threat to their civil liberties. To understand the implications of that belief, we need briefly to trace the complicated historical relation between civil liberties and civil rights.

A recent textbook offers a standard contemporary understanding of the difference between the two. "Civil liberties refer to the freedoms that individuals enjoy and that governments cannot invade. Civil rights refer to the powers and privileges that belong to us by virtue of our status as citizens."[5] This distinction is helpful, but there are obvious complications. For instance, in the United States almost all of our civil liberties derive from the Bill of Rights, which would seem to imply that rights and liberties blend into one another. Thus, if we include as civil rights the "privileges that belong to us by virtue of our status as citizens," many of our civil liberties are also civil rights. In fact, prior to the Civil War "civil liberties" and "civil rights" were used interchangeably.

For instance, in *The Rights of Man* when Thomas Paine refers to what today we associate with civil liberties—such as freedom of speech—he calls them civil rights.[6] Likewise, when Clement Vallandigham criticized Lincoln's crackdown on what today we would call civil liberties, he protested Lincoln's violation of civil rights, even though he staunchly defended a state's right to maintain slavery. Indeed, at this time, civil rights were not distinguished from civil liberties but from political rights, with political rights having to do with rights in relation to the government, such as the right to vote, and civil rights having to do with rights within civil society. This distinction was, in turn, related to William Blackstone's distinction between civil and political liberty. Political liberty, for him, involved people's participation in rule, whereas civil liberty meant "nothing more than the impartial administration of equal and expedient laws." In fact, Blackstone himself used the term "civil privileges" to refer to "the right of personal security, the right of personal liberty, and the right of private property." In 1833 the American Anti-Slavery Society's constitution drew on Blackstone to demand the equality of "civil privileges" for whites and blacks.[7]

In the meantime, various states set the stage for our present distinction between civil liberties and civil rights when, either authorized by or providing support for Justice Taney's famous declaration in *Dred Scott* that African Americans had no rights that a white man had to respect, they began to use "civil rights" to designate privileges and immunities guaranteed to whites but not to free blacks. For instance, in 1859 a court in Mississippi held that "free negroes or persons of color . . . are entitled to no such rights. They are to be regarded as alien enemies or strangers *prohibiti*, and without the pale of comity, and incapable of acquiring or maintaining rights of property in this State."[8] With the end of the Civil War, the Fourteenth Amendment was ratified and various "civil rights" acts were passed to undo such rulings as well as *Dred Scott*, which covered free blacks as well as slaves. Together they were designed to guarantee equal rights for freedmen. As a result, "civil rights" began to be distinguished from the "civil liberties" guaranteed by the Bill of Rights.

The civil rights movement of the twentieth century reinforced this distinction, so that in 1968 Milton Konvitz could write, "Although the terms 'civil rights' and 'civil liberties' are often used interchangeably, when they are differentiated the latter generally denotes the rights of *individuals*, while the former refers to the constitutional and legal status and treatment of *minority groups* that are marked off from the majority by race, religion, or national origin."[9] At the same time, the civil rights movement also helped to efface the traditional distinction between civil and political rights. Dictionary entries as late as the early 1960s defined civil rights as nonpolitical rights guaranteed by a government. But, since blacks were clearly denied the franchise because of their status as a group, present definitions refer to civil rights as those rights guaranteed by the Fifteenth Amendment as well as the Thirteenth and Fourteenth. For the period after the Civil War, however, civil rights were still clearly distinguished from political rights, and they were starting to be distinguished from civil liberties. *Ex parte Milligan* shows how important the latter distinction was for Reconstruction politics.

Like the Vallandigham case, *Ex parte Milligan* grew out of the Lincoln administration's practice of trying in military courts civilians suspected of sympathizing with the Confederates. A partisan Democrat from Indiana, Lambdin P. Milligan criticized Lincoln's policies during the war, especially his crackdown on "civil rights" through the institution of the draft and the suspension of habeas corpus. Thought to be a member of the Sons of Liberty, which allegedly conspired with the Confederates, Milligan was accused of trying to prevent enlistments and encouraging desertion. Denied habeas corpus and tried by a military tribunal, he was sentenced to hang. Unsuccessfully petitioning first Lincoln and then Andrew Johnson for a pardon, he eventually had his sentence commuted to life imprisonment, which allowed him to pursue his legal challenge to the Supreme Court. Along with Vallandigham, Milligan was the most famous victim of Lincoln's crackdown on civil liberties. Together they serve to remind us of a conflict over the origins of civil liberties in the United States. On one hand, the ideal of liberty has been associated with a cosmopolitan tradition, traceable to the Stoics and eventuating in doctrines of the "rights of man" and "human rights." On the other, it has frequently been seen as the special inheritance of Englishmen, who considered it a birthright, confirmed by the Magna Charta but traceable to around A.D. 450 when Britons invited from the continent the liberty-loving Angle warriors Hengst and Horsa.[10] Siding with Edmund Burke in his debate with Paine, Vallandigham and Milligan subscribed to the latter view. Indeed, both were featured in a book published soon after the war called *American Bastille*.

Republished in 1883, this book champions the Magna Charta, arguing that for more than five centuries there was a conflict between the "sovereign and people, the one for royal prerogative, the other for the rights of personal liberty."[11] With the formation of the American republic, in which the people became sovereign, this age-old conflict seemed to resolve itself. Nonetheless, the author claims, it reappeared with the election of Lincoln, who instituted a regime of military despotism that gave the government the power of arbitrary arrests. "There was a time when the proudest appellation a man could bear was that of American citizen. 'I am an American citizen,' implied liberty and safety—protection and justice. Then, the national shield was, indeed, a shield with arms — a shield which defended the citizen against every act of tyranny and usurpation — a shield which guarded him on land and sea, at home and abroad." Lincoln, however, turned the shield into the service of military rule, trampling on the liberties of citizens. In doing so he defamed the national symbol of the liberty bell. For instance, his Secretary of State William Seward is quoted telling an English lord, "My lord, I can touch a bell on my right hand, and order the arrest of a citizen of Ohio; I can touch a bell again, and order the imprisonment of a citizen of New York; and no power on earth, except that of the President, can release them. Can the Queen of England do so much?"[12]

The quotation attributed to Seward is probably a fabrication, even if it was frequently repeated during the nineteenth century. Milligan's case, in contrast, was real, and it resulted in a landmark decision by the Supreme Court. The case for the government was primarily argued by Attorney General A. G. Speed and General Benjamin Butler. Butler had gained notoriety during the Civil War for the harsh martial law he imposed as commanding officer over occupied New Orleans. For instance, one New Orleans citizen was hanged for tearing down the U.S. flag. The incident that got him the most publicity, however, was his insult to southern womanhood when he declared, "Any lady who shall by word or gesture express contempt of any Federal officer or soldier shall be liable, without protection or redress, to be treated as common prostitutes are treated."[13]

Arrayed against him was a formidable team of legal minds. David Dudley Field, born in New England, was the brother of Supreme Court Justice Stephen S. Field and Cyrus W. Field, the man responsible for the transatlantic cable. In 1848 David Field had written a code of civil procedures for the state of New York that became the basis of civil law reform in the United States and abroad. The Field Code influenced the English Judicature Acts of 1873 and 1875, which were then adopted by many British colonies. Among other things, as a democratic reform aimed at an institution once associated with the crown, it abolished courts of equity, thus denying Melville's fictional lawyer in "Bartleby" some easily earned income. By inclination a Democrat, Field had such strong antislavery convictions that he joined the Republican Party and helped nominate Lincoln. Nonetheless, he had a very different sense of the nation from Sumner. As the war came to a close, he urged the federal government to crush the last vestiges of rebellion and then to restore the union "with the rights of the States and the rights of individuals as clearly defined and as firmly secured as the rights of the nation."[14] Working with Field was Jeremiah S. Black, a former chief justice of Pennsylvania and attorney general under President James Buchanan. Black also recruited a rising Republican from Ohio, General James Garfield, who would be elected president in 1880.

The crucial issues at stake were the extent of the president's power in wartime and whether he could authorize a military commission to try a civilian when, as was the case in Indiana, civil courts were open. Since the latter was an issue in the Vallandigham case, the government argued that it had already been decided when the Supreme Court refused to hear that Copperhead's appeal. But in Ex parte Vallandigham (1864) the Court had relied on a technicality, ruling it could not hear an appeal from a military commission because it was not a court of record. That situation did not hold for Milligan's case. On the substantive issues, both sides drew on examples from history to offer opposing accounts of "the progress and development of Anglo-Saxon liberty."[15] Milligan's attorneys argued that their client had been denied rights guaranteed by the Constitution and that those rights could not be suspended during wartime. Reminding the Court that executive power is not a kingly power, they insisted that the only theory of government "compatible with civil liberty" is one that restricts the power of the executive (31). At the same time, the framers of the Constitution were wise enough not to restrict those powers too much. As Black insisted, "This government of ours has powers to defend itself without violating its own laws; it does not carry the seeds of destruction in its own bosom. It is clothed from head to foot in a panoply of defensive armor" (81–82).

Butler agreed, but only if the Court granted the president powers during war that Milligan's lawyers would deny him. "We insist only that the Constitution be interpreted so as to save the nation, and not let it perish" (104). Civil courts might have been open in Indiana, but only "because the strong arm of the military upheld them" (87). Getting in a dig at Black, he alluded to Buchanan's helplessness in the face of secession. One danger to the nation that Black did not consider, he gloated, was "imbecility of administration; such an administration as should say that there is no constitutional right in a State to go out of the Union, but that there is no power in the Constitution to coerce a State or her people, if she choose to go out" (89).

The Court sided with Milligan, unanimously ruling that the president had no authority to try a civilian in military courts when civil courts were open. According to Justice David Davis, "No graver question was ever considered by this court, nor one which more nearly concerns the rights of the whole people" (118–19). Contrary to the Constitution, Milligan had been denied trial by a proper court of law and trial by jury. To the objection that conditions of rebellion and war created special circumstances, Davis replied,

LIBERTY. (on banner)

CONSTITUTION

SIC SEMPER TYRANNIS

Drawn by   Eng^d by J A. O'Neill. N.Y.   A. Will
Copyright J A Marshall 1880.

LIBERTY BELL 1776.

Proclaim Liberty throughout all the Land, unto all the Inhabitants thereof.

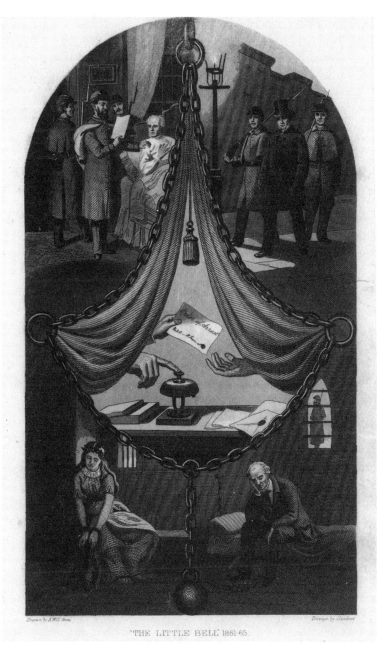

Drawn by S.Wild from.

Design by Quuchert

"THE LITTLE BELL" 1861-65.

This frontispiece to *American Bastille* contrasts the Liberty Bell of 1776 surrounded by images of George Washington, Lady Liberty, the American Eagle, the Constitution affixed to the American shield, and the Virginia state motto — "Thus always to tyrants" — with Secretary of State Seward's "Little Bell" that allegedly was rung to bring about the arbitrary arrests and imprisonments portrayed around it.

The Constitution of the United States is a law for rulers and people, equally in war and in peace, and covers with the shield of its protections all classes of men, at all times, and under all circumstances. No doctrine, involving more pernicious consequences, was ever invented by the wit of man than that any of its provisions can be suspended during any of the great exigencies of government. Such a doctrine leads directly to anarchy or despotism, but the theory of necessity upon which it is based is false; for the government, within the Constitution, has all the powers granted to it, which are necessary to preserve its existence; as has been happily proved by the result of the great effort to throw off its just authority. (120–21)

To the objection that the military commission was justified by martial law, Davis replied, "Civil liberty and this kind of martial law cannot endure together; the antagonism is irreconcilable; and, in the conflict, one or the other must perish" (124–25). For the Court it was paramount that civil liberty survive.

To get a sense of the differences between Justice Davis's reasoning and Lincoln's we can return to the *Somers* affair that we briefly examined in the preceding chapter. One of the complaints against Captain Mackenzie was that he hanged the alleged mutineers without proof that a real mutiny was about to take place. But, according to Sumner, that proof was unnecessary. What was important was whether Mackenzie felt an *"apparent necessity."*[16] According to legal precedent, the distinction between an apparent and a real necessity lies at the foundation of the right of self-defense. After all, when someone feels threatened by someone wielding what looks like a loaded pistol, if that person were required by law to make certain that the pistol were really loaded, he or she might well be dead before having a chance to respond. Stopping a mutiny, according to Sumner, is clearly a form of self-defense and adheres to the same logic. For Lincoln that logic also extended to putting down an insurrection to save the national ship of state. Thus, in his response to Corning, he argues that, in the case of rebellion threatening the very existence of the nation, he should not have to wait to arrest people "until defined crimes shall have been committed" but, instead, should be able to arrest people if there is an apparent necessity to do so to help to save the country.[17]

In *Ex parte Milligan* Justice Davis denies the analogy between an individual's self-defense and a nation's. There was, he claimed, no reason to declare martial law in Indiana at the time, because there was no immediate military threat. "Martial law cannot arise from a *threatened* invasion. The necessity must be actual and present; the invasion real, such as effectively closes the courts and deposes the civil administration" (127). A nation cannot respond to a threatened invasion in the same way that individuals can respond to threats to their lives for a variety of reasons, but most importantly because the nation's identity—or at least the identity of the United States—depends upon the value it places on civil liberties. If in trying to defend itself it violated one of the sacred principles it stands for, the nation would no longer be the same nation. As Justice Davis put it, "A country, preserved at the sacrifice of all the cardinal principles of liberty, is not worth the cost of preservation" (126).[18] As Black put it, first employing the metaphor of national suicide that we discussed in the preceding chapter, "A violation of law on the pretense of saving such a government as ours is not self-preservation, but suicide" (81).

☆ ☆ ☆ Soon after World War I, Charles Warren noted that *Ex parte Milligan* had been "long recognized as one of the bulwarks of American liberty."[19] Soon after World War II, Allan Nevins ventured that "the heart of the decision is the heart of the difference between the United States of America and Nazi Germany or the Soviet Union."[20] *Milligan* owes part of its reputation to what appears today to be the nonpartisan nature of the decision. Lincoln himself had appointed five members of the Court, including Justice Davis, his friend and campaign manager. Garfield's presence on Milligan's team was also telling. Garfield knew that he would be attacked by some partisan Republicans for serving "in defense of traitors." But even though he had been a brigadier general, had denounced Copperheads, and had signed the order transferring Vallandigham to the Confederacy, he had, in his own words, "resisted some attempts to extend the power of Military Commissions so far as to try civilians who were interfering in any way with the war—such fellows as Vallandigham. I had resisted that as being un-American and contrary to the old English spirit of liberty." Thus when the opportunity came to help defend Milligan, he wrote to a friend, "I was willing to subject myself to the misunderstanding of some for the sake of securing the supremacy of the civil over the military authority."[21]

Praised today, the case, at the time, was controversial. First, when the full opinion appeared in December 1866, it seemed retroactively to declare the military trial of Lincoln's assassins unconstitutional. Second, it raised questions about trying Jefferson Davis in a military court. Third, and most important, if the Court unanimously held that the military commission authorized by the president was unlawful, it split over another, extremely contentious issue. Although the circumstances of the case did not require them to do so, five justices ruled that Congress, as well as the president, had no constitutional power to create military commissions during wartime. Their opinion provoked a strong dissent from the other four justices, including Chief Justice Salmon P. Chase. They agreed with their colleagues that the way Milligan was tried violated the March 3, 1863, act of Congress that authorized the suspension of habeas corpus but placed various conditions upon the executive branch when it did so. Once that point was established, however, they felt that the Court's business was done. They very much disagreed with the majority that the Constitution forbid even Congress, the voice of the people, from establishing military commissions during wartime. "Congress has the power not only to raise and support and govern armies but to declare war. It has, therefore, the power to provide by law for carrying on war. This power necessarily extends to all legislation essential to the prosecution of war with vigor and success, except such as interferes with the command of the forces and the conduct of campaigns. That power and duty belong to the President as commander-in-chief. . . . The power to make necessary laws is in the Congress; the power to execute in the President" (139). To be sure, Congress did not choose to exercise its power to create military commissions. Even so, the minority insisted, "in such a time of public danger, Congress had power, under the Constitution," to authorize military trials, even when civil courts were open (140).

This split in the Court was mirrored in the public, which debated the wisdom of the majority decision. The Democratic *Baltimore Sun* rejoiced that the "miserable plea of military necessity is torn from human liberty, and men feel again that the chains of despotic power are utterly riven." In contrast, the Radical Republican *Washington Chronicle*, claimed that "the denial of Congressional power has elicited universal condemnation from the people of the country." The majority's decision, it protested, "places the rights of the individual before the safety of the whole people."[22] The debate over how the Court's decision affected the balance between national security and civil liberty has persisted through today.

An important figure for critics of the majority opinion is John W. Burgess, who in 1890 held the Lieber Chair of Political Science at Columbia University. "The minority opinion," he wrote,

> is the only view which can reconcile jurisprudence with political science, law with policy. It is devoutly to be hoped that the decision of the Court may never be subjected to the strain of actual war. If, however, it should be, we may safely predict that it will necessarily be disregarded. In time of war and public danger, the whole power of the State must be vested in

the General Government, and the constitutional liberty of the individual must be sacrificed, so far as the Government finds it necessary for the preservation of life and the security of the State. This is the experience of political history and the principle of political science.[23]

Burgess's reasoning was powerful enough to cause even Warren to temper his praise of Ex parte Milligan by noting that "there was a serious and well-founded criticism" of the Court's ruling on the power of Congress.[24]

Others have gone much farther. Their criticism provides ample evidence of how the Lincoln legend affects historical judgment. For instance, in an influential book with a chapter called "The Irrelevance of the Milligan Decision," Mark E. Neely Jr. works as hard as he can to defend Lincoln's record on civil liberties. Providing valuable empirical evidence showing that the actual number of political arrests—by his definition—was smaller than normally assumed, he goes on to argue that the highly publicized cases of Vallandigham and Milligan are relatively unimportant. "The real legacy of Ex parte Milligan," he confidently concludes, "is confined between the covers of the constitutional history books. The decision itself had little effect on history."[25] Adopting a "realistic" stance that accepts hard evidence, not idealistic pronouncements in books, Neely's argument would be better served if he were a better reader of the words contained in books.

For instance, his reading of Milligan completely ignores the split in the Court and the consequences of that split.[26] Ironically, he also forgets some of the most memorable lessons of the man he tries to defend. For Neely to argue that Milligan is irrelevant is like saying that the Gettysburg Address is irrelevant because the country has not lived up to its ideal of equality.[27] But, as Lincoln knew, statements of principle, such as those uttered by Justice Davis in Milligan, can have a profound effect on history even when they are not always adhered to. They can because they establish standards that help to guide, in Lincoln's words, the "better angels of our nature."[28] Indeed, to a large extent, "Honest Abe" has been mythologized because he more than almost any other political leader is felt to have matched his words with his deeds. He is remembered for pronouncing the famous words about a nation "dedicated to the proposition that all men are created equal" and for giving substance to that proposition by announcing the Emancipation Proclamation. He is revered for honoring those who "gave the full measure of devotion" so that the nation could "have a new birth of freedom" and for giving his own life to that cause.[29]

Neely's interpretation is less indebted to Lincoln himself than to Lincoln as interpreted by Edward S. Corwin, a noted advocate of a strong executive during national emergencies. Unlike Burgess, Corwin dismissed even the minority opinion as unrealistic. As Rossiter, who dedicates his book to Corwin, puts his mentor's position, "What Lincoln did, not what the Supreme Court said, is the precedent of the Constitution in the matter of presidential emergency power."[30] Exploiting Lincoln's reputation as a plain stylist, Corwin attacked what he considered the inflated rhetoric of Justice Davis's principled opinion: "To suppose that such fustian would be of greater influence in determining presidential procedure in a future great emergency than precedents backed by the monumental reputation of Lincoln would be merely childish."[31] That a noted political "realist," without a touch of irony, could attack Justice Davis's language as being out of touch with reality while allowing someone's reputation to override the precedent of an actual Supreme Court decision is ample illustration of the power of Lincoln's civic mythology to affect history.

Faulting Justice Davis for "fustian," Corwin's own pronouncement has proven eminently quotable. Both Neely and Rossiter cite it to help wrap up their arguments against the practicality of *Milligan*.[32] What neither acknowledges, however, is that in later editions of his book on the president's powers, Corwin himself dropped this particular criticism of Justice Davis and replaced it with much more temperate language, perhaps in response to a growing awareness of the dangers of an imperial presidency. To his credit, Rossiter, writing in 1948, could not have known about Corwin's revision. Furthermore, he acknowledges the dangers of having a great constitutional scholar like Corwin argue that we should trust a precedent based on someone's "monumental reputation" rather than one based on a Supreme Court decision. Insisting that "Lincoln's actions form history's most illustrious precedent for constitutional dictatorship," Rossiter, nonetheless, warns that Lincoln "set a precedent for bad men as well as good. It is just because Lincoln's reputation is so tremendous that a tyrant bent on illegal power might successfully appeal to this eminent shade for historical sanction of his own arbitrary actions."[33]

In making this point, Rossiter, a critic of *Milligan*, ends up echoing the justice that Corwin so harshly mocked. "This nation, as experience has proved," Justice Davis wrote, "cannot always remain at peace, and has no right to expect that it will always have wise and humane rulers, sincerely attached to the principles of the Constitution. Wicked men ambitious of power, with hatred of liberty and contempt of law, may fill the place once occupied by Washington and Lincoln; and if this right is conceded, and the calamities of war again befall us, the dangers to human liberty are frightful to contemplate" (125). The irony, however, does not end with Rossiter's unacknowledged agreement with Justice Davis. Even though a unanimous Court in *Milligan* rebuked Lincoln's wartime policies, it too helped to perpetuate the myth that arose almost immediately after his assassination.

If critics of *Milligan* argue that it was easy and almost cowardly to declare Lincoln's actions during the war unconstitutional after victory had been secured, *Milligan* itself suggests that it was much easier to praise Lincoln after he died than while he was living. As Justice Davis's quotation shows, less than two years after Lincoln's death, the majority placed him in the austere company of Washington. Not to be outdone, the minority called him "that upright and patriotic President under whose administration the Republic was rescued from threatened destruction" (141). Earlier the minority went so far as to suggest that, if Lincoln had not become the "victim of an abhorred conspiracy," he might have pardoned Milligan himself (132). Playing on Lincoln's growing reputation as a man of mercy, despite the fact that under his leadership more members of the U.S. military were executed than in all other U.S. wars combined, this suggestion relies on a crucial component of Lincoln's mythologization: unconstrained speculation about the might-have-been if he had lived. For some, *Milligan* confirmed Lincoln's sincere attachment to the principles of the Constitution and his promise to be merciful to the defeated South.[34] For others, it threatened to undercut efforts to avenge his horrible death and to carry out his dream of making equality the rule of the land.

The debate that ensued over *Milligan* soon after it was decided dramatizes the tensions that arose when those like Sumner claimed that the nation Lincoln died for was one that provided for both liberty and equality. At stake, many felt, was the policy of Reconstruction that depended on both military rule of the South and strong congressional measures. *Milligan*'s defense of individual civil liberties, they argued, would hamstring efforts to guarantee equal civil rights for freedmen. If the debate over whether *Milligan* unbalances competing claims between civil liberties and national security is still very much with us, the debate that pitted its defense of civil liberties against civil rights has largely been forgotten. It needs to be revisited.

☆ ☆ ☆ The extent to which *Milligan* had the potential to prompt that debate is illustrated by the government's argument. On one hand, Attorney General Speed and Butler used language, according to a respected twentieth-century legal scholar, "suited to the royal Stuarts in times before the prerogative had been bound by law and custom of the constitution."[35] With the onset of war, they declared, the president was the "sole judge of the exigencies, necessities, and duties of the occasion, their extent and duration. During the war his power must be without limit" (18). On the other hand, it was Butler who raised a point that seems obvious to people today. Responding to arguments about constitutional protections of liberty, he reminded the Court, "The Constitution provides that 'no person' shall be deprived of liberty without due process of law. And yet, as we know, whole generations of people in this land—as many as four millions of them at one time—people described in the Constitution by the same word, 'persons,' have been till lately deprived of liberty ever since the adoption of the Constitution, without any process of law whatever" (103). Many who shared Butler's desire to make former slaves equal citizens compared the case Nevins would call "a great triumph for the civil liberties of Americans in time of war or internal dissension" to the infamous case of *Dred Scott*.[36]

Most defenders of civil liberties today would probably agree with Justice Davis, who countered his critics by arguing that *Dred Scott* served the interests of slavery, whereas *Milligan* spoke for liberty.[37] Nonetheless, the comparison made perfect sense to Radical Republicans at the time. In both cases, they felt, the Supreme Court catered to Southern interests. *Milligan*, like *Dred Scott*, limited the power of Congress. *Dred Scott* did so by overruling the Missouri Compromise, which gave Congress power over U.S. territories. *Milligan* did so by limiting Congress's power to establish military tribunals to try civilians. In both, the controversial rulings were made in dicta of split decisions, not necessary for the outcome of the case. Furthermore, both majorities justified their rulings in the name of civil liberties. *Dred Scott* was the first Supreme Court decision to evoke the Bill of Rights to overturn congressional legislation. It did so when Justice Taney cited the due process clause of the Fifth Amendment to argue that the Missouri Compromise deprived a U.S. citizen of "his liberty or property, merely because he brought his property [a slave] into a particular Territory of the United States."[38] *Milligan* asserted the supremacy of civilian over military rule by guaranteeing citizens the right to be tried in civil courts.

In a letter to Chief Justice Chase, John Jay expressed great concern about the majority decision. "If, as the public begin to fear, their denial of the powers of Congress is any index to the view they are prepared to take of the great questions that will come before them in reference to Reconstruction, our situation is certainly a grave one." Thaddeaus Stevens, the driving force behind congressional Reconstruction, felt that *Milligan*, "although in terms not as infamous as the Dred Scott decision, is yet far more dangerous in its operation upon the lives and liberties of the loyal men of this country." *Harper's Weekly* fumed, "The action in regard to the Supreme Court need not be misunderstood. It is not, whether in time of peace in loyal States the civil

Courts shall be supreme, which nobody questions. It is, whether loyal men or rebels shall reorganize the Union."[39] It went on to advocate packing the Court to turn the five-judge majority into a minority. These fears seemed justified when President Andrew Johnson immediately stopped all military trials of civilians in the occupied South and read the decision as endorsing his plan to stop military rule as soon as possible. In the end, however, the fears of Radical Republicans were not completely justified, since the Court did not declare military rule of the South unconstitutional.[40]

Even so, the Court never came close to endorsing Sumner's vision of a unified nation dedicated to both liberty and equality. For Sumner, the "essential conditions of national life" were "*one sovereignty, one citizenship, one people*" (Nation 61). Achieving that unity would, he felt, transform the "whole face of the country. . . . There will be concord for discord, smiles for frowns. There will be a new consciousness of national life, with a corresponding glow. The soul will dilate with the assured unity of the Republic, and all will feel the glory of its citizenship. Since that of Rome, nothing so commanding" (Nation 63–64). But even before the end of the war Justice Davis had written a friend about Sumner's plans for Reconstruction, "The negro can never be elevated to social & political rights in this country & all wise statesmen know it."[41] Less than a decade after the end of the war, the *Slaughter House Cases* (1873) made it clear that there were still two citizenships: state and federal. If that case did not involve the rights of freedmen, one decided soon thereafter did. The case of *United States v. Cruikshank* (1876) resulted from events on Easter Sunday 1873 in Colfax (named after Republican Vice President Schuyler Colfax) in the newly established Grant Parish in Louisiana. When the Republican governor appointed some of his supporters, including blacks, to local offices, a newly established White League and other paramilitary groups with access to riverboat cannons resisted, storming the local courthouse occupied by outmanned but armed blacks. Two whites were killed, while from 69 to more than 100 blacks were killed. Federal troops captured a number of whites, who were brought to trial. Of the nearly 100 defendants, William Cruikshank and two others were convicted under the 1870 Federal Enforcement Act of conspiracy to "injure, oppress, threaten, or intimidate" African Americans trying to exercise their rights as citizens. On appeal, the case made its way to the Supreme Court.[42]

The Court overturned the convictions by maintaining a strict separation between federal and state citizenship. "There is in our political system," the Court summarized, "a government of each of the several States, and a government of the United States. Each is distinct from the others, and has citizens of its own, who owe it allegiance, and whose rights, within its jurisdiction, it must protect. The same person may be at the same time a citizen of the United States and a citizen of a State; but his rights of citizenship under one of these governments will be different from those he has under the other." Although "within the scope of its powers," the U.S. government is "supreme and beyond the States," its scope is limited. It "can neither grant nor secure to its citizens rights or privileges which are not expressedly or by implication placed under its jurisdiction." Since the right in question, "the right of the people peacefully to assemble for lawful purposes," existed "long before the adoption of the Constitution," it does not come within the scope of federal powers but is instead a right to be protected by the states. "Sovereignty, for the protection of the rights of life and personal liberty within the respective States, rests alone with the States."[43] As a result, the rights Cruikshank was accused of violating were not covered under the Enforcement Act, and responsibility for protecting them rested with individual states whose sovereignty predated the Constitution.

A clear rebuke to Sumner's ideal of one sovereignty and one citizenship, *Cruikshank* confirms his belief that the rights of African Americans would not be protected without granting imperial power to a centralized national government. As such, it is a terrible blot on the reputation of the Court. But even as we condemn it, we need to recognize that, from the perspective of the Court and of Cruikshank's lawyers, it rested on some of the same principles of constitutional liberty that underlay the *Milligan* case. In *Milligan* Justice Davis declared that "it is the birthright of every American citizen when charged with crime, to be tried and punished according to law" (119). Similarly, in *Cruikshank* the Court ruled, "In criminal cases, prosecuted under the laws of the United States, the accused has the constitutional right 'to be informed of the nature and cause of the accusation.' The indictment must set forth the offence with clearness and all necessary certainty, to apprise the accused of the crime with which he stands charged, and every ingredient of which the offence is composed must be accurately and clearly alleged."[44] The government had not heeded this guarantee. As a result, adopting the logic of some justices in *Milligan*, who felt that, even though Milligan had acted improperly, he should not be convicted if the government violated fundamental principles of civil liberty, the Court in *Cruikshank* came out on the side of civil liberties. It is worth speculating about what stand the American Civil Liberties Union would have taken on this case, if it had existed at the time.

What we do know is that the same David Dudley Field who argued Milligan's case argued Cruikshank's, employing some of the same rhetoric. Field felt that if the Enforcement Act was allowed to stand, "the substance of American constitutional government, as received from the fathers, will have gone, and the forms will not be long in following."[45] He was joined by Reverdy Johnson, who as a senator had passionately argued against trials by military commissions because they disregarded "all the safeguards and rules of evidence, adopted after the experience of centuries."[46] We also know that even some moderate Republicans, including Carl Schurz, who was both antislavery and a great defender of civil liberties, claimed that the Enforcement Act and the accompanying Ku Klux Klan Act threatened the status of the states as "depositories of the rights of the individual."[47] The Ku Klux Klan Act even had a provision authorizing the suspension of habeas corpus. That provision points to how complicated the relation between civil liberties and civil rights was in the period. In 1867 Radical Republicans had passed the Habeas Corpus Act because they felt it was necessary to allow blacks and white Unionists in the South to appeal to federal, not state, courts. What they could not anticipate was that, when Republican-controlled state governments tried to crack down on the Klan, suspected members used it for their own benefit. Thus, four years later, those passing the Ku Klux Klan Act felt that the protection of blacks and white Unionists now depended on the possibility of suspending habeas corpus.

☆ ☆ ☆ If the Court's decision in *Cruikshank* seemed to spell the end of Sumner's vision of equal rights for all citizens, 1875 had seen the passage of a civil rights act that promised to move closer to that ideal. Congress had passed important civil rights legislation in 1866 and again in 1870. Even so, Sumner tried a number of times to bring into law a new act that provided more extensive federal guarantees. On January 15, 1872, he made a memorable speech supporting his bill. Calling the "Declaration of Independence our Magna Charta," he declared that "equality in rights is not only the first of rights, it is the axiom of political truth." The real issue of the Civil War, he insisted, pitting comments of Jefferson Davis against those of Lincoln, was the South's refusal to accept this axiom. Quoting from the Gettysburg Address, he evoked the "prophet-President, soon to be a martyr," for his cause, asking Congress to pass his bill to finish the work Lincoln dedicated his life to achieving. Waxing eloquent, he enthused, "There is beauty in art, in literature, in science, and in every triumph of intelligence, all of which I covet for my country; but there is a higher beauty still in relieving the poor, in elevating the down-trodden. There is true grandeur in an example of justice, making the rights of all the same as our own." Then, as he had in 1867, he linked the ideal of civil equality with victory in the Civil War. "Only by maintaining Equality will you maintain the great victory of the war."[48]

Sumner's bill was so important to him that, as he lay dying in 1874, he urged his friends E. R. Hoar and Frederick Douglass to dedicate themselves to its passage. A major roadblock to that deathbed wish arose in the 1874 fall election when Democrats, for the first time since the war, took control of the House. Sparked into action, a lame-duck Republican Congress, partly in tribute to Sumner, passed the 1875 Civil Rights Act, even though it lacked Sumner's cherished provision outlawing segregated schools. It was pushed through by the notorious Benjamin Butler, who had argued the case against Milligan. Watered down, it was still a powerful statement that banned acts of racial discrimination in housing, theaters, and trains. Resisted and challenged in the South, this bill was on the books for only eight years.[49] In its October 1883 session, the U.S. Supreme Court by an eight-to-one majority declared most of its provisions unconstitutional. The opinion of the Court was written by Justice Joseph P. Bradley.

Bradley had played a crucial role in the disputed election of 1876 when November results gave Democrat Samuel Tilden a clear majority over Republican Rutherford Hayes in the popular vote but left the electoral college vote in dispute because three southern states—South Carolina, Louisiana, and Florida—had rival sets of electors, one committed to Hayes, the other to Tilden. The controversy threatened to divide the country only eleven years after the end of the Civil War. Some Democrats went so far as to chant, "Tilden or Blood!" Even if armed insurrection was unlikely so long as Republicans were in charge of the presidency and the army, Democrats in Congress still could have stopped the count of electors and made the job of any new president impossible. But cooler heads prevailed.

Coming together, Democratic and Republican congressmen used their constitutional authority to create a special electoral commission of fifteen to decide disputes in the three states. The commission was made up of five members of the House and five members of the Senate, evenly divided by party. Republican representatives included Garfield. The commission also had five Supreme Court justices: two Republicans, two Democrats, and, it was planned, Justice Davis, a nominal Republican but, especially because of his role in Milligan, someone trusted more by Democrats than by Republicans. Davis, however, was appointed senator in Illinois. His replacement was Justice Bradley, a Republican but recently applauded by Democrats for helping to bring Cruikshank to the Court. By an eight-to-seven majority, along strict party lines—with Bradley delivering the deciding vote—the commission awarded all three states to Hayes and gave him a one-vote victory in the electoral college. Intent on healing the country, Hayes unofficially agreed to one of the Democrats' most important demands. Federal troops in the South would be returned to their barracks and not used to prop up Republican rule in states of the former confederacy. Reconstruction ended when the new president took office in March 1877 by announcing his "New Departure."

When Bradley penned the decision in the 1883 Civil Rights Cases, some felt that he was paying Southerners back for his role in the 1876 election. Whether that speculation is true or not, the decision was a stunning blow to advocates of civil rights. Douglass, for instance, who was silent when Hayes ended Reconstruction, spoke out forcefully against the decision.[50] Indeed, given Douglass's faith in rule by law, one reason he might not have protested the events of 1877 was the fact that the Civil Rights Act of 1875 was on the books, providing for federal intervention in cases of racial discrimination. From our present perspective, Douglass's anger seems fully justified. After all, the Fourteenth Amendment adopted in 1868 guarantees "equal protection of the laws," which was all that the 1875 act seemed to do. The Court's decision, however, was based on a careful reading of the exact words of the amendment.

Deemed necessary because the Thirteenth Amendment forbade slavery and involuntary servitude without guaranteeing citizenship to African Americans, the Fourteenth Amendment has four clauses. The citizenship clause makes all "persons born or naturalized in the United States, and subject to the jurisdiction thereof," citizens. The second clause forbids states from abridging "the privileges or immunities" of U.S. citizens. The third clause forbids states from depriving "any person of life, liberty, or property, without due process of law." Likewise, the fourth forbids states from denying "to any person within its jurisdiction the equal protection of the laws." The problem with the 1875 act, according to the majority, was that it forbade discrimination in acts involving private parties, whereas in fact the Fourteenth Amendment addresses only "state action." To grant the federal government power to forbid individual states from denying people equal protection was not, it argued, to give the federal government the power to police the relations between individuals. That power is the responsibility of individual states. Thus the 1875 act overstepped its authority and was unconstitutional.

The most unsavory part of Bradley's decision came in his dismissal of the U.S. government's claim that the 1875 act was authorized not only by the Fourteenth but also by the Thirteenth Amendment. Soon after the Thirteenth Amendment was passed, the Court had ruled that it forbade not only the institution of slavery but any badges and incidents of slavery. Because slavery had given rise to the sense of black inferiority, racial discrimination, the government argued, was a badge of slavery. Bradley strongly disagreed. Mere discrimination on the basis of race or color did not, he emphasized, stamp blacks with a badge of servitude linked to the institution of slavery. After all, *free* blacks in the antebellum period had also experienced discrimination. Declaring an end to what he saw as the federal government's paternal protection of freedmen, he pronounced, "When a man has emerged from slavery, and by aid of beneficent legislation has shaken off the inseparable concomitants of that state, there must be some stage in the progress of his elevation when he takes the ranks of a mere citizen, and ceases to be the special favorite of the law, and when his rights as a citizen or a man are to be protected in the ordinary modes by which other men's rights are protected."[51]

If that misguided sentence is frequently quoted, a more telling passage for the purposes of this chapter comes when Bradley links the attempt to enforce equal civil rights with a threat to individual liberty. For the federal government to try to "cover the whole domain of rights appertaining to life, liberty, and property" would, Bradley declared, "establish a code of municipal law regulative of all private rights between man and man in society." Enforced civil equality, Bradley and seven other justices agreed, posed a risk to individual liberty.[52]

The majority opinion elicited a powerful dissent from Justice John Marshall Harlan, the only Southerner on the Court at the time and a former slaveholder. The dissent did not come easily, however. Noticing the difficulty that her husband was having writing, Harlan's wife placed Taney's inkstand—a prized memento of the couple—in a noticeable position on his desk. The memory of the role that Taney's inkstand had played in *Dred Scott* seemed to motivate Harlan, who overcame his writer's block and soon finished his dissent.[53] It argued that, through "subtle and ingenious verbal criticism," Bradley had sacrificed the "substance and spirit of the recent amendments."[54]

Shortly before the Court announced its decision in the Civil Rights Cases, Mark Twain finished the manuscript of a novel he had been intermittently working on since 1876 when the Court announced its decision in *Cruikshank*. He called it *Adventures of Huckleberry Finn*. In the next chapter we will examine how Twain's famous book relates to questions of citizenship and civil rights.

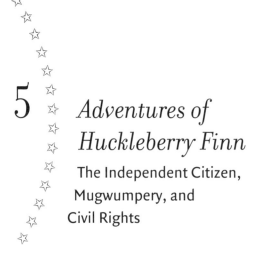

5   *Adventures of Huckleberry Finn*

The Independent Citizen, Mugwumpery, and Civil Rights

Shortly after Samuel Clemens died in 1910, his friend William Dean Howells concluded his *My Mark Twain* with a famous comparison. "Emerson, Longfellow, Lowell, Holmes—I knew them all and all the rest of our sages, poets, seers, critics, humorists; they were like one another and like other literary men; but Clemens was sole, incomparable, the Lincoln of our literature."[1] Howells's comparison of these two incomparables reminds us that Twain has been mythologized almost as much as Lincoln.[2] In large part due to the popularity of *Adventures of Huckleberry Finn*, Twain has come as close as anyone to being anointed the national poet of the United States. But the comparison does more. If, on one hand, it simply implies that Twain stands out as much among the major figures of American literature as Lincoln stands out among the major figures of American politics, on the other, it both confirms and helps to produce a perception that Twain's literary artistry has political lessons for the nation. Since at least the twentieth-century civil rights movement, for many Americans that lesson has had to do with the persistence of racism. Documentary filmmaker Ken Burns reveals just how much Twain and his book have been mythologized on this score when he claims that Twain "was willing to confront race before anyone else was, to put a human face on an African American for the first time in all of literature."[3]

Such mythologization grows out of the nation's need to reconcile the contradiction between its professed ideal of equality and its history of racism. Thus, both Lincoln and Twain are frequently evoked as heroes in what Charles Flint Kellogg calls the story of a "frayed and almost broken thread" between the antislavery movement and the twentieth-century civil rights movement:[4] Twain for his devastating portrayal of slavery in *Huckleberry Finn* along with its egalitarian image of Huck and Jim, both of which were used as a weapon against racism during and after the civil rights movement; Lincoln as the Great Emancipator, whose affirmation of the proposition that all men are created equal was evoked by Martin Luther King Jr. when he shrewdly staged his "I Have a Dream" speech by the Lincoln Memorial. Both can be heroes in that story because, as Richard Hill writes, Twain "has been called the 'Lincoln of our literature,' and like Lincoln he believed that truth and justice always outweighed expedience."[5] Thus, when Arthur Schlesinger Jr. needs examples of the independent cast of mind that epitomizes America at its best, he turns to both Twain and Lincoln.[6]

But just as Lincoln has his share of detractors, so Twain, especially because of *Huckleberry Finn*, has, in recent years, had his. Chastising him for his use of the "N-word" and a stereotyped portrait of Jim that denies black agency, critics charge that *Huckleberry Finn* indulges in its own bigotry.[7] Whether the heated controversy over the book has arisen because of its intrinsic qualities or because of its iconic stature is hard to determine. For instance, as we saw in Chapter 1, Jonathan Arac praises the book for its aesthetic power but decries the politics of what he calls its hypercanonization. *Huckleberry Finn*, he fears, has become so identified with the nation that many of its defenders act as if national culture itself is threatened when it is not taught.[8] Certainly, if *Huckleberry Finn* were not required reading in many schools, it would not be attacked as often as it has been.

Nonetheless, it is still worth pondering what about the work led to its canonization. There is, of course, its use of language. Robert Penn Warren, for instance, interprets Howells's comparison by saying that "as Lincoln freed the slave, Twain freed the writer."[9] A linked possibility is suggested by Lionel Trilling when he claims that some artists "contain a large part of the dialectic [of their culture] within themselves, their meaning and power lying in their contradictions; they contain within themselves, it may be said, the very essence of their culture."[10] There is, however, a problem with Trilling's formulation when it comes to *Huckleberry Finn*. Trilling's image of a contained dialectic implies a sense of formal control that *Huckleberry Finn* does not always have. *Huckleberry Finn* does not so much "contain" a dialectic as have it spill out of its pages. Indeed, part of the formal difficulty Twain faced was his inability to resolve or contain contradictions that arose as he told his story. Thus, a more accurate formulation than Trilling's is Myra Jehlen's argument that the power of *Huckleberry Finn* comes from its "dissonance." Arguing that "classics typically mediate a culture's founding contradictions," she notes that many nineteenth-century works project visions of the "contradictions in the national culture." But "Twain's novel is not only about contradiction, it is itself radically contradictory. . . . That this funny book for boys has glimpsed the heart of the national darkness is . . . generally recognized; and one essential power of a classic is to see in the dark."[11]

Many of the debates about the book result from readers trying to resolve contradictions that it cannot contain. For Jehlen, the primary source of its dissonance is its treatment of individualism, which it both "celebrates and abhors."[12] For the historian David Hollinger, Twain is our national poet because he is "an emblem for the many contradictions within . . . 'the political culture' of the United States and the 'black' elements within 'white' culture."[13] In this chapter I want to explore these questions of individualism, politics, and race by focusing on the ideal of the independent citizen that was dear to Twain's heart. To do so I will look at three different historical moments: the book's moment of representation, its moment of production, and its moment of reception. Its moment of representation is the time in which the book is set, the age of slavery in the Mississippi River Valley. Its moment of production is after the Civil War, when the contentious issue was not slavery but, as we saw in the preceding chapter, whether African Americans should have equal political and civil rights. Its moment of reception is, in fact, many moments, from the time it was published to today.

Twain's idealization of the independent citizen is indicated by his mugwumpery. Mugwumps were former loyal Republicans who in 1884 bolted from their party to support Grover Cleveland, the Democratic candidate for president. In doing so, they became synonymous in American English with independence from partisan politics. They were also, for the most part, cultural elitists. That elitism would seem to come into conflict with Huckleberry Finn's populist appeal. Indeed, the tension between the book's mugwumpery and its populism complicates standard readings of the book that champion Huck for an improvisational independence that allows him to overcome inherited prejudices and help a runaway slave. My point is not to deny the undeniable power of Huck's moments of moral courage. It is to argue that Twain's notorious inability to sustain those moral high points reveals an accommodationist as well as an oppositional streak in Huck. The book, in other words, works on, as well as with, the great American myth that social injustices can be remedied by courageously independent individuals, a myth Twain shared with his culture and helped to shape.

It is this myth that sustains the narrative of continuity between abolitionism and civil rights protests, since both, it is felt, depended on people who, like Huck, were willing to defy unjust laws to help a black man. Ironically, however, what that narrative leaves out is the period after the Civil War when the problem was not unjust laws but lack of support for laws guaranteeing freedmen civil rights, a period of time in which Twain was writing his novel. To chart the complicated relation between Twain's mugwumpery and that nineteenth-century civil rights movement helps us better understand the book and the history of its reception, a history that is further illuminated when it is related to how the early effort to achieve civil rights failed and was then revived years later. The point is not to tie *Huckleberry Finn*'s racial politics to either its moment of representation or its moment of production. It is, instead, to use those moments to help understand how the book has been read and continues to be read today. At the same time, insofar as the history of civil rights remains a work in progress, Twain's book, through its internal contradictions, can help us see both the strengths and weaknesses of relying on his ideal of independence to combat the ongoing problem of racism.

☆ ☆ ☆ Looking at changes in voting practice—"the central act of democratic citizenship"—Michael Schudson has identified four different models. In the colonial and early Republican period there was a "politics of assent," in which propertied, white males voted publicly for prominent community members who acted more as guardians than as representatives. With Jacksonian America, the politics of assent was, for the most part, replaced by the "politics of affiliation," which transferred authority from the personal realm to an interpersonal realm presided over by parties rather than by gentlemen. Reacting against corruption associated with the politics of affiliation and responding to the extension of the franchise, a third model, the "politics of the informed citizen," arose. Schudson's fourth model is that of "the rights-bearing citizen," which, he argues, emerged in the wake of the civil rights movement of the twentieth century.[14]

If Schudson provides a loose historical account of these four models, it would be a mistake to assume that one completely displaced the other. All four exist today, competing with and sometimes complementing one another. Likewise, even in the era of the politics of assent or the politics of affiliation there were arguments made for the informed citizen. Similarly, both the politics of assent and of the informed citizen are linked to the ideal of an independent citizenry—the politics of assent because a propertied elite could stand above partisan interests and make decisions for the good of the whole, the politics of the informed citizen because educated voters should have the same capacity. A major concern of this chapter will be to show how the combined ideal of the informed, independent citizen came into existence in part as a response to an early version of the rights-bearing citizen. But first we need to see how the link between the informed citizen and the ideal of political independence influenced both *Huckleberry Finn*'s composition and what Arac calls its hypercanonization.

We can do so by remembering that Twain was a confirmed Mugwump. Asked by his teenage daughter to make a statement about himself for a biography she was writing, he proclaimed, "I am a Mugwump and a Mugwump is pure from the marrow out."[15] Retrospectively describing his decision to become an independent, he proudly noted, "I have never voted a straight ticket from that day to this. I have never belonged to any party from that day to this. I have never belonged to any church from that day to this. I have remained absolutely free in those matters. And in this independence I have found a spiritual comfort and peace of mind quite above the price."[16]

Twain's pride in his mugwumpery indicates a number of views he had about citizenship at the time of *Huckleberry Finn*'s publication. It would be a mistake, however, to assume that the book simply registers beliefs Twain already had. On the contrary, they developed as he wrote the book. Then, once it was finished, Twain became its most important reader and turned Huck into a model and an inspiration for his own acts of citizenly independence. Likewise, *Huckleberry Finn* is not simply a reflection of mugwumpian positions. If Twain identified Mugwumps with purity, he was by no means a pure Mugwump. The very independence that attracted him to mugwumpery kept him from identifying it with a set of doctrines. More important than revealing *what* Twain thought, *Huckleberry Finn* gives insight into *how* he thought. Mugwumpery was, for him, more an independent cast of mind than a particular set of beliefs.

At least part of the dissonance of *Huckleberry Finn* comes from the pressure it places on particular political positions taken by Mugwumps. It also places pressure on the ideal of independence itself. Celebrating that ideal, the book has a countercurrent suggesting its limits, a sign that the "absolute freedom" Twain associates with mugwumpery was not so easy to obtain, a sign that while writing his novel he was haunted by his later belief that it is a "sweet-smelling, sugar-coated [lie]" that "there is such a thing in the world as independence: independence of thought, independence of opinion, independence of action."[17] But before we can recognize the pressure the book places on Twain's ideal, we need to understand the views and the cast of mind of Mugwumps.

Historians frequently dismiss Mugwumps as unrealistic, ineffective reformers. Even so, they, better than any group, brought together the ideal of the independent citizen with that of the informed citizen taught in civics classes today. For them that ideal was an amalgam of classical republicanism and Jacksonian liberalism. Republican in linking virtue with political independence, it was Jacksonian in the way its stress on the individual privatizes virtue.[18] Mugwumps were able to bring republicanism and liberalism together because of their faith in education to train citizens to choose the good of the whole over self- or party interest. For instance, according to the Mugwump president of Harvard University, Charles W. Eliot, writing in 1884, the goal of a liberal education is to "enlarge the intellectual and moral interests of the student, quicken his sympathies, impel him to the side of truth and virtue, and to make him loathe falsehood and vice."[19]

Mugwumps may have inherited a republican rhetoric that articulated public responsibility in the language of duty, trust, and the sacrifice of self-interest, but they did not locate those virtues primarily in the realm of politics. On the contrary, they, like liberals, felt that political liberty demanded that virtue remain independent of politics. Indeed, like Emerson and Thoreau, Mugwumps considered the traditional realm of politics so corrupt that it could not be reformed from within. Their sense of how that reform would come about was, however, very different from that of the Transcendentalists. Many, for instance, urged the application of business practices to government. Just as a business was concerned primarily with the efficiency of its operations, so too should government be. One way to ensure that efficiency was to eliminate handing out governmental jobs as political favors by instituting a professional, nonpartisan civil service system.

Although Mugwumps helped to graft a classical republican vocabulary of virtue onto Jacksonian liberalism, they did not embrace the extreme individualism so frequently associated with liberalism today. Opposed to a *politics* of affiliation, not affiliation itself, Mugwumps were great advocates of associations within civil society, especially those of educated professionals. Seventy-nine learned societies were established in the 1870s and 121 in the 1880s. Mugwumps played an important role in the most important ones, such as the American Economic Association, the American Chemical Society, the American Historical Association, and the Modern Language Association. Those organizations could exert powerful influence. According to one historian, Seth Low, who had tried to bring business practices to municipal government, "very likely achieved more for reform as president of the National Civic Federation from 1908 to 1916 than he had as mayor of New York City earlier."[20] Rather than abandon the concept of civic virtue, Mugwumps moved it from the political sphere to the voluntary organizations of civil society. It was in those organizations, free from the partisan bickering of politics, that disinterested knowledge could be produced by what C. S. Peirce called professionally trained communities of the competent, and it was disinterested knowledge in both the arts and the sciences that Mugwumps sought.

The professionalism of the Mugwumps kept them from succumbing completely to the privatization of virtue, but their ideal of civic virtue did rely on the moral integrity of individual citizens. For instance, one important Mugwump innovation in the law was the development of a right to privacy.[21] Similarly, the most successful Mugwump reform had to do with how individuals voted. Civil service reform, they felt, would eliminate self-interest as a motive for some voters. More direct electoral reforms prohibited electioneering close to polling places and required voter registration and the so-called Australian or secret ballot.[22]

The modern electoral system began in the 1820s when courts accepted the use of printed ballots. Nonetheless, consistent with the politics of affiliation, ballots were provided by parties, who listed only a slate of candidates along party lines. A party's ballot was easily recognized at a distance, which made it difficult to cast a secret ballot, thus encouraging bribery. By the 1880s Mugwumps and third party candidates like Henry George demanded replacing the existing system with the secret ballot. Massachusetts in 1888 was the first state to adopt the reform, which was quickly copied by other states. By 1910 only two did not have the Australian ballot. Under the new system, standard ballots were printed not by the parties but by the state for each electoral district. Those ballots listed all candidates who qualified. A positive reform on the whole, the Australian ballot nonetheless generated its own problems. Illiterate voters obviously had a difficult time with it, as did some who could read. Ballots were so confusing in New York that special schools were established to instruct people how to mark them. Furthermore, third parties found it harder to get a voice. Rather than print up and distribute ballots with their candidates, now they had to meet official qualifications in order to be included on the standard ballot. Indeed, the new system helped to move the electoral process from the party—third party or not—to the individual voter. As Schudson puts it, "The ballot now hailed a private individual making rational choices about policy preferences where the party-printed ballot had beckoned with the pleasures of affiliation and comradeship."[23]

But how to ensure that the individual being hailed made the right choices for the country? The answer, for the most part, was education. That education, as Eliot emphasized, was more about training a person how to think than about imparting a particular content. The reading of literature—good literature—was crucial. Not directly part of the electoral system, works of literature also hailed individual citizens and inculcated in them not so much information as the proper sensibility to help make distinctions needed to elect the best leaders for the nation.

It is important to remember that Twain was a Mugwump, because, on the basis of what Mugwumps stood for, few readers would identify *Huckleberry Finn* as mugwumpian. Huck, after all, does not conform to the mugwumpian ideal of the informed citizen. Although he has the capacity to act independently, he is unschooled in the education Mugwumps felt necessary to produce that independence. On the contrary, Huck helps reinforce the populist myth that the political wisdom of the American people comes from inherently good hearts guided by practical experience, not from formal education. "Dickens," Jehlen shrewdly argues, "wrote popular classics," but "the vernacular *Huckleberry Finn* is better described as a *populist* classic, a work animated by its defiance of high culture,"[24] a high culture, we should note, with which Mugwumps identified. Overshadowing the book's mugwumpian premises, its populism contributes to its popular appeal. Attractive to Mugwumps, Twain's novel is not simply a Mugwump tract. On the contrary, much of *Huckleberry Finn*'s popularity comes from Twain's refusal to let mugwumpery become a fixed set of ideas. In Twain's mind, *Huckleberry Finn*'s dramatization of a populist version of mugwumpery was more mugwumpish than mugwumpery itself. Indeed, there was a populist streak in Twain's initial decision to become a Mugwump.

The 1884 campaign was one of the ugliest in U.S. history. Republicans had nominated James S. Blaine, who was attacked for his links to corruption, especially the Credit Mobiler scandal. In response, Cleveland ran on a reform platform backed by a well-deserved reputation for public honesty. But Cleveland, a bachelor, had fathered an illegitimate child by a widow and former mistress. Attacks on his personal morality matched those on Blaine's political morality. In the midst of this bitter campaign, with *Adventures of Huckleberry Finn* in press, Twain and Howells exchanged letters. In one Twain asked Howells to read proofs. Howells responded, "If I had written half as good a book as Huck Finn, I shouldn't ask anything better than to read the proofs; even as it is I don't," and added that he would continue to support the Republicans. Twain disagreed. Defending Cleveland, he wrote back, "To grown men, apparently in their right mind, seriously arguing against a bachelor's fitness for President because he has had private intercourse with a consenting widow! Those grown men know what the bachelor's other alternative was—& tacitly they seem to prefer that to the widow."[25]

Howells, a great admirer of Hester in *The Scarlet Letter*, had already joked,

"What I ought to do is vote for Cleveland's widow." Now he responded that, even if it were true that Cleveland's "private life may be no worse than that of most men," as "an enemy of that contemptible, hypocritical, lopsided morality which says 'a woman shall suffer all the shame and a man none,[']] I want to see him destroyed politically by his past." Howells's continued resolve to vote for Blaine prompted a spirited reply from Twain.

Somehow I can't seem to rest quiet under the idea of your voting for Blaine. I believe you said something about the country & the party. Certainly allegiance to these is well; but as certainly a man's *first* duty is to his own conscience & honor—the party & the country come second to that, & never first. . . .

It is not necessary to vote for Cleveland; the only necessary thing to do, as I understand it, is that a man shall keep *himself* clean, (by withholding his vote for an improper man,) even though the party & the country go to destruction in consequence. It is not *parties* that make or save countries or that build them to greatness—it is clean men, clean ordinary citizens, rank & file, the masses. Clean masses are not made by individuals standing back till the *rest* become clean.

As I said before, I think a man's first duty is to his own honor; not to his country & not to his party.[26]

Much of Twain's reasoning is recognizably mugwumpian—for instance, his implied distinction between true political morality and narrow moralism as well as, most obviously, his distrust of party affiliation. But his faith in "ordinary citizens, rank & file, the masses" is populist—populist, but not a view that would cause Twain to support the Populist Party. Skeptical about the masses' ability as a group to effect meaningful political reform, Twain stays true to his belief that individuals are the basis of virtuous political action. Even so, for him, those individuals come not, as most Mugwumps believed, from the professionally educated elite but from the "rank and file."

No critic has been able to express the power of Twain's mixture of populism and mugwumpery better than Trilling. Trilling wrote long after Mugwumps were a presence in American politics. Nonetheless, in his 1948 introduction to a widely used textbook edition, he sounds almost mugwumpian as he both praises Huck's independence and argues that reading Twain's novel helps produce independent citizens. For Trilling, reading literature—at least a certain kind of literature—is especially important in a society like the United States where "liberalism is not only the dominant but even the sole intellectual tradition."[27] In an age in which liberalism has become the "L-word," Trilling's characterization might seem curious. He is, however, using "liberalism" similarly to how a 1946 *Life* editorial used it. Contrasting it to socialism, on one hand, and conservatism, on the other, the editorial distances liberalism from a belief in laissez-faire economics and then cites three liberal principles: (1) that government needs to acknowledge some outside limit to its own power, (2) that good ends never justify dubious means, and (3) that no political system—even those based on rationality—can offer a perfect answer. Liberalism, as a result, demands endless compromise in politics at the same time that "no man can be a liberal who does not believe that faith and morals are independent of politics, more important than politics and essential to political liberty."[28]

In such a society, Trilling argues, "a criticism which has at heart the interests of liberalism might find its most useful work not in confirming liberalism in its sense of general rightness but rather in putting under some degree of pressure the liberal ideas and assumptions of the present time." To combat "the tendencies of liberalism to simplify," Trilling turns to literature, "the human activity that takes the fullest and most precise account of variousness, possibility, complexity, and difficulty."[29] It is precisely these qualities that make *Huckleberry Finn*, for him, a great work.

"Wherein does its greatness lie?" Trilling asks. "Primarily in its power of telling the truth." Twain, he concludes, echoing previous criticism, "is the great master of style that sounds in our ears with the immediacy of the heard voice, the very voice of unpretentious truth."[30] The book's ability to tell the truth makes it a "subversive" work—subversive, but not destructive, since it has both an aesthetic and a political foundation in "moral realism," the "perception of the dangers of the moral life itself." Thus, *Huckleberry Finn*'s subversion helps to produce independent citizen-readers capable of questioning prevailing moral and political assumptions. If this makes Trilling sound like Harvard's President Eliot, who, after all, edited the Harvard Classic series of "great books," Trilling's celebration of Huck, the uneducated outcast, shows how well he appreciates Twain's populist streak. For Trilling, Huck's moral character challenges the false morality of moralistic figures, like the Widow, as well as that of the book's professionally trained elite that fails to recognize the immorality of slavery.

The book's high point occurs, therefore, in chapter 31, when Huck, the self-professed bad boy, is willing to go to hell rather than return his friend Jim to slavery. "No one who reads thoughtfully the dialectic of Huck's great moral crisis," Trilling asserts, "will ever again be wholly able to accept without some question and some irony the assumptions of the respectable morality by which he lives, nor will ever again be certain that what he considers the clear dictates of moral reason are not the engrained customary beliefs of his time and place." No wonder, then, that in the midst of his analysis Trilling pauses to note that Tom Blankenship, "the original of Huck," like Huck himself, lit "'out for the Territory,' only to become a justice of the peace in Montana, 'a good citizen and greatly respected.'"[31]

More than any other academic critic, Trilling influenced how nonaca-demic, democratically minded guardians of culture read—and continue to read—Twain's novel. To take just one example, Academy Award–winning screenwriter Jeremy Larner, citing Huck's moral courage, calls *Huckleberry Finn* the most important political novel written in the United States.[32] The problem with such Trilling-inspired readings is, as others have pointed out, that Huck is not quite the exemplary hero they make him out to be. Huck's moral courage may exert itself in the book's high points, but he is also easily swayed by the influence of others, a model not of independence but of the sort of uninformed voter the Mugwumps feared. Thus, if much of the book's appeal comes from how Twain interweaves populism with mugwumpery, in the end the two do not rest easy with one another. Just as *Huckleberry Finn*'s populism undercuts mugwumpish pretensions to high culture and trained sensibilities, so Twain's mugwumpery calls into ques-tion the book's embrace of populism.[33]

The seeming answer to this contradiction is that Huck is only a boy and that he simply needs to assert his independent spirit more consistently. Thus Trilling tries to turn the book into a bildungsroman by implying that when Huck grows up, he will, like Tom Blankenship, become a model citi-zen. But *Huckleberry Finn* is anything but a bildungsroman. Huck ends not having learned from experience but back under the sway of Tom Sawyer, the seeming rebel who trusts what he learns in books more than what he learns from experience.

Huckleberry Finn's attitude toward literature nicely illustrates the tensions between its populism and its mugwumpery. A product of the high culture embraced by Mugwumps, books in *Huckleberry Finn* do not help train sen-sibilities as equipment for living. They lead instead to a distorted sense of reality. Far better, it seems, is the glimpse of unmediated reality that we get from Huck's eyes. Twain, however, is fully aware that even Huck's portrayal of life "as it is" cannot escape the mediation of books. Beginning by hav-ing Huck refer to his existence in another book, *Huckleberry Finn* unfolds with one adventure after another based on literary models: Huck's encoun-ter with Jim on Jackson Island recalls *Adventures of Robinson Crusoe*; the feud between the Sheperdsons and Grangerfords, *Romeo and Juliet*; and the Wilks incident in which thieves are robbed in order to return goods to their rightful owners, *Henry IV, Part 1*. If only an educated class of readers catches such allusions, the education in sensibility that *Huckleberry Finn* offers challenges any sense of mugwumpian superiority that such readers might entertain.

The tension between *Huckleberry Finn*'s mugwumpery and its populism is primarily a conflict of ideas, but Twain's attraction to mugwumpery as a cast of mind complicates another factor that made Trilling's reading so popular. Trilling's praise of Huck's moral courage had special poignancy in a country that continued to deny equal civil rights to African Americans. For a generation of readers about to experience a widespread attack on Jim Crow, Huck's willingness to go to hell rather than return Jim to slavery was a model for how to respond to unjust laws of racial division. This is not to say that people read chapter 31 and marched off to a sit-in. But it is to say that, read how Trilling read it, *Huckleberry Finn* generated what Raymond Williams would call a "structure of feeling" inclined to make readers sympathize with the budding civil rights movement.[34] *Huckleberry Finn* had already been anointed a quintessentially American work for its celebration of Huck's "shrewdness" and his "insatiable hunger" for "freedom."[35] Its hypercanonization after World War II linked those qualities to the battle for racial equality.

Huck's display of courage in chapter 31 is so powerful that Twain himself seems to have drawn on it when faced with the difficult task in 1884 of defying the authority of the Republican Party and thus taking a political stand at odds with almost all of his friends at Nook Farm. Just as Huck defies the socially accepted standards of his time and place and risks going to hell rather betray his black friend, so Twain spoke of the "hellish design" of his mugwumpery.[36] A hellish design to those around him but, like Huck's act, a morally sound one in Twain's eyes, since he clearly linked mugwumpian independence with the ability to cast off racial prejudices and help the cause of African Americans. For instance, on the same day he wrote Howells urging him to join "all other honest & honorable men (who are independently situated)" in refusing to vote for Blaine, Twain hastened to send a follow-up letter relating the following incident:

> Before I forget it I must tell you that Mrs Clemens has said a bright thing. A drop letter came to me asking me to lecture here for a church debt. I began to rage over the exceedingly cool wording of the request, when Mrs. Clemens said "I think I know that church; & if so, this preacher is a colored man—he doesn't know how to write a polished letter—how should he?"
>
> My manner changed so suddenly & so radically that Mrs. C. said: "I

will give you a motto, & it will be useful to you if you will adopt it: 'Consider every man colored till he is proved white.'"[37]

Twain's well-documented sympathy for African Americans seems to support the belief that *Huckleberry Finn* is a "weapon against racism." But if we relate Twain's mugwumpery to the battle over civil rights raging at the time of his book's publication, a problem arises. One of the best discussions of the ways in which *Huckleberry Finn* attacks southern beliefs, including its racism, is Louis Budd's in *Mark Twain: Social Philosopher*. Budd's discussion comes in a chapter titled "The Scalawag," which follows one called "The Solid Citizen."[38] Referring to white Southerners who turned Republican during Reconstruction, "Scalawag" is an appropriate label for Twain, whom Howells described as "the most desouthernized Southerner I ever knew."[39] Scalawags even shared with Mugwumps the quality of independence Twain so valued, overcoming blind loyalty to region and race while Mugwumps overcame blind loyalty to party. Nonetheless, politically Twain the Scalawag comes into tension with Twain the Mugwump, who, with dire consequences for African Americans' civil rights, deserted the Republican Party in 1884 and joined forces with the very Democrats Scalawags opposed. Inspired by Trilling and others, many readers have joined Twain in believing that political independence serves the cause of civil rights. But at the time of *Huckleberry Finn*'s publication, the rights-bearing and the independent models of citizenship existed at best in an uneasy relation to each other. It is time, therefore, to turn to *Huckleberry Finn*'s relation to debates over civil rights at the time of its production.

☆ ☆ ☆ For many readers, *Huckleberry Finn* is the most poignant portrayal of the shadow slavery cast over the promised land. Indeed, as we evaluate characters, what ultimately counts is whether or not they are willing to help Jim escape slavery. In the end, it does not matter if they are, like Jim and Huck, outcasts, such as Pap, the Duke and the King, and others. Nor does it matter if they are exceptional figures, like Colonel Sherburn and the Shepersons and the Grangerfords, who stand out from the masses. It does not even matter if, like Judge Thatcher, the doctor who treats Jim, and the doctor and lawyer who expose the King and the Duke as frauds, they are part of an educated professional elite that stands above the narrow-mindedness, sentimentality, and naive self-interest that make most townspeople so vulnerable to being duped and manipulated. Anointed by Mugwumps the guardians of public virtue, these community leaders have a positive role that too often is overlooked. But even their professional training does not keep them from supporting slavery. Thus, for readers as well as for Twain, it is uneducated Huck who occupies the book's moral center.

As important as slavery is for the book's action, however, the book was not written during the age of slavery. It was written, instead, from 1876 to late August 1883 in the midst of the national debate examined in the preceding chapter over whether African Americans, who had been emancipated for a generation, would retain the political and civil rights granted to them during Reconstruction.[40] This difference between the book's moment of representation and its moment of production has sparked a critical controversy.

For debunkers the popular tendency to emphasize the book's moment of representation over its primarily post-Reconstruction moment of production has led to exaggerated accounts of its antiracist message. Challenging the piety by which *Huckleberry Finn* has been celebrated as an antislavery masterpiece, they note that hardly anyone at that time, even in the "redeemed South," argued publicly for a return to slavery. If almost all of Twain's readers were already convinced that slavery was wrong, how, they wonder, can Huck's moral struggle subvert their sense of morality? As Evan Carton puts it, "Huck's moment of greatest moral risk is for Twain and his readers, a moment of moral comfort, even complacency."[41] The much maligned ending in which Tom and Huck laboriously work to free Jim even though he is already free can be read in similar terms. According to James M. Cox, "If Tom is rather contemptibly setting a free slave free, what after all is the reader doing, who begins the book after the *fact* of the Civil War? This is the 'joke' of the book—the moment when, in outrageous burlesque, it attacks the sentiment which its style has at once evoked and exploited."[42] Whereas it was quite easy to marshal public sentiment against the horrors of slavery, it was a much more difficult task to arouse the public about the threat to African American rights in the post-Reconstruction era.

Contrasting critics like Carton and Cox are those who argue that the book's focus on slavery needs to be read allegorically. For some, that allegory is about the absurdity of having "to free" people who were naturally free in the first place. For instance, in 1959 Lynn Altenbernd argued that "the rescue of Jim from the cabin . . . is simply an allegorical way of saying that the conditions for the slave's freedom had already existed before the Civil War, and the South could have acknowledged this fact and turned him loose."[43] For others, it comments on contemporary efforts "to re-enslave" freedmen by denying them newly won rights. After all, to create a memorable image of a black man and a white boy sharing a raft at a time when the country was debating whether blacks should have equal access to public accommodations is to invite allegorical commentary.[44]

For example, when Huck consents to the King and the Duke's establishment of hierarchical rule on the raft, he rationalizes, "It took away all the uncomfortableness, and we felt mighty good over it, because it would have been a miserable business to have any unfriendliness on the raft; for what you want, above all things, on a raft, is for everybody to be satisfied, and feel right and kind towards the others."[45] Just as attempts to avoid unfriendliness between white North and South led to selling the interests of freedmen down the river, so Huck's desire to keep peace on the raft eventually leads to Jim's reenslavement, a reminder that entrusting Jim's fate to someone claiming to be the lost heir of Louis XVI is as much a mistake as entrusting the fate of freedmen to the "Bourbon" regimes of the New South. Similar passages caused Budd, also in 1959, to claim, "To readers in a country in which there were now no slaves, the novel took on fresh meaning as a judgment of the South's conduct after the withdrawal of federal troops had paroled it to its own conscience."[46] In readings like Budd's, Huck's act in chapter 31 is anything but a moment of moral complacency. It served, in Twain's day, to appeal to the conscience of the nation, as it did during the civil rights movement that Budd was in the process of experiencing.[47]

Both *Huckleberry Finn*'s debunkers and its champions have a point. Both, however, tend to simplify the post-Reconstruction era during which Twain composed most of *Huckleberry Finn*. It in no way minimizes the historical importance of Hayes's 1877 "New Departure" to note that the effects of Reconstruction did not vanish overnight. Whereas today we are prone to mark 1877 as a decisive turning point, we need to remember that, while Twain was writing, the white supremacist rule of the South was still being contested. For instance, the Democratic Party was successfully challenged in a number of Southern states, most notably Virginia, where in 1879 a coalition of Republicans and "Readjusters" won the state House of Representatives and sent the maverick General William Mahone to the Senate and in 1881 triumphed in the race for governor.[48] More important, whereas redeemed Southern regimes were intent on keeping freedmen in their place, segregation during these years was de facto, not de jure. As we saw in Chapter 4, from 1875 to 1883 the most extensive Civil Rights Act of the period was on the books, giving freedmen more legal rights than they had ever had.

To understand *Huckleberry Finn*'s racial politics, we need to remember that Twain began writing it a year after passage of the 1875 Civil Rights Act and finished it while that act was still on the books. But we also need to remember that, in one of those historical events that an author cannot control, by the time the book was published (in Great Britain in late 1884 and in the United States in 1885), the Supreme Court had declared the 1875 act unconstitutional. In other words, what so far I have been calling *Huckleberry Finn*'s moment of production consists in fact of two "moments": the book's time of composition and its time of publication. The status of civil rights for African Americans changed dramatically from one to the other. Any account of Twain's original intention needs to acknowledge that *Huckleberry Finn*'s composition coincided almost exactly with the existence of a piece of legislation that gave the federal government power to outlaw cases of individual racial discrimination. Likewise, any account of the book's initial impact needs to acknowledge that by the time the book appeared, that legislation had been declared unconstitutional. At the same time, both accounts have to acknowledge that most readers are unaware of either of these facts, which means that they cannot have influenced their reading of the book. This historical evidence can, however, clarify the debate between Twain's champions and his debunkers.

For instance, if we remember that political and civil rights were in force while Twain was writing, it seems unfair to fault him for failing to campaign for them. What he does do is make an affective appeal demanding sympathy and respect for freedman. Prior to the Civil War, Francis Lieber noted that "the first basis of all justice, sympathy, is wanting between the two races."[49] As far as Twain was concerned, that situation had not changed with emancipation. In a world in which rights were in force but rarely enforced, blacks were clearly not getting the respect they deserved.

Even so, the fate of Sumner's Civil Rights Act also causes problems for the book's champions. For instance, Shirley Fisher Fishkin and Carl F. Wieck evoke Twain's act of composition in relation to the Civil Rights Act of 1875 to argue that *Huckleberry Finn* advocates civil rights for freedmen. But they ignore the fact that in the 1884 election Twain supported Democrats who applauded the outcome of the Civil Rights Cases.[50] Equally important, allegorical readings of chapter 31 do not work. Huck's greatest moment of moral crisis appealed to those experiencing the civil rights movement of the twentieth century because it illustrates the need to defy unjust laws. While Twain was writing his book, however, the situation was quite different. When Budd argues that the end of Reconstruction paroled the South "to its own conscience," he is only partly right. From 1875 to 1883 the federal government had the power in many cases to punish individuals in the South whose consciences saw nothing wrong with discriminating against blacks. Antislavery works like Harriet Beecher Stowe's *Uncle Tom's Cabin* or Frederick Douglass's *Narrative* had as their targets unfair laws. But while Twain was writing his book, the problem was not unfair laws; it was the failure to obey and to enforce fair ones. As Douglass himself put it in an 1880 speech in Twain's Elmira, New York, "It is a great thing to have the supreme law of the land on the side of justice and liberty. . . . But today, in most of the land on the southern states, the fourteenth an the fifteenth amendments are virtually nullified. The rights which they were intended to guarantee are denied and held in contempt."[51]

The narrative of continuity from the antislavery movement to the civil rights movement of the twentieth century relies on the fact that both abolitionists and civil rights leaders protested unfair laws. What it neglects, however, is that moment after the Civil War in which laws protected the civil rights of freedmen. To remember that Twain wrote *Huckleberry Finn* while the 1875 Civil Rights Act was on the books forces a reconsideration of the role of the law in his book.

Because of the emphasis placed on Huck's defiance of the law in chapter 31, *Huckleberry Finn* is frequently seen as questioning the legal order. In fact, its author was, for the most part, an advocate of rule by law, which he felt fostered citizenly independence. For instance, during the time *Huckleberry Finn* was in progress, Twain wrote — then suppressed — a passage for *Life on the Mississippi* advocating the need to maintain civil order. According to him, in the South one hotheaded murderer too frequently defied conviction by intimidating witnesses, juries, and judges. That defiance, he claims, led to the high number of lynchings in the South. The cause of this deplorable state of affairs was not that the South had a higher proportion of hotheads or that the average Southerner was naturally more timid than his Northern cousin. It resulted instead from a lack of respect for the law. "One thing the average Northerner" has over "the average Southerner," Twain notes, is that "he bands himself with his timid fellows to support the law, (at least in the matter of murder,) to protect judges, juries, and witnesses, and also to secure all citizens for personal danger and from obloquy or social ostracism on account of opinion, political or religious." Lack of such protection in the South led not only to "unpunished murder, against the popular approval" but also to "the decay and destruction of independent thought and action in politics."[52]

In making political independence dependent on rule by law Twain repeats a paradox at the heart of classical liberal thought's advocacy of civil society. Religious and political diversity are possible only when people agree to submit to a legal system that protects them. People are, Twain argues, naturally diverse. "Human beings are so constituted, that given an intelligent, thinking, hundred of them, or a thousand, or a million, and convince them that they are free from personal danger or social excommunication for opinion's sake, it is absolutely impossible that they shall tie themselves in a body to any one sect, religious or political." The South, which "purports to be free," is "'solid' for a single political party" because, without legal protection, people do not feel free to speak their minds.[53]

There are a number of incidents in Huckleberry Finn reinforcing the importance of rule by law. As Budd points out, Twain's comments in his suppressed Life on the Mississippi passage about hotheaded murderers anticipate Colonel Sherburn's murder of Boggs.[54] Similarly, the feud between the Sheperdsons and the Grangerfords dramatizes how violence can escalate outside rule by law. Whereas Colonel Sherburn illustrates how one powerful figure can dominate a community not bound together through the force of law, the feud shows how a conflict of equally courageous groups can result in vendettas that, as we saw in the chapter on Hawthorne, legal codes were designed to stop. What makes the feud particularly absurd is the inability of either side to remember its cause. It persists because neither family can escape the bondage of an outworn code of honor. As this and many other incidents show, the ultimate problem for Twain is not the law—even though he knows that unjust ones exist—it is slavery, mental as well as physical.

Twain's debunkers are literalists. Slavery for them is the historical institution that existed in antebellum America. For Twain it is that and more. Twain uses the injustices of slavery, as a historical institution, to generate sympathy and respect for the freedmen who suffered under it. He also, in Budd's words, "challenged the memory of the old regime" by forcefully undercutting the myth of the "happy slave" propagated by Joel Chandler Harris and Thomas Nelson Page, a challenge that caused Jay B. Hubbell to complain that Twain borrowed a "little too much of the abolitionist legend of the Deep South."[55] Furthermore, he uses it, as Trilling correctly noted, to force readers to think critically about the sanctity of prevailing codes of morality. Debunkers may argue that, because slavery had been abolished for a generation, chapter 31 gives readers a sense of moral comfort. But most readers were—and are—perfectly capable of recognizing that the change in attitudes toward slavery from the time of the book's moment of representation to its moment(s) of production is a poignant illustration of how what one generation thought was moral can be condemned by the next.

Even so, slavery is not just one example of many in which moral codes can change. For Twain it is absolutely wrong. Huck's moral struggle in chapter 31 might invite us to question existing codes of morality, but it is not intended to challenge our assumption that slavery is wrong. Those wrongs are not confined to the actual institution. Slavery for Twain encompasses any cast of mind that keeps people from thinking independently. Indeed, one of the book's most obvious messages is that people who believe in slavery are as enslaved mentally as Jim is physically. Such mental slavery was not abolished with emancipation, and for Twain, the Mugwump, one of its worst forms is uncritical allegiance to party. Thus, in his *Autobiography* he calls Mugwumps "a little company made up of the unenslaved of both parties."[56]

Likewise, soon after the 1884 election, facing charges of disloyalty by Republicans, Twain gave a speech called "Consistency." Equating blind party loyalty with slavery, he asks, "What slave is so degraded as the slave who is proud that he is a slave? What is the essential difference between a life-long Democrat and any other kind of life-long slave?" It is "this idea of consistency—unchanging allegiance to party—" that "has lowered the manhood of the whole nation—pulled it down and dragged it in the mud." In fact, since "change is the law of his being," the "really consistent man" is one who changes, even if willingness to do so in the face of powerful opposition takes the courage Huck has to risk going to hell. The world's major reforms, Twain insists, depend upon such courageously independent individuals. The "Mugwump has a great history at his back" and "he comes of a mighty ancestry. He knows that in the whole history of the race of men no single great and high and beneficent thing was ever done for the souls and the bodies, the hearts and brains, of the children of this world, but a Mugwump started it and Mugwumps carried it to victory. And their names are the stateliest in history: Washington, Garrison, Galileo, Luther, Christ. Loyalty to petrified opinions never yet broke a chain or freed a human soul in this world—and never will."[57]

In *Huckleberry Finn* Twain is not trying to convince people to oppose an institution that legally had been abolished for a generation. If he were, charges of generating moral comfort would be justified. As Twain fully knew, whether or not slavery would survive as an institution was a closed issue at the time he was writing. What was not decided at that time—and still today—was how best to combat social injustices, like slavery. For Twain, mugwumpery was the answer. It was because the root cause of social injustice is people's enslavement to petrified opinions. Only those willing to escape such enslavement are capable of leading the way to emancipation.

As strongly as Twain argues this belief in essays like "Consistency," when he tries to embody it in *Huckleberry Finn*, a problem arises. To be sure, at times Huck proves to be the courageous individual who becomes a model for Twain's own mugwumpery. But at other times he is not so noble. To put this dilemma in Twain's terms, insofar as Huck's independence is linked to a perpetual openness to change, it also means that he is not as consistent a hero as we would hope. Or to put it slightly differently, *Huckleberry Finn* itself does not provide a completely consistent endorsement of Twain's stated beliefs about independence. Since this view of the book's inconsistency is not consistent with the prevailing critical consensus, I need to elaborate on what I mean.[58]

☆ ☆ ☆ Twain's faith in the individual as a foundation for virtuous political action places him in a long American tradition. Where he differs from others, according to Robert Penn Warren, is in his refusal to believe that there is a higher-law standard guiding moral action. Twain, he argues, "is as much against the arrogance of an antinomian who would take his conscience as absolute as against that of any established order. Huck's free consciousness comes not from any version of revelation, but from a long and humble scrutiny of experience." In Huck, "Twain, in a revolutionary and literally radical way, is undermining impartially both conventional society and religion, and the tradition of antinomianism in America. Twain was simply against all notions of revelation, and to him the 'higher law,' the idea that one with God is a majority, and an encyclical all looked alike; any quarrels among Mrs. Grundy, Henry David Thoreau, Theodore Parker, the Pope of Rome, and a certified case of paranoia were, according to Twain's theory, strictly intramural." Huck, he concludes, is closer to William James than Emerson, "an antinomian of an educable 'consciousness,' not of the absolute 'conscience.'"[59]

As helpful as it is, Warren's corrective is complicated by *Huckleberry Finn*'s dramatic action. If Huck's sound heart does not express a transcendent standard of right and wrong, what keeps it open to education through experience is its profound capacity for sympathy. Sympathy, as we saw in *The Scarlet Letter*, is a crucial component of a democratic sensibility. Not bound by barriers of race, class, gender, and other forms of affiliation categorized by status, Huck's sympathy for Jim gives him the courage to defy accepted codes of morality, even those claiming higher authority. Thus, according to Trilling, the defining characteristic of Huck's "intense moral life" is a "sympathy" that is "quick and immediate."[60]

Nonetheless, as we saw in *The Scarlet Letter*, the appeal to sympathy has important political limitations. If its cultivation is a necessary condition for justice, it is not a sufficient one. Extremely effective in protesting unjust laws, it alone cannot be the foundation of just ones. For instance, an affective appeal against slavery is easier to make than an affective appeal for civil rights. Indeed, insofar as *Huckleberry Finn* focuses on the evils of slavery, it is not clear to what extent the historical fact of slavery dictates the need for civil rights beyond the basic one of emancipation. Furthermore, an appeal to sympathy provides no help in distinguishing among differing sympathies.

Trilling tries to provide the basis for such a distinction by noting that Huck's sympathy is "never sentimental." He may display "tenderness," but it is always tempered by "the assumption that his fellow men are likely to be dangerous and wicked. He travels incognito, never telling the truth about himself and never twice telling the same lie, for he trusts no one and the lie comforts him even when it is not necessary."[61] What Trilling fails to note, however, is the dilemma Huck's deceptions create for a book celebrated for its power to tell the truth. Huck may not indulge in sentiment, but one reason he has no qualms about lying to the book's rascals is that he thinks he is one of them. Thinking himself wicked, he not only lies to them; he often sympathizes with them, from the Duke and the King to the would-be murderers on the *Walter Scott* to a runaway slave to the owner of Jim's children. As important as Huck's lack of false pathos is, it does not help him discriminate among this group. On the contrary, from his point of view the slave owner is more worthy of sympathy than Jim. To be sure, when Huck's sympathies for Jim trump those for the slave owner, we applaud. What, however, is the logic by which Huck discriminates among his various sympathies?

Well aware of the irony that Huck thinks he is doing wrong when he does right, most readers assume that Huck simply inverts categories in order to act morally. But that assumption keeps them from looking closely at Huck's actual logic. As Steven Mailloux has noted, "Viewing Huck's conflict as a debate between racist ideology and Huck's natural goodness may be a useful way to get at the ideological point of his inner struggle, but it is not very helpful in capturing the rhetorical dynamics of the internal dialogue." In fact, whereas we associate Huck's "heart" with good and his deformed conscience with bad, in Huck's actual working out of his moral dilemmas, only the conscience evokes questions of right and wrong. Huck's own rationalization of what he does follows, according to Mailloux, "pragmatic considerations about feeling happy and about actions being troublesome, considerations that tend to break down simple distinctions between good and evil."[62] For instance, when Huck does not turn Jim in to the men looking for fugitive slaves, he originally feels "bad and low" for having "done wrong" (127). But he then realizes that he would also feel bad if he had betrayed his friend. "Well, then, says I, what's the use you learning to do right, when it's troublesome to do right and ain't no trouble to do wrong, and the wages is just the same? I was stuck. I couldn't answer that. So I reckoned I wouldn't bother no more about it, but after this always do whichever come handiest at the time" (128).

Huck is not the only one who is stuck. Twain is too. Twain was a moralist. In 1882, when Howells praised his "indignant sense of right and wrong" and "his ardent hate of meanness and injustice," Twain responded by hoping "the public will be willing to see me with your eyes."[63] He wanted a moral basis to political action. On the whole, he found it, as did Mugwumps, in educated voters. Nonetheless, recognizing that even educated voters can be mistaken, he places his ultimate trust in Huck. Thus, years after he wrote his book, he retrospectively claimed that Huckleberry Finn dramatizes the triumph of Huck's sound heart over his socially conditioned and depraved conscience. Huck's heart, however, is not quite able to sustain the pressure Twain places on it.

In chapter 31 Huck's willingness to do wrong because it is equally troublesome to do right may lead him to help Jim, but at other times his desire to remain free and easy by avoiding what is troublesome both accommodates him to the status quo and hurts Jim's interests. Responding to the King and the Duke taking control of the raft and transforming its egalitarian space into a hierarchical one with Jim again in the role of a slave, Huck rationalizes, "It didn't take me long to make up my mind that these liars warn't no kings nor dukes, at all, but just low-down humbugs and frauds. But I never said nothing, never let on; kept it to myself; it's the best way; then you don't have no quarrels, and don't get into no trouble. If they wanted us to call them kings and dukes, I hadn't no objections, 'long as it would keep peace in the family; and it warn't no use to tell Jim, so I didn't tell him. If I never learnt nothing else out of Pap, I learnt that the best way to get along with his kind of people is to let them have their own way" (165). Written at a time when newly won freedoms for African Americans were being threatened in order to restore peace to the "family" of northern and southern whites, this passage gives quite a different sense of Huck's "sound heart" from the one we get in his efforts to help Jim.

To be sure, there seems to be a clear difference between Huck's acts of accommodation and his acts of courageous independence. The former maintain the peace; the latter promise to cause Huck difficulty. The latter are motivated by a sense of loyalty to Jim; the former follow Pap's depraved sense of values. Given Pap's racist sentiments, Huck's loyalty to a black man would seem to be a clear break with his father. In fact, Huck attributes that loyalty to his upbringing. Resolving to go to hell rather than do the right thing, he concludes that he "would take up wickedness again, which was in my line, being brung up to it" (271). His wicked ways, as he knows from long experience, might get him into difficulty down the road, but Huck has learned to live with the short-term rather than the long-term consequences of his acts, which is one reason he can face the prospect of eternal damnation. For instance, Huck knows that accommodating the King and the Duke will most likely cause problems in the future, as it does. But he accommodates them anyway. What controls Huck's decision making is not a concern about the future—certainly not a concern about its possibility for justice—but how he feels at the moment. Huck's loyalty to Jim may defy what others think, but it still accommodates Huck to how he himself feels. Since deciding to turn Jim in would make him internally "full of trouble" (269), he decides, as he does in giving in to the wishes of the King and the Duke, to do what is easiest. He will confront the consequences of that choice when they arise as he floats along dealing with life as it comes.

Of course, Huck is an unreliable narrator who is not aware of the moral consequences of his acts. Since readers are, their awareness might seem to be the result of a difference in education—if not a formal one, at least one of experience. But the power of the novel depends on the fact that Huck makes a choice that his more educated and experienced elders would not. Twain's intent may be to use Huck to educate his "betters," but the education he offers cannot, as we have seen, be derived from an internal logic within Huck's consciousness. Nor is it based on a solid foundation of moral principles.

As often is the case, we get insight into Twain's views on such serious matters in a humorous incident. Not long after chapter 31, Huck again is forced to ponder whether he is doing right or wrong in helping Jim escape bondage. As he and Tom work to free Jim from the Phelps's farm, Tom insists that they do it the right way, the way dictated by the books he has read about prison escapes. That means digging Jim out with case knives. Finding the work slow and difficult, Huck suggests that, even though it "ain't right, and it ain't moral," they should use pickaxes instead. Intrigued with the idea, Tom continues to insist that "right is right, and wrong is wrong, and a body ain't got no business doing wrong when he ain't ignorant and knows better." He then solves their dilemma by coming up with the legal fiction of imagining that a pickax is in fact a case knife. "Give me a case-knife," he says to Huck. Huck responds.

> He had his own by him, but I handed him mine. He flung it down, and says: "Give me a *case-knife*."
> I didn't know just what to do—but then I thought. I scratched around

among the old tools, and got a pick-ax and gave it to him, and he took it and went to work, and never said a word.

He was always just that particular. Full of principle. (307)[64]

One of many incidents contrasting Huck's practicality with Tom's romanticism, this passage makes an important point for Twain. Slavish adherence to principles of right and wrong can keep people from accomplishing the pragmatic task at hand. It is Twain's recognition that the complexities of life do not conform to a priori principles that makes him, along with fellow literary realists Howells and Henry James, part of what Morton G. White called the "revolt against formalism."[65] But how are we to distinguish between right and wrong in the absence of clear-cut principles? One answer is that we are persuaded an action is right by effective rhetoric. In the case of Huckleberry Finn, that would be the effective rhetoric of Twain's story. For instance, readers are confident that Huck does the right thing in chapter 31 because of the skill by which Twain tells his story up to that point. True, but as effective as Twain's rhetoric is, its power to persuade would not be as great as it is without his readers' prior belief that the institution of slavery is wrong. That belief comes primarily not from a formal education, not from dialectical logic, and not even from solid moral principles, but from historical hindsight.

According to Stacey Margolis, Twain builds such hindsight, a "retrospective account of action," into the structure of the book. As she puts it, "Characters repeatedly come to know what they really did (or what their actions really mean) only after the fact, only retrospectively." For instance, "Miss Watson's will casts a shadow over the entire plot, redefining what everyone has been doing to Jim." A formal component of the book, this retrospective account of action forces "readers into the same kind of recognition that Huck and Jim experience in the world of the novel."[66] The question is, however, What does that recognition entail?

On one hand, it might seem to confirm Warren's argument about Twain's belief in an educable consciousness, since readers are educated by the passage of history to recognize the morality of Huck's actions. On the other, it reminds us that, when we act, we have no way of knowing what the future consequences of our actions will be. Thus, the one perspective someone in the midst of a moral dilemma can never have is a retrospective view of it. The first sort of recognition can easily lead those in the present to feel morally superior to those in the past. The second deflates that pretentious belief. Indeed, if Huck is an example of an educable consciousness, in the book his education is never finished. And Huck's is not the only one.

A mugwumpian document in its stress on the need to educate the moral faculties, *Huckleberry Finn* reminds us, as Trilling points out, that even an educated sense of morality needs continual correction. Aimed at training the moral discrimination of readers who must complete an education that Huck never finishes, the book offers the disconcerting lesson that such an education can never be complete.

In making this point, I am not denying the importance of Huck's acts on behalf of Jim. What I am suggesting is that translating the moral force of that action into a model for how to act outside the book is more difficult than many tend to think. If Twain retrospectively appeals to Huck's sound heart to explain the action of the book, we would be better advised to trust the opening "Notice" that warns us against finding such a moral. We can get a sense of what I mean by comparing *Huckleberry Finn* to "The Private History of a Campaign That Failed," the first piece Twain published after *Huckleberry Finn*.

This semiautobiographical account of Twain's desertion from the Confederate army has numerous parallels to *Huckleberry Finn*. It begins with a description of Twain's life in the army as the carefree adventure of an inexperienced youth from town bound together with his peers for a weekend outing in the country. As Tom Quirk has suggested, the similarities between the Marion Rangers and Tom Sawyer's band of robbers would have given Twain ample reasons to explain why he deserted when confronted with the first realities of combat. "Like many new recruits at the time, Twain had mixed loyalties, which, coupled with his own lack of training and discipline, created in him an ambivalence, if not a moral confusion." But if those circumstances would have *excused* Twain's desertion, they would not have *sanctified* it, which is what Twain does when he fashions a highly moral reason for abandoning his duty.[67]

As the Rangers prepare one night for their first encounter with the enemy, they fire blindly at and kill a man who happens to ride by. "The thought," Twain reports, "shot through me that I was a murderer, that I had killed a man—a man who had never done me any harm. That was the coldest sensation that ever went through my marrow." Preyed on by the thought of this dead man, Twain decides to abandon "this vocation of sham soldiership while I could save some remnant of my self-respect."[68]

Twain's account of this killing, especially his own involvement, is almost certainly a retrospective fabrication, a fabrication that transforms what others might see as an act of disloyalty or cowardice into an act of moral independence. One obvious purpose of that fabrication is to challenge the numerous celebrations of heroism on both sides of the Civil War written at that time. Indeed, Twain's sketch appeared in the midst of a volume replete with Civil War reminiscences. But Twain's fabrication also gives moral sanctity to his first important change of allegiance, his first step toward becoming a Scalawag. If most likely that first step was simply the result of a youthful desire to remain free from responsibilities and duties, Twain retrospectively makes it a moral act just as he adopts a high moral tone in explaining his desertion from the Republican Party. Twain defines a Mugwump as one who is pure from the marrow out, and it is the cold sensation that his imagined killing has on his marrow that leads to his desertion.

As Quirk points out, "A Campaign That Failed" is not the first work in which Twain identifies with Huck. Earlier, however, he seems to have identified with Huck's free and easy lifestyle, not his moral integrity. For instance, while still working on *Huckleberry Finn*, Twain published *A Tramp Abroad*, in which Huck's raft gets transported to Germany for a carefree trip down the Neckar. Similarly, "A Campaign That Failed" begins with a somewhat satiric, but clearly affectionate, treatment of the young recruits' lack of discipline and purpose. Out of that carefree youthful response to the world, Twain creates, without explanation, a highly developed moral consciousness, thus suggesting that moral and political independence can spring miraculously out of an unencumbered life of youthful freedom. By including this moral point of view within his sketch, Twain justifies the switch of loyalties that made him a Scalawag just as in "Consistency" he justifies the switch of loyalties that made him a Mugwump. But even though he retrospectively imposed a similar moral on *Huckleberry Finn*, the book itself does not consistently sustain that point of view. In fact, despite similarities, Twain's narratives in his book and in his sketch have significant differences.

In the sketch Twain sympathizes with a dead man because he was a "man who never done me any harm"; in the book Huck uses almost the same phrase to describe the slave owner who would suffer if Jim were to steal his children. If in the sketch Twain's sympathies are aligned with his moral response, in the book Huck's are frequently out of alignment. Twain's proper sorting out of sympathies in the sketch implies that a happy-go-lucky youth develops into a morally sensitive one, a development made credible by the presence of Twain's adult consciousness. The youth, we are made to believe, becomes the adult who wrote the sketch he is in. But the novel places us in the midst of Huck's moral confusion without a guiding adult consciousness. Rather than present us with a developmental narrative, Twain moves Huck from his moment of high moral courage into slapstick comedy. If, as John Gerber notes, both the sketch and the novel share a similar pattern of action in which the protagonist "lights out" after getting into a "series of scrapes of increasing complexity and annoyance," the move west in Huckleberry Finn is fraught with moral ambiguity.[69] Evoking the myth of the West as a place of unconstrained freedom at the same time that it marks Huck's renewed subservience to Tom Sawyer's romantic fantasy, the book ends with Huck imagining campaigns among "the Injuns, over in the Territory" (361). Just as Huck succumbs to Tom's thirst for adventure by acquiescing to a plot to free a black man who is already free, so he succumbs to Tom's desire to find new adventures with Native Americans as the source of fun.

To point out that Huck is not as consistent a hero as Twain's retrospective account of the book makes him is not to deny Twain's claim in "Consistency" that the cause of liberty has often been served by courageously independent thinkers. But it is to suggest that, if Huck is Twain's model for his own mugwumpish acts of independence, those acts might not be as consistently virtuous as Twain would like them to be. Indeed, if Twain's brand of mugwumpery displayed consistent sympathy for African Americans, it also came into tension with an alternative strategy for furthering their cause, one that does not fit so easily into the narrative connecting courageous abolitionists with civil rights protesters. To see why, we can turn to a scene that would seem to prove an exception to my claim that Huckleberry Finn does not, for good historical reasons, make an explicit case for African American political and civil rights. Helping to prove Twain's debunkers wrong by showing that the book does indeed address such issues, it also reveals the limits of Twain's mugwumpery in promoting those rights.

☆ ☆ ☆ Early in the book Pap launches into a tirade after he encounters a black professor with the right to vote in his home state of Ohio. "Well, that let me out," Pap exclaims. "Thinks I, what is the country a-coming to? It was 'lection day, and I was just about to go and vote, myself, if I weren't too drunk to get there; but they told me there was a State in this country where they'd let that nigger vote, I drawed out. I says I will never vote agin" (34). According to Mailloux, this passage "requires little rhetorical work from a reader. . . . The racism remains on the surface of the discourse, and the striking contrast between the speaker's ethos and his well-educated black target—'a p'fessor in a college'—makes the ideological point."[70] Indeed, few readers miss the point that Pap is much less qualified to vote than this educated black man.

But if the passage requires a reader to do little rhetorical work to catch its "ideological point," it does require quite a bit of historical reconstruction if a reader is to understand its full implications. According to Mailloux, Twain's rhetorical appeal can be understood historically by reference to a speech Blaine made soon after losing the 1884 election. Republicans in that campaign faced a challenge more difficult to overcome than Blaine's reputation. As the South became more and more solid, Republicans were forced to counter by carrying almost the entire North (and in the long run by admitting more western states) to level the political playing field. To be sure, as I have already argued, even as late as 1884 the South was not as solid as it became in 1888. Thus, Republicans devised the strategy of "Carrying the war into Africa"—that is, of trying to capture a few key southern states. But when that strategy failed, the election turned on New York, Cleveland's home state. Although the results were extremely close, Blaine was not able to squeak out a victory as had James Garfield four years earlier. Venting a frustration that he could not express during the campaign for fear of losing votes in the South, Blaine lashed out a few days after the results were clear, blaming his defeat (somewhat justifiably) on election practices in which blacks were "deprived of free suffrage and their rights as citizens [were] scornfully trodden under foot." A system of "cruel intimidation," "violence," and "murder" that deprived blacks of "all political power," he concluded, had also deprived him of victory.[71]

Mailloux is certainly correct to note that Pap's tirade helps us to understand the system that provoked Blaine's tirade. What he fails to note is that in the 1884 election Twain sided not with Blaine but with the Democrats Blaine castigated. Twain may have identified his mugwumpery with Huck's willingness to risk social condemnation and go to hell rather than betray Jim, but that very mugwumpery helped to put into office a president who benefited from electoral abuses generated by people sharing Pap's racist prejudices.

Occurring after Twain finished composing *Huck Finn*, the 1884 election could not have affected his intentions in writing the book. Nonetheless, the retrospective perspective that the election affords highlights an aspect of this passage that most of today's readers overlook. They, like Mailloux, read the passage as an attack on efforts to deny blacks their newly won right to vote. In fact, it makes a case not for all blacks but for an educated black. If today we think of the disenfranchisement of blacks as a class, at the time Twain was writing, many people distinguished between educated and uneducated blacks. For instance, describing the situation in the South prior to disenfranchising legislation, the Englishman James Bryce, whose best American friends were Mugwumps, favorably noted that "the comparatively small minority of educated and property-owning colored people suffer less . . . because they are less frequently interrupted in going to the polls." At the same time he felt that, if the South found a way legally to keep uneducated blacks from voting, the measures should also be applied to uneducated whites, most of whom were immigrants.[72]

When people read Twain's passage as supporting the Fifteenth Amendment, they are right. But they too often forget the limits of that amendment. It does not, as is commonly assumed, grant the right to vote to all black males. It simply prohibits denying someone the right to vote on the basis of race. If that was a great advance, there were still all sorts of ways to deny people the right to vote. If today we read Pap's tirade primarily as a comment on African American rights, it is just as importantly an argument against uneducated voters. Indeed, it makes its rhetorical point about the folly of denying educated blacks the vote by playing on another racial stereotype at the time—the uneducated, drunken Irish who, along with uneducated blacks, were blamed for destroying responsible government. Far from sending the message that the franchise should be extended, it implies that the system Pap rails against will be better off if uneducated, prejudiced Pap Finn sticks to his vow never to vote again.[73]

Twain most likely composed this passage in late 1876 or early 1877. Its message is very similar to a December 9, 1876, cartoon by his friend Thomas Nast called "The Ignorant Vote—Honors Are Easy" that depicts a scale, one side labeled "South" and the other "North." Sitting on the Southern scale, labeled "black," is the caricature of a former slave, balanced on the Northern scale by the an Irish immigrant, labeled "white," even though in his simianlike caricature he is almost as dark as the African American.[74] A year earlier, the year of the 1875 Civil Rights Act, Twain had published "The Curious Republic of Gondour" anonymously in the *Atlantic Monthly*. Concerned about ignorant and incompetent voters, especially in comparison with the more elitist British system, Twain satirically proposed means to take elections out of the hands of "the ignorant and non-taxpaying classes." Gondour did not repeal its guarantee of universal suffrage, but it did grant up to nine additional votes depending on a person's education. Accumulated property could also increase an individual's vote, but regulations ensured that the educated would outvote the rich in order to protect the interests of the "great lower rank of society."[75] Combined with civil service reform, which was a foundation of the Mugwump platform, this weighted system of voting results in immediate improvement.

Twain's stress on the educated voter in this satiric piece and elsewhere might seem in direct conflict with his celebration of Huck in the work that followed. But adolescent, nonvoting Huck is not so much a part of the political process as an equitable corrective to it. Indeed, as a comment on

December 9, 1876

The Ignorant Vote—Honors Are Easy.

Thomas Nast's "The Ignorant Vote—Honors Are Easy" appeared in the December 9, 1876, *Harper's Weekly.* Often sympathetic to the plight of freedmen, Nast hated the Irish, whom he blamed for corruption at Tammany Hall.

those eligible to vote, Twain's ironic portrayal of uneducated Pap demanding that an educated black professor not be allowed to vote would have been received more warmly by Mugwumps than by supporters of Blaine. For instance, the *New York Times*, with Mugwump leanings, reported Blaine's post-election outburst under the following headline: "Smarting under Defeat / Mr. Blaine Makes a Very Foolish Speech. / He Waves the Bloody Shirt Vigorously, and Plays upon the Prejudices of the Ignorant."[76] The ignorant the *Times* has in mind includes both blacks and whites; nonetheless, it was blacks who were the primary targets of intimidation in the South. Though not as prone to upsetting the Northern public, genteel arguments for the need of informed voters also turned out to be an effective weapon keeping freedmen from voting.

The point is not, of course, to encourage uninformed voters. It is instead that, formulated at the time it was and in the way it was, the Mugwump ideal of the independent, informed voter was in tension with the ideal of the rights-bearing citizen that advocated the right of all freedmen to vote. In fact, in *Huckleberry Finn* Twain consistently mocks those claiming rights, from the desperadoes Huck and Jim see on the *Walter Scott* to members of the mob asserting a right to see Bogg's dead body to Tom in the overdrawn escape scene, who grants Jim a right, not as a citizen, but as a prisoner. The most memorable of all, however, is Pap, who protests granting an African American the right to vote with "They call that govment! A man can't get his rights in a govment like this" (33).[77] To be sure, Twain's satiric deployment of the language of rights should not be interpreted as a blanket attack on the notion of the rights-bearing citizen. Just because the language of rights can be abused does not mean there are no legitimate claims to rights. If Twain's mugwumpian ideal was in tension with the rights-bearing model, it was not in direct opposition to it.

On the contrary, most Mugwumps had antislavery backgrounds, and in the 1884 election they never would have supported a Democrat who stood for the values of the Old South. As the prominent Mugwump Richard Gilder made clear in an editorial in the *Century* magazine titled "A Grave Responsibility," President Cleveland would lose their support if he did not guarantee the rights of Southern blacks.[78] What Gilder does not mention, however, is that the rights of blacks had been dramatically reduced as a result of the 1883 Civil Rights Cases. In supporting the Democrats in the 1884 election, Mugwumps refused to make that decision an issue in the campaign. Silently—and sometimes vocally—they were willing to trust the goodwill of the South, especially its respected and educated classes, to treat blacks fairly.

Mugwumps' trust in educated Southern whites is a major reason why most blacks were so vehement in their denunciation of them. To be sure, some blacks also blamed the Civil Rights Cases on a predominantly Republican Court. But Republicans were not called, as one black newspaper called Mugwumps, "a thing without heart or soul. It is the impersonation of hypocrisy and the excrescence of all that is contemptible; it subsists on pretense and grows fat on treason."[79]

Blacks' animosity toward Mugwumps increased by the end of Cleveland's first term. A native of Buffalo, Cleveland was not a Southern Democrat, and he went out of his way soon after his election to reassure the nation that blacks would be treated fairly. Nonetheless, even though freedmen's fears that Cleveland's election would bring about a return to slavery were unfounded, the Democratic victory did effect important changes. As one chronicler of the 1884 election puts it, "With a Democrat executing the federal election laws, white Southerners hardly needed waste their time trying to repeal them. They could cheat and steal as much as they liked."[80] The black vote, he notes, was almost completely wiped out. If Twain complained of the "solid" South in his suppressed passages in *Life on the Mississippi*, his moral decision to bolt from the Republican Party helped to solidify it and ensure its continuity, all in the name of national unity.

In his inaugural address Cleveland stressed above all the end of sectional division in the country. That message was one of Cleveland's main attractions to Mugwumps who attributed much of the partisan bickering that characterized North/South politics to ignorant voters, whose prejudices did not allow them to transcend local interests in order to see the greater national good. The fact that former Republicans could see beyond party loyalty to vote for a Democrat was in itself a sign of the potential for reform. But for reform to be lasting, the vote had to be entrusted to educated voters.

The argument for an informed electorate is so rational and so compelling that it is hard to fault. It certainly appears to be color-blind. Like Bryce, reformers expressed concern about uneducated immigrants in the North as well as African Americans in the South. In fact, later in the century some former bolters spearheaded the movement to restrict immigration through the use of a literacy test, a proposal that failed but nonetheless became a model for policies adopted in racist pockets of Bryce's British Empire, like South Africa and Australia, as well as for the tests used in the South to exclude black voters. Indeed, despite the Mugwumps' genteel rhetoric, the fact remained that blacks were affected much more than whites by demands to ensure informed, independent voters. The racist motive behind the arguments of some Mugwumps are made explicit in Gilder's 1883 comment that "Negroes constitute a peasantry wholly untrained in, and ignorant of, those ideas of constitutional liberty and progress which are the birth right of every white voter; . . . they are gregarious and emotional rather than intelligent, and are easily led in any direction by white men of energy and determination."[81] Prominent Mugwumps like Charles W. Eliot and Charles Francis Adams Jr. agreed and consistently supported segregation. Similarly, the views of William A. Dunning, the famous historian critical of Reconstruction, are, according to David Donald, those of a Mugwump.[82]

My point is not to imply through a logic of association that Twain was a racist. His views on race are closer to those of Mugwumps like Samuel Bowles of the Springfield Republican, William Hayes Ward of the Independent, William Lloyd Garrison Jr., and Horace White, who recognized that their trust in the goodwill of the South had been misplaced and early in the twentieth century joined sixty people calling for a national conference on racism. That conference led to the foundation of the National Association for the Advancement of Colored People (NAACP), whose first president was former Mugwump Moorfield Storey. Such careers make it easy to assume that what provided continuity between the antislavery movement and the twentieth-century civil rights movement was a mugwumpian brand of political independence.

Not having an antislavery background himself, Scalawag Twain, primarily because of the moral force of Huck's actions in chapter 31, fits nicely into that narrative of continuity. But that narrative obscures the existence of an alternative way of supporting freedmen at the time Twain was writing. Twain might have supported the Fifteenth Amendment, and he might have created a sympathetic portrayal of Jim, but those two together do not add up to making a case for uneducated and superstitious Jim to have the right to vote. For Twain and many other Mugwumps, if African Americans as a class should not be denied the right to vote, the uneducated as a class should not be given that right. There were, however, people who did support the right to vote for people similar to Jim. They were also deeply concerned about producing more educated voters, but not at the expense of the vast majority of freedmen.

☆ ☆ ☆ Four years before Cleveland stressed the end of sectionalism in his inaugural address, James Garfield began his by emphasizing the importance of the Constitution and the president's executive duty to uphold the supremacy of national law. Making it clear that he was alluding to federal laws upholding the political and civil rights of freedmen, Garfield highlighted the monumental duty of elevating "the negro race from slavery to the full rights of citizenship." To those who resisted that elevation, he warned, "under our institutions" there is "no middle ground for the negro race between slavery and equal citizenship." He followed that warning with a section on the need to preserve "freedom of the ballot" and another on the need for a national educational policy that would help to ensure informed voters by addressing the problem of illiteracy. Of course, Mugwumps also drew attention to the dangers of a large number of illiterate voters, but their solution was much different. Garfield insisted that "there can be no permanent disenfranchised peasantry in the United States" and called on the nation to educate its voters.[83] Mugwumps, in contrast, stressed the importance of requiring education first and then allowing people to vote.

During this time there were a number of calls for the federal government to give financial aid to solve the problem of uneducated voters. These programs would be financed by a large budgetary surplus created by a tariff on imported goods, a tariff that Twain as an advocate of free trade opposed. One of the most vocal proponents was lawyer/novelist Albion W. Tourgée, an outspoken defender of African American rights who later in the century would defend Homer Plessy. While Twain was seeing *Huckleberry Finn* through the press, Tourgée rushed to finish *An Appeal to Caesar* in time for the 1884 election. His book minutely outlined the dangers of an illiterate electorate and argued for a solution much more elaborate than one proposed by New Hampshire senator Henry Blair. Tourgée opposed Blair's bill because it channeled money through individual states. Tourgée worried, probably correctly, that Southern states would give disproportionate amounts to white schools. Thus, he advocated giving money directly to the local schools most in need of it. Although recent debunkers of Twain, such as Arac and Jane Smiley, pit *Huckleberry Finn* against Stowe's *Uncle Tom's Cabin*, Tourgée's works, better than anyone's, present an alternative view of black civil rights.[84]

In 1880 Tourgée published *Bricks without Straw*, set during Reconstruction with telling portraits of two former slaves. One, having fought for the Union army during the Civil War, establishes himself as an independent and productive farmer, and the other, though physically crippled, is a gifted teacher and speaker.[85] Dramatizing reasons for Reconstruction's failure by showing how intimidation by the Ku Klux Klan and white opposition destroys the promising efforts of these two at self-sufficiency and improvement, the book ends by suggesting that the only hope is a coalition of whites and blacks. Twain in all likelihood read Tourgée's important but now neglected novel, since he bought a copy the year it was published, a year in which he returned to his efforts to finish his own novel about black and white relations.[86] But in *Huckleberry Finn*, as in Stowe's *Uncle Tom's Cabin*, the primary black figure, if sympathetic, is not a model for developing a new class of independent citizens. This difference between Tourgée's and Twain's novels is due in large part to conflicting views about the connection between education and the right to vote as well as the notion of citizenly independence itself.

Like Garfield, whose memory *An Appeal to Caesar* evokes, Tourgée felt that it was paramount to protect African American voting rights. In a direct rebuke to calls by Mugwumps to reform the electoral process, he dismissed the argument against universal suffrage as "not only absurd, but cowardly and unjust in the extreme." The problem, he claimed, was not with "the ignorant masses" but with the "general neglect of the more important functions by the *intelligent masses*." Nonetheless, hand in hand with protecting voter rights was the responsibility to provide the education needed to exercise that right properly.[87]

A major mistake of Reconstruction, Tourgée felt, was the belief that hundreds of years of history could be overcome through a formal change in the status of African Americans from slave to citizen. For instance, Charles Sumner "exulted too quickly when he declared that by giving the ballot to the freedmen we had 'chained him to the chariot-wheel of American progress.'"[88] Change would come only gradually and through education directed at both the culturally ingrained prejudices of whites and the ignorance of most freedmen. Whereas "the mass of ignorance may be instinctively right in purpose, it is naturally unable to judge the instrumentalities with which it works."[89] Almost as if he were describing Huck, Tourgée warned that "the ignorant man cannot exercise the power of the citizen with any sort of assurance that he is acting rightly."[90]

Tourgée envisioned two major threats to the republic: the possibility that the ignorant masses would not be able to implement their basically sound intentions and the possibility that ambitious individuals would place their self-interests above those of the whole. Education alone, he admitted, cannot make good citizens out of individuals with ambitious inclinations. "An educated man," he acknowledges, "may not be a good citizen because he will not perform the duties which he understands. . . . Mere intelligence is not enough to insure the performance of public duties, any more than it is a sufficient safeguard against private crime. Knowledge simply gives to the individual the power to be a good citizen, not the inclination."[91] Nonetheless, a program of general education can empower the masses so that their basically good intentions will hold ambitious individuals in check. That process would succeed, however, only if all citizens actively participated in politics.

"Politics," Tourgée writes in his 1888 *Letters to a King*, "is the broadest, richest, and most important field of Christian endeavor." Discounting the ballot reforms advocated by Mugwumps, he rejects the idea that "political evils may be cured by cunningly contrived devices." A citizen's political duty cannot be discharged by "a mere perfunctory exercise of the electoral franchise." Similarly, civil service reform for him was not a disinterested measure that would restore virtue to the republic by eliminating the partisan rewards of the spoils system. On the contrary, it would lessen citizen participation in government and replace it with a class of professional administrators. Far from restoring virtue, it would destroy it by creating a European brand of the modern bureaucratic state that people so love to hate. For Tourgée, political parties, as the best instrument for hearing the will of the people, were less a cause of corruption than a powerful check on it. Through them the "supremely dangerous factor of personal ambition" has been held in check, since "the political leader has become the mere agent and creature of his party." If some might criticize this "strange agency" of the party, it is through the party system that "the ultimate power" has been taken "from the leader and the caucus and placed in the hands of the rank and file." [92]

The "King" in Tourgée's title is the citizen, who in a republic shares sovereignty with all other citizens. Aware that this sovereignty can become simply "a figure of speech not literally consistent with fact," Tourgée claims that the citizen, as voter, does indeed possess sovereign power, but only if he exercises it in conjunction with other "kings." "Though the sovereignty vested in him is absolute, it must be exercised jointly with that inhering in his fellows; though the right is several, the possession is joint." Thus, it is through the "voluntary republic" of a political party that "the citizen's power may be made effective" by allowing him to exercise his sovereign power. [93]

Both Mugwump Twain and Republican Tourgée had populist streaks. Twain, for instance, shared Tourgée's belief that "political error is possible to the most highly cultured community," [94] and both turned to the "rank and file" to guard against such errors. But Twain turned to isolated, independent individuals—whenever Huck aligns himself with others, Jim excepted, he loses his independence [95]—whereas Tourgée felt that the rank and file had power only in a political party that placed constraints on ambitious individuals. For Twain the politics of affiliation threatened an independent citizenry; for Tourgée it enabled it. Twain envisioned the possibility of "absolute freedom" in mugwumpery; Tourgée imagined the possibility of "absolute" sovereignty only through the maintenance of party loyalty.[96] Not opposed to the notion of the independent citizen, Tourgée proposed a completely different account of what independence entails. "Genuine political independence," he claimed, is not the "weak, sniveling thing that passes by that name." It requires instead the strength and confidence needed for someone to "do his duty as a partisan in order that his duty as a citizen may be more easily and certainly performed." For Tourgée the so-called independent voter mistakenly believes that he can stand outside politics in order to make a reasoned judgment that allows him to choose sides before descending into its fallen realm. But solutions to the nation's problems, he argued, cannot be generated in a realm outside politics. They arise instead through political debate. Mocking those "falsely claiming to be 'the better classes,'" who think themselves the guardians of government by standing above partisan politics, Tourgée declared "partisanship . . . the very foremost duty of the citizen." Independents put forth "clamorous pretense of fairness and virtue," but Tourgée dismissed them as "malcontents" and "intractables" with "weak and vacillating natures" that have "not positiveness of character enough to have party affiliations, strong and earnest." Far from virtuous, this class of voter, casting its lot first with one party and then the next, is "in all its forms . . . purchasable, and always in the market—waiting to be bid for."[97]

As strange as it might sound to people in the early twenty-first century to have someone link independence with partisanship, Tourgée clearly anticipated how the rise of the "independent" voter would generate politicians whose campaigns are guided by opinion polls, not by independent ideas. As recent elections have shown, when the outcome depends on the fluctuating vote of independents, candidates too often focus on a few issues of concern to swing voters. In purchasing their votes, a politician might get elected, but not by addressing issues affecting the interests of the nation as a whole. Indeed, in abandoning the Republican Party to join the Democrats, Mugwumps might have prided themselves in their independence, but for Tourgée they failed to stay committed to the most important, if not popular, principle of the newly amended Constitution: the principle of equal citizenship for all of the nation's citizens, black and white. A major reason Tourgée advocated the duty of partisanship was his recognition that it was necessary to establish and to protect the rights of freedmen, one of the most blatant examples being the passage of the 1875 Civil Rights Act by a lame-duck Republican Congress. In contrast, he accused independents of creating an "unstable element" in our politics. To emphasize their vacillation, Tourgée drew on a metaphor popular at the time and called independents "'the floating vote.'"[98] That metaphor can help us understand why the politics of *Huckleberry Finn* itself has seemed to fluctuate from reader to reader and generation to generation.

In this book most identified as quintessentially American, freedom is imagined as floating down a river on a raft. John Barth has called that image one of the most memorable created in world literature, an image "larger than the stor[y] in which [it] appear[s]."[99] Indeed, Huck cannot be envisioned apart from his raft, just as the raft cannot be envisioned without Jim, and just as Huck, Jim, and their raft cannot be envisioned apart from the Mississippi River. Much of the power of the raft as image comes from its suggestion of freedom. In his highly influential *On Civil Liberty and Self-Government* Francis Lieber listed "as one characteristic of American liberty, the freedom of our rivers. The unimpeded navigation of rivers belongs to the right of free locomotion and intercommunication."[100] Yet, as Huck's and Jim's voyage down the heart of the country shows, slavery greatly restricted that freedom. Given those restrictions, what precisely is the significance of Huck's and Jim's freedom on the river?

On one hand, it is a freedom that Huck and Jim, as fellow fugitives, have from the restraints and subservient roles imposed on them by a corrupt society. This freedom becomes a positive freedom as black man and white boy create their own "world elsewhere,"[101] which becomes a model for how "clean men, clean ordinary citizens, rank & file" can "make or save countries." On the other hand, freedom on the river suggests a childlike fantasy, "a purely lazy, relaxed, floating-down-the-river freedom, categorically on holiday, categorically an escape from all responsibility. . . . It is not a freedom to do anything; it is not even freedom *from* anything important. It is freedom from table-manners and formal clothes, and evening prayers."[102] An image of both freedom made possible by independence from established and constraining affiliations and a freedom in which Huck and Jim have no more direction and purpose than the flotsam and jetsam that drifts by them on the river, the raft recalls the freedom of independent citizenship idealized by Twain and the Mugwumps. On one hand, it can be a freedom that, emancipated from prejudices caused by blind loyalty to party, can virtuously put the needs of the country ahead of those of any interest group. On the other, it can be an irresponsible freedom of accommodation that, in Tourgée's words, simply contents itself with "drifting back and forth in the eddies of the great political current."[103] Huck, T. S. Eliot observed, "gives the book style," but the "river with its strong, swift current is the dictator to the raft."[104] Indeed, as Huck and Jim float along, the river dictates their course, taking them deeper and deeper into the heart of slavery.

Huckleberry Finn, in other words, seems simultaneously to endorse Twain's belief that the true test of independence is to buck the tides of popular political opinion and to raise the possibility that what appears to be independent action may, in fact, be nothing more than going with the flow. That doubleness haunts Twain's writings. If, on one hand, he made powerful public defenses of mugwumpery, on the other, they are shadowed by doubts about the morality of his acts of independence. "Consistency," for instance, is fraught with concerns about disloyalty, treason, and desertion.[105] Providing no easy formula by which to distinguish right from wrong, Huckleberry Finn also provides no easy way to determine whether Twain's scalawagish and mugwumpish tendency to switch sides is a sign of true independence or a lack of consistent principles. Indeed, if Twain self-consciously used Huck as a model for independent moral action in his public life, that life revealed an accommodationist streak of its own, one that raises questions about the independence of self-proclaimed nonpartisan writers, like Twain.

For Tourgée writers had the same partisan duty as citizens. There was no more room for disinterested "independence" in aesthetics than there was in politics. Thus, Tourgée strongly advocated "the novel with a purpose." Partisan works of the imagination were for him an important weapon on the battlefield of political rhetoric and helped citizens avoid the great sin of standing "idly by and see[ing] evils prevail while expecting to be held guiltless."[106] In contrast, Twain adhered much closer to the mugwumpian ideal that a work of literature should take a disinterested stance above partisan politics. It is, therefore, no accident that excerpts from Huckleberry Finn as well as the first literary appreciation of Twain appeared in the mugwumpian Century magazine. Nor is it an accident that its editor Gilder derided Tourgée's view of aesthetics. Writing to George Washington Cable about his manuscript John March, Southerner, he complained that it was "a tract, not a story. Instead of a return to literature: an attempt to fetch everything into literature save & except literature itself . . . Shades of Tourgée!"[107] Gilder clearly thought differently about Twain's southern novel.

Tourgée seems to have as well. He corresponded with Cable, encouraging his support of freedmen's rights. Then, in 1888, when he challenged writers to make the links between slavery and the new condition of African Americans the new field for fiction, he faulted literary realists for failing to take up the challenge without even mentioning Huckleberry Finn.[108] Indeed, for him, Twain could well have illustrated the purchasable conscience of Mugwumps.

From the fall of 1884 to February 1885 Twain went on a reading tour with Cable to publicize their new books.[109] While they were on tour, Gilder published Cable's controversial "The Freedman's Case in Equity," which makes a case for treating African Americans as equal citizens. Evoking the higher-law standard of equity because of the recent Civil Rights Cases, Cable argued that unfair treatment of blacks is no longer a question of "whether constitutional amendments, but whether eternal principles of justice are violated."[110] Cable's argument made him, a former Confederate officer, the most hated man in the South, and the Century's publication of his essay might seem to align it with his views. But Gilder was also careful to publish a rebuttal by Henry Grady, the most articulate spokesman for the New South. Titled "In Plain Black and White," Grady's essay proposed a very different sense of what equitable treatment for freedmen entailed. Using measured and respectful language—"nigger," for instance, is studiously avoided—the essay never refers to blacks as citizens. On the contrary, Grady divided "the revolution" of Reconstruction into three steps: the abolition of slavery, the Fifteenth Amendment, and the Civil Rights Act of 1875. "The first step, right by universal agreement, would stand if the law that made it were withdrawn. The second step, though irrevocable, raises doubts as to its wisdom. The third, wrong in purpose, has failed in execution and has been overturned by the highest court in the land."[111]

Adopting a position above partisan politics, the Century stood for reasoned debate about the issue, refusing to take a particular stand, even though it did not allow the young Charles Chesnutt to publish a response articulating a black point of view. Similarly, according to Arthur G. Pettit and Stephen Railton, Twain, on tour, declined to comment on either the Civil Rights Cases or Cable's essay.[112] Twain's silence might seem a violation of his celebration of political independence, but it can also be seen as an attempt, like that of the Century, to maintain it. Conducting the tour to help market Huckleberry Finn, Twain would not have wanted to be identified with North or South but with the entire American people.

Celebrated for its stance of disinterestedness, political independence can have its own partisan effects. Grady, for instance, knowing the national audience of the Century, argues that the solution to the "race problem" will come from neither sentimental views about blacks nor partisan politics. Instead, he calls for "clear views, clear statement, and clear understanding" as well as trust in "the common sense and courage of the American people." When Cleveland won the 1884 election, Grady had praised the same people, striding down the aisle of the Georgia legislature shouting, "Mr. Speaker, a message from the American people."[113]

Looked at from this perspective, Twain's aesthetic independence seems less a commendable ability to tell the truth than a compromised effort to maintain a national audience for his books at the same time that, like Mugwumps, he appeals to national unity while contributing to the silencing of blacks. Indeed, if Tourgée was accused of raising the bloody shirt in his fiction, the only bloody shirt in Huckleberry Finn is the one Huck and Tom steal from Aunt Sally's clothesline for Jim to write on with his own blood.

The extent to which Twain accommodated himself to the demands of a national audience is illustrated by the passages he suppressed from Life on the Mississippi. Their critical view of the South certainly seems the work of a Scalawag. Twain, after all, lamented how the South's lack of respect for rule by law allowed a few hothead murderers to intimidate the entire population and thus lead to the violent extralegal means of lynching. But what he fails to mention is that most lynchings involved more than a few hotheads. They were instead an important part of the paramilitary violence committed against blacks and their Scalawag supporters. Nor does Twain mention—although he certainly knew about it because of publicity in newspapers and conversations with, among others, Cable—that the most notorious lack of respect for rule by law in the South at this time was violation of civil rights acts designed to protect the rights of freedmen.

To be sure, later in his life Twain wrote "The United States of Lyncherdom." But he agreed with his publisher to wait until he died to bring it out for fear that it would cut back sales of his other books in the South.[114] Similarly, one critic speculates that Twain suppressed the passages from Life on the Mississippi because he recognized that they "may have offended certain prospective subscribers to the book, back in 1883, when it first appeared: particularly those in the South—and perhaps those in the North, too, who sentimentalized over what they thought of as the 'good old days' and prided themselves on the delicacy of their sensibilities."[115] If Twain's suppression of these passages seems to violate his celebration of independence, it also helped him to remain independent of partisan squabbles between North and South, an independence that both reinforced his belief in the importance of national reconciliation and helped him to become identified as a national rather than as a regional writer. That such an identity would help the nationwide sales of his books is not a consequence that Twain the businessman would have taken lightly. Mugwumps may have been among the first to advocate applying business principles to the practice of government, but Twain was one of the first writers self-consciously to turn the production of literature into a business enterprise. Adopting a stance of political independence in order to appeal to a national audience, Twain found himself governed by the dictates of the marketplace. Just as Huck's accommodationist streak is at odds with the heroic image of him, so this aspect of Twain is at odds with the, in part self-created, image of him as courageously independent.

Rather than undercut Twain's ideal of mugwumpish independence, however, such a demystified image of Twain catering to the market makes that ideal even more attractive. Indeed, despite Tourgée's attacks on Mugwumps, he could well fit Twain's definition of an independent. Having placed his faith in the partisan politics of the Republican Party only to find it abandoning the cause of rights for, as he put it, dimes and dollars, he became an almost solitary voice within the white community uncompromisingly speaking out for African American rights. If history has closed the book on the morality of slavery, it remains open on how essential the values Twain associates with mugwumpery are for dealing with the country's ongoing politics of race. The citizenly independence Twain celebrated may not be sufficient, in itself, to bring about the racial equality promised by the image of Huck and Jim's friendship on the raft. But, until it is realized, it is hard to imagine people working for it without Huck's ability, occasional as it is, to buck the tide of communal opinion. This despite the fact—or maybe because of the fact—that our imaginations have been conditioned by the most marketable political myth of all: the one of courageously independent citizens making a difference.

☆ ☆ ☆ I have spent considerable time looking at *Huckleberry Finn*'s complicated relation to Twain's mugwumpery and the debate over civil rights at the time of the book's production. It would be a mistake, however, to tie its racial politics to that moment. Its politics have changed as conditions in the country have changed. In fact, as we have seen, its politics changed from the moment of the book's composition to that of its publication because of the intervening decision in the Civil Rights Cases. If Twain had no control over that event, he certainly had no control over events in the future that would continue to alter how the book has been received. This is not to say that attention to complications at the book's moment of production is irrelevant for an understanding of its future reception. On the contrary, the way in which those complications contributed to the book's internal dissonance sets the terms for the changing history of its reception.[116]

For instance, in his careful study of contemporary reviews Mailloux discovered that, despite heated debates about the "race question" and despite the fact that Twain conducted that well-publicized reading tour to promote his new book with Cable, one of the most prominent figures in those debates, no one linked *Huckleberry Finn* to them. Similarly, as we have seen, in 1888 when Tourgée challenged writers to make the condition of blacks in the South the new subject matter of fiction, he faulted literary realists for failing to take up the challenge without even mentioning *Huckleberry Finn*. Ten years later the noted African American classicist W. S. Scarborough mentioned Tourgée, Page, Harris, Cable, Howells, Harriet Beecher Stowe, E. P. Roe, Ruth McEnery Stuart, and Allen Dromgoole in an essay titled "The Negro in Fiction as Portrayer and Portrayed" but did not mention Twain.[117] As late as 1916 Chesnutt made no reference to *Huckleberry Finn* or Twain in "The Negro in Books."[118] Certainly, all three authors knew about Twain. Why, then, did they neglect to comment on that aspect of *Huckleberry Finn* that receives the most attention today: the portrayal of Jim?

The most credible answer to that question is that, for many people, Twain's account of Jim was not all that remarkable. It was not because, as we have seen, *Huckleberry Finn* stresses the need for respectful treatment of African Americans rather than making a case for specific civil rights. If there are good historical reasons for that emphasis, and I think there are, it, nonetheless, helped accommodate the book to an audience that, for the most part, had little enthusiasm for maintaining comprehensive civil rights for African Americans. "Respectful," after all, can mean different things to different people. Even segregationists, like Grady, insisted on treating African Americans with respect. To be sure, the Civil Rights Act of 1875 created a legal standard of "respectful" behavior that they resisted. But the Civil Rights Cases, decided between the time Twain finished his book and the time of its publication, eliminated that awkwardness, as now "respectful" treatment could conform to the law of the land. If today we think that Jim would have won even segregationists' respect because of the minstrel-like characteristics that Twain sometimes gives to him, it is just as likely that he would have won it for his honesty and loyalty, the same characteristics that win him respect from the doctor that treats Tom Sawyer's bullet wound at the end of the book. Jim may not be Uncle Tom, but he is certainly not a threat.

If in the early years of its reception *Huckleberry Finn* was not enlisted in debates about race, it was still controversial. Controversy, however, centered on whether swearing and smoking Huck was a proper model for young boys, and it led to Concord's notorious banning of the book. *Huckleberry Finn* was also controversial in another, less publicized way. A celebrity in his time, Twain was as well known as a comic lecturer as a best-selling author. His reputation as a funny man hindered *Huckleberry Finn*'s ability to be recognized as a great work of literature. As Jay B. Hubbell notes, "Until after the end of the century few of the literary historians recognized Twain as a major American writer."[119] To be sure, some, like Barrett Wendall of Harvard and Brander Matthews of Columbia, followed Howells and celebrated the book's literary merits. But not until 1921 did *Huckleberry Finn* achieve "official sanction" with Carl Van Doren's ranking of it along with *The Scarlet Letter* as the greatest of American novels and with Stuart P. Sherman's adulatory chapter on Twain in *The Cambridge History of American Literature*. Its canonization, if not its hypercanonization, was sealed with the massive praise by DeVoto and Hemingway in the 1930s, although even then Twain's comic reputation plagued him, as some critics followed Van Wyck Brooks's 1920 judgment that, whereas he was a masterful humorist, Twain lacked the moral seriousness of the great satirists writing in English, such as Swift. Variations of this judgment persist, most prominently in the debate over whether Twain's reliance on slapstick humor in the scene in which Tom and Huck help Jim escape from Phelps's farm botches the ending, but also in Arac's claim that *Huckleberry Finn* is a wonderfully funny book, even if not a nationally representative one.[120]

Within the context of these various debates over the book, the controversy over race came only *after* it had achieved canonical status. We can trace different stages of that debate by looking at responses by some African American writers. When Twain died in 1910, the focus was so much on the antics of Huck and Tom that Booker T. Washington felt compelled to remark, "It is possible that the ordinary reader of this story has been so absorbed in the adventures of the two white boys that he did not think much about the part that 'Jim' . . . played in all these adventures. . . . I cannot help feeling that in [Jim] Mark Twain has, perhaps unconsciously, exhibited his sympathy and interest in the masses of the negro people."[121] When the civil rights movement of the twentieth century began to stir, the situation changed. By 1937 black author and critic Sterling Brown provided a more forceful reading of Twain's book. "In *Huckleberry Finn* (1884) the callousness of the South to the Negro is," Brown notes, "indicated briefly, without preaching, but impellingly. . . . Jim is the best example in nineteenth century fiction of the average Negro slave (not the tragic mulatto or the nobel savage) . . . clinging to his hope for freedom and completely believable."[122] With Jim Crow laws increasingly attacked as disrespectful, the book's message for the respectful treatment of blacks began to read as a protest against legalized segregation. It is at this time that chapter 31 takes center stage in readings of the book.

In the post–civil rights era, with the Civil Rights Act of 1964 on the books, the definition of respectful treatment changed yet again, with many arguing that Twain's use of racial epithets and caricatures is anything but respectful. Ralph Ellison's complicated response to the book, praising it while noting its racial stereotypes, marks the transition from the civil rights era to the post–civil rights era.[123] Developing at that time, the Black Power movement and its emphasis on black agency highlighted Jim's frequent lack of it. If the resolution of Huck's moral crisis in chapter 31 appealed to many white readers, it too easily affirmed the view in the 1940s and 1950s that combating racial oppression was "a test of white morality, a matter of individual conscience rather than of social structure."[124] As Arthur Schlesinger Jr. put it in 1949, "The sin of racial pride still represents the most basic challenge to the American conscience. We cannot dodge the challenge without renouncing our highest moral principles." Schlesinger's "we" is clearly coded "white," just as Gunnar Myrdal's extremely influential study of race, *An American Dilemma* (1944), described primarily a white dilemma.[125]

Equally important, as Schudson argues, the legal successes of the civil rights movement helped the rights-bearing model of citizenship gain increased prominence. Making the "polling place less clearly the central act of political participation" by diffusing "the political" into "everyday life,"[126] the rights-bearing model has gone hand in hand with increased attention to "cultural politics," including the politics of *Huckleberry Finn's* representations of race. Indeed, insofar as one of the rights afforded to each citizen is assumed to be the right to an ethnic identity, an important role of literature, it can be argued, becomes its ability to promote that identity. As Arac puts it, "If civil rights mean anything, shouldn't it mean that African Americans ought to have a real voice in public definitions of what counts as a model of enlightened race relations?"[127]

The history of *Huckleberry Finn's* reception that I have sketched is, like the book itself, full of ironies. For instance, today's attacks on *Huckleberry Finn*, at least in part, result from the very civil rights movement that helped lead to its hypercanonization, since without integrated classrooms there would be much less controversy about the book's representation of blacks.[128] Similarly, if, at the time of *Huckleberry Finn's* production, the Supreme Court had decided the Civil Rights Cases differently, the civil rights movement itself would have been very different. To be sure, powerful forms of de facto segregation would probably have persisted, just as they do today. But protests would not have manifested themselves in acts of civil disobedience. On the contrary, protesters would have insisted—as supporters of black rights did in the seven-year period in which Twain wrote—that people's private consciences conform to the law. In that context, it is unlikely that chapter 31 would have been praised in the same way it has been.

But the most telling irony about *Huckleberry Finn*'s reception—one that reminds us of the contingent nature of literary reputations and politics—has to do with what I have been calling the book's accommodationist streak. If that streak kept it from making as strong a case for African American civil rights as Douglass's, Cable's, and Tourgée's principled but partisan works, it also helped it do progressive political work in the future. Only because *Huckleberry Finn* had the capacity to appear independent from the partisan politics of its moment of production was it able to accrue the cultural capital that allowed it later to be enlisted in the twentieth-century fight for civil rights. Within the history I have outlined, therefore, it is not at all surprising that, once that legal struggle was won, *Huckleberry Finn* began to be attacked. After all, there is a certain appropriateness in the fact that, written at a time when the country rejected the rights-bearing model, it is now the object of attack by many embracing that model. Indeed, it is not too much of an exaggeration to claim that today's controversies about the book are frequently between those honoring the values of the independent citizen and those advocating the values of the rights-bearing citizen.

That much said, the question still remains: How did *Huckleberry Finn* accrue the cultural capital it did? If there is no easy answer to that question, we can get a sense of the conditions that helped make Twain's masterpiece a national, rather than a regional, work by returning to where we started: Howells's comparison of Twain to Lincoln.

☆ ☆ ☆ Although Howells's 1910 comparison is the one remembered today, it was not the only one he made between Twain and Lincoln. Writing an appreciation for the *Century* in 1882, he compared Twain to Grant as well as to Lincoln. "Mark Twain's humor," he claims, "is as simple in form and as direct as the statesmanship of Lincoln or the generalship of Grant."[129] In 1901 Howells again evoked both Lincoln and Grant, but the comparison had become much more complicated, in part because in the interim Twain had published Grant's *Memoirs*. No longer about statesmanship or generalship, it is now about how Twain uses words as "single-mindedly as Grant did to express the plain, straight meaning their common acceptance has given them with no regard to their structural significance or their philological implication." Just as Grant's straightforward military tactics are expressed in his language—and vice versa—so Howells implies that Twain's use of language is also linked to a particular way of conducting affairs of state—a particularly American way. The focus on language allows Howells to make a case for Twain as a great literary artist, not simply a humorist. In fact, Twain is an exceptional artist *because* his language has more in common with the language of two of the great political leaders of the country than with that of its best artists. Twain, Howells goes on,

writes English as if it were a primitive and not a derivative language, without Gothic or Latin or Greek behind it, or German and French beside it. The result is the English in which the most vital works of English literature are cast, rather than the English of Milton and Thackeray and Mr. Henry James. I do not say that the English of the authors last named is less than vital, but only that it is not the most vital. It is scholarly and conscious; it knows who its grandfather was; it has the refinement and subtlety of an old patriciate. You will not have with it the widest suggestion, the largest human feeling, or perhaps the loftiest reach of imagination, but you will have the keen joy that exquisite artistry in words can alone impart, and that you will not have in Mark Twain. What you will have in him is a style which is as personal, as biographical as the style of any one who has written, and expresses a civilization whose courage of the chances, the preferences, the duties, is not the measure of its essential modesty. It has a thing to say, and it says it in the word that may be the first or second or third choice, but will not be the instrument of the most fastidious ear, the most delicate and exacting sense, though it will be the word that surely and strongly conveys intention from the author's mind to the reader's. It is the Abraham Lincolnian word, not the Charles Sumnerian; it is American, Western.[130]

Howells's description of Twain's language as if it were primitive rather than derivative prepares the way for Hemingway's famous claim that all modern American literature derives from *Huckleberry Finn*. Prior to Twain, Hemingway claims, there was "Emerson, Hawthorne, Whittier, and Company," who "did not know that a new classic does not bear any resemblance to the classics that have preceded it." Writing "like exiled English colonials from an England of which they were never a part to a newer England that they were making," they "did not use the words that people always have used in speech, the words that survive in language." There was also Melville, a "writer of rhetoric," who is praised for his rhetoric, "which is not important." Unlike Melville, Twain does not wrap knowledge in "rhetoric like plums in a pudding."[131] Indeed, as Howells already claimed in 1901, Twain's "great charm is his absolute freedom in a region where most of us are fettered and shackled by immemorial convention. He saunters into the trim world of letters, and lounges across its neatly kept paths, and walks about on the grass at will, in spite of all the signs that have been put up from the beginning of literature, warning people of dangers and penalties for the slightest trespass."[132]

Contrasted to the patrician style of Milton, Thackeray, and Henry James, Twain's emancipatory style is a democratic one, a point Howells makes by moving Twain from the company of a politician to that of literary figures and then back to that of politicians. He ends, however, not with Grant but with Lincoln, a western American who is in turn contrasted with Charles Sumner. If we want to understand some of the forces at play helping *Huckleberry Finn* "[express] a civilization" through a "word" that is "American, Western," we need to understand the significance that both Grant and Sumner played in the 1901 comparison and why it is important that neither is mentioned in the famous 1910 comparison.

In 1882, when Howells and Twain were both loyal Republicans, the coupling of Grant and Lincoln would have been natural. Even after Twain's defection from the Republican Party in 1884, Grant was an obvious figure of comparison because of Twain's publication of his *Memoirs*. Nonetheless, for Twain to be recognized, as Howells recognizes him, as "entirely American"[133] and not a Scalawag, comparisons with Grant would have to go—not because of Grant's role in the Civil War, which Southerners had forgiven especially because of the image of his honorable handshake with Lee, but because of his presidency during Reconstruction.

In contrast, if Grant could never be completely forgiven, Lincoln, in part because of his death and in part because of beliefs he actually held, was seen by many Southerners as someone who would have saved them from the dishonor of Reconstruction. In Thomas Dixon's *The Clansman*, for instance, Lincoln sympathizes with the defeated South and resists efforts at Radical Reconstruction.[134] When D. W. Griffith brings Dixon's novel to the screen in *Birth of a Nation*, the newspaper announcing Lincoln's assassination is called the *New South*. Appropriately, in his speech to the New England Society of New York called "The New South," Henry Grady drew on Lincoln's western origins to anoint him the "first typical American," one who unites "Puritans and Cavaliers."[135] Grady was not the only one identifying the West as a place to reconcile sectional conflict between North and South. Frederick Jackson Turner's famous "frontier thesis" also saw the West as a place where people from different backgrounds melted together to become Americans.

Speaking of Lincoln in 1901, Twain himself sounds more than a little like Grady. As chairman of the celebration of Lincoln's ninety-second birthday in New York, Twain identified himself as a Southerner who had fought for the Confederacy. Quoting the Gettysburg Address to make the dead refer to those of both North and South, he tells his Northern audience, "The old wounds are healed. You and we are brothers again." Jointly to honor Lincoln, "the greatest citizen, and the noblest and best after Washington, that this land or any other has yet produced," was to let Northerners and Southerners forget that they were "ever enemies" and remember that "we are indistinguishably fused together and nameable by one common great name—Americans."[136]

Sumner could never have performed the same reconciliatory function. The father of the Civil Rights Act of 1875, he had helped to sponsor much Reconstruction legislation. To be sure, some Southerners, if not all, showed him great respect, due in part to guilt over the horrible beating inflicted upon him in the Senate chambers in 1856 by South Carolina representative Preston Brooks, but mostly due to his great sense of honor. Whereas other Radical Republicans were thought to be motivated by a spirit of revenge, Sumner in 1872 had risked displeasure in his home state of Massachusetts by unsuccessfully trying to pass a bill designed to ease memories of the recent conflict by erasing the names of Civil War battles from the Army Register and from the regimental colors of the United States. What betrayed Sumner, Southerners felt, was not his honor but a false sense of idealism. Misguided as Sumner's brand of idealism was, Southerners praised his devotion to principles, as Senator L. Q. C. Lamar had done in a stirring eulogy. One characteristic that united Horace-quoting Lamar and Sumner was their mastery of classical oratory.

It is Sumner's reputation as a model of Ciceronian rhetoric that most obviously accounts for Howells's contrast between him and Lincoln. Even so, the Charles Sumnerian "word" carried with it implications far beyond those of a particular brand of rhetoric. First, it implied a noble but outdated republicanism shared by advocates of both old North and old South, which had been supplanted by the new American style of the West, the style of both Lincoln and Twain. Second, it connoted a false idealism, especially in matters of race. For instance, in his infamous opinion in *Plessy v. Ferguson* (1896) Justice Henry Billings Brown went out of his way to interrupt a quotation from the antebellum Massachusetts case of *Roberts v. Board of Education*, in which Chief Justice Lemuel Shaw (Melville's father-in-law) established a precedent for separate but equal schools, to insert parenthetically Sumner's name and to identify him as the attorney for the black plaintiff.[137] Since at the turn of the century Sumner's idealism was epitomized by his efforts to ban segregated schools, Brown's allusion helped to establish the *Plessy* decision as a realistic solution to the "race problem," a solution endorsed by most of the country North and South, if not by Sumner's biographer, onetime Mugwump Moorfield Storey.

Storey, as we have seen, like Twain, was a Mugwump, one who reassessed his 1884 trust in the educated South to treat blacks fairly and became the first president of the NAACP, an organization founded by W. E. B. Du Bois and others the same year that Twain died and Howells made his famous comparison between him and Lincoln. The NAACP grew out of a national conference of concerned citizens that gave special honor to the memories of William Lloyd Garrison, Tourgée, and Douglass, Sumner's trusted friend. In identifying with Sumner, Storey made a clear statement about his commitment to renew the struggle for civil and political liberty. From our present perspective it makes perfect sense that the NAACP's founders would also have associated themselves with Lincoln, as they did by calling for their conference on February 12, 1909, the one-hundredth anniversary of his birthday. Indeed, far overshadowing figures like Sumner and Tourgée, unknown to many Americans today, Lincoln is the most important figure in the national narrative that establishes a continuity between efforts to abolish slavery and the civil rights movement of the twentieth century. But if the appropriation of Lincoln's prestige by the founders of the NAACP has largely succeeded today, the situation in 1910 was quite different. For instance, that year saw publication of a revised edition of James Bryce's Mugwump-influenced *The American Commonwealth*, which first appeared in 1888. Including new chapters on "the Negro Problem," Bryce favorably quoted Grady, whom he described as a "brilliant Southerner," while noting skeptically Du Bois's impatient efforts at political organization.[138] A year earlier he had published the third in an annual series of Yale Lectures on Responsibilities of Citizenship. Stressing the importance of "the principle of Independence," he listed as major hindrances to good citizenship indolence, private self-interest, and party spirit. In his conclusion, describing how to overcome these obstacles, he turned to Lincoln, who by his example and words as well as by "the quiet patience, dignity, and hopefulness which he showed in the darkest hours" inspired citizens to appeal to "their best interests."[139] Lincoln, the Great Emancipator, is not mentioned.

Thus, it should come as no surprise to learn that, when Chesnutt gave a speech in 1913 enlisting Lincoln for the cause of civil rights, he had to insist that the great man's finest achievement was the abolition of slavery. He needed to stress that point because "in the modern era of harmony and good feeling, as the result of which no painting of a Civil War battle is allowed in the National Capital, this service of Lincoln for humanity has been minimized and sometimes slurred." Indeed, "it was pitiable how little was said, in the late Lincoln Centennial celebration, about Lincoln the Emancipator. Perhaps this was inevitable, because to give emancipation its proper importance it would be necessary to properly characterize slavery, and to do this would be, by implication, to criticize the slave-holder, and in our time this is not considered good taste. So warm has become the *rapprochement* between North and South, that slavery is almost regarded in some quarters as a beneficent patriarchal institution, which *Uncle Tom's Cabin* grossly slandered."[140]

In light of Chesnutt's remarks, it is clear that Twain's portrayal of slavery in *Huckleberry Finn* could have had a potentially positive effect even at the time of his death. And there is no doubt that he sympathized with many of the goals of the NAACP. Thus it makes sense that in the national narrative that establishes the continuity between efforts to abolish slavery and the civil rights movement, he occupies, for many, the same position of importance as a writer as Lincoln does as a politician, a similarity generated and reinforced by Howells's famous comparison. Ironically, however, when Howells made that comparison, it had the power to help establish Twain as a writer identified with the nation only because in most people's minds Lincoln was not identified primarily as the Great Emancipator but as the great reconciler of North and South.

Twain's complex relation to the struggle for civil rights is illustrated by the combined facts that the NAACP's first major campaign was against lynching and that Twain, as we have seen, had already produced a manuscript about its horrors. But, as we have also seen, Twain agreed to suppress his manuscript until after his death, most likely because its publication would have hurt the national sales of his other books. Similarly, as Howells sensed, in order for his "my" Mark Twain to become the "our" Mark Twain of the nation, Twain had to be distanced from Sumner, although he would continue to be well served by a comparison to Lincoln, who represented so many things to so many people while embodying for all of them the value of honest independence.

If, at the time of Twain's death, Lincoln was admired by most for an independent cast of mind that, overcoming partisan bickering, could have united North and South, he was also available, not without reason, to be evoked as a hero for the civil rights movement. Similarly, Twain, that Southerner who lived much of his life in the North while being identified with the West and the American spirit, was also available, not without reason, to be enlisted in the fight against racism—so much so that Howells's famous comparison of politician and writer goes in two directions, not just one. For instance, in order to emphasize how Lincoln effected a revolution in style in political language, Garry Wills evokes Hemingway's praise of *Huckleberry Finn*. "It is," he asserts, "no greater exaggeration to say that all modern political prose descends from the Gettysburg Address." Intent on showing how "Lincoln's Address created a political prose in America . . . to rank with the vernacular excellence of Twain," Wills gauges Lincoln's excellence by measuring him against Twain's standards for the effective use of words. Most important, citing a passage from *Huckleberry Finn*, he concludes that "Lincoln and Twain both knew how to sneak around the frontal defenses of prejudice and find a back way into agreement with bigots."[141]

The agreement both Lincoln and Twain found with bigots has raised reasonable questions about their commitment to civil rights. Nonetheless, we are still left with undeniable evidence of the effect their most memorable words have had on the nation. Celebrating independence while suggesting its limits, combining the values of a Mugwump with those of a Scalawag, making a populist appeal that only isolated members of the populace can fulfill, *Huckleberry Finn* has added to the nation's civic consciousness an unforgettable image of a white boy and a black man floating through the nation's heartland. A community of saints Trilling called them, a community whose utopian promise of racial equality Twain cannot imagine within the legal order of civil society. And yet, precisely for that reason, those working for its realization still have much to learn from Twain's novel understood in relation to the country's still-incomplete history of civil rights.

6 ☆ China Men

The Immigrant Citizen,
Wong Kim Ark, and
Civil Talk

In *China Men* Maxine Hong Kingston accomplishes the difficult task of honoring her male ancestors at the same time that she challenges their patriarchal customs.[1] Celebrating those ancestors' imaginative and physical efforts to establish and transform a new home despite resistance to their presence, *China Men* is part autobiography; part retold and altered Chinese and European myths, legends, and works of fiction; and part legal chronicle. Indeed, the book's middle chapter is called "The Laws." Summarizing legislation and court decisions that have affected persons of Chinese descent living in the United States, this chapter complicates the already complicated effort to determine the genre of a book that self-consciously resists preset categories. Not knowing quite what to do with Kingston's second book, the publishers label it "Nonfiction/Literature." One blurb on the paperback cover calls it "a history," and libraries comply by placing it with other historical accounts of the Chinese American experience. But another blurb says that the book consists of "the myths and stories that emerge from the lode of a culture's deepest realities." This defiance of easy generic classification is appropriate for a book illustrating the dangers of fixing people's identities.

The location of "The Laws" at the book's formal center is not accidental. Laws, Kingston implies, played a central role in Chinese immigrants' experience of Americanization. For instance, prior to "The Laws" we have a chapter called "The Father from China," and after it we have one called "The American Father," a reminder that the father from China has to negotiate the complicated field of American laws to become an American father. That was not an easy task. For instance, "The Laws" describes harsh and discriminatory provisions against Chinese in the 1879 California constitution, the notorious Chinese Exclusion Act of 1882, and its various extensions. Measures such as these drastically determined and limited possibilities for Chinese in America. Even so, Kingston's chronicle also makes clear that Chinese immigrants were determined not to have their lives completely determined by unfair laws. Not simply victims, they appropriated the legal system's egalitarian promise to find ways to protect rather than to abridge their rights.

Thus, in the midst of listing various repressive laws, Kingston also records "a victory. In *Yick Wo v. Hopkins*, the U.S. Supreme Court overturned San Francisco safety ordinances, saying that they were designed to harass laundrymen of Chinese ancestry."[2] In such victories, the Chinese did more than advance their own cause; they changed how the legal system affected all Americans. *Yick Wo*, for instance, rules that if discriminatory intent can be inferred from unfair administration, a law that appears fair can, in fact, be unconstitutional. As a result, the NAACP included *Yick Wo* as part of its legal strategy to end segregation. If *Yick Wo* is an important case, the second victory Kingston lists is even more important. Under the year 1898, we learn of "another victory. The Supreme Court decision in *The United States v. Wong Kim Ark* stated that a person born in the United States to Chinese parents is an American. The decision has never been reversed or changed, and it is the law on which most Americans of Chinese ancestry base their citizenship today" (155–56).

This chapter looks at both this 1898 Supreme Court case and Kingston's 1980 work of the literary imagination. To bring the two together is to offer an understanding of a potential within U.S. citizenship that we would not get if they were kept apart. I will start with an extended discussion of *Wong Kim Ark* and end with *China Men*, since Kingston's vision of citizenship in part depends upon conditions made possible by the legal case — but only in part, because as important as the results of *Wong Kim Ark* are, they are limited. For instance, no formal legal definition can ultimately determine what the nature of citizen participation in civic life will be. Obviously, works of the imagination, like Kingston's, cannot either. Nonetheless, insofar as politics is, as Aristotle called it, the art of the possible, imaginative visions like hers have a crucial role to play in our understanding of possibilities contained in the notion of citizenship.

To be sure, laws, such as those concerned with voting rights, can enhance possibilities for active citizenly participation. Furthermore, almost every court decision concerning citizenship implies at least a minimal vision of what it entails. *Wong Kim Ark*, for instance, refuses to base citizenship by birth on racial descent. In doing so it highlights a special feature of *China Men*, a book about Kingston's descent that refuses to endorse a determination of citizenship by descent. Kingston pulls off that difficult feat by working on/with myths of the nation's founding fathers as well as the myths of her ancestral fathers. If, as Gary Jacobsohn has argued, "American citizenship is a source of identity as well as rights," Kingston imagines a continually reconstructed sense of "We, the People" through a dynamic interaction among citizens that acknowledges the importance of one's ethnic heritage without concluding that it ultimately determines one's identity.[3] Such a civic vision requires, in Kingston's world, the capacity for civil talk among citizens and groups of citizens.

☆ ☆ ☆ There is a long tradition of nativism in the United States hostile to all sorts of immigrant groups. In the antebellum period much of that hostility was directed against the Irish. In the late nineteenth century it was directed against immigrants from southern and eastern Europe as well as the Chinese. For instance, in "Unguarded Gates" (1892), Thomas Bailey Aldrich, editor of the *Atlantic Monthly*, decries a "wild and motley throng" that "presses" through the country's "wide open and unguarded gates," by naming "men from the Volga and Tartar steppes . . . Malayan, Scythian, Teuton, Kelt, and Slav," along with the "featureless figures of the Hoang-Ho."[4] At the time, however, Congress passed exclusion acts against only the Chinese.

As Erika Lee and Mae Ngai have recently shown, efforts to exclude the Chinese led to the development of the Immigration and Naturalization Service (INS), a large and powerful governmental bureaucracy designed to police immigration, as well as the need for visas, passports, alien registration cards, and documents deemed necessary to distinguish between legal and illegal immigrants. In turn, pressure to deport illegal immigrants added to the INS's gatekeeping responsibilities the power to patrol immigrant communities in search of illegals while giving immigration officials a measure of judicial authority over cases once reserved for federal courts, which tended to be more sympathetic to the plight of immigrants. Finally, even if, with the 1924 Johnson-Reed Act, Congress dramatically limited European immigration, those limits were based on national origin, whereas Chinese were limited as a race.[5]

When an ethnic Chinese born in Hong Kong claimed exemption from the 1882 Exclusion Act because he was a British subject, not a subject of China, an 1883 circuit case denied his claim by declaring that the act was intended to exclude laborers of the Chinese race, no matter what their nationality.[6] Indeed, by 1917 Congress barred all natives of the "Asiatic zone," stretching from Afghanistan to Japan, creating a composite group that continues to determine how Asian Americans are legally defined. Persisting today, the tendency to think of illegal immigration in racial terms originated with the 1882 act. It is within this context that we need to understand the case of Wong Kim Ark.

There are two ways to become a citizen: by birth or by naturalization. Birthright citizenship is determined by the Fourteen Amendment; Congress decides who can be naturalized. The first Naturalization Act of 1790 restricted the right to "any alien, being a free white person."[7] Although the act was modified at various times, that language remained through the Civil War. But in 1870 the right was extended to "aliens of African nativity, and to persons of African descent."[8] During congressional debate, Charles Sumner, with Chinese and other Asians clearly in mind, had proposed removing the word "white" from all acts pertaining to naturalization. But his proposal and another by Lyman Trumbull failed. Thus, the 1870 act did not open up naturalization for persons of Asian descent. Nonetheless, they would still seem to be eligible for birthright citizenship under the Fourteenth Amendment.

The citizenship clause of the Fourteenth Amendment states, "All persons born or naturalized in the United States, and subject to the jurisdiction thereof, are citizens of the United States and of the State wherein they reside." As we saw in Chapter 4, this clause was necessitated by Justice Taney's infamous opinion in *Dred Scott v. Sandford* (1857) that placed the power of the federal government squarely behind the institution of slavery. Scott, a slave, argued that he had become free when his master took him into a free territory. One issue facing the Court was whether he had the right to bring suit, a right often reserved for citizens. As a result, Taney made some of the Supreme Court's first rulings on citizenship, a concept contained but not defined in the Constitution.

Working within what sounds like an egalitarian framework, Taney argued that "the words 'people of the United States,' and 'citizens,' are synonymous terms, and mean the same thing. They both describe the political body, who, according to our republican institutions, form the sovereignty, and who hold the power and conduct the government through their representatives. They are what we familiarly call the 'sovereign people,' and every citizen is one of this people, and a constituent member of this sovereignty."[9] If Taney's definition confirmed the republican belief that "the people" consists of only one class of citizens, he used it to deny citizenship to free blacks as well as slaves. Since there is only one class of citizens, he argued, the "deep and enduring marks of inferiority and degradation" implanted on blacks excluded them from the community that originally constituted the sovereign people of the nation.[10]

The citizenship clause of the Fourteenth Amendment was designed to nullify Taney's ruling. Not specifically mentioning African Americans, it nonetheless guaranteed them both U.S. and state citizenship. That is because almost all persons of African descent living in the United States in 1868 had been born there. At the same time, the clause's general language would seem to apply to everyone, including those of Chinese descent. That assumption was challenged, however, when the government denied Wong Kim Ark citizenship.[11]

Wong Kim Ark was born in San Francisco in 1873 to Chinese parents legally in the United States who, nonetheless, by U.S. law could not become naturalized citizens. When his parents moved back to China in 1890, Wong Kim Ark visited them, returning to San Francisco on July 26, 1890. Despite the 1882 Exclusion Act, collector Timothy Phelps admitted him as a citizen. In 1894 he again visited China. Returning in August 1895, he was denied entrance by the anti-Chinese collector John H. Wise, who claimed that, because he was not a citizen, the existing Chinese exclusion act applied. Wong Kim Ark hired prominent attorney Thomas Riordon, who claimed that Wong Kim Ark was a citizen by birth under the citizenship clause of the Fourteenth Amendment. In contrast, U.S. District Attorney Henry S. Foote argued that someone born in the United States of Chinese parents was a subject of China, not a citizen of the United States.

Wong Kim Ark was in part a victim of political pressure. Elected president again in 1892, Grover Cleveland relied on the support of Democratic labor unions that were notoriously anti-Chinese. Indeed, earlier in the year they had helped push through the Geary Act, officially listed as "an act to prohibit the coming of Chinese persons into the United States."[12] It extended the 1882 Exclusion Act and, for the first time, made illicit residence a federal crime, punishable by a year's imprisonment at hard labor *before* deportation. It also created the first internal passport system in the United States requiring Chinese laborers legally here to carry identity cards. An early version of the act required photographic identity, but because of protests from, among others, Tsui Kuo-yin, China's minister to the United States, this requirement was removed. Nonetheless, a year later it was reinstated in an amended bill, bringing about the first widespread use of this new technology for such purposes.[13] While the bill, still containing the photographic requirement, was debated, Congressman Thomas Geary of California defended it with pro-labor and xenophobic defenses of citizenship that anti-immigrant sentiment often unleashes.[14]

Responding to critics' claims that requiring photo identity cards was degrading, Geary proclaimed, "Such an argument is unworthy of notice.

From the resemblance which all Chinamen bear to one another no other means of identifying them than by photograph could be selected."[15] In fact, he argued, identity cards and their accompanying papers benefited the legal immigrant by giving him, "under the seal of government, a justification for his presence, and the written testimony always with him to free himself from this inconvenience and annoyance, while his right to remain could only be questioned and the production of his certificate required by a regularly appointed federal officer, who we cannot presume would use his position to violate the spirit of the law or harass and annoy."[16] Dismissing the complaint that a law virtually excluding an entire group of people from the country was unfair, Geary, waxing eloquent, appealed to the importance of citizenship.

Some people will condemn all restriction laws, because from the fatherhood-of-God and brotherhood-of-man standpoint, all men being equal, all men should be permitted the same degree of freedom and liberty in the practice of their trades and callings, and in the enjoyment of whatever fruits may come to them from their own industry, and all laws that interfere with the individual man, restricting his opportunities, or denying him the right to enjoy life and liberty, must be condemned by humanitarians and Christians. But this beautiful sentiment finds no application in the exercise of governmental powers, because the first duty of governments is to their own citizens, and in securing to them the protection and the enjoyment of their life and liberty the consideration of the effect on other people is not of consequence.[17]

If similar sentiments could be marshaled against immigrants in general, Geary argued that the Chinese were different from other immigrant groups because of their vast numbers and ways of life.

The Chinese laborer brings here no wife and children, and his wants are limited to the immediate necessities of the individual, while the American is compelled to earn income sufficient to maintain the wife and babies. There can be but one end to this. If this immigration is permitted to continue American labor must surely be reduced to the level of the Chinese competitor, the American's wants measured by his wants, the American's comforts no greater than the comforts of the Chinaman, and the American laborer not having been educated to maintain himself according to this standard, must either go down into a darkness too gloomy to contemplate, or else take up his pack and leave his native land. The protection of American labor is an essential duty of the American Government; and protection against such competition is not only advisable but necessary, if we wish to continue the government we now have.[18]

Highlighting the always present danger of the need to define the citizen against the noncitizen, Geary's bill helped create new and important legal consequences based on that distinction. The Chinese challenged the act's constitutionality, claiming that its procedures for deportation denied immigrants due process as guaranteed by the Fifth Amendment. But a divided Supreme Court ruled that, as aliens, Chinese did not have the same Fifth Amendment rights as citizens. While in the United States, aliens were entitled "to the safeguards of the Constitution, and to the protection of the laws, in regards to the rights of person and property, and to their civil and criminal responsibility," but Chinese laborers, as denizens or otherwise, had no right "to be or remain in this country, except by the license, permission, and sufferance of Congress."[19] Thus, if Congress decided to remove them, they had no recourse to constitutional protections. As Justice Brewer warned in dissent, that ruling would apply to all aliens, not just Chinese. As a result, "the case established the basic principle that would distinguish immigration law from other branches of administrative law: aliens might have privileges, but, unlike citizens, they could not invoke the specific rights protected by the Bill of Rights against the government in administrative proceedings."[20]

In making these distinctions between citizens and aliens, the Geary Act shows why it is so important not to deny the benefits of citizenship to any particular group. Indeed, Geary's ultimate goal was not simply to protect American workers by restricting immigration; it was to make sure that Chinese did not become citizens. To grant Wong Kim Ark citizenship simply because he was born here would mean that children born to other Chinese in the country would become citizens and thus part of the group Geary, at least in theory, defended. This concern, as much as the often-cited fears of prostitution, accounts for why, under their provisions, the exclusion acts made it even more difficult for Chinese women to enter the country than for Chinese men, a point that Geary did not mention when he lamented the fact that the "Chinese laborer brings here no wife and children."[21] Combined with antimiscegenation laws, the exclusion acts aimed at eliminating Chinese from the country. To grant one Chinese citizenship would threaten that goal and, according to many, threaten U.S. citizenship itself.

Arguing the case against Wong Kim Ark in the U.S. District Court for the Northern District of California in 1895, Foote claimed that "to force upon us as natural born citizens, persons who must necessarily be a constant menace to the welfare of our Country," would imperil the "very existence of our Country."[22] Foote lost his argument when Judge William Morrow, relying on the 1884 circuit court decision of *In re Look Tin Sing*, ruled for Wong Kim Ark, "It is enough that he is born here whatever the status of his parents."[23] But when the case was appealed to the Supreme Court, George D. Collins, a San Francisco lawyer who filed an amicus curiae brief supporting the U.S. government, made an even stronger argument than Foote had by appealing to the myth of the founding fathers.

There certainly should be some honor and dignity in American citizenship that would be sacred from the foul and corrupting taint of a debasing alienage. Are Chinese born in this country to share with the descendants of the patriots of the American Revolution the exalted qualification of being eligible for the Presidency of the nation, conferred by the Constitution in recognition of the importance and dignity of citizenship by birth? If so, then verily there has been a most degenerate departure from the patriotic ideals of our forefathers; and surely in that case American citizenship is not worth having.[24]

With the Cleveland administration and the Democratic regime in California under fire for failing to enforce rigidly the almost unenforceable Geary Act, the government's refusal to grant Wong Kim Ark citizenship helped rally waning political support. Indeed, if Homer Plessy's now famous case received little attention when it was argued before the Supreme Court in 1896, Wong Kim Ark's now largely forgotten case received wide attention as it came before the Court in 1898.[25] In a six-to-two decision the Court ruled in Wong Kim Ark's favor. The case turned on interpretation of the citizenship clause's phrase "subject to the jurisdiction thereof." Was jurisdiction territorial or national?

Wong Kim Ark claimed that it was territorial, that because anyone within the territorial limits of the United States is subject to its jurisdiction, anyone born within those limits is a citizen. The government disagreed. If birthright citizenship were defined territorially, it argued, the phrase "subject to the jurisdiction thereof" would be unnecessary, since it would mean the same thing as "born or naturalized in the United States." Instead, the phrase should be defined nationally, since even when citizens or subjects of a country are outside its territorial limits, they are still subject to its jurisdiction. Indeed, when a U.S. couple outside the country gives birth to a child, the government reasoned, the child is a U.S. citizen because it, like its parents, is assumed to be under U.S. jurisdiction. Similarly, when a child of Chinese parents is born in the United States, it, like its parents, should be subject to Chinese jurisdiction and thus become a Chinese subject. The issue facing the Court was Does the United States determine citizenship by birth according to *jus soli* (by soil) or *jus sanguinis* (by blood)? Thirty years after the amendment's enactment, the Court finally had to rule on how to interpret one of its crucial phrases.

Writing for the six-judge majority, Justice Horace Gray began by noting that the Constitution uses but does not define the terms "citizen of the United States" and "natural-born citizen of the United States." As a result, following the Court in *Minor v. Happersett* (1875), he turned to the common law. Operating according to *jus soli*, English common law had been definitively established by Justice Edward Coke's 1608 ruling in *Calvin's Case*, which declared that all children born within the king's realm were subjects of the king.[26] There were, to be sure, some exceptions, such as persons born to foreign ambassadors or to alien enemies occupying part of the king's dominions, since such children could not be said to be "born within the allegiance, the obedience, or the power, or, as would be said at this day, within the jurisdiction of the King."[27] Common-law doctrine, Gray asserted, was adopted by the United States. The Fourteenth Amendment did not change that situation; it merely reaffirmed it in such a way as to overturn Taney's *Dred Scott* ruling that limited U.S. citizenship to whites. The phrase "subject to the jurisdiction thereof" was included for two reasons. First, it emphasized the common-law exceptions of children of ambassadors and occupying armies. Second, it excluded "children of members of the Indian tribes, standing in a peculiar relation to the National Government, unknown to the common law" (682). The latter was ruled upon by the Court in *Elk v. Wilkins* (1884), the first case that substantively interpreted the phrase in question.

The case resulted when John Elk, an American Indian, renounced his tribal loyalty and claimed American citizenship under the Fourteenth Amendment. Writing for a seven-to-two majority, Justice Gray denied his claim, arguing that although loyal members of Indian tribes are in a "geographical sense born in the United States," they are "no more 'born in the United States and subject to the jurisdiction thereof,' within the meaning of the first section of the Fourteenth Amendment, than the children of subjects of any foreign government born within the domain of that government, or the children born within the United States, of ambassadors or other public ministers of foreign nations."[28] As a result, even though Elk had renounced his tribal loyalty, he could not claim automatic citizenship at birth. The only way for him to become a citizen, therefore, was through naturalization.

But American Indians were a special case.[29] To confirm his argument that the phrase "subject to the jurisdiction thereof" should be read territorially, Gray pointed to the final clause of Section 1 of the Fourteenth Amendment: the equal protection clause, which declares that no state shall "deny to any person within its jurisdiction the equal protection of the laws." "It is impossible," Gray wrote, "to construe the words 'subject to the jurisdiction thereof,' in the opening sentence as less comprehensive than the words 'within its jurisdiction,' in the concluding sentence of the same section: or to hold that persons 'within the jurisdiction' of one of the States of the Union are not 'subject to the jurisdiction of the United States'" (687).

Ending his argument for a territorial interpretation, Gray contended that an interpretation excluding children born to aliens within the United States from the jurisdiction of the United States would "deny citizenship to thousands of persons of English, Scotch, Irish, German, or other European parentage, who have always been considered and treated as citizens of the United States" (694). The only remaining question for the Court to decide, he declared, was whether the citizenship clause applied to Chinese as well. Citing a number of Supreme Court cases involving Chinese, he concluded that "Chinese persons born out of the United States, remaining subjects of the Emperor of China, and not having become citizens of the United States, are entitled to the protection of and owe allegiance to the United States, so long as they are permitted by the United States to reside here; and are 'subject to the jurisdiction thereof,' in the same sense as all other aliens residing in the United States" (694). The fact that Congress had passed exclusion acts and had not allowed Chinese to become naturalized citizens did not affect the provisions concerning citizenship by birth proclaimed by the Fourteenth Amendment. Born in the United States, Wong Kim Ark was a natural-born citizen. Since he had not renounced his citizenship, he remained a citizen and should be allowed reentry.

The dissent was written by Chief Justice Melville W. Fuller, joined by Justice Harlan. Fuller took issue with the majority's appeal to common law. Citing a number of authorities, he showed that common law had not simply been adopted by the United States, especially on the issue of citizenship. In fact, he argued, the common-law doctrine of jus soli was a feudal doctrine that had no place in American law. It had "no more survived the American Revolution than the same rule survived the French Revolution" (710). Common law assumed a subject's indissoluble loyalty. The United States, however, was founded on the right to alter allegiance. Declaring their independence, former colonial subjects asserted their right to form a new political entity. A country of immigration, the United States was founded on the implicit recognition of the right of individuals to expatriate from their former countries.

Explicitly, the United States had acknowledged the right of expatriation in a law passed by Congress on July 27, 1868, the same year that the Fourteenth Amendment was adopted. Still on the books today, this act declared expatriation to be a "natural and inherent right of all people, indispensable to the enjoyment of the rights of life, liberty, and the pursuit of happiness."[30] It led to naturalization treaties with a variety of countries, including, in 1870, one with Great Britain, thus giving official British recognition of U.S. citizenship for anyone still alive who had been born in the colonies prior to the American Revolution. Expressing a consensual view of citizenship, the Expatriation Act, for Fuller, marked a clear break by the United States with common-law doctrine and ruled out a common-law reading of the amendment.

Another argument against the common-law interpretation depended on a distinction between subjects and citizens. In an 1895 law review essay Collins, who filed an amicus curiae brief for the U.S. government, pointed out that under common law "the question was not what constituted a citizen of the nation, but what constituted a subject of the king." The "subordinate status of subject . . . , however appropriate to monarchy, is fundamentally repugnant to republican institutions."[31]

Collins could have reinforced his argument by referring to Dred Scott. In Dred Scott slaves were certainly subject to the jurisdiction of the United States. But they were not citizens. Thus, even if prior to the Fourteenth Amendment the United States had adopted common law, Dred Scott made clear that it did not make all subjects automatic citizens. Indeed, Taney denied citizenship not only to slaves but to free blacks by including them as part of a subject race. Commenting on a provision in the Articles of Confederation that determined each state's quota for the armed forces in proportion to its "white inhabitants," he declared, "Words could hardly have been used which more strongly mark the line of distinction between the citizen and the subject—the free and the subjugated races."[32] Since it was universally granted that the purpose of the Fourteenth Amendment was to overturn Dred Scott, it would seem to follow that in granting citizenship to blacks, the Fourteenth Amendment broke with feudal practices of subjection, including the common-law doctrine associated with them. In the nineteenth century, the standard way for countries to move from feudal to republican practices was to determine citizenship by descent. Thus it made perfect sense to argue that with the Fourteenth Amendment the United States followed that method.

Fuller found textual evidence for a *jus sanguinis* reading in the 1866 Civil Rights Act. Passed two months before the same Congress proposed the Fourteenth Amendment, it states "that all persons born in the United States and *not subject to any foreign power*, excluding Indians not taxed, are hereby declared to be citizens of the United States" (719–20, qtd. by Fuller [emphasis added]). "The words 'not subject to any foreign power,'" Fuller insisted, "do not in themselves refer to mere territorial jurisdiction, for the persons referred to are persons born in the United States. All such persons are undoubtedly subject to the territorial jurisdiction of the United States, and yet the act concedes that nevertheless they may be subject to the political jurisdiction of a foreign government. In other words, by the terms of the act all persons born in the United States, and not owing allegiance to any foreign power, are citizens" (720). Passed in part with the intention of guaranteeing the constitutionality of the 1866 act, the Fourteenth Amendment carried the same meaning in the crucial phrase of its citizenship clause.[33]

In his law review essay Collins argued that if the framers of the amendment had wanted to indicate jurisdiction territorially, they would have written "subject to the jurisdiction of its laws," since clearly anyone within U.S. territory, except for mutually agreed-upon representatives of foreign countries, is subject to its laws. But they had instead used a phrase that indicated national, not territorial, jurisdiction.[34] When they wanted to indicate territorial jurisdiction, as in the equal protection clause, they were perfectly capable of doing so.

To be sure, the majority claimed that a *jus sanguinis* ruling would deny citizenship to many children born of immigrant aliens in this country. But for Fuller this argument was wrong. *Elk v. Wilkins* held that the crucial phrase means "not merely subject in some respect or degree to the jurisdiction of the United States, but completely subject to their political jurisdiction, and owing them direct and immediate allegiance."[35] Immigrant aliens permanently domiciled in the United States had implicitly acknowledged a break with their home country, so that when their children were born, they were completely subject to the jurisdiction of the United States. But the situation of Chinese, Fuller argued, was different. Forbidden by the Chinese government from expatriation and forbidden by U.S. law from naturalization, Chinese "seem in the United States to have remained pilgrims and sojourners" (726). Since they were not completely subject to the jurisdiction of the United States, their children could not become automatic citizens by birth.

Pointing to an inconsistency in the majority's argument, Fuller noted that the Court had granted the government power to expel or deport aliens, but not citizens. To grant citizenship to children of people forbidden from becoming citizens themselves was to allow the government to break up families by expelling parents but not children. Furthermore, if the *jus soli* interpretation were granted, all children born abroad of U.S. citizens since 1868 would be denied citizenship, since they were not born in the United States. A *jus sanguinis* interpretation would account for their citizenship because both they and their parents were still subject to the jurisdiction of the United States.

Despite Fuller's argument, the Court decided in favor of Wong Kim Ark. As a result, according to an expert quoted by Gray, "The right of citizenship [in the United States] never *descends* in the legal sense, either by the common law, or under the common naturalization acts. It is incident to birth in the country, or it is given personally by statute" (665).

☆ ☆ ☆ *Wong Kim Ark* is a storehouse of conflicting views on U.S. citizenship that illustrate Rogers Smith's claim that it has been determined by complicated interactions between republicanism, liberalism, and "inegalitarian, ascriptive traditions of Americanism."[36] Indeed, it shows that both republicanism and liberalism are capable of aligning themselves with ascriptivism.

In the classical liberalism of Locke, to be designated a citizen is not to add to one's basic rights; it is, instead, to be called on to participate in honoring, protecting, and preserving rights granted at birth. According to Étienne Balibar, for those lodged within this tradition, "the men of 1776 and 1789, the men of liberty and revolution, became 'citizens' because they had universally won access to *subjectivity*. Better said: because they had become conscious (in a Cartesian, or Lockean, or Kantian way) of the fact that they were indeed free 'subjects,' always already destined to liberty (by their 'birthright')."[37] As "free" as they were, however, they also knew that citizenship entails subjection to civil rule. Thus, the basic tenet of liberal citizenship is the doctrine of consent. Citizens, for liberals, have to consent to their own subjection.

Although it has some similarities with liberalism, classical republicanism offers a different view of citizenship. Within it, rights do not precede political and civil society; they are a product of it.[38] As a result, citizenship does more than protect already existing rights; it is the very condition of having rights. It is also the right to participate, as part of the res publica (the public body), in the construction of those rights, which is why classical republicanism, much more than classical liberalism, emphasizes active citizenly participation in the public sphere. If the stress on active participation is one of its strengths, a potential weakness is its particularism. Not sharing liberalism's universalistic assumption that all people share the same rights at birth, republicanism insists that rights are the product of a particular political order. As a result, it is much more prone to stress the difference between citizens and noncitizens. It is also more likely to define "the people" as the original founders of the republic, a definition making it difficult to redefine "the people" in light of changing circumstances.

The dangers of this view are illustrated by Taney in his *Dred Scott* decision, which restricted citizenship to white descendants of "the people" who originally founded the republic. Of course, Taney's decision has long been the object of criticism. Thus, a more telling illustration of potential dangers in republican thought is Justice Harlan. Harlan is most famous for his courageous and lone dissents in the Civil Rights Cases of 1883 and *Plessy v. Ferguson* (1896). Nonetheless, his decision to join the dissent in *Wong Kim Ark* lets us see how the republicanism that generated his dissents in cases involving African Americans can justify exclusions as well as inclusions.

Harlan's dissent in *Wong Kim Ark* might seem inconsistent with his famous dissent in *Plessy v. Ferguson* and other cases in which he resisted the tendency to define the United States as an Anglo-Saxon country. For instance, in *Downes v. Bidwell* he dissented when the majority denied full constitutional protections for inhabitants of the Philippines and Puerto Rico, acquired by the United States after the Spanish-American War. Justifying this ruling that gave these people the status of subjects rather than citizens, Justice Henry Billings Brown wrote, "There are certain principles of natural justice inherent in the Anglo-Saxon character which need no expression in constitution or statute to give them effect."[39] To which Harlan responded, "The wise men who framed the Constitution, and the patriotic people who adopted it, were unwilling to depend for their safety upon such inherent principles. They proceeded upon the theory—the wisdom of which experience has vindicated—that the only safe guaranty against governmental oppression was to withhold or restrict the power to oppress. They well remembered that Anglo-Saxons across the ocean had attempted, in defiance of law and justice, to trample on the rights of Anglo-Saxons on this continent."[40]

Harlan also dissented when the majority denied citizenship to John Elk. In his dissent he even provided a third interpretation of the citizenship clause. For the majority in that case and for the majority and minority in *Wong Kim Ark*, the phrases "born and naturalized in the United States" and "subject to the jurisdiction thereof" refer to the same temporal moment. But Harlan thought differently. Admitting that Elk, born a member of an

Indian tribe, was not, at birth, completely subject to the jurisdiction of the United States, Harlan pointed out that when later he renounced his tribal loyalty, he was. Thus, Harlan argued, he satisfied the two conditions of the citizenship clause, even if he did not satisfy them at birth. As Harlan put it, the citizenship clause allowed persons born in the United States to "claim the rights of national citizenship from and after the moment they become subject to the complete jurisdiction of the United States."[41]

Given these cases, why did Harlan join Chief Justice Fuller in trying to deny birthright citizenship to Wong Kim Ark? One reason is suggested in his famous *Plessy* dissent. Arguing why blacks should not be forced to ride in separate railroad cars, Harlan evokes the Chinese.

There is a race so different from our own that we do not permit those belonging to it to become citizens of the United States. Persons belonging to it are, with few exceptions, absolutely excluded from our country. I allude to the Chinese race. But by the statute in question, a Chinaman can ride in the same passenger coach with white citizens of the United States, while citizens of the black race in Louisiana, many of whom, perhaps, risked their lives for the preservation of the Union, who are entitled by law, to participate in the political control of the State and nation, who are not excluded, by law or reason of their race, from public stations of any kind, and who have all the legal rights that belong to white citizens, are yet declared to be criminals, liable to imprisonment, if they ride in a public coach occupied by a citizen of the white race.[42]

If Harlan was intent on overturning Taney's republican sense of the people, he did so by appealing to a new founding moment: the Civil War and the amendments that reconstituted the nation. For Harlan, there was a place for African Americans and Native Americans in that view of the nation, but not one for Chinese Americans.

Harlan frequently ruled against Chinese.[43] He joined the Court when it upheld the 1888 Scott Act that denied Chinese laborers, even those with valid return certificates issued before the act was passed, the right to reenter the United States. Ruling that the right to exclude aliens was a condition of national sovereignty not limited by existing treaties, it claimed that the Chinese "remained strangers in the land, residing apart by themselves, and adhering to customs and usages of their own country. It seemed impossible for them to assimilate with our own people, or make any changes in their habits of living."[44] Although he did not participate in the Court's support of the Geary Act's requirement that even legal Chinese aliens without proper identification cards could be deported, in other cases he cited the Court's reasoning with approval.[45] Indeed, only a year before *Plessy*, he supported granting immigration officials judicial authority to rule on whether various Chinese could be excluded.[46]

In his *Plessy* dissent Harlan declared, "In view of the Constitution, in the eye of the law, there is in this country no superior, dominant, ruling class of citizens. There is no caste here. Our Constitution is color-blind, and neither knows nor tolerates classes among citizens. In respect of civil rights, all citizens are equal before the law."[47] Because of its sweeping claims, this passage has led many to assume that Harlan opposed racial discrimination on broad, cosmopolitan humanitarian grounds. But they fail to note his repeated use of "citizen."[48] For Harlan a republic cannot operate unless all citizens are equal before the law. But that does not mean that all people are equal before the law, nor that all are eligible for citizenship. On the contrary, his republicanism caused him to sympathize with Geary's view that "the first duty of governments is to their own citizens."

Harlan's republicanism was so strong that it caused him to misread important language in the Constitution. Even though the Fourteenth Amendment makes a crucial distinction by referring to "citizens" in its citizenship and privileges and immunities clauses while referring to "persons" in its due process and equal protection clauses, in both his *Plessy* and Civil Rights Cases dissents, Harlan acts as if the latter two protections are reserved only for citizens. In the case of Chinese immigrants, who were excluded from citizenship, that mistake was a telling one.

In 1883 Harlan's son asked his father for advice for a college debate in which he had to support the 1882 Exclusion Act. Harlan suggested that he argue, "We are not bound upon any broad principle of humanity, to harm our own country in order to benefit the Chinese who may arrive here. . . . Now if by introduction of Chinese labor we jeopardize our own laborers, why not restrict immigration of Chinese?"[49] Because he was simply suggesting a strategy of debate for his son, Harlan did not necessarily agree with this line of reasoning; nonetheless, it is consistent with other remarks he made about immigration in general. Harlan, after all, began his political career as a member of the anti-immigrant Know-Nothing Party, and whereas he was not opposed to all immigration, he did proclaim in a law school lecture that "we could exclude any particular race anywhere on earth from our country by act of Congress."[50]

Harlan's attitude toward the Chinese is a powerful example of how the tradition of civic republicanism could lend support to a system of racial exclusion. His reminder that Congress has the power to exclude any race from this country also calls attention to the limits of liberalism's ideal of consensual citizenship. We can see those limits in Rogers Smith's interpretation of *Wong Kim Ark*.

Given Harlan's ascriptivism, it would seem that Smith would side with the majority in *Wong Kim Ark*. Indeed, he admits that the majority opinion "genuinely served liberal, inclusive positions." But he also claims that it "fit the ascriptive, nationalistic, and often mystical spirit of [nineteenth-century ideas of racial homogenization] better than the rationalistic, consensual account of citizenship that Fuller presented" in dissent.[51] Smith sticks to this interpretation despite admitting that evidence about both Fuller and Harlan does not support it.[52] His reason for doing so is revealed in a book he coauthored with Peter H. Schuck.

Schuck and Smith claim that birthright citizenship for children of illegal immigrants undermines the principle of consensual citizenship they trace to Locke. Even so, they do not join many anti-immigrant groups in demanding that the citizenship clause of the Fourteenth Amendment be eliminated. On the contrary, they praise it for giving an "expansive, but not universal" shape "to the American political community."[53] What they do instead is argue against the way *Wong Kim Ark* has been interpreted to grant citizenship to children of immigrants not legally in the country. Parents, like those of Wong Kim Ark, legally here have the nation's consent to be here. Thus, children born to them, like Wong Kim Ark, should be granted citizenship. But parents illegally here do not have the nation's consent to be here. Thus, the ruling in *Wong Kim Ark* should not apply to them, and the Court was wrong to imply that it does in the 1982 case of *Plyer v. Doe*.[54] "Concessions to prudence, fairness, and liberal humanitarianism should not be taken to deny to the American community the essence of a consensual political identity — the power and obligation to seek to define its own boundaries and enforce them. If Congress should conclude that the prospective denial of birthright citizenship to the children of illegal aliens would be a valuable adjunct of such a national self-definition, the Constitution should not be interpreted in a way that impedes that effort."[55]

Schuck and Smith raise an interesting legal point about the scope of *Wong Kim Ark*, but in doing so they also reveal the capacity of their consensual view of citizenship to join Harlan's republicanism in aiding nativist American ascriptivism. Smith dismisses the majority, not the minority, opinion as ascriptive because it bases its ruling on the common-law doctrine affirmed by Justice Coke in *Calvin's Case*. In contrast, he calls Fuller's account of citizenship consensual because it follows Emmerich Vattel, the eighteenth-century Swiss author of *The Law of Nations*, who was intent on breaking with medieval doctrines, such as the one affirmed by Justice Coke.

Vattel did so by arguing that international law should follow a *jus sanguinis* determination. A territorial determination for him denied any consideration of consent because it relied on an outmoded notion of sovereignty in which anyone born in the king's territory was a lifetime subject of the king. In contrast, a determination by descent, he argued, implies the consent of the child through the agency of his parents, or more accurately, through that of his father. That consent, he continued, would become explicit by allowing the child, upon reaching majority, to choose its country of allegiance.

Compared to the medieval doctrine of *jus soli*, Vattel's doctrine of *jus sanguinis* is more consensual. But when Congress passed the Expatriation Act the same year the Fourteenth Amendment was ratified, the United States no longer adhered to medieval doctrine. Fuller may have cited the 1868 Expatriation Act to support his argument for *jus sanguinis*, but he failed to note how it also had the potential to transform the common-law doctrine of birthright citizenship. Coupled with the right of expatriation, a *jus soli* determination no longer entailed perpetual allegiance. On the contrary, it now came closer to the consensual ideal than a *jus sanguinis* determination. After all, as the distinction between civic and ethnic nations makes clear, today consensual accounts are most often opposed to ones based on descent, not to ones based on where a person was born. Appropriately, in *Wong Kim Ark* the great principle established by the majority's *jus soli* decision is that in the United States the right of citizenship never descends.

Smith praises Fuller's account of citizenship as "rationalistic" rather than ascriptive.[56] But it is precisely the doctrine of mutual consent that grants the "people," as sovereign, the right to deny citizenship to any individual or group that it chooses. Indeed, when that outspoken proponent of economic liberalism Justice Stephen Field spoke for a unanimous Court in what has come to be known as the *Chinese Exclusion Case*, he granted unchecked power to the people to exclude a group such as the Chinese, a power that could be limited only by, in his words, the "consent of the people."[57] In contrast, *Wong Kim Ark* proclaims a principle that both limits the power of the people to exclude an entire race from birthright citizenship and imposes an obligation upon the nation to grant the protections of citizenship to everyone born within its jurisdiction, no matter of what descent. To be sure, in imposing that obligation *Wong Kim Ark* retains some of the paternalism derived from the medieval origins of *jus soli*. In it the sovereign protects subjects in exchange for loyalty. But perhaps the civic ideal that the nation will care for all born in its territory should trump that of mutual consent.

As important as that ideal was and remains for a more inclusive vision of American citizenship, it was and is limited. A formal definition of who can be a natural-born citizen does not provide a vision of the type of civic life a citizen will be born into. For instance, whether a country has a *jus soli* or *jus sanguinis* determination of citizenship has little or no effect on how citizens interact with one another or the relation between citizens and the political body that governs them. Another limitation is that the Court's decision does not govern naturalization laws, which remain in the hands of Congress. In many ways, inclusive laws of naturalization are more important for guaranteeing a heterogeneous citizenry than rulings deciding eligibility for citizenship at birth. After all, if naturalization laws do not discriminate according to race, within a generation children of many races will be born citizens even when a country adheres to *jus sanguinis*.

But to point to these limits is not to imply that the Court's decision in *Wong Kim Ark* lacks importance. According to Jacobsohn, its refusal to allow descent to determine citizenship means that "henceforward the ability of the native-born to share in the aspirational content of American national identity was formed only by one's relation to the physical boundaries of the United States."[58] In establishing that principle, the case had important practical effects. Although it did not overrule existing exclusion acts, it did open a small but significant opportunity for those of Chinese descent—as well as other excluded groups—living in the United States. In a country with liberal naturalization laws, distinctions between *jus soli* or *jus sanguinis* are not so important, but the United States at the turn of the century was not such a country. In fact, soon after the Court's decision, Congress tightened restrictions on Asian immigration. Within that context, *Wong Kim Ark* countered those who wanted to restrict citizenship according to race. Insofar as people of different races—citizens or not—inhabited the territory under U.S. jurisdiction, as they did, children of different bloods would most likely be born and become automatic citizens, as indeed they have been.[59]

As a result, *Wong Kim Ark* provided a corrective to yet another limit of classical republicanism: its stress on group identity. Citizens, according to classical republicanism, participate with equal rights in the public sphere, but they do so as representatives of groups (estates) that determine who they are. This vision has direct relevance to the political situation in the United States today where people continue to be identified in terms of race. Because race has been used to exclude various people from citizenship, people intent on current racial justice challenge those static aspects of classical republicanism that rule out a perpetual redefinition of how "the people" are racially defined. Even so, the emphasis on group identity can risk limiting the possibilities of identity as much as classical republicanism's identification of someone as a member of an estate.

Addressing the complicated problem of how to conceive of a public sphere that both recognizes the dangers of confining an individual's identity to membership in a group and the reality that group membership plays a determinant role in shaping one's identity, Robert Post writes, "Democratic public culture must . . . be understood as distinct from the cultures of particular groups and communities. Even though we know that in actuality the identities of individuals are formed through socialization into the specific mores of specific and historical groups and communities, the ideal of self-determination requires that public culture always maintains the possibility of citizens imagining themselves as something other than what in fact they are."[60]

One consequence of Wong Kim Ark has been to foster conditions for a heterogeneous citizenry in which people continually confront people different from themselves. One of the strengths of China Men is its dramatization of such interaction and its vision of how it can lead to a more democratic public culture. Just as Kingston's work resists existing generic categories, so it provides a way of constructing identities that works on/with existing racial and national categories. In doing so, it generates a model for a public culture in which citizens can acknowledge the group—or groups—to which they belong while still imagining themselves to be other than what they are, a capacity that leads to a dynamic, rather than to a fixed, sense of individual, cultural, and national identity. It is time, then, to return to Kingston's work of the literary imagination.[61]

☆ ☆ ☆ If Wong Kim Ark provides a legal standard for more inclusive national membership in terms of birth, China Men lets us see the numerous and complicated factors that generate a sense of national belonging. "Belonging" has at least two overlapping meanings. On one hand, to belong means to be possessed by someone or something, as a piece of property belongs to a person. On the other hand, a sense of belonging implies that one fits in or feels at home. A sense of national belonging, as we saw in Chapter 3, can be linked to both a territory—a country—and to a group of people—a nation. If Hale implies that a person belongs to a country and Lincoln insists that a country belongs to its people, Kingston gives a sense of both. She also explores the complications of belonging to a people. On one hand, a sense of belonging depends on being accepted as a member by the group. On the other, it depends on people's subjective feelings that they fit in. In fact, the two interact, since a group's exclusion can make people feel out of place, and a sense that they do not fit can legitimate denial of membership to a particular people. To achieve a sense of national belonging, Chinese, like all immigrants, had to go through a process of Americanization. That is accomplished legally through naturalization. The special obstacles the Chinese had to overcome are indicated by the fact that they were not allowed to naturalize. *Wong Kim Ark* was such an important victory because it gave legal and symbolic sanction to the idea that Chinese could indeed be members of the American nation. Even so, a legal designation of membership by no means guarantees a sense of belonging. It does not because Americanization has a cultural as well as a legal component. For instance, in 1885 anti-immigrant Josiah Strong lamented, "Many American citizens are not Americanized."[62] What Strong meant, of course, was that, despite their legal status, these immigrants remained linguistic and cultural "outsiders." From Strong's point of view, still shared by many today, the only way to become truly American was to go through a process of cultural assimilation.

Accused of having no desire to assimilate, Chinese were also considered incapable of doing so. Indeed, since a major reason given for denying them the right to naturalize was their failure to assimilate, the legal and cultural obstacles they had to overcome were linked. For instance, explaining why Wong Kim Ark should not be considered a citizen, District Attorney General Foote declared that he had "been at all times, by reason of his race, language, color, and dress, a Chinese person."[63] Even after some Chinese were granted citizenship by *Wong Kim Ark*, Foote's belief that they were and would always remain Chinese, not Americans, persisted. They were, as a result, labeled "other." *China Men* dramatizes how the Chinese are able to transform that sense of otherness into a sense of belonging.

Maxine, the narrator, describes how during the Korean War elementary school children had to wear "dog tags" and participate in preparedness drills.

We had to fill out a form for what to engrave on the dog tags. I looked up "religion" in the *American Chinese Dictionary* and asked my mother what religion we were. "Our religion is Chinese," she said. "But that's not a religion," I said. "Yes, it is," she said. "Well, tell the teacher demon it's Kung Fu Tse, then," she said. The kids at school said, "Are you Catholic?" "No." "Then you're a Protestant." So our dog tags had O for religion and O for race because neither black nor white. Mine also had O for blood type. Some kids said O was for "Oriental," but I knew it was for "Other," because the Filipinos, the Gypsies, and the Hawaiian boy were O's. (276)

This sense of otherness made Chinese Americans victims of what W. E. B. Du Bois famously called double consciousness.

Resulting from a world in which an American is assumed to be white, double consciousness, Du Bois argues, imparts to African Americans a sense of "two-ness," a sense of being both an "American" and a "Negro." Deprived of "self-consciousness," the African American instead sees "himself through the revelation of the other world," a world that considers him incapable of becoming a "true" American. That perspective makes African Americans prone to internalizing a sense of inferiority. "It is," Du Bois writes, "a peculiar sensation, this double-consciousness, this sense of always looking at one's self through the eyes of others, of measuring one's soul by the tape of a world that looks on in amused contempt and pity."[64] Chinese Americans, Kingston makes clear, are prone to a similar sense of "two-ness."

Although the "father from China" and his friends try to fit in by wearing American clothes and adopting American habits, their sense of not belonging is betrayed by their use of words. In "The Laws" Kingston quotes Justice Field's claim that Chinese immigrants were distinguished from others because they were simply "sojourners" with their real home still in China (155). Yet she portrays China Men themselves assuring their wives that they were "Sojourners only," a self-identification that helped justify their exclusion (44). Similarly, characters frequently use the term "American" to refer to whites, thus excluding themselves linguistically in the same way Strong had.

Even so, as both Kingston and Du Bois know, double consciousness need not produce a negative sense of self. It can, for instance, as Du Bois notes, generate the gift of "second-sight," a critical capacity often missing in those who fit in too easily. If the negative aspect of double consciousness arises when an American identity is assumed to be a fixed category that certain groups cannot achieve, its positive aspects open up the possibility of transforming the established sense of American identity. Indeed, cultivating the capacity for second-sightedness in her readers by portraying it in her characters, Kingston imagines and tries to produce a world that revises what it means to be an American. In that world Americanization is not simply a process of assimilation.

Having the root meaning of "making similar," assimilation implies that immigrants need to take on existing customs in order to belong. Kingston challenges that implication in three overlapping ways. Most obviously, she joins advocates of cultural and multicultural citizenship by embracing cultural difference. America, for multiculturalists, is constituted by many different cultures, not by a dominant one to which all others have to conform. As important as recognition of cultural difference is for Kingston, however, she is aware, as are many others, that it runs the risk of turning individual cultures into fixed categories of their own.[65] Thus, she complicates arguments for cultural difference by working on/with another popular account of Americanization, one frequently discounted today, that of the melting pot.

In his 1893 description of the closing of the frontier, Frederick Jackson Turner provides a famous variation on the melting pot metaphor. Challenging the model by which immigrants assimilate to an already existing culture, he imagines a process of dynamic interaction among various groups that produces a new and unique American identity. In the "crucible" of the frontier, he argues, "immigrants were Americanized, liberated, and fused into a mixed race."[66] Kingston, like Turner, imagines a process of dynamic cultural interaction with the potential to alter existing cultural formations and bring new ones into existence. But whereas Turner implies that this interaction generates a new homogeneous and unique American culture, for Kingston differences of some sort persist.

Unlike Turner, Kingston is acutely aware of unequal power relations among different groups, an inequality that led to the legal exclusion of Chinese and the legal segregation of African Americans. For instance, writing a year earlier than Turner, Congressman Geary, drawing on a different meaning of "frontier," stressed the need to maintain "guards and inspectors upon our frontiers and at our different seaports, in order to prevent the infraction of our laws by a race of people who never have shown any respect for them."[67] As Justice Thurgood Marshall once quipped, the problem with the metaphor of the melting pot is that some groups were never allowed in the pot.[68] If Marshall's comment was directed against advocates of a color-blind standard in the law, it also suggests limits to naive celebrations of cultural difference. American culture may not be homogeneous; nonetheless, there is still some cultural entity—call it a "culture" of multicultural interaction—more accessible to members of some groups than others. Confronted with a history of cultural exclusion that denied them the possibility of assimilation, Chinese Americans developed a strategy of cultural appropriation.

If "assimilation" means "to make similar," "appropriation" means "to make one's own." We have already seen this strategy at work as Chinese learned to appropriate the legal system that so often was a source of repression and to turn it to their advantage. We also saw how in the process of protecting their rights, they altered the legal system for all Americans. In the chapters surrounding "The Laws," Kingston shows a similar strategy at work in the realm of culture, with the Chinese altering the meaning of cultural practices that labeled them "other."

Encouraged to take on an American name as a way of fitting in, the father from China is aware of the "power of naming" (242). Thus he calls himself "Edison." In order to explain to his wife why he chose that name, he takes her to the film *Young Tom Edison*. "They both liked the scene where the mother took Ed-Ah-Son into the barn but only pretended to thrash him; she faked the slaps and crying and scolding to fool the strict father, the father 'the severe parent,' according to Confucius, and the mother 'the kind parent.' ('My bones, my flesh, father and mother,' said Tu Fu.) After the movie, Ed explained to his wife that this cunning, resourceful, successful inventor, Edison, was who he had named himself after. 'I see,' she said. 'Ed-Da-Son. Son as in *sage* or *immortal* or *saint*'" (71). Appearing as if he is simply trying to assimilate to his new world, the father appropriates an American name, giving it a new meaning that does not cancel out the American meaning but that, nonetheless, adds a Chinese component to it, just as the husband and wife give a product of American popular culture a Chinese interpretation.

China Men is full of moments such as these in which the capacity for second-sightedness unfixes stereotypes and makes possible new, more affirmative identities. For instance, for years "chinamen" (111) was a pejorative label, a collective term signaling the inability of those using it to see Chinese as individuals. Kingston, however, appropriates the term for her title, changing its meaning by separating "china" from "men" and giving individual men the dignity of upper case. At other times, Kingston uses multilingual puns to give new meaning to staples of American culture. For example, in "The Adventures of Lo Bun Sun," she retells, with a decidedly Chinese inflection, the story of Robinson ("Lo Bun Sun") Crusoe that had such a powerful influence on the early American imagination.

In *China Men* appropriation is closely aligned with a process of adoption. Derived from the Latin *optave*, meaning to choose or to desire, "adoption" can involve a set of beliefs or cultural practices as well as a child. In adapting to their new country by adopting American customs and American culture, immigrants, Kingston shows, need not simply assimilate to them; they can also give them new meaning. Even so, they still have to face charges, like those leveled by Collins, that they cannot become true Americans because they do not descend from "the patriots of the American Revolution."

The most obvious response to such arguments is that, except for the Daughters of the American Revolution, most white Americans are not direct descendants from patriots either. Nonetheless, a widespread and dangerous civic myth is that, through a mystical process, a nation's culture and history can be racially inherited. Indeed, the myth of cultural inheritance is not confined to xenophobes. Horace M. Kallen, the early-twentieth-century proponent of cultural pluralism, offered what he thought was an irrefutable argument for the unchanging persistence of ethnic identities by pointing out that people cannot choose their grandfathers.[69] Countering such narratives of deterministic descent, Mary Antin, a Russian Jewish immigrant, much to the chagrin of some nativists, claimed the nation's forefathers as her own. In The Promised Land (1912), she writes, "Naturalization, with us Russian Jews, may mean more than the adoption of the immigrant by America. It may mean the adoption of America by the immigrant."[70] Following in Antin's footsteps, Kingston shows how a culture and a history can be adopted as well as inherited. In doing so she perpetuates the spirit of one of the most important national forefathers: Abraham Lincoln.

"A nation," according to Lincoln, "may be said to consist of its territory, its people, and its laws."[71] But it is also defined by what, at the end of his First Inaugural, he calls "mystic chords of memory."[72] That metaphor could be interpreted in an exclusive sense that would confine the mystical process of memory only to persons with a racial connection to the country's founding fathers. But in Lincoln's hands it becomes a metaphor of inclusion. Not something that descends to individuals, a nation's culture and history is, for him, available to anyone who learns and adopts it through a mystic process of memory. For instance, in the Gettysburg Address, when Lincoln evokes "our fathers," who "brought forth . . . a new nation," he does not exclude any members of his present and future audience from adopting them as their "fathers."[73] At the same time, as we have seen, in adopting those Revolutionary patriots, he also subtly alters their vision to produce a founding document of a second American Revolution brought about by the Civil War.

Working within this Lincolnian tradition, Kingston adopts the country's history and culture at the same time that she works on/with the myths it has generated about both, including myths of the founding fathers. Describing the China Men's labor building the nation's railroads, she writes, "They built railroads in every part of the country—the Alabama and Chattanooga Railroad, the Houston and Texas Railroad, the Southern Pacific, the railroads in Louisiana and Boston, the Pacific Northwest, and Alaska. After the Civil War, China Men banded the nation North and South, East and West, with crisscrossing steel. They were the binding and building ancestors of this place" (146). In working on myths of the nation's founding fathers, Kingston alters the traditional sense of American identity.

A standard question within American studies is What makes an American? *China Men* answers that question by posing another one: Who made America? To answer that question is to remind us of the material, as well as the political, making of the country.[74] China Men, the book shows, had an important role in that making. If Lincoln claimed that the country's "vast extent, and its variety of climate and population" had been turned into an "advantageous combination for one united people" by "steam, telegraphs, and intelligence,"[75] Kingston details the important contribution of the Chinese to that task. Imagining a grandfather at the ceremony celebrating the completion of the transcontinental railroad, the narrator proclaims, "The white demon officials gave speeches. 'The Greatest Feat of the Nineteenth Century,' they said. 'The Greatest Feat in the History of Mankind,' they said. 'Only Americans could have done it,' they said, which is true. Even if Ah Goong had not spent half his gold on Citizenship Papers, he was an American for having built the railroad" (145).

Relying on questionable historiography, Taney's exclusive racial definition of "We, the People" confined the term to descendants of the whites who had participated in the original constitution of the country. Kingston's inclusive definition opens the term to all who contributed to the country's making. And since the country is in a perpetual process of remaking, she allows for the inclusion of new generations of founding fathers, for the perpetual making of more Americans. If Locke felt that, in making the land productive, people's labor gave them possession of the land, Kingston suggests that people's labor gives them a claim to belong to the land.

Nonetheless, as Kingston knows, both now and in the past, a number of immigrants contributing to the land's productivity came into the country illegally. The conflict between their claim to belong and their legal status generates what is perhaps the most controversial aspect of Kingston's book: its complication of the opposition between legal and illegal immigrants that frames today's ongoing debates about immigration and provides the foundation for Schuck and Smith's notion of a citizenship based on mutual consent.

☆ ☆ ☆ Unable to get her father to tell her how he arrived in the United States, Maxine imagines three different possibilities. In one he entered the country legally; in another he was born in the United States and received automatic citizenship; in another he entered illegally. This uncertainty over the legality of the father's entrance makes an important point: his contribution to the country remains the same no matter how he arrived. Speaking to the many ways in which China Men ended up American citizens, these different accounts also question whether it is always so easy to distinguish between legal and illegal entries.

The "illegal" father travels from China to Cuba, where he rolls cigarettes and cigars and works in sugarcane fields. Seeking the aid of a professional smuggler, he hides inside a crate shipped from Cuba to New York, where he successfully sneaks into the country. The non-native-born "legal" father comes through San Francisco. Although he should be allowed to enter even under existing exclusion acts because he qualifies under an exception for scholars, friends warn him that immigration officials will not let him in. "Listen, stupid, nobody gets to be classified 'Scholar.' You can't speak English, you're illiterate, no scholar, no visa. 'Coolie.' Simple test" (45).

Aware that immigration officials might not honor his legitimate examination certificate, he searches for documents that they will honor. First, his relatives' families "unburied their documents—visas, passports, reentry permits, American birth certificates, American citizenship papers" (46). He also lets it be known that he was on the market to buy documents from locals who are legal citizens of the United States. "These Americans had declared the birth of a new son for every year they had been visiting in China and thereby made slots for many 'paper sons.' When a Sojourner retired from going-out-on-the-road or died, he made another slot. Somebody took his place" (46). The father goes, therefore, "with two sets of papers: bought ones and his own, which were legal and should get him into the Gold Mountain according to American law. But his own papers were untried, whereas the fake set had accompanied its owners back and forth many times" (46–47). About to face officers of the law who might not recognize an authentic document, the "legal" father comes prepared to gain entrance with fake papers. Then, at Angel Island in the San Francisco Bay, he undergoes a demeaning and ritually rigorous interrogation in which he must prove the identity established by his papers. Passing this test, as he passed the Imperial Examination to become a scholar in China, he is finally allowed to enter the country "legally."

If the "legal" father's potentially "illegal" entrance into the country blurs the boundary between legal and illegal immigrants, further blurring occurs because of a historical accident. Describing the burning of the Hall of Records after the San Francisco earthquake of 1906, Kingston writes, "Citizenship papers burned, Certificates of Return, Birth Certificates, Residency Certificates, passenger lists, Marriage Certificates—every paper a China Man wanted for citizenship and legality burned in that fire. An authentic citizen, then, had no more papers than an alien. Any paper a China Man could not produce had been 'burned up in the fire of 1906.' Every China Man was reborn out of that fire a citizen" (150).

It is the San Francisco fire that generates the possibility of the father's birthright citizenship. In the very next paragraph, the one just before the chapter on "The Laws," we are told that Maxine's grandfather was "seen carrying a child out of the fire, a child of his own in spite of the laws against marrying" (151). At the start of "The American Father," Kingston glosses this passage. "In 1903 my father was born in San Francisco where my grandmother had come disguised as a man. Or, Chinese women, once magical, she gave birth at a distance, she in China, my grandfather and father in San Francisco. She was good at sending. Or the men of those days had the power to have babies. If my grandparents did no such wonders, my father nevertheless turned up in San Francisco a citizen" (238). As the phrase "turned up" suggests, the legality of the father's claim to citizenship might very well be in question.

In celebrating how the Chinese circumvented the law, Kingston may seem scandalously to encourage illegal immigration. What she actually does is deploy an imaginative re-creation of history to complicate simplistic oppositions between legal and illegal immigrants. Her point is not to champion illegality at the expense of legality. It is instead to point to the injustice of laws and practices that would force a "legal" immigrant to enter the country as an "illegal" one. She reinforces that point by juxtaposing the experiences of the "legal" father in San Francisco and the "illegal" father in New York.

In the myth of America as the land of opportunity, no place occupies a more important symbolic role than New York harbor, with Ellis Island and the Statue of Liberty. In contrast, San Francisco, because of Angel Island, raises serious questions about that myth. Indeed, the San Francisco–based *Wasp* published a well-known anti-Chinese cartoon "A Statue for Our Harbor," with a derogatory image of a China Man replacing that of Lady Liberty. Thus, it is with a mischievous sense of irony that Kingston has the "legal" father come through San Francisco while the "illegal" father comes through New York, where so many European immigrants entered with the blessing of the law. Indeed, as the "illegal" father makes his way into the country, he looks up to see the Statue of Liberty. "'Is she a goddess of theirs?' the father asked. 'No,' said the smuggler, 'they don't have goddesses. She's the symbol of an idea.' He was glad to hear that the Americans saw the idea of Liberty so real that they made a statue of it" (52–53). Then,

Drawn by George Frederick Keller after the Statue of Liberty was conceived but before it was erected, "A Statue for Our Harbor" appeared in the *Wasp*, November 11, 1881. Keller replaces Lady Liberty with a Chinese coolie holding an opium pipe and places junks in the San Francisco harbor illuminated by a Chinese moon. The words on the halo read "Ruin to White Labor" and "Diseases," "Immorality," and "Filth."

with his first spending money, Ed buys a postcard of the statue and pastes it into his album before adding any personal snapshots. Honoring the ideal of liberty, he is, nonetheless, forced to sneak into the country illegally, while his "legal" counterpart has to contemplate using fake papers in order to achieve the entrance he is entitled to.

Confronted with laws at odds with the country's professed universalistic civic ideals, Chinese immigrants used their imaginations to get around them. If doing so calls attention to the sometimes arbitrary distinction between "legal" and "illegal," it by no means undermines the need to implement fair laws. For instance, even though Congress denied Chinese citizenship by naturalization, Wong Kim Ark countered that unfairness by making citizenship possible by birth. Without that ruling Kingston's play between "legal" and "illegal" immigration would have no historical force. After all, if even "real" sons were "illegal," it would have been useless to create paper sons. Before Wong Kim Ark the promise of U.S. citizenship for those of Chinese descent was a fraud. Kingston, for instance, tells of a "citizenship judge" who tricks the grandfather working on the transcontinental railroad into buying worthless citizenship papers. After Wong Kim Ark, however, the promise of citizenship was no longer a fraud. On the contrary, even a child born of illegal immigrants could receive valid papers. Despite Schuck's and Smith's argument, there is perhaps no more poignant example of the egalitarian implications of the decision in Wong Kim Ark than the fact that, in the eyes of the law, children of illegal immigrants have the same right to citizenship as children of long-standing citizens. Making descent irrelevant, Wong Kim Ark places each child born within the United States under the protective shield of the Constitution.

Certainly, if the majority had not prevailed, Kingston would have been forced to tell a very different story about the transformation of the "Father from China" into the "American Father." Telling the story she does, she is able to honor her male ancestors not only through what she says but also through how she says it. Denied citizenship by restrictive laws, those ancestors imaginatively used documents to create legal citizens. Imagining stories about them, Kingston works within the tradition they established by using the document she is writing to reinforce their right to belong. And she does more than simply work within the tradition she honors. She also works on it through her own act of adoption. If Kingston's male ancestors created and adopted "paper sons," she, a woman, creates and adopts paper fathers and grandfathers. Telling a story about her own relatives, she acknowledges as her ancestors all China Men who helped make her life in America possible.

In *Wong Kim Ark* the minority responded to the argument that Chinese could become citizens by the accident of birth by quoting Vattel on the international law of citizenship: "The true bond which connects the child with the body politic is not the matter of an inanimate piece of land, but the moral relations of his parentage" (708, qtd. by Fuller). In contrast, for Kingston the land has become animated by the labor of her ancestors working on/with it to make it productive.

On the island of Oʻahu in the Hawaiʻian Islands, the narrator wanders into the sugarcane fields cultivated by Bak Goong, her great-grandfather. "I have heard the land sing," she writes. "I have seen the bright blue streaks of spirits whisking through the air. I again search for my American ancestors by listening in the cane" (90). Imagining her grandfather in the fields, she details how the laborers had not been allowed to talk while working. Her grandfather, however, was a "talk addict" (110) and needed to express himself. Tricking the overseer, he led workers into the cane, where they dug a deep hole and yelled into it.

They had dug an ear into the world, and were telling the earth their secrets.

"I want home," Bak Goong yelled, pressed against the soil, and smelling the earth. "I want my home," the men yelled together. "I want my home. Home. Home. Home. Home."

Talked out, they buried their words, planted them. "Like cats covering shit," they laughed.

"That wasn't a custom," said Bak Goong. "We made it up. We can make up customs because we're the founding ancestors of this place."

(118)

Listening to the cane years later, Kingston draws on her own mystic chords of memory to conjure up the lives of the workers who cultivated the land. "Soon the new green shoots would rise, and when in two years the cane grew gold tassels, what stories the wind would tell" (118).[76]

For Kingston, more than buried words of her once-silenced ancestors animate the land. The spirits of their buried bodies animate it as well. In a law school lecture, Justice Harlan supported his belief that Chinese were simply sojourners by claiming that, when they die, "no matter how long they have been here, they make arrangements to be sent back to their Fatherland."[77] If *Wong Kim Ark* gave Chinese born in the United States the possibility for U.S. citizenship, *China Men* also establishes their right to belong because of the graves of their forefathers.

Kingston's most explicit argument for the right of Chinese Americans to belong comes in the story of Kau Goong, the narrator's great-uncle. The "longest-lived and biggest human being [Maxine] had ever seen" (179), Kau Goong is urged to go to China to reunite with his wife, whom he left behind many years ago. But to the chagrin of his relatives, he balks, claiming that he does not want to live under Communism. Then his wife, more than ninety years old, smuggles herself out of the People's Republic to Hong Kong in order to be with him. "He has to go now, I thought; he cannot leave her alone and old in a foreign country. But Great Uncle, who was standing by the window, the profile of his big head against the glass and peach trees, the long tendons of his neck stretching, his big Adam's apple bobbing, said 'I've decided to stay in California.' He said, 'California. This is my home. I belong here.' He turned and, looking at us, roared, 'We belong here'" (184). Anticipating the title of one of the best books arguing for inclusive American citizenship—*Belonging to America*—Kau Goong stakes his claim to a new home.[78]

Kau Goong's affirmation that he belongs in California is an important part of the process by which those who have helped to make America are recognized by themselves and others as Americans. His roaring "*We* belong here" signals Kingston's recognition of the pull of a diasporic identity.[79]

☆ ☆ ☆ "Diaspora" derives from the Greek word *speirein*, which means to sow or scatter. The United States, it could be argued, is made up of numerous diasporic communities that often feel a special kinship with their various "homelands." As the travels of the China Men back and forth between the United States and China demonstrate, movement within these communities is often two-way, leading to what has come to be called a transnational or border identity. Constituted by the multiple subjectivities that people have from occupying spaces within or between different cultures, this hybrid identity points to the seeming arbitrariness of national boundaries—and thus national citizenship—in an increasingly mobile global society. If the concept of citizenship is to be preserved at all, it would seem to require redefinition in terms of different geographic units such as cities or in terms of multiple or at least dual nationalities.[80]

For instance, in *Wong Kim Ark* an argument against adopting a *jus soli* policy for the United States while much of the world retained *jus sanguinis* was that doing so created possibilities for dual citizenship. Commenting on *Wong Kim Ark*, the *Harvard Law Review* concluded, "This difficulty, however, is more apparent than real. When a child is born in America of Chinese parents, China claims him by *jus sanguinis*, America by *jus soli*. It is not a question whether he is an American or a Chinaman; he is both. . . . The duality of citizenship is a fact only in a third country. In China, he is a Chinaman; in America, an American."[81]

The title page of Kingston's book seems to endorse this conclusion. In addition to the English title of *China Men*, Kingston includes the Chinese written character for "Gold Mountain Warriors," the name adopted by Chinese journeying to California, which was known as the Gold Mountain.[82] Even so, these two titles have a significantly different effect from what the *Harvard Law Review* concludes about Wong Kim Ark's status. The title in Chinese identifies the book's protagonists with the United States; the title in English, with China. Rather than belonging to both America and China, the book's protagonists might seem to belong to neither. In fact, Kingston makes clear that they belong in America.

As much as Kingston recognizes the existence of multiple subjectivities and ties to multiple identities, she also works on diasporic mythology and border theorists' romance with displacement.[83] Indulging in diasporic nostalgia, some immigrants continue to imagine roots in their lost "homeland" that, they feel, determine their "authentic" identity. That nostalgia is so powerful that Kingston herself seems to indulge in it. For instance, telling an old Chinese legend, she remembers her father remarking, "'All Chinese know this story,'" and then adds, "If you are an authentic Chinese, you know the language and the stories without being taught, born talking them" (256). But if Kingston was born talking them, she changes them, leading to accusations that she does not tell the "real" stories. What such criticism fails to understand, however, is that Kingston is self-consciously challenging dreams of cultural authenticity. Advocating a dynamic, not a static, sense of culture, she portrays a world in which to retell myths is continually to alter them. Just as she gives a Chinese inflection to the story of Robinson Crusoe, so she gives an American one to Chinese myths and legends. We should, for instance, not miss the irony that Kingston refers to "an authentic Chinese" directly after a chapter called "The American Father."

The notion of an authentic culture risks creating rigid racial classifications that generate the sorts of racial stereotypes that Kingston is intent on undermining. This goes for Chinese culture as well as for American culture. Whereas there has been much criticism of Eurocentric thought, Kingston knows that decentering is also necessary for a culture that named itself the "Middle Kingdom." Thus, she plays with our notion of what is authentically Chinese by including "black Chinese Red Communists" (86), the narrator's black cousin and uncle living in the People's Republic. She also undercuts beliefs in epiphanies of diasporic connection. "The Making of More Americans" ends when Maxine's mother phones a brother in Singapore she has not seen for fifty years. The result: "Nothing significant said" (219).

Acutely aware of how individual identity is shaped by one's cultural heritage, Kingston does not consider it ultimately determinant. On the contrary, for her, identity is fashioned as much by where people live and with whom they interact as by where they come from. As we can see from the last chapter devoted to her father, she also knows that people want to feel at home where they live.

The myth juxtaposed to "The American Father" is about China's earliest known poet, who spent most of his life wandering in exile.[84] The juxtaposition reminds us that, although the father was a scholar in China, his learning is rarely appreciated in his new country. But, even though this neglect and the hardships he faces contribute to his silence, it would be a mistake to conclude that he ends his life in exile. On the contrary, the last paragraph of "The American Father" begins with a standard component of the immigration novel. "So my father at last owned his house and his business in America." It ends, "He planted many kinds of gourds, peas, beans, melons, and cabbages—and perennials—tangerines, oranges, grapefruit, almonds, pomegranates, apples, black figs, and white figs—and from seed pits, another loquat, peaches, apricots, plums of many varieties—trees that take years to fruit" (255). Diaspora may mean dispersion, but it also suggests the need to take root after sowing. Planting a mixture of Chinese and American plants, the father cultivates a space for their seeds to root. Redefining what it means to be an American, Kingston does not abandon the term itself. The "American Father" is here for the long term.

This image of the "American Father" creating a sense of rooted identity could easily conclude Kingston's book. Rather than end with the father, however, Kingston adds a chapter devoted to the next generation of China Men. Guarding against a falsely optimistic view of what U.S. citizenship entails, "The Brother in Vietnam" details the travails he must face. The brother, it turns out, has many similarities with his father. For instance, in a subtle variation on the typical immigrant story in which immigrants are Americanized in public schools, the brother is a high school teacher, just as his father had been in China. Most important, the brother, like his father, has to face a military draft. "Freedom from the draft," we are told, was the reason for the father "leaving China in the first place. The Gold Mountain does not make war, is not invaded, and has no draft. The government does not capture men and boys and send them to war" (269). The reality is, of course, quite different. "The War" Maxine had written in a composition during the Korean War. But "the teacher corrected 'Which war?' There were more than one" (276). Citizenship and war is an age-old theme. A traditional argument against the right to expatriation was that it would allow someone to escape military duty in the midst of battle. Conversely, those who serve during wartime can make a claim for citizenship. In the late nineteenth century, as many in the United States lobbied to restrict citizenship, France liberalized its citizenship laws to make more people eligible for military service. About the same time, in his *Plessy* dissent Justice Harlan argued for African American citizenship by noting how African Americans risked their lives during the Civil War. Their ability to do so was enabled by Lincoln's use of executive power in wartime. Arguing that the Emancipation Proclamation would place Lincoln in "universal history," George Bancroft called it a "military necessity" that "decided the result of the war. It took from the public enemy one or two millions of bondmen, and placed between one and two thousand brave and gallant troops on the side of the Union."[85] Lincoln also successfully instituted a military draft. Nothing, perhaps, is a more poignant reminder that citizenship entails duties as well as privileges than compulsory service during wartime.

Even though some refuse to recognize the brother as a "real" American, in the eyes of the law, he is eligible for the draft. Opposed to the war but having no religion by which he could be classified a conscientious objector and wanting to avoid being drafted into the infantry, he has two options: "go to Canada or enlist in the Navy." Although he has relatives in Vancouver Chinatown, he decides against Canada for personal and historical reasons. Unlike the country of his birth, Canada has no interpersonal attachments for him. "He had no friends there. He had never even met those relatives. He did not want to live the rest of his life a fugitive and an exile." The brother's refusal to become a man without a country reminds us that the myth of China's exiled poet, located between the brother's chapter and the father's, comments on the brother's life as well. The brother's decision is also influenced by past efforts to intimidate those of Chinese descent into leaving the country. "He would not," he vows, "be driven out" (283). So he enlists in the navy.

A communication specialist because of his academic qualifications, he has to undergo a security check. Reminiscent of the "legal" father's interrogation on Angel Island, the security check, invasive of privacy as it is, definitively establishes the family's right to be in the country. As the narrator ironically puts it, "The government was certifying that the family was really

American, not precariously American but super-American, extraordinarily secure—Q Clearance Americans. The Navy or the FBI had checked his mother and father and not deported them. Maybe the grandfather's Citizenship Judge was real after all. . . . The government had not found him un-American with divided loyalties and treasonous inclinations" (299). If the security clearance establishes the brother's citizenship in the government's eyes, being shipped to Asia establishes it in his own eyes.

Reversing the movement of earlier chapters, "The Brother in Vietnam" charts a journey from the United States to Asia. Playing on the myth that for children of Chinese immigrants that journey is a "return," Kingston writes, "In Taiwan he was for the first time in a country of Chinese people. The childish dream was that he would find like minds, and furniture that always fit his body. Chinese Americans talk about how when they set foot on China, even just Hong Kong, their whole lives suddenly make sense; their youth had been a preparation for this visit, they say. They realize their Americanness, they say, and 'You find out what a China Man you are'" (294). Led to expect a moment of diasporic connection as he finally returns "home," the brother is made aware of how different he is from those raised in a different land. "He had not," we are told, "'returned.'" China might mean the Middle Kingdom, but for the brother, "the Center was elsewhere" (301).

For Kingston, the center is always elsewhere. Early in the book she describes how Chinese, who thought of themselves as from the Center, "landed in a country where we are eccentric people" (15). By the end of the book she has created a world in which no group is at the center of the world, a world in which all people are eccentric people. In such a world, we know who we are only through encounters with what we are not, encounters that would be impossible if all people were the same, encounters that have the capacity to alter who we are. To belong to America, Kingston insists, is not to have a fixed identity. It is instead to have the opportunity to participate in a process of reconstructing one's self that interaction with numerous groups makes possible. If similar interactions take place elsewhere, no interaction is exactly the same as the one taking place within the United States. In suggesting a model for that interaction, Kingston makes her contribution to the vision affirmed in *Wong Kim Ark* when the Court refused to base citizenship by birth on descent and thus made it possible for people of all races to share the same territory.

☆ ☆ ☆ Kingston's dynamic model of citizenship brings us to a topic that links literary and political concerns: representation. We have already seen how Lincoln's ideal of a government of the people, by the people, for the people raises important questions about political representation. We have also seen how the debate over Huckleberry Finn raises questions about the ability of one work of literature to represent America or the American spirit. Within the American literary tradition the writer who most self-consciously claimed to represent the nation is Walt Whitman, who himself idealized Lincoln. Whitman made a claim to be representative by adopting a literary strategy that embraced the nation's diverse citizenry through an expansion of the self. He was especially intent on speaking for those who had been silenced. As revolutionary as he was, however, Whitman, like Lincoln, assumed the right to speaking for others. China Men formally embodies a subtly different strategy of representing how persons within a given territory interact with and affect one another.[86]

Unlike Whitman's "I," Kingston's narrator makes no claim to speak for those she is not, although she does continually imagine who she is not, especially when she, a woman, takes on the difficult task of telling the story of China Men. In order to accomplish that task, she goes to the closest source she has, her father, and tries to get him to speak. But he is silent about his past. Confronted with that silence, Kingston makes no claim to speak for him. On the contrary, the imaginative accounts that follow and constitute the rest of the book are designed to provoke him into speaking for himself. "I'll tell you what I suppose from your silences and few words," she says, "and you can tell me that I'm mistaken. You'll just have to speak up with the real stories if I've got you wrong" (15). Making no claim to tell the real story of her father, China Men also makes no claim to be the authentic account of the Chinese American experience. It certainly makes no claim to provide the definitive account of what it means to be an American. It is, instead, an imaginative reconstruction that invites readers of all ethnic backgrounds to speak up and tell their own stories if it has gotten the account of Americanization wrong.[87]

Kingston's invitation for readers to tell their own stories in response to hers grows out of the tradition of "talk story" popular on the Hawai'ian Islands, where she once taught and where so many different groups of people interact. In "talk story" listeners show respect not by trying to interpret a story but by telling, one by one, their own related but different stories, each prompted by the ones coming before. A mode of discourse capable of creating bonds between people from diverse groups, "talk story" is Kingston's model for how citizens in a diverse nation can interact with one another. There may be no fixed, substantive American culture, but there can be a "culture" of civil talk enhancing the interaction and learning between and among individuals and groups.

In *China Men*, Kingston offers a self-consciously fictionalized narrative that, rather than claiming to speak for those who have been silenced, provokes diverse voices into speaking for themselves. Not a naive celebration of identity politics, the book, through its formal structure, stresses the possibility of creating common bonds through a dialogue of multiple voices that need not efface their differences.[88] This dialogic structure is emphasized by the book's first and last chapters. Titled "On Discovery," the first works on/ with myths of discovery by drawing on Chinese legends to offer an account of the discovery of America across the Pacific as well as across the Atlantic. Bringing readers to an imagined world of America, it also introduces them to the world of the book, which, Kingston hopes, will be a world of discovery. The title of her final chapter is "On Listening," a reminder that discovery comes not only from speaking one's voice and representing one's interests but, equally important, from listening to others. This dynamic process of provoking new voices into a dialogue of speaking and listening opens up possibilities for perpetually redefining both the constitution of the body politic and the identities of the individuals it embodies. If American citizens must subject themselves to the country's laws, Kingston imagines how, through civil talk, their participation in a heterogeneous society can subject what it means to be an American to continual revision.

7 ☆ Conclusion

Keeping Discussions of U.S. Citizenship Open

Modeled on "talk story," *China Men* keeps a dialogue with its readers open. In this conclusion, I want to keep my discussion of citizenship open by bringing the four works I have written about and their authors into dialogue. That dialogue will, in turn, expand into a brief exchange with recent calls for "transnational," "postnational," and "global" citizenships that I mentioned in Chapter 1. But first, a review of the book's three goals.

Selected works of literature have a role to play in civic education, I have argued, by supplementing, not displacing, other forms of discourse. For instance, works of literature rarely teach students, as much civic education should, about the makeup of civic institutions. They can, however, supply an important affective component to that instruction. If traditionally they have been used to generate loyalty and patriotism, they also have a very different use. "The literature of citizenship," Julia Lupton argues, "is never simply civic, never fully coterminous with the public spaces that it maps." Confronting us with the complicated dilemmas, choices, and even sacrifices that citizens must face, "the literature of citizenship provokes collective and individual processes of evaluation, deliberation, and debate."[1]

An example is the way all four of my works test the great civic ideal, poignantly expressed by Lincoln, that "reverence for the laws" should become "the political religion of the nation"[2]: *The Scarlet Letter* through Dimmesdale's, Hester's, and Chillingworth's defiance of the law; *Huckleberry Finn* through Huck's disregard of the laws of slavery; *China Men* through questioning the opposition between legal and illegal immigrants; and even "The Man without a Country," which, despite its clear message of patriotism, reminds us that in the very act of publishing Nolan's story, Ingham risks punishment for disobeying orders. In testing that ideal, none of the four denies the importance of rule by law. What they do instead is dramatize various conflicts citizens subject to rule by law confront. If, unlike much political discourse, they do not resolve those conflicts by providing models of substantive or even procedural justice, they do alert readers to the inevitable emotional as well as intellectual contradictions and tensions that citizenship entails.

Indeed, each narrative I have treated is generated by almost unresolvable conflicts: *The Scarlet Letter* by potential clashes between the pursuit of happiness and the demands of justice; "The Man without a Country" by calls for loyalty in a country founded on the right to alter loyalties; *Huckleberry Finn* by ongoing tensions between the ideals of liberty and equality; and *China Men* by conflicts between attachments to an ethnic heritage and affinities for a new home. Yet, even as they dramatize these conflicts, these narratives also keep open the hope of redemption for fallen, discredited, or eccentric people, whether Hester, Philip Nolan, Huck and Jim, or Maxine's relatives.[3]

If those similarities give these works a role in civic education, they are not enough to answer a question linked to a second goal, which is to speculate on what allows works like *The Scarlet Letter*, *Huckleberry Finn*, and "The Man without a Country" to achieve almost mythical status themselves. I have already spent considerable time accounting for how Twain's work achieved that status and how Hale's lost it. But I have not yet taken a stab at explaining why *China Men* lacks it. The most obvious explanation is age. For a story to become a myth, it has to be retold over a number of generations. Although *China Men* participates in the retelling of numerous myths and legends, the book itself is not that old. Even so, more than age is, I think, at stake.

According to Henry Nash Smith, myth "fuses concept and emotion into an image."[4] Smith's emphasis on the image might seem to ignore the narrative component of myth. In fact, it highlights a particular aspect of it. As Richard Slotkin writes, through "periodic retelling," the "formal qualities and structures" of a narrative "are increasingly conventionalized and abstracted, until they are reduced to a set of powerfully evocative 'icons' — like the landing of the Pilgrims, the rally of the Minutemen at Lexington, the Alamo, the Last Stand, Pearl Harbor."[5] In a shrewd analysis of *Huckleberry Finn*, Robert Penn Warren describes how such images work in literature. "There are," Warren acknowledges, "incoherences in *Huckleberry Finn*. . . . But the book survives ultimately because all is absorbed into a powerful, mythic image. That mythic image, like all great myths, is full of internal tensions and paradoxes. . . . In its fullness, the myth is not absorbed formally into the novel. It bursts out of the novel, stands behind the novel, overshadows the novel, undercuts the novel."[6]

The Scarlet Letter generates similarly powerful images that have the capacity to burst out of the novel, such as Hester on the scaffold and Hester and Dimmesdale in the forest, images that have led readers to misread the novel itself. Likewise, for generations the image of Nolan alone and lonely on a ship at sea was identical with the nation's sense of what it meant to be a man without a country, even for those who had only been told of the story and not actually read it. In contrast, *China Men*, comprised of so many stories, does not easily coalesce into one image. This is not an aesthetic judgment. Though episodic, Kingston's work is formally more successful than *Huckleberry Finn*. But it does help to explain why Kingston's book is less likely to achieve the mythic status that the other three have or once had.

Even without that status, however, it greatly contributes to this book's primary goal. Some sort of civic mythology is, I have argued, not only inevitable but indispensable. For instance, to avoid being immobilized, the United States needs some way to negotiate the conflicts that arise between its civic ideals of liberty and equality. The civic mythology surrounding Lincoln helps it do so. Indeed, given the utopian, democratic potential of the Great Emancipator's vision, the Lincoln legend is preferable to many alternatives that might arise. At the same time, it needs to be perpetually worked on as well as with. Similarly, I have tried to show, the capacity of selected works of literature to work on/with civic myths can add to our understanding of citizenship: *The Scarlet Letter* through work on/with the myth of the Puritan origins of American democracy; "The Man without a Country" through work on/with the Spirit of '76; *Huckleberry Finn* through work on/with the myth of the independent citizen; and *China Men* through work on/with myths of the founding fathers. In choosing these works, I have not tried to generate a classificatory system that covers all possibilities of citizenship. Good, patriotic, independent, and immigrant citizens are not the only kinds of citizens. Nor are they mutually exclusive categories. For some, a good citizen is a patriotic citizen. At the same time, there is nothing to keep immigrant citizens from being patriotic, or good or independent. Potentially overlapping and at times reinforcing one another, these four types signal different emphases more than strict oppositions. Even so, they can generate tensions, both within themselves and between one another.

In individual chapters, I have already explored tensions within particular kinds of citizenship. *The Scarlet Letter* moves us from the notion of good citizenship as the obedient subject to that of the good neighbor, who operates more in the realm of civil society than within the civic sphere of politics. Delivering a sermon on patriotism, "The Man without a Country" distinguishes between loyalty to one's government and to one's country. *Huckleberry Finn* celebrates the independent citizen while dramatizing its limitations, limitations highlighted by a comparison between Twain's notion of independence and Tourgée's. Portraying how immigrants adopt the laws and cultures of their new country, *China Men* differentiates between those who assimilate to both from those who alter their terms through acts of appropriation.

If these are some of the tensions within particular kinds of citizenship, a dialogue between the four works and their authors can highlight overlaps and tensions between their different visions. We can start with the two most well-known works: *The Scarlet Letter* and *Huckleberry Finn*. Both provoked controversy upon their publication. *Huckleberry Finn* was banned by the Concord Public Library as an immoral influence on young boys; *The Scarlet Letter* sparked debates because of caricatures in "The Custom-House" and its treatment of adultery. Nonetheless, by the 1920s *Huckleberry Finn* had joined *The Scarlet Letter* as one of the generally acknowledged American classics. In 1921, for instance, Carl Van Doren's *The American Novel* called *The Scarlet Letter* and *Huckleberry Finn* the two greatest American novels.[7] Although as late as 1894 in the journal *Education* E. W. Barrett advocated assigning *Twice-told Tales* or *The Marble Faun* rather than *The Scarlet Letter* because students should not "associate with those who are constantly dejected or morbidly sensitive," today textbook sales indicate that Hawthorne's and Twain's books are the most widely taught American works in colleges and, along with *To Kill a Mockingbird* and *The Great Gatsby*, are the most frequently taught in high schools: public, Catholic, and independent.[8]

Their pedagogical value comes in part from their depiction of two important moments in American history: Puritan New England and antebellum slave society. Equally important, both speak to potentially alienated young people by treating outcasts whose rebellions end in possible redemption. Indeed, given the fact that both Hawthorne and Twain champion the artist for nonpartisanship—Hawthorne through his attack on the spoils system in "The Custom-House" and Twain through his mugwumpery—Hawthorne's good citizen seems to share numerous characteristics with Twain's independent citizen. There are, however, important differences, which are linked to differences in their formal structures.[9]

Warren calls Hawthorne's book "the first American novel to be truly 'composed,' in the sense that we shall find Henry James using the term; that is, the first novel to consider form as, in itself, an expression of emotion and meaning."[10] In contrast, *Huckleberry Finn* is episodic, and, whereas there have been a number of efforts to grant it a complex formal unity, even most of its outspoken supporters admit that it is formally flawed. For instance, as masterfully as Twain creates Huck's voice to tell his story, it is not clear what kind of story he is telling. On one hand, he seems to describe his initiation into adulthood; on the other, he seems to offer social satire. Initiation and satire come into conflict, however, since we have no desire for Huck to be successfully initiated into the society that Twain so effectively satirizes.

Huck's failure to be initiated into society points to a crucial difference between Twain's and Hawthorne's senses of independence. A specific example shows how. Although Hawthorne and Twain were firmly committed family men, both write about dysfunctional families. Both also describe custody battles in which the state threatens to take a child away from a single parent; in *The Scarlet Letter*, from the mother; in *Huckleberry Finn*, from the father. In Hawthorne's romance our sympathies are with the mother, against the state, but in Twain's novel we hope that Huck does not have to return to his drunken father. Even so, our distrust of Pap does not mean that we sympathize with the state. Although it is clear that Huck is better off in a foster home than with Pap, Twain undercuts the "civilizing" code imposed on Huck by the widow, Miss Watson, and Aunt Sally. The constraints they place on Huck suggest that our differing sympathies about these two custody battles are not simply the result of the developing cultural assumption—fostered by *The Scarlet Letter*—about the nurturing role of mothers. On the contrary, the fact that the state battles with a mother in one book and with a father in the other highlights a more important difference between the two books.

Pearl, as we have seen, is completely unimaginable without her mother. Huck, however, is almost unimaginable with a mother. To have given Huck a mother would have greatly complicated Twain's attack on the sentimental codes of civilization embodied in the book through women. It is one thing to have Huck rebel against the widow. It would have been quite another to have had him rebel against a mother, especially for Twain, who was extremely sentimental about motherhood. Likewise, if Huck's independence depends on a dysfunctional father, Pearl's lack of an acknowledged father is felt to be a major loss. In *The Scarlet Letter* isolation is dangerous, while family relations—and by extension familylike communal relations—help to foster Hester's independence from too-rigid conformity to the state. In contrast, in *Huckleberry Finn* Huck's independence depends on breaking ties of both filiation and affiliation. On one hand, Huck needs to escape his father's ignorant prejudices; on the other, he needs to resist communal prejudices of even the educated with whom he might forge attachments, including the prejudices of his friend Tom Sawyer, whose influence Huck can never totally shake. If *The Scarlet Letter* stresses the importance of civil society's voluntary associations, *Huckleberry Finn* points to their dangers.

The major—and crucial—exception to Huck's need to break bonds of filiation and affiliation is his relation with Jim, who acts like a brother and a father to Huck. Yet nothing differentiates *Huckleberry Finn* from *The Scarlet Letter* more than the community established between Huck and Jim on the raft. Both books are about relationships condemned by the civil societies in which they live, one about a man and a woman, the other about a white boy and a black man. But whereas Hawthorne sympathizes with, but ultimately condemns, the relation between Hester and Dimmesdale because of its location outside civil society, Twain both sympathizes with and condones the relation between Huck and Jim, even though he cannot imagine a place for it within civil society. To be sure, Hawthorne's condemnation of Hester and Dimmesdale's adultery does not sanctify the civil order they contemplate escaping. Quite the opposite. The idea of civil society, as we have seen, developed in contrast to the idea of religious society. The problem with Puritan society, as Hawthorne portrays it, is that it is not civil enough. Hester is able to suggest an alternative order because she does not follow Dimmesdale's effort to find salvation in an order completely bound to a religious one. In *Huckleberry Finn*, however, no viable alternative civil order seems capable of being forged out of Huck and Jim's "community of saints," a community with which we are expected to sympathize but a community that seems incapable of being sustained. Paradoxically, then, hope for an alternative civil society comes in a book considered tragic in its mode, whereas a book celebrated for its humor offers little hope for such an alternative.

In the chapter on *Huckleberry Finn*, we saw how Twain, turning to the ideal of the independent citizen in response to his distrust of the politics of affiliation, also exposes the limits of his ideal. There are potential limits to Hawthorne's view of the good citizen within civil society as well. Most obviously, to stress the importance of activities within civil society is to risk minimizing the importance of activities within the traditional realm of politics. That risk becomes apparent when we turn to the issue of slavery that so concerned Twain.

Acknowledging the conflict between loyalty to an one's state and to the federal union, Hawthorne searched for a reason to fight the Civil War. Writing to his friend Horatio Bridge, he identified the issue of slavery. "If we are fighting for the annihilation of slavery . . . it might be a wise object, and offers a tangible result, and the only one which is consistent with a future Union between North and South. A continuance of the war would soon make this plain to us; and we should see the expediency of preparing our black brethren for future citizenship by allowing them to fight for their own liberties, and educating them through heroic influences."[11] Whereas the annihilation of slavery was indeed the basis for restoring the Union, a truly equitable citizenship for blacks was, as we have seen, derailed by the reconciliation of white North and South.

Even though he died in 1864, Hawthorne unintentionally anticipates a reason for those derailed efforts in his metaphoric descriptions of the scarlet letter. The letter is called variously a mark, a brand, a badge of shame, and a stigma. What Hawthorne could not have known was that a few years after *The Scarlet Letter* appeared, Justice Taney in the *Dred Scott* case would use similar metaphors to deny citizenship to anyone of African descent—free or slave. Since in a republic there is only one class of citizens, Taney, as we have seen, argued that "the deep and enduring marks of inferiority and degradation" implanted on blacks had so "stigmatized" them that they were excluded from the sovereign body constituting the nation.[12] In an effort to undo the damage done by *Dred Scott*, the Supreme Court, after the Civil War, ruled that the Thirteenth Amendment forbade not only slavery but also all "badges and incidents" of slavery. The difference between a badge and a stigma is significant. A badge can be removed; a stigma, coming from the Greek word for a brand, is implanted for a lifetime—and for Taney could be passed from generation to generation.[13]

The Scarlet Letter ends by giving Hester a choice whether or not to wear her "badge of shame." She willingly chooses to wear it, in part because through her own agency the letter has "ceased to be a stigma."[14] In contrast, the possibility of achieving the status of model citizen through individual effort was denied African Americans because their race meant that, as a group, they inherited a badge of slavery, whose stigma persisted. The civil society argument about "uncoerced human associations" by itself is not adequate to deal with that problem.[15] Instead a much more traditional argument about active citizen participation in the political sphere would seem to be called for. As Reinhold Niebuhr argued in 1932, "It may be possible, though it is never easy, to establish just relations between individuals in a group purely by moral and rational suasion and accommodation. In inter-group relations this is practically an impossibility. The relations between groups must therefore always be predominantly political rather than ethical, that is, they will be determined by the proportion of power which each group possesses as much as by any rational and moral appraisal of the comparative needs and claims of each group."[16]

The risk of emphasizing good citizenship in civil society is political quietism of the sort that Hawthorne succumbed to in the 1850s when he argued that slavery would wither and die of its own accord. Whereas it is far too simple to consider that quietism the final word on the "politics" of Hawthorne's most famous novel, it does point to limits to his view of the good citizen.[17] It also reiterates how important slavery has been for defining the terms of U.S. citizenship, since, as we have seen, the citizenship clause of the Fourteenth Amendment was explicitly intended to help undo slavery's effects. At the same time, as we have also seen, there are dangers in framing issues of citizenship only in black and white terms. The citizenship clause was designed to combat the effects of slavery, but as *United States v. Wong Kim Ark* makes clear, it has affected all sorts of groups. Indeed, if we stick for a moment with the metaphors of badges and stigmas, we can see how even the Thirteenth Amendment, which banned the institution of slavery, has potential application to other groups.

In *Hodges v. United States* (1906) the Supreme Court rendered the Thirteenth Amendment "such a weak reed" that until *Bell v. Maryland* (1968) it was of little use in combating the lingering effects of slavery.[18] Alluding to the Geary Act in his opinion of the Court in *Hodges*, Justice Brewer noted, "In slave times in the slave States not infrequently every free Negro was required to carry with him a copy of a judicial decree or other evidence of his right to freedom or be subject to arrest. That was one of the incidents of slavery. By the act of May 5, 1892, Congress required all Chinese laborers within the limits of the United States to apply for a certificate, and anyone who after one year from the passage of the act should be found within the jurisdiction of the United States without such a certificate, might be arrested and deported."[19] Even though the certificates Chinese were required to wear were real, not metaphoric, badges, no one, he reminded the Court, challenged the act under the Thirteenth Amendment. Brewer's reminder was clearly intended for the ears of Justice Harlan, one of two dissenters in *Hodges*, who, nonetheless, unlike Brewer himself, had little concern for the plight of the Chinese.

Just as the effect of the Civil War amendments on questions of citizenship goes beyond the issue of slavery, so does the effect of the war itself. Historically, the end of slavery coincided with the transformation of a union of states into a modern nation. Logically, however, the two need not be connected. The increased power granted to the federal government during and after the war altered the nature of citizenship in the United States in ways that go beyond issues of race. Most importantly, by giving priority to national over state citizenship, it significantly changed the citizen's relation to the federal government. We can get a sense of what is at stake in that transformation by comparing our two New Englanders: Hawthorne and Hale.

A year before "The Man without a Country" appeared, Hawthorne published his own piece in the *Atlantic Monthly*. In it he explains Southerners' national disloyalty by stressing their loyalty to their state or region.

It is a strange thing in human life, that the greatest errors both of men and women often spring from their sweetest and most generous qualities; and so, undoubtedly, thousands of warm-hearted, sympathetic, and impulsive persons have joined the Rebels, not from any real zeal for the cause, but because, between two conflicting loyalties, they chose that which necessarily lay near the heart. There never existed any other Government against which treason was so easy, and could defend itself by such plausible arguments as against that of the United States. The anomaly of two allegiances (of which the State comes nearest to home to a man's feelings, and includes the altar and the hearth, while the General Government claims his devotion only to an airy mode of law, and has no symbol but a flag) is exceedingly mischievous in this point of view; for it has converted crowds of honest people into traitors, who seem to themselves not merely innocent, but patriotic, and who die for a bad cause with as quiet a conscience as if it were the best. In the vast extent of our country, — too vast by far to be taken into one small human heart, — we inevitably limit to our own State, or at farthest, our own section, that sentiment of physical love for the soil which renders an Englishman, for example, so intensely sensitive to the dignity and well being of his little island, that one hostile foot, treading anywhere upon it, would make a bruise on each individual breast.[20]

In his First Inaugural Lincoln appealed to "bonds of affection . . . stretching from every battle-field and patriot grave, to every living heart and hearth-stone, all over this broad land."[21] In contrast, Hawthorne describes how the "altar and the hearth" bind citizens' hearts to the state, not to the nation. Even so, Hawthorne is careful to call Southerners' disloyalty a mistake, a mistake, it turns out, with remarkable similarities to Hester's mistake in the novel that made Hawthorne famous. Hester, after all, like Southerners, errs by following generous sympathies close to her heart and feels attachment to a piece of land because of interpersonal relations, not "an airy mode of law." Aware of the power of such attachments, Hale aids Lincoln's cause by combating them with an affective tale of his own. Whereas Hawthorne acknowledges the "anomaly of two allegiances," Hale insists on one. If Hawthorne describes the heart's attachment to individual states through the altar and the hearth, Hale tries to transfer that attachment to the country's vast territory by comparing it to one's mother and by evoking the national symbol of the flag.

It is tempting to label Hawthorne's views "Southern" and Hale's "Northern." But, as we have seen, there were numerous Northerners who were firm defenders of the Union and still shared Hawthorne's understanding of local and regional attachment. He, and they, had a Jacksonian, not a Lincolnian, sense of the nation. Hawthorne's views were, for instance, very similar to those of Robert Rantoul, a prominent Jacksonian Democrat in Massachusetts. Rantoul, who once ran for office against Charles Upham, the Whig politician responsible for Hawthorne losing his position in the Custom House, shows why it is a mistake to assume that antislavery sentiment was unthinkable without a Lincolnian sense of the nation. As we have seen, Lincoln's views were heavily indebted to Daniel Webster and Justice Joseph Story. A vocal critic of slavery, Rantoul fought Story over the codification of Massachusetts law and defended Thomas Sims, the first victim in Massachusetts of Webster's Fugitive Slave Act, which gave new powers to the federal government. For Rantoul the Union was a "limited partnership," and Hawthorne would have agreed.[22] In contrast, Hale viewed it as an organic, corporate entity. That difference demands a bit of explanation, since it affects the relation citizens have to the nation.

As the nineteenth-century German legal historian Otto Gierke noted, the corporate form goes back to Roman law, which recognized two kinds of associations: the *universitas* and the *societas*. In the former, members lose their individual identities to form a corporate whole; in the latter, members retain their individual identities to form a contractually based partnership. When Renaissance political thinkers conceptualized the modern state, Gierke claimed, they drew on the legal concept of *societas*, such as in theories of social contract. Similarly, for many people in the antebellum period, the United States were conceived as a *societas*, not a corporate entity. But during the nineteenth century, the corporate, organic model gained force, imported to the United States by thinkers like Francis Lieber. When the Civil War decided that the United States would become a singular, not a plural, entity, with individual states subordinate to the central government, the corporate model prevailed.[23] With the victory of the corporate model, why, then, does The Scarlet Letter, with its sense of local attachment, continue to have such force?

The obvious answer, as we saw in Chapter 2, is that, although The Scarlet Letter expresses ideas about sympathies and attachments similar to those in Hawthorne's Atlantic Monthly piece, Hawthorne's novel is not about the "anomaly" of the U.S. federal system. The corporate notion of the nation with its concentration of power in a centralized federal government has prevailed, but the structure of feeling expressed in Hawthorne's novel is very much with us. If sometimes it gets expressed in terms of states' rights, it more often gets expressed in local attachments. One telling example is the attachment to local sports teams, professional and collegiate, that compete in groups called the National or American Leagues, the National Football League, or the National Collegiate Athletic Association. It also, very importantly, gets expressed in the civil society argument I discussed in conjunction with The Scarlet Letter, one in which a primary function of the government in liberal democracies is to create a space for local attachments to flourish through voluntary associations. We can see its persistence in China Men.

Like Hawthorne, Kingston recognizes people's important attachments to groups, not simply to an abstract nation. Maxine's family may get confirmed as "Q Clearance Americans" by the brother's FBI security check, but he decides to enlist in the navy and not leave the country because of ties to friends and family. This does not mean that he lacks a sense of what it means to be an American, but it does mean that his sense of national belonging differs from how Benedict Anderson has influentially described it.

By describing a nation as an "imagined community," Anderson offers a compelling, if corporate, explanation as to why nationalism became such a potent force in the nineteenth century.[24] Many people at that time were threatened by a move from the familiarity of face-to-face communities to what they considered a fragmented and alienated modern society. To imagine the nation as an extended community was to give it great ideological power by having people think of it as a Gemeinschaft (community), not as a Gesellschaft (society).[25] With citizenship described by thinkers as different as Lauren Berlant and J. M. Barbalet as "participation in or membership of a community," in the nineteenth century it became inextricably bound to the nation.[26] Even so, Hawthorne, writing before Anderson's sense of the nation dominates, and Kingston, writing in the late twentieth century, conceive of the nation more as an imagined society than as an imagined community. Consisting of different and often overlapping communities, this nation as imagined society acknowledges national citizenship, but communal identification occurs on a more local level. At the same time, harmonious and dynamic relations among the nation's different communities depend on skills of sociability developed in voluntary associations.

Twain, too, to a certain extent, thinks of the nation more as a societas than as a corporate entity. But his distrust of affiliation makes him think of it as a society of discrete individuals rather than one of interconnected groups that, for both Hawthorne and Kingston, are the basis of communal attachments. Having little faith in the ability of such intermediary forms of association between the nation and the individual to create communal attachments, Twain imagines a world in which the independence of isolated individuals is constantly threatened by "society," conceived of in his case as an indistinguishable mass that allows for no individuality. Evoking the metaphor of the ship of state, Hale had countered threats of secession by warning that disunion "would be like breaking up a noble ship, which whatever its imperfections, still bears those on board safely across the seas, in order that the dismembered and scattered crew might find greater safety and independence on the loose rafts constructed out of the fragments."[27] *Huckleberry Finn* charts the course of a loose raft, not of the ship of state itself.

Another way to measure similarities and differences between Hawthorne, Hale, Twain, and Kingston is to look at their portrayals of burial and gravestones. Indeed, even though citizenship is frequently determined by birth, affective connections to a country can be determined as much by the dead as by the living. Lincoln, for instance, memorably appealed to the graves of patriots on battlefields to try to forge bonds of affection between citizens. Similarly, at the end of his story, Hale highlights Nolan's love of country through the inscription on the stone placed in his memory at Fort Adams, even though Nolan is buried at sea, which had become his home in exile. *The Scarlet Letter* and *China Men* also dramatize how tombstones and memorials to the dead establish connections to the land, but their emphases are quite different from the one implied by Hale. One reason Hester feels the pull to return to Boston is the presence of Dimmesdale's grave. But, unlike Nolan, Hester is bound by an interpersonal relationship, not by patriotism. If Nolan elicits readers' loyalty to the United States by comparing his country to a mother, Hawthorne's Hester feels bound to Boston because of her attachment to her lover.

In *China Men*, as well, buried loved ones establish Chinese immigrants' claims to belong to the land, even though, as the comic story of Mad Sao shows, immigrants sometimes have to come to terms with the ghosts of relatives buried in China. Having "firmly established his American citizenship by serving in the U.S. Army in World War II,"[28] Mad Sao was the most "Americanized" of those in Maxine's immigrant community. But from her grave in China his mother continues to haunt him. Only when Mad Sao returns to perform the proper rituals of respect can he feel at home in his new land.

Like Kingston, Twain transforms the serious rituals of burial into a source of humor. He, however, is outright irreverent in his handling of Peter Wilks's corpse. A product of Twain's impatience with the superstitions of Christian burial, his portrayal of burials in *Huckleberry Finn* also reveals a different attitude about people's attachment to the land. When people die in *Huckleberry Finn*, such as the crooks on the *Walter Scott* and Pap, they find a final "resting place" at the bottom of the Mississippi, not in a firm piece of land. Describing Twain's attitude toward funerals and adding a footnote about his fondness for cremation, Louis Budd argues that in 1884 Twain was moving toward mugwumpery "from motives wider than just voting for the public servant instead of the party hack."[29] All customs, political or social, that tried to fix one's identity, including burial, were to him suspect. Lacking Kingston's sense of rootedness to the land, Twain, nonetheless, anticipates her by working on and with founding myths that would fix the American "character."

If many of Twain's contemporaries appealed to myths of the Cavaliers of Virginia or the Puritans of New England, Twain takes on both, delivering a devastating criticism of the "First Families of Virginia" in *Pudd'nhead Wilson* and mocking the symbol of Plymouth Rock in an 1881 speech to the New England Society of Philadelphia. Describing the Pilgrims as a "hard lot," he notes that they "took good care of themselves, but they abolished everybody else's ancestors." Asking "where are my ancestors," he replies, "My first American ancestor, gentlemen, was an Indian—an early Indian. Your ancestors skinned him alive." He goes on to list Quakers and Salem witches as other ancestors, saving his trump card for last. "The first slave brought into New England out of Africa by your progenitors was an ancestor of mine—for I am a mixed breed, an infinitely shaded and exquisite Mongrel."[30]

Twain's call "to get up an auction and sell Plymouth Rock" might seem a challenge to Hawthorne, who is so identified with the culture of New England. But, as we have seen, Hawthorne also works on the myth of the Puritan origins of American citizenship as much as he works with it. Indeed, his mythical creation of morally rigid and authoritarian Puritans may well have resonated with people like Clement Vallandigham, who criticized the Puritans for self-righteousness. In his 1862 *Atlantic Monthly* piece, for instance, Hawthorne complicates the myth of the Puritans as the lovers of liberty by evoking the *Mayflower* to establish a connection, not between Puritans and Cavaliers, but between the Puritans and the slaves of Virginia. "There is a historical circumstance known to few, that connects the children of the Puritans with these Africans of Virginia, in a very singular way. They are our brethren, as being lineal descendants from the Mayflower, the fated womb of which, in her first voyage, sent forth a brood of Pilgrims upon Plymouth Rock, and in a subsequent one, spawned slaves upon the Southern soil, —a monstrous birth, but with which we have an instinctive sense of kindred, and so are stirred by an irresistible impulse to attempt their rescue, even at the cost of blood and ruin."[31]

What Hawthorne himself could not have known was that by the late nineteenth century, competing narratives of national origins frequently pitted Plymouth Rock against another national symbol, the recently erected Statue of Liberty. If, before the Civil War, the story of Plymouth Rock, like that of Nathan Hale, was, for the most part, a regional one, increased immigration after the war helped give it national importance. As Werner Sollors puts it, "The more heterogeneous the country was perceived to be, the more Plymouth Rock came to be stressed as a mark of distinction."[32] Indeed, to compete with narratives about the United States as a land of immigrants, a national monument to the forefathers in Plymouth depicting Faith was dedicated on August 1, 1889. Strongly resembling Lady Liberty, Faith, nonetheless, rests her left foot upon the firm foundation of a piece of what is supposed to be Plymouth Rock and holds in her left hand a Bible, not the Declaration of Independence.

Designed to discredit the potential citizenship of Ellis Island immigrants, appeals to Plymouth Rock and *Mayflower* ancestry did not go unchallenged. For Russian Jewish immigrant Mary Antin, Ellis Island and Plymouth Rock are linked rather than opposed. Interpreting the Statue of Liberty "to mean that the love of liberty unites all races and all classes of men into one close brotherhood, and that we Americans, therefore, who have the utmost of liberty that has yet been attained, owe the alien a brother's share," she argues that, because both immigrants and the Pilgrims arrived on American shores after long ocean voyages, "the ghost of the Mayflower pilots every immigrant ship, and Ellis Island is another name for Plymouth Rock."[33]

If Antin works on/with the myth of Plymouth Rock and the *Mayflower* to include immigrants, just as Hawthorne and Twain had included Native Americans and African Americans, Kingston works on/with Antin's appropriation of it. Using her opening chapter of "On Discovery" to remind us of those who came to America by voyaging across the Pacific as well as the Atlantic, Kingston complicates Antin's celebratory narrative by having the "illegal" father enter the country in New York under the shadow of the Statue of Liberty, while making the "legal" father undergo the travails of Angel Island in San Francisco. Destabalizing simple narratives about legal and illegal immigration, Kingston refuses to let us forget a history that unfairly excluded Chinese from the land of opportunity.

Of these four authors, Kingston is clearly the most concerned about the immigrant citizen. But she is not alone in her interest. Stating in "The Custom-House" that "human nature will not flourish, any more than a potato, if it be planted and replanted, for too long a series of generations in the same worn-out soil,"[34] Hawthorne reminds readers of the Puritans' immigrant status by using metaphors of transplantation to describe their adaptation to a new world. Preaching patriotism to those born on its soil, Hale's "The Man without a Country" might seem to have little pull on the immigrant imagination. But it had a profound impact on Antin. As one of his many public services, Hale had established Hale House for immigrants in Boston. In *The Promised Land* Antin speaks glowingly of her experiences there and her encounters with Hale himself, who invited her to his house, gave her access to his library, and encouraged her writing. Meeting in the early morning they were, she reports, "busy in the interests of citizenship and friendship." Earlier in the book, Antin alludes to "The Man without a Country" when she notes that a life of exile in Russia for Jews, as a "people without a country," intensified her love for "her new country."[35] As late as 1949, teaching editions of *The Promised Land* were used in public school civics classes, just as when I started work on this book one of the few places "The Man without a Country" was still in print was for a series designed for students of English as a second language.[36]

Antin's love of her country clearly shows how the immigrant citizen can become the most patriotic of citizens. But if Antin seems to endorse Hale's notion of patriotism, Hawthorne, Twain, and Kingston suggest alternatives. Because of his awareness that people's love of country is as likely to derive from attachments to the altar and hearth as from those to the symbol of the flag, Hawthorne was accused by some of treason during the Civil War. Likewise, as we have seen, although the brother in *China Men* chooses not to become a man without a country and go to Canada or Sweden to escape military service during the Vietnam War, he is motivated more by interpersonal attachments and a refusal to be driven out than by an abstract love of country. The most explicit challenge to Hale's version of the patriotic citizen comes, however, from Twain and his notion of citizenly independence.

In the last years of his life Twain, like Hale, was actively involved in helping immigrant citizens. In them he saw a potential model for patriotism, just as he turns Huck, the son of Irish Pap Finn, into a "quintessential American." Indeed, in 1907 Twain described his favorite project, the Children's Theater for immigrants on the Lower East Side of Manhattan, as if it were the training ground for a slew of young Hucks, freed by its sponsoring

Educational Alliance from enslaving indoctrination by parents, falsely moralistic Miss Watsons, or corrupt Tom Sawyers.

> It may be . . . that we must learn our lessons of citizenship on the East Side in the Children's Theater. There the true principles of life which mean true citizenship are being taught to those boys and girls who are to be the future citizens of America. . . . Their morals are watched; they are educated in the practical things of life—the things that make for this very citizenship which we, as a nation, have lost. We have good reason to emulate these people of the East Side. They are reading our history and learning the great questions of America that we do not know and are not learning, and they are learning them first hand and are doing their own thinking.

The activities of these independent, self-thinking new citizens starkly contrast with rituals that pass as patriotism, like salutes to the flag and support of unjust wars. In mugwumpian fashion, Twain attributes such "so-called patriotism" to love of party, not country. It is "derived second hand from certain men who seek to influence us to their way of thinking, and their way of thinking is generally in a direction that will subserve their own private ends or the ends of the party which they represent." Chief among the doctrines "employed for the benefit of political parties" is the slogan "My country, right or wrong, my country."[37]

Twain was especially disdainful of this slogan because it was the rallying cry for the Spanish-American War and its imperialist aftermath. It was also, as we have seen, associated with "The Man without a Country." Indeed, Hale had evoked his famous story in support of the government's turn-of-the-century imperialist adventures. In contrast, although Twain himself had initially supported the war as one of liberation, when the United States took over former Spanish colonies and violently suppressed the Philippine quest for independence, he became a staunch anti-imperialist. Branded a traitor, he insisted that the truly patriotic citizen is one with enough independence to protest when the country's noble civic ideals are violated. As frequently was the case, he evoked Huck Finn as a model.[38]

Alerted that *Huckleberry Finn* was banned by the Denver public library, Twain blamed General Frederick Funston, a hero of the Philippine War stationed nearby, and compared Huck to the general. "No, if Satan's morals and Funston's are preferable to Huck's, let Huck's take a back seat; they can stand any ordinary competition, but not a combination like that." The difference was between republican and monarchical patriotism.

In the one government and the king may rightfully furnish you their notions of patriotism; in the other, neither the government nor the entire nation is privileged to dictate to any individual what the form of his patriotism shall be. The gospel of the monarchical patriotism is: "The King can do no wrong." We have adopted it with all its servility, with an unimportant change in the wording: "Our country, right or wrong!" We have thrown away the most valuable asset we had:—the individual's right to oppose both flag and country when he (just he, by himself) believed them to be in the wrong. We have thrown it away; and with it all that was really respectable about that grotesque and laughable word, Patriotism.

Patriotism of this sort, he argued, should not be mistaken for citizenship. "Citizenship? We have none! In place of it we teach patriotism which Samuel Johnson said a hundred and forty or a hundred and fifty years ago was the last refuge of a scoundrel—and I believe that he was right. I remember when I was a boy and I heard repeated time and time again the phrase, 'My country, right or wrong, my country!' How absolutely absurd is such an idea. How absolutely absurd to teach this idea to the youth of the country."[39]

It is, of course, easy to side with Twain, since he is attacking a war that, viewed retrospectively, is, for the most part, unpopular—which is almost as easy as siding with Huck when he disobeys the laws of slavery in 1885. But, as Twain well knew, it was not easy to chart a course of independence when the tide of public opinion was against him—or Huck. For him, really to value dissent requires a willingness to defend the rights of those who take unpopular points of view. In Zechariah Chafee's words, "We all believe in freedom of speech, but the question is, do we believe in it when it is disagreeable to us?" Defending the right of people to disagree with the entry of the United States into World War I, a war he supported, Chafee added, "I think this war is right, but the people who opposed it, who were wrong this time, may be right next time, as they were right in the Mexican War."[40]

For Twain, the problem with formulas like "Our country, right or wrong" is that they relieve people of making judgments of right and wrong precisely when those judgments are most called for but difficult to make. Indeed, it should come as no surprise that even the patriotic slogan Twain despised has a more complicated history than usually assumed.

As we saw in the chapter on Hale, the phrase is attributed to Stephen Decatur, who responded to an 1816 toast honoring his service to the country with a toast of his own. Newspapers of the day reported him saying, "Our country! In her intercourse with foreign nations, may she always be right and always successful, right or wrong." In Mackenzie's 1846 biography this "memorable" toast was altered to "Our country! In her intercourse with foreign nations, may she always be in the right; but our country, right or wrong." Then, by the end of the century, it had been reduced to the simple "Our country, right or wrong," thus altering the meaning of what were, most likely, Decatur's original words.[41]

Indeed, Decatur's own, unequivocal patriotism did not keep him from disagreeing with the government when he thought it threatened the success of the country. In 1804 he met Samuel Taylor Coleridge, who was serving as secretary to the governor of Malta. Thirty years later Coleridge remembered Decatur for criticizing the Louisiana Purchase, which he felt threatened the compactness of territory essential for national success.

> In an evil hour for my country did the French and Spaniards abandon Louisiana to the United States. We were not sufficiently a country before; and should we ever be mad enough to drive the English from Canada, and her other North American provinces, we shall soon cease to be a country at all. Without local attachment, without national honor, we shall resemble a swarm of insects, that settle on the fruits of the earth to corrupt and consume them, rather than men who love and cleave to the land of their forefathers. After a shapeless anarchy, and a series of civil wars, we shall at last be formed into many countries; unless the vices engendered in the process should demand further punishment, and we should previously fall beneath the despotism of some military adventurer, like a lion consumed by an inward disease, prostrate, and helpless, beneath the beak and talons of a vulture, or yet meaner bird of prey.[42]

Little did those who evoked Decatur's (reputed) quotation to justify the expansionist aftermath of the Spanish-American War know that the naval hero himself opposed a policy of territorial expansion as a threat to true love of country.

Decatur's fears suggest that U.S. citizenship is open to charges of being simultaneously too inclusive and too exclusive. It is too inclusive because the vast expanse of U.S. territory forces national citizenship to compete, as Hawthorne recognized, with local attachments. It is too exclusive because it is not cosmopolitan enough. Thus, it makes sense that nationally based citizenship is being challenged by ideas of "transnational," "postnational," and "global" citizenships. The formal legal status of citizenship may still be defined by the nation-state, but, as Linda Bosniak argues, many other aspects of citizenship exist "both above and below the state."[43] For increasing numbers of people, for instance, active political engagement takes place in the "form of transnational social movements, including those of labor rights activists, environmentalists, feminists, and human rights workers." Similarly, "when citizenship is approached psychologically, as an experience of identity and solidarity, . . . people increasingly maintain identities and commitments that transcend or traverse national boundaries."[44]

Although the primary focus of this book has been on national citizenship, there is no reason why the literary works we have looked at cannot engage Bosniak's argument by extending their work on/with civic myths to the myth of national citizenship itself. Twain, for instance, was a tireless advocate of rights around the globe, as evidenced by his attacks on imperialism and his advocacy of an international copyright agreement, an issue he understood so well because of the worldwide circulation of his works—none more so in recent years than *Huckleberry Finn*. To take one example, in Weimar, the cultural capital of Germany, a moving company for large musical instruments names itself after Huck and uses the image of him on his raft as its icon. The mythic image of Huck's raft, which Warren says bursts out of the novel, also crosses national borders. Likewise, with its attention to the flows of people and ideas back and forth between the United States and China, *China Men* has an obvious transnational element. But so too does *The Scarlet Letter*. Carrying with them thoughts of their European roots, Hawthorne's characters have a diasporic imagination powerful enough for the book to challenge the traditional story of immigration by having second-generation Pearl "return" to the "Old World." Hawthorne's own sense of belonging in England was so strong that Mark Van Doren titled a chapter about Hawthorne's time there "Man without a Country."[45] Similarly, if, as Bosniak argues, to characterize transnational political "activism as 'citizenship,' . . . requires recognition of citizenship practices in the domain of civil society,"[46] *The Scarlet Letter* brings about that recognition through Hester's good citizenship, a form of citizenship whose commitment to local attachments potentially transcends national boundaries. Indeed, the passages I quote from Michael Walzer on civil society are in a collection called *Toward a Global Civil Society*.

Even Hale's story about love of country has a transnational aspect, but one that ironically poses a challenge to postnational advocates. Preaching loyalty to one's country, not to a country associated with particular institutions and civic ideals, the patriotic message of "The Man without a Country" was easy to translate to other countries. For instance, in an 1897 edition, Hale reported that to his "great pleasure" a Spanish translation was "printed in Peru for the encouragement of the patriots of that country in their contest with Chile."[47] According to a 1925 account, "Prior to the World War, the Germans adapted the story to fit their ideas of patriotism and published it anonymously. Upon Italy's entrance into the World War in 1917, the Italian Government distributed millions of copies of the story to its people."[48] Hale may overstate the case when he claims that his story about love of country expresses a universal sentiment, but the ease by which it has been translated reveals its capacity to work on myths of cosmopolitan citizenship.

Much of the power of "The Man without a Country" comes from Hale's skill at convincing readers that their country is their home. For good reasons, advocates of postnational citizenship have challenged that identification. Nonetheless, they still have to reckon with people's desire to feel at home—somewhere. That desire is not limited to characters in Hale's story. Hester feels it, as do the China Men in Kingston's work. Most people who share this desire associate a home with a piece of land. Notable exceptions are Huck and Jim, who seem to feel most at home floating on their raft. But, as we have seen, the sense of freedom their mobility gives them comes at a cost, as Twain cannot imagine a space for them anchored within civil society. The mobility associated with global citizenship might come at a similar cost. Indeed, its detractors argue that citizenship is meaningless unless it is "rooted in a bounded political community."[49] Global citizenship, they protest, is a bloodless doctrine that fails to acknowledge the special moral ties and obligations that go with attachment to a specific community.

Important as it is, this challenge has in turn been challenged. Critics of the notion of universal obligation, Henry Shue has shown, imagine people as if they were a pebble thrown in a pond with their duties "exactly like the concentric ripples around the pebble: strongest at the centre and rapidly diminishing towards the periphery."[50] But, Shue notes, the metaphor of concentric circles does not necessarily describe how people, in fact, sense their duties and obligations. For instance, someone involved in a global environmental movement can feel more obligations to fellow members miles away than to antienvironmentalist neighbors. To be sure, counterexamples of this sort do not fully answer the challenges posed to advocates of universal obligation. After all, even my counterexample depends on making distinctions between degrees of obligation. Indeed, although cosmopolitan advocates of global citizenship see it as an alternative to national citizenship, there is no inherent reason why global citizens will not, like Melville's Cosmopolitan in *The Confidence Man*, see their primary obligation to themselves rather than to humankind. What, after all, is to keep transnational citizens from being interpellated as deracinated consumers by a global capitalist economy?

In response to similar questions, Veit Bader makes a case for "rooted cosmopolitanism."[51] Similarly, the cosmopolitan nationalist David Hollinger appropriates the metaphor of concentric circles to argue for the expansion of one's duties and obligations. As we saw in the Hawthorne chapter, loyalty to the nation has long been seen as a natural expansion of loyalties developed first in the family, then the local community, and finally in the "imagined community" of the nation. An advocate of "civic" over "ethnic" nations, Hollinger expands the circle of sympathy even further. A liberal democratic state's commitment to universal civic ideals, he argues, helps to extend national sympathies to identification with the entire human species. "The civic nation," he argues, "is located midway, so to speak, between the ethnos and the species. It can mediate between them, and all the more significantly when the society is diverse: a civic nation mediates between the species and those ethno-racial varieties of humankind represented between its borders."[52]

But Hollinger's solution has problems of its own, as shown by his otherwise commendable attempt to distinguish "cosmopolitan" from "universal." Hollinger prefers cosmopolitanism to universalism because, for him, cosmopolitanism is rooted in knowledge of other cultures, a knowledge that can place one's own culture under critical scrutiny. As such it is like the positive double consciousness fostered in Kingston's China Men, one that creates a critical perspective of second-sightedness that destabilizes any culture's claim to be the "center." But when Hollinger distinguishes between civic and ethnic nations, he slides back into universalism, a universalism he claims is best exemplified by the United States, which he finds "unusual in the extent and passion with which its ideological spokespersons accept and defend the nation's negotiated, contingent character within a broad canopy of universalist abstractions derived from the Enlightenment." This, even though elsewhere he insists that the "democratic aspirations" of the United States have been "inherited largely from England."[53] Insofar as, for Hollinger, other nations do not embody these universal civic ideals as well as the United States, his argument dramatizes the danger of having one nation or culture project its values as universal. When that is the case, as so often it is, the nation's role as a mediator between the ethnos and the species is called into question. Indeed, Hollinger never fully explains why the nation and not some other entity has to perform that mediating function.

As I note in Chapter 1, my own reasons for continuing to focus on national citizenship are more pragmatic. As important as it is to imagine alternatives to it, no one has yet made a compelling case that we should, therefore, stop trying to understand it. On the contrary, if it is as ideologically corrupt as its harshest critics maintain, we should be even more motivated to understand it. Furthermore, given the world we live in, for transnational political activity to be effective, it still has to influence national politics.[54] At the same time, given the powerful influence that U.S. national politics have around the globe, it would seem that those interested in transnational issues would want to understand the civic mythologies that help to motivate them. Finally, if transnational citizenship really made it unnecessary to continue working on/with the civic mythologies of national citizenship, its advocates should give up the passports that allow them to move from country to country. But none that I know have done so. Nations, after all, remain the most important protectors of citizens' rights.

Pointing to "international human rights regimes that have developed in the post–World War II period," Bosniak argues that such rights "are no longer exclusively guaranteed at the national level."[55] To a certain extent she is right, but if these "supranational" guarantees were sufficient, stateless individuals would not be at risk. Yet, according to Judith N. Shklar, "To be a stateless individual is one of the most dreadful political fates that can befall anyone in the modern world."[56] Poignant awareness of such a dreadful fate is one reason Hannah Arendt argues that a citizen "is by definition a citizen among citizens of a country among countries. His rights and duties must be defined and limited, not only by those of his fellow citizens, but also by the boundaries of a territory."[57] As important as it is to imagine alternatives to national citizenship, it is also important to remember that Arendt's argument is rooted in historical experience. Describing how one of the first steps in the "final solution" was to render Jews stateless, she concludes, "the Jews had to lose their nationality before they could be exterminated."[58]

As Chapters 3, 4, and 5 make clear, civil liberties and civil rights are some of the most important privileges and immunities of citizenship. They are called civil liberties and civil rights—not human liberties and human rights—because they are guaranteed by a particular civil order. Varying from civil order to civil order, particular civil liberties and civil rights help to define the quality of citizenship in different nations, even ones professing universal ideals. In contrast, declarations of human rights, lacking a state to enforce them, remain largely symbolic. That does not mean that they are irrelevant. As we have seen, when a government is unwilling to enforce them, civil rights acts and constitutional guarantees of civil liberties can also become largely symbolic, but they continue, nonetheless, to create standards by which judgments of justice can be measured. Likewise, declarations of human rights can place needed pressure on individual nations to live up to the ideals that they represent. Nonetheless, without the power of a state, the supranational organizations associated with them are limited in what they can do.

When Gertrude Himmelfarb claims that citizenship "has little meaning except in the context of a state," it by no means follows that the state has to be linked to a nation.[59] But it does mean that even alternatives to national citizenship cannot escape the three contradictions and tensions of citizenship I identified in Chapter 1. Promising self-governance and possibilities of emancipation, citizenships imagined as alternatives to national citizenship will still entail some form of subjection if they hope to have any practical effect. Likewise, even postnational, transnational, or global citizenships will be compelled to define members against nonmembers, citizens against noncitizens. Finally, alternative forms of citizenship will still have to wrestle with the dilemma that equality of membership does not necessarily eliminate other forms of inequality between fellow citizens.

Civic myths will remain as long as such contradictions and tensions remain. "There is," Shklar writes, "no notion more central in politics than citizenship, and none more variable in history, or contested in theory."[60] Conducting a historical investigation by interweaving legal and literary analysis, this book has explored some of the dilemmas of U.S. citizenship while trying to give new insight into four works of literature. If that is more than enough to try to accomplish in one book, I will, nonetheless, end by speculating that, insofar as a number of the dilemmas of citizenship I have explored will persist, those works—and ones still to be written—will, very likely, remain valuable resources for anyone interested in working on/with civic mythologies generated in the future.

Notes

Preface

1 Brook Thomas, "Opening Statement," *Cross-Examinations of Law and Literature: Cooper, Hawthorne, Stowe, and Melville* (New York: Cambridge University Press, 1987), 16. Although I state my position as clearly as I can, Florence Dore, who herself claims to find a "logic" of censorship common to both law and literature, cites *Cross-Examinations* as an example of the tendency to see law as "the omitted fact—the historical key that will unlock the ambiguous literary text" (*The Novel and the Obscene: Sexual Subjects in American Modernism* [Stanford: Stanford University Press, 2005], 10). For a brief restatement of my position, see *The New Historicism and Other Old-Fashioned Topics* (Princeton: Princeton University Press, 1991), 13. For a more extended discussion, see "Reflections on the Law and Literature Revival," *Critical Inquiry* 17 (1991): 510–39.

2 F. O. Matthiessen, *American Renaissance: Art and Expression in the Age of Emerson and Whitman* (New York: Oxford University Press, 1941), xv–xvi.

Chapter 1

1 Will Kymlicka and Wayne Norman, "The Return of the Citizen: A Survey of Recent Work on Citizenship Theory," *Ethics* 104 (1994): 352–81. The essay is reprinted in Ronald Beiner, ed., *Theorizing Citizenship* (Albany: SUNY Press, 1995). Another helpful collection of essays is Gershon Shafir Jr., ed., *The Citizenship Debates* (Minneapolis: University of Minnesota Press, 1998). See also the journal *Citizenship Studies*, whose first issue appeared in 1997.

2 Arjun Appadurai, "Disjuncture and Difference in the Global Cultural Economy," *Public Culture* 2 (1990): 1–23.

3 Among many others, see Rainer Bauböck and John Rundell, eds., *Blurred Boundaries: Migration, Ethnicity, Citizenship* (Aldershot: Ashgate Press, 1998); Stephen Castles and Alastair Davidson, *Citizenship and Migration: Globalization and the Politics of Belonging* (New York: Routledge, 2000); Rob Kroes, *Them and Us: Questions of Citizenship in a Global World* (Urbana: University of Illinois Press, 2000); and Seyla Benhabib, *Transformations of Citizenship: Dilemmas of the Nation State in the Era of Globalization* (Assen: Koninklijke Van Gorcum, 2001).

4 Thomas Hammar, *Democracy and the Nation-State: Aliens, Denizens and Citizens in a World of International Migration* (Aldershot: Avebury Press, 1990).

5 See the special issue "Cities and Citizenship," *Public Culture* 8 (1996).

6 Will Kymlicka, *Multicultural Citizenship* (Oxford: Clarendon Press, 1995).

7 Renato Rosaldo, "Cultural Citizenship and Educational Democracy," *Cultural Anthropology* 9 (1994): 402. See also Jan Pakulski, "Cultural Citizenship," *Citi-*

zenship Studies 1 (1997): 73–86, and Nick Stevenson, ed., *Culture and Citizenship* (London: SAGE, 2001).

8 Jürgen Habermas, "Citizenship and National Identity: Some Reflections on the Future of Europe," in Beiner, *Theorizing Citizenship*, 255–82, quotation at 264. See also Habermas's "Multiculturalism and the Liberal State," *Stanford Law Review* 47 (1995): 849–54, and Étienne Balibar, "Is European Citizenship Possible?," *Public Culture* 8 (1996): 355–76, and *We the People of Europe: Reflections on Transnational Citizenship*, trans. James Swenson (Princeton: Princeton University Press, 2004).

9 For one example, see Toby Miller, *The Well-Tempered Self: Citizenship, Culture, and the Postmodern Subject* (Baltimore: Johns Hopkins University Press, 1993).

10 T. H. Marshall, *Citizenship and Social Class and Other Essays* (Cambridge: Cambridge University Press, 1950).

11 Chantal Mouffe, *Dimensions of Radical Democracy: Pluralism, Citizenship, Community* (London: Verso, 1992).

12 Mark S. Weiner, *Black Trials: Citizenship from the Beginning of Slavery to the End of Caste* (New York: Knopf, 2004), 5–6.

13 David Cole, *Enemy Aliens: Double Standard and Constitutional Freedoms in the War on Terrorism* (New York: New Press, 2003).

14 Kymlicka and Norman, "Return of the Citizen," 352.

15 A representative sample can be found in *American Literary History* 18 (Summer 2006). See also Aihwa Ong, *Flexible Citizenship: The Cultural Logic of Transnationality* (Durham: Duke University Press, 1999). Ong is an anthropologist.

16 Glenn Hendler, "Citizenship and United States Writing: Perspectives from the American Literature Divisions" (presentation at MLA convention, Washington, D.C., December 28, 2005); Lauren Berlant, "Citizenship," in *Keywords of American Cultural Studies*, ed. Bruce Burgett and Glen Hendler (forthcoming). A few of the best recent books on citizenship by scholars of American literature are Lauren Berlant, *The Queen of America Goes to Washington City: Essays on Sex and Citizenship* (Durham: Duke University Press, 1997); Bruce Burgett, *Sentimental Bodies: Sex, Gender, and Citizenship in the Early Republic* (Princeton: Princeton University Press, 1998); Glenn Hendler, *Public Sentiments: Structures of Feeling in Nineteenth-Century American Literature* (Chapel Hill: University of North Carolina Press, 2001); Monica Brown, *Gang Nation: Delinquent Citizens in Puerto Rican, Chicano and Chicana Narratives* (Minneapolis: University of Minnesota Press, 2002); Russ Castronovo, *Necro Citizenship: Death, Eroticism, and the Public Sphere in the Nineteenth-Century United States* (Durham: Duke University Press, 2001); Gregg D. Crane, *Race, Citizenship, and Law in American Literature* (New York: Cambridge University Press, 2002); Dana D. Nelson, *National Manhood: Capitalist Citizenship and the Imagined Fraternity of White Men* (Durham: Duke University Press, 1998); David Leiwei Li, *Imagining the Nation* (Stanford: Stanford University Press, 1998); Lisa Lowe, *Immigrant Acts: On Asian American Cultural Politics* (Durham: Duke University Press, 1996); Michael Moon and Cathy Davidson, eds., *Subjects and Citizens: Nation, Race, and Gender from "Oroonoko" to Anita Hill* (Durham: Duke University Press, 1995); Rosura Sánchez, *Telling Identities: The California Testimonies* (Minneapolis: Univer-

sity of Minnesota Press, 1995); and Priscilla Wald, *Constituting America* (Durham: Duke University Press, 1995).

17 Balibar, *We the People of Europe*, 12.

18 Rogers M. Smith, *Civic Ideals: Conflicting Visions of Citizenship in U.S. History* (New Haven: Yale University Press, 1997), 3.

19 I self-consciously use "work" instead of "text." Referring to literary artifacts as "texts" rather than "works" no longer has what Roland Barthes called a "subversive force in respect of the old classifications." It has instead become a cliché. By calling those artifacts "works," I recall Northrop Frye's argument that "the efficient cause of civilization is work, and poetry in its social aspect has the function of expressing, as a verbal hypothesis, a vision of the goal of work and the forms of desire." My use of "work" over "text" is intended to call attention to literature's connection with the work of civilization as well as to the labor that went into its formal shaping and production. See Roland Barthes, "From Work to Text," *Image-Music-Text*, trans. Stephen Heath (New York: Hill and Wang, 1977), 158, and Northrop Frye, *Anatomy of Criticism* (Princeton: Princeton University Press, 1957), 106.

20 David Donald, *Lincoln Reconsidered*, 2nd ed. (New York: Random House, 1959), 144.

21 James H. Kettner, *The Development of American Citizenship, 1608–1870* (Chapel Hill: University of North Carolina Press, 1978); Kenneth L. Karst, *Belonging to America: Equal Citizenship and the Constitution* (New Haven: Yale University Press, 1989); Judith N. Shklar, *American Citizenship: The Quest for Inclusion* (Cambridge: Harvard University Press, 1991); Michael Schudson, *The Good Citizen: A History of American Civic Life* (New York: Free Press, 1998); T. Alexander Aleinikoff, *Semblances of Sovereignty: The Constitution, the State, and American Citizenship* (Cambridge: Harvard University Press, 2002); and Linda Bosniak, "Citizenship," in *Oxford Handbook of Legal Studies*, ed. Peter Crane and Mark Tushnet (Oxford: Oxford University Press, 2003), 1285–1325.

22 René Wellek and Austin Warren, *Theory of Literature: New Revised Edition* (New York: Harcourt Brace Jovanovich, 1962), 191.

23 Smith, *Civic Ideals*, 34.

24 Michael Ignatieff, "The Myth of Citizenship," in Beiner, *Theorizing Citizenship*, 53–78, quotation at 58.

25 Garry Wills, *Cincinnatus: George Washington and the Enlightenment* (Garden City, N.Y.: Doubleday, 1984).

26 Many of the most prominent were identified by the "myth and symbol" school of American studies. See, for instance, Nicholas Cords and Patrick Gerster, eds., *Myth and the American Experience*, 2nd ed. (Encino, Calif.: Glencoe, 1978).

27 Robert Michels, *Der Patriotismus* (Munich: Dunker and Humblot, 1929).

28 Max Lerner, "Constitution and Court as Symbols," *Yale Law Journal* 46 (1937): 1295.

29 Smith, *Civic Ideals*, 34.

30 Claude Lévi-Strauss, *Structural Anthropology*, trans. C. Jacobson and B. G. Schopf (New York: Basic Books, 1963). My understanding of Lévi-Strauss is indebted to

Fredric Jameson, *The Political Unconscious: Narrative as Socially Symbolic Act* (Ithaca: Cornell University Press, 1981).

31 Robert M. Cover, "Nomos and Narrative," *Harvard Law Review* 97 (1983): 4–5. See also Peter Fitzpatrick, *The Mythology of Modern Law* (London: Routledge, 1992). For more on cultural narratives and their implications for interdisciplinary work within law and literature, see Brook Thomas, "An Opening Statement," in *Cross-Examinations of Law and Literature: Cooper, Hawthorne, Stowe, and Melville* (New York: Cambridge University Press, 1987), 1–18, and Sara Maza, "Stories in History: Cultural Narratives in Recent Works in European History," *American Historical Review* 101 (1996): 1493–1515. For a definition, see James Phelan, *Living to Tell About It: A Rhetoric and Ethics of Character Narration* (Ithaca: Cornell University Press, 2005), 8–10, 214.

32 J. G. A. Pocock, "The Ideal of Citizenship since Classical Times," in Beiner, *Theorizing Citizenship*, 29–52.

33 Max Weber, "Citizenship in Ancient and Medieval Cities," in Shafir, *Citizenship Debates*, 43–52.

34 Peter Riesenberg, *Citizenship in the Western Tradition: Plato to Rousseau* (Chapel Hill: University of North Carolina Press, 1992), xi, xvii. See also Veit Bader, ed., *Citizenship and Exclusion* (New York: St. Martin's Press, 1997).

35 *The Compact Edition of the Oxford English Dictionary* (Oxford: Oxford University Press, 1971), 1:44.

36 Peter H. Schuck and Rogers M. Smith, *Citizenship without Consent: Illegal Aliens in the American Polity* (New Haven: Yale University Press, 1985).

37 Michael Ignatieff, *Blood and Belonging: Journeys into the New Nationalism* (New York: Farrar, Straus and Giroux, 1994), 4–5.

38 David Hollinger, *Postethnic America: Beyond Multiculturalism* (New York: Basic Books, 1995), 134, and Werner Sollors, *Beyond Ethnicity: Consent and Descent in American Culture* (New York: Oxford University Press, 1986).

39 Bernard Yack, "The Myth of the Civic Nation," *Critical Review* 10 (1996): 193–211, and Anthony Smith, *The Ethnic Origin of Nations* (Oxford: Basil Blackwell, 1992). See also Brook Thomas, "Civic Multiculturalism and the Myth of Liberal Consent," *New Centennial Review* 1 (2001): 1–35.

40 Smith, *Civic Ideals*, 9. Acknowledging that the classification of nations as either ethnic or civic "is misleading," Rogers Smith agrees with Anthony Smith "that all nations are defined in ways that combine 'ethnic-genealogical' or ascriptive traits and 'civic-territorial' features emphasizing shared political beliefs as well as land" (ibid., 518 n. 55). But he also insists that "all efforts to mythologize nations or peoples as somehow 'prepolitical', as families or primordial kinship groups, must be rejected" (ibid., 10–11).

41 Karl Marx, "On the Jewish Question," in *The Marx-Engels Reader*, 2nd ed., ed. Robert C. Tucker (New York: Norton, 1978), 26–52; Anatole France, *Le Lys Rouge* (Paris: Calmann-Levy, 1923), 113 (my translation).

42 This dilemma has caused many in literary studies to attack the "decorporealizing" abstraction of "formally equivalent" citizenship. See, for instance, Michael Warner, "The Mass Public and the Mass Subject," in *Habermas and the Public*

Sphere, ed. Craig Calhoun (Cambridge: MIT Press, 1992), 377–401. In contrast, others, in the tradition of Marshall, argue that "formally equivalent citizenship" should be expanded to include more rights. For such an argument in terms of sexuality, see Morris Kaplan, *Sexual Justice: Democratic Citizenship and the Politics of Desire* (New York: Routledge, 1997).

43 *Perez v. Brownell*, dissenting, 356 U.S. 44 (1958) at 64.

44 David J. Brewer, *American Citizenship* (New York: Scribner, 1902), 15, 14.

45 Quoted in *United States v. Wong Kim Ark* 169 U.S. 649 (1898) at 665. Gray first cited this passage in an essay that he wrote as a young lawyer refuting Taney's decision in *Dred Scott*. See Horace Gray, *A Legal Review of the Case of Dred Scott as Decided by the Supreme Court of the United States from the Law Reporter for June, 1857* (Boston: Crosby, Nichols, and Co., 1857), 15.

46 Louis Althusser, "Ideology and Ideological State Apparatuses (Notes towards an Investigation)," in *Lenin and Philosophy, and Other Essays*, trans. Ben Brewster (New York: Monthly Review Press, 1971), 127–86, quotation at 175. For Althusser this interpellation is accomplished by "ideological state apparatuses" that control all aspects of civil society through institutions, like the family and the educational system, as well as by the state's traditional apparatuses, like the police and the legal system. By subordinating all institutions of civil society to the state, Althusser ignores the way in which modern democracies, as we will see in Chapter 2, can define citizenship to allow people to develop subjectivities in civil society. For a different challenge to Althusser's account of interpellation, see Judith Butler, "'Conscience Doth Make Subjects of Us All,'" *French Yale Studies* 88 (1995): 6–26.

47 Simon Schama, *Citizens: A Chronicle of the French Revolution* (New York: Knopf, 1989), 858.

48 Étienne Balibar, "Citizen Subject," in *Who Comes after the Subject?*, ed. Eduardo Cadava, Peter Connor, and Jean-Luc Nancy (New York: Routledge, 1991), 38–39. See also "Subjection and Subjectivation," in *Supposing the Subject*, ed. Joan Copjec (New York: Verso, 1994), 7–15, and "Propositions on Citizenship," *Ethics* 98 (1988): 723–30.

49 In the United States, for instance, unlike France, educational policy varies not only from state to state but also frequently from school district to school district. In a federal system, in other words, the "state" is not as monolithic as Althusser implies. Indeed, he works within a tradition of absolutist thinkers that includes Thomas Hobbes and Jean Bodin, the Renaissance theorist of French absolutism.

Neglecting the complications of the U.S. federal system has also led critics, mistakenly, to evoke Rousseau's notion of the "general will." For instance, Lisa Lowe claims that the incorporation of U.S. citizens into the state "asks that individual differences (of race, ethnicity, class, gender, and locality) be subordinated to the general will of the collective polity" (*Immigrant Acts*, 144). Donald E. Pease equates the U.S. notion of a "public will" with Rousseau's "general will" in *Visionary Compacts: American Renaissance Writings in Cultural Context* (Madison: University of Wisconsin Press, 1987), 74. Iris Marion Young provides a "critique of the ideal of universal citizenship" that mistakenly confuses the ideal of a "common good" with that of a "general will" ("Polity and Group Difference: A Critique of the Ideal of Universal Citizenship," *Ethics* 99 [1989]: 250–74, quotation at 253). In the U.S. context, appeals to the will of the people are not the same as Rousseau's somewhat mystical appeals to the "general will."

50 Kenneth Burke, "Literature as Equipment for Living," in *Philosophy of Literary Form* (Baton Rouge: Louisiana State University Press, 1941), 293–304.

51 According to Richard Slotkin, "Myth does not argue its ideology, it exemplifies it" (*The Fatal Environment: The Myth of the Frontier in the Age of Industrialization, 1800–1890* [New York: Antheneum, 1985], 19).

52 Smith, *Civic Ideals*, 33.

53 Ibid., 34.

54 Ibid., 504.

55 Ibid., 505.

56 Ibid., 33.

57 Wolfgang Iser, *The Fictive and the Imaginary: Charting Literary Anthropology* (Baltimore: Johns Hopkins University Press, 1993).

58 Lauren Berlant, *The Anatomy of National Fantasy: Hawthorne, Utopia, and Everyday Life* (Chicago: University of Chicago Press, 1991), 14.

59 According to Richard Slotkin, "Myths are stories, drawn from history, that have acquired through usage over many generations a symbolizing function that is central to the cultural functioning of the society that produces them" (*Fatal Environment*, 16).

60 *Loving v. Virginia*, 388 U.S. 1 (1967).

61 William H. McNeil, "The Care and Repair of Public Myth," *Foreign Affairs* 61 (1982): 1–13, quotations at 1, 6, 9, 6.

62 Hans Blumenberg, *Work on Myth*, trans. Robert Wallace (Cambridge: MIT Press, 1985).

63 Wellek and Warren, *Theory of Literature*, 190–91.

64 Harry Levin, "Some Meanings of Myth," in *Myth and Mythmakers*, ed. Henry A. Murray (New York: George Braziller, 1960), 10.

65 Ernst Cassirer, *The Myth of the State* (New Haven: Yale University Press, 1946).

66 Julia Lupton, *Citizen-Saints: Shakespeare and Political Theology* (Chicago: University of Chicago Press, 2005), 207.

67 Charles Warren, *The Supreme Court in United States History* (1922; rev. ed., Boston: Little, Brown, 1926), 2:427.

68 On the method of "cross-examination," see Thomas, *Cross-Examinations*.

69 George Armstrong Kelly, "Who Needs a Theory of Citizenship?," in Beiner, *Theorizing Citizenship*, 79–104, quotations at 88–89.

70 Schudson, *Good Citizen*, 3.

71 See Nancy Isenberg, *Sex and Citizenship in Antebellum America* (Chapel Hill: University of North Carolina Press, 1998), on how historians of antebellum feminism emphasize the campaign for suffrage at the expense of other issues concerning citizenship.

72 Richard Hofstadter, "Abraham Lincoln and the Self-Made Myth," in *The American Political Tradition and the Men Who Made It* (New York: Knopf, 1948), 92.

73 Roy P. Basler, *The Lincoln Legend* (Boston: Houghton Mifflin, 1935), 296.

74 Harold Holzer, Gabor S. Boritt, and Mark E. Neely Jr., *The Lincoln Image: Abraham Lincoln and the Popular Print* (New York: Scribner, 1984), 149. See also Waldo W. Braden, ed., *Building the Myth* (Urbana: University of Illinois Press, 1990), and William W. Betts Jr., ed., *Lincoln and the Poets* (Pittsburgh: University of Pittsburgh Press, 1965).

75 Peter Karsten, *Patriot Heroes in England and America* (Madison: University of Wisconsin Press, 1978), 98.

76 Acknowledging the strength the Lincoln legend gathers from "the Christian theme of vicarious atonement and redemption," Hofstadter goes on to emphasize how "Honest Abe" personified the myth of the self-made man; see "Abraham Lincoln and the Self-Made Myth," 92.

77 Karsten, *Patriot Heroes*, 98.

78 Barry Schwartz, *Abraham Lincoln and the Forge of National Memory* (Chicago: University of Chicago Press, 2000), 296–97.

79 John A. Hayward, "Who Are Citizens?," *American Law Journal* 2 (1885): 315.

80 Aristotle, *The Politics* (London: Clarendon Press, 1946), 134.

81 Edmund S. Morgan, *Inventing the People: The Rise of Popular Sovereignty in England and America* (New York: Norton, 1980).

82 Brian C. J. Singer, "Cultural versus Contractual Nations: Rethinking Their Opposition," *History and Theory* 33 (1996): 334.

83 Michael Johnson, "Introduction: Abraham Lincoln, Wordsmith," in *Abraham Lincoln, Slavery, and the Civil War: Selected Writings and Speeches* (Boston: Bedford/St. Martins, 2001), 1–10.

84 Basler, *Lincoln Legend*, 296.

85 Henry Steele Commager, "The Search for a Usable Past," *American Heritage* 16 (1965): 96.

86 Quoted in James A. Schiff, "*The Scarlet Letter* as Myth," in *Updike's Version: Rewriting "The Scarlet Letter"* (Columbia: University of Missouri Press, 1992), 8.

87 Sara de Saussure Davis and Philip D. Beidler, eds., *The Mythologization of Mark Twain* (Tuscaloosa: University of Alabama Press, 1984).

88 Commager, "Search for a Usable Past," 96.

89 James Bryce, *Promoting Good Citizenship* (Boston: Houghton Mifflin, 1909).

90 Charles Edward Merriman, *The Making of Citizens: A Comparative Study of Methods of Civic Training* (Chicago: University of Chicago Press, 1931).

91 Learned Hand, "A Plea for the Open Mind and Free Discussion," in *The Spirit of Liberty: Papers and Addresses of Learned Hand* (New York: Vintage, 1959), 210.

92 Sandra Stotsky, *Connecting Civic Education and Language Education: The Contemporary Challenge* (New York: Teachers College, 1991).

93 Jonathan Arac, *Huckleberry Finn as Idol and Target: The Functions of Criticism in Our Time* (Madison: University of Wisconsin Press, 1997), vii.

94 Ibid., 16.

95 Ibid., 11.

96 Ibid., 218. For an ironic account of principled action, see my discussion in Chapter 5 of Huck and Tom's attempt to use case-knives to free Jim.

97 A better solution to the idolatry that so concerns Arac is, it seems to me, Gerald Graff and James Phelan's strategy of using the critical controversies about Twain's book to foster classroom debates. See Mark Twain, *Adventures of Huckleberry Finn*, 2nd ed., ed. Gerald Graff and James Phelan (Boston: Bedford, 2004).

98 Arac, *Idol and Target*, 218.

99 Lionel Trilling, *The Liberal Imagination: Essays on Literature and Society* (New York: Viking, 1950), xi–xii.

100 To be sure, Arac feels that he himself provides a nuanced and critical view of Lincoln. Granting that Lincoln's leadership "did most to create that confusion among 'State, nation, and government' that [Randolph] Bourne condemned," Arac writes that "I cannot end simply by praising Lincoln" (*Idol and Target*, 217). Nonetheless, a page later, he, in fact, ends with the idealized appeal to him I have already quoted.

101 Ibid., 4.

102 Donald, *Lincoln Reconsidered*, 144.

103 Since many of those attacks come from African Americans, the referent for Arac's "we" becomes troublesome.

104 Bernard DeVoto, *Mark Twain's America* (Moscow: University of Idaho Press, 1932), 320–21.

105 Charles Edward Merriman, *American Political Ideas: Studies in the Development of American Political Thought, 1865–1917* (New York: Macmillan, 1923), 473.

106 Ibid., 159. Citing Woodrow Wilson's argument in *Mere Literature* (1898), Merriman does claim that "alongside of the civic training through the philosophers and perhaps more powerful in depth and intensity of appeal, are the poets and dramatists who serve as transmitters of group traditions, or sometimes as the shapers of custom and laws" (ibid.).

107 When I taught a unit on Lincoln's most memorable speeches and "The Man without a Country" in conjunction with the Vallandigham dispute to a class of 1,200 freshmen, their course evaluations indicated that they preferred reading Hale's story to Lincoln's speeches.

Chapter 2

1 Nathaniel Hawthorne, *The Scarlet Letter*, centenary ed., vol. 1 (Columbus: Ohio State University Press, 1962), 55. Future references will be included parenthetically within the text.

2 Larry J. Reynolds, *European Revolutions and the American Literary Renaissance* (New Haven: Yale University Press, 1988). For an understanding of this scene in the context of antebellum debates over capital punishment, see John Cyril Barton, "The Anti-Gallows Movement in Antebellum America," *REAL* 22 (2006): 145–78.

3 Frederick Newberry, *Hawthorne's Divided Loyalties: England and America in His Work*

(Rutherford, N.J.: Fairleigh Dickinson University Press, 1987), and Charles Ryskamp, "The New England Sources of *The Scarlet Letter*," *American Literature* 31 (1960): 237–72.

4 J. G. A. Pocock, *The Machiavellian Moment: Florentine Political Thought and the Atlantic Republican Tradition* (Princeton: Princeton University Press, 1975), 335. Hobbes in *De Cive*, published in Latin in 1642 and translated into English in 1651, did use "citizen" to designate membership in a commonwealth. But he did not use it as Aristotle did to designate a member of a republic who has the capacity to both rule and be ruled. Instead, like the French absolutist Bodin, he distinguished citizens, who had specific benefits, from other subjects, like denizens, who did not have all or any of them. See *On the Citizen*, trans. Richard Tuck and Michael Silverthorne (Cambridge: Cambridge University Press, 1998). In *Leviathan* (1651) Hobbes uses "citizen" more in the sense of a city dweller. For instance, he writes of a man, "Let him therefore consider with himself, when taking a journey, he armes himselfe, and seeks to go well accompanied; when going to sleep, he locks his dores; when even in his house he locks his chests; and this when he knows there bee Lawes, and publike Officers, armed to revenge all injuries shall be done him; what opinion he has of his fellow subjects, when he rides armed; of his fellow Citizens, when he locks his dores; and his children, and servants, when he locks his chests." "Fellow Citizens" are clearly those "fellow subjects" who dwell in close proximity to the man. See *Leviathan* (New York: Penguin, 1986), 186–87.

5 Edmund S. Morgan, *The Puritan Dilemma: The Story of John Winthrop* (Boston: Little, Brown, 1958), 91. Morgan also uses the term "good citizen" when he acknowledges that the Puritans' phrase would have been "civil man" (*Puritan Family* [New York: Harper, 1966], 1).

6 R. B. Nye, *George Bancroft* (New York: Knopf, 1945), 102.

7 Anon., "Bancroft's History of the United States," *American Jurist and Law Magazine* 2 (1838): 229–31, quotation at 230.

8 Ibid., 229.

9 For an excellent summary of speeches by people, like Daniel Webster, Joseph Story, and Edward Everett, who share Bancroft's view of the Puritans' republican institutions, see John P. McWilliams, *Hawthorne, Melville, and the American Character: A Looking-Glass Business* (New York: Cambridge University Press, 1984), 25–36. On Bancroft, see David Levin, *History as Romantic Art* (Stanford: Stanford University Press, 1959).

10 Lauren Berlant, *The Anatomy of National Fantasy: Hawthorne, Utopia, and Everyday Life* (Chicago: University of Chicago Press, 1991); Michael J. Colacurcio, "'The Woman's Own Choice': Sex Metaphor and the Puritan 'Sources' of *The Scarlet Letter*," in *Doctrine and Difference* (New York: Routledge, 1997), 205–28; and Donald E. Pease, *Visionary Compacts: American Renaissance Writings in Cultural Context* (Madison: University of Wisconsin Press, 1987).

11 Judith N. Shklar, *American Citizenship: The Quest for Inclusion* (Cambridge: Harvard University Press, 1991).

12 Jean Cohen and Andrew Arato, *Civil Society and Political Theory* (Cambridge: MIT

Press, 1992), ix. Informed by events in the former Soviet bloc in 1989, where the economic sphere was controlled by the state, this and other current definitions do not include the economic in civil society as did Adam Smith, Adam Ferguson, and Georg Wilhelm Friedrich Hegel.

13 My point is not that Hawthorne set out to write a story arguing for the importance of an independent civil society in the way that a political economist might. His goal was to write the most compelling story that he could. Nonetheless, in its reception, especially the role it has played in education in the United States, *The Scarlet Letter* and its representation of people's desires and how those desires can best be fulfilled imparts certain attitudes, values, and structures of feeling that coincide with the attitudes, values, and structures of feeling associated with civil society arguments. Furthermore, even if Hawthorne did not self-consciously set out to make an argument for an independent civil society, he would have known about such arguments through the Scottish Enlightenment figures of Adam Smith and Adam Ferguson. On "structures of feeling," see Raymond Williams, *Marxism and Literature* (Oxford: Oxford University Press, 1977), 128–35.

14 Rufus Choate, "The Importance of Illustrating New England History by a Series of Romances Like the Waverley Novels," in *The Works of Rufus Choate with a Memoir of His Life*, 2 vols., ed. Samuel Gilman Brown (Boston: Little, Brown, 1862), 1:319–46, quotations at 344. Choate alludes to a passage from *An Account of a Conversation Concerning a Right Regulation of Governments for the Common Good of Mankind in a Letter to the Marquis of Montrose, the Earls of Rothes, Roxburg and Haddington* (1703). See David Daiches, ed., *Andrew Fletcher of Saltoun: Selected Political Writings* (Edinburgh: Scottish Academic Press, 1979), 108. It might seem ironic that in making a plea for the United States to unite and to forget regional differences Choate quotes a Scottish nationalist. But Fletcher advocated a federal union of Scotland and England, so he could be said to have anticipated the federal system of the United States.

15 Will Kymlicka, *Multicultural Citizenship* (Oxford: Clarendon Press, 1995), 189.

16 Choate, "Importance," 340, 339.

17 Herman Melville, *Billy Budd, Sailor (An Inside Narrative)* (Chicago: University of Chicago Press, 1962), 55.

18 On Hawthorne and a national literature, see Neal Frank Doubleday, "Hawthorne and Literary Nationalism," *American Literature* 12 (1942): 447–53. See also Jonathan Arac, who argues that *The Scarlet Letter* is an aesthetic narrative, not a national narrative, and that it became representative of the nation only through a retrospective process of canonization that devalued national narratives. Arac's provocative argument reminds us that literature can do many more things than give us compelling stories about national membership and values. Indeed, many works do not even have the potential to become civic myths. Nonetheless, *The Scarlet Letter*'s engagement with the myth of Puritan origins clearly gives it that potential. More important, Arac focuses on a work's form and content, but form and content alone do not make a narrative national; its reception plays a role as well. Thus, even if we grant Arac's basic premise, the important ques-

tion for me is Why do Arac's "aesthetic narratives," like *The Scarlet Letter* and *Adventures of Huckleberry Finn*, retain the status of civic myths while more explicitly national or patriotic narratives, like "The Man without a Country," have lost favor over time? Chapter 5 will directly address that question in terms of Twain's novel, but to raise the question now is to suggest that literature's relation to nationalist ideologies is a complicated one. Answering it shows, as I try to do in this chapter, that those ideologies are more complicated than the ones that many recent literary critics are so intent on demystifying. See Jonathan Arac, "Narrative Forms," in *The Cambridge History of American Literature*, ed. Sacvan Bercovitch (New York: Cambridge University Press, 1995), 2:605–777. On *The Scarlet Letter*'s reception, see Richard Brodhead, *The School of Hawthorne* (New York: Oxford University Press, 1986).

19 George Dekker, *The American Historical Romance* (New York: Cambridge University Press, 1987), 148.

20 On how the Puritans differ from the image created by Hawthorne, see Carl N. Degler, "Were the Puritans Puritanical?," in *Out of Our Past*, rev. ed. (New York: Harper, 1970), 9–20. Some of the most provocative—if conflicting—accounts of Hawthorne's relation to the Puritans are Michael Davitt Bell, *Hawthorne and the Historical Romance of England* (Princeton: Princeton University Press, 1971); Sacvan Bercovitch, *The Office of "The Scarlet Letter"* (Baltimore: Johns Hopkins University Press, 1991); Colacurcio, "'Woman's Own Choice,'" and "Footsteps of Ann Hutchinson: The Context of *The Scarlet Letter*," ELH 39 (1972): 459–94; and Pease, *Visionary Compacts*. Michael T. Gilmore, "Hawthorne and the Making of the Middle Class," in *Discovering Difference*, ed. Christoph K. Lohman (Bloomington: Indiana University Press, 1993), 88–104, and T. Walter Herbert, *Dearest Beloved: The Hawthornes and the Making of the Middle-Class Family* (Berkeley: University of California Press, 1993), argue that *The Scarlet Letter*'s major characters have a nineteenth-century moral outlook. Both follow Nina Baym, who claims that Hawthorne "has created an authoritarian [Puritan] state with a Victorian moral outlook"; see "Passion and Authority in *The Scarlet Letter*," *New England Quarterly* 43 (1970): 209–30, quotation at 215.

21 William Dean Howells, "Hawthorne's Hester Prynne," in *The Critical Response to Nathaniel Hawthorne's "The Scarlet Letter*," ed. Gary Scharnhorst (Westport, Conn.: Greenwood Press, 1992), 105, 108.

22 John Winthrop, *Winthrop's Journal: "History of New England*," ed. J. K. Hosmer (New York: Scribner, 1908), 2:83–84, 238–39.

23 Charles Beard and Mary Beard, *The Rise of American Civilization* (New York: Macmillan, 1927), 1:775.

24 Nathaniel Hawthorne, *The House of the Seven Gables*, centenary ed., vol. 2 (Columbus: Ohio State University Press, 1963), 8.

25 On sympathy in Hawthorne, see Gordon Hutner, *Secrets and Sympathy: Form and Disclosure in Hawthorne's Novels* (Athens: University of Georgia Press, 1988), and Edgar Dryden, *Nathaniel Hawthorne and the Poetics of Enchantment* (Ithaca: Cornell University Press, 1977).

26 Arthur Cleveland Coxe, "The Writings of Hawthorne," in *Church Review and Eccle-*

siatical Register, rpt. in *Nathaniel Hawthorne: The Contemporary Reviews*, ed. John L. Idol Jr. and Buford Jones (New York: Cambridge University Press, 1995), 149–51.

27 David Leverenz provides an excellent analysis of the tension between the narrator's perspective and that of the dramatic action in "Mrs. Hawthorne's Headache: Reading *The Scarlet Letter*," *Nineteenth-Century Fiction* 37 (1983): 552–75.

28 Herbert, *Dearest Beloved*, 187.

29 Puritans in fact allowed divorce.

30 For Marcuse, see *Eros and Civilization: A Philosophical Inquiry into Freud* (1955; reprint, New York: Random, 1962). My use of Marcuse is indebted to Robert Milder. But whereas Milder argues that "the crux of Hawthorne's problem in *The Scarlet Letter*—and consequently our own reading of it—is that he could envision no social or moral space between the repressiveness of Puritan Boston and the wildness of the forest" ("*The Scarlet Letter* and Its Discontents," *Nathaniel Hawthorne Review* 22 (1996): 20), I argue that he conceives of such a space in the nascent formation of a relatively independent civil society. Arac also appeals to Marcuse and his analysis of "The Affirmative Character of Culture" in his reading of *The Scarlet Letter*. See "The Politics of *The Scarlet Letter*," in *Ideology and Classic American Literature*, ed. Sacvan Bercovitch and Myra Jehlen (New York: Cambridge University Press, 1986), 247–66, esp. 249. On Bercovitch and Marcuse, see Thomas Claviez, "Dimensioning Society: Ideology, Rhetoric, and Criticism in Sacvan Bercovitch and Herbert Marcuse," *REAL* 11 (1995): 173–205.

31 Nathaniel Hawthorne, *The Blithedale Romance*, centenary ed., vol. 3 (Columbus: Ohio State University Press, 1964), 114.

32 Ibid., 50.

33 Nathaniel Hawthorne, *The Marble Faun*, centenary ed., vol. 4 (Columbus: Ohio State University Press, 1968), 430.

34 Thomas R. Mitchell, *Hawthorne's Fuller Mystery* (Amherst: University of Massachusetts Press, 1998), makes a strong case for the influence of Margaret Fuller's views of marriage on *The Scarlet Letter*.

35 Herbert, *Dearest Beloved*, 111.

36 See Claire McEachern, *"This England": Literature and the Nation, 1590–1612* (Cambridge: Cambridge University Press, 1996).

37 See Linda K. Kerber, *No Constitutional Right "To Be Ladies": Women and the Obligations of Citizenship* (New York: Hill and Wang, 1998), 13, and Mary Beth Norton, *Founding Mothers and Fathers: Gendered Power and the Forming of American Society* (New York: Knopf, 1996).

38 Merril D. Smith, *Breaking the Bonds: Marital Discord in Pennsylvania, 1730–1830* (New York: New York University Press, 1991), 51.

39 Mitchell, *Hawthorne's Fuller Mystery*, 141–46, gives the best explanation as to why Hawthorne names his villain after William Prynne, the seventeenth-century Presbyterian lawyer who, after being branded with the letters S.L. ("seditious libeler") for criticizing King Charles I and Bishop Laud, eventually turned against his fellow Presbyterians and, importantly, disagreed with Milton on divorce.

40 Robert M. Ireland, "The Libertine Must Die: Sexual Dishonour and the Un-

written Law in the Nineteenth-Century United States," *Journal of Social History* 23 (1989): 27–44, quotation at 32. For more on cases involving the "unwritten law," see Ireland, "Insanity and the Unwritten Law," *American Journal of Legal History* 32 (1988): 157–72; Hendrik Hartog, "Lawyering, Husbands' Rights, and 'the Unwritten Law' in Nineteenth-Century America," *Journal of American History* 84 (1997): 67–96; and Melissa J. Ganz, "Wicked Women and Veiled Ladies: Gendered Narratives of the McFarland-Richardson Tragedy," *Yale Journal of Law and Feminism* 9 (1997): 255–303.

41 Herbert, *Dearest Beloved*, 201.

42 Gilmore, "Middle Class," 93; D. H. Lawrence, *Studies in Classic American Literature*, rpt. (Garden City, N.Y.: Doubleday, 1951); Jeremy D. Weinstein, "Adultery, Law, and the State: A History," *Hastings Law Journal* 38 (1986): 195–238, quotation at 225.

43 Adultery has a complicated history in Anglo-American law. It was not a criminal act in common law but was dealt with in ecclesiastical courts. As a result, the legal fiction of criminal conversation developed to allow common-law courts to rule on adultery, even if under an assumed name. See Laura Hanft Korobkin, *Criminal Conversations: Sentimentality and Nineteenth-Century Legal Stories of Adultery* (New York: Columbia University Press, 1998). Then in 1650, Puritans in England criminalized adultery. Even before that event a number of colonies, including Massachusetts, had criminalized the act. For the actual laws of adultery in seventeenth-century New England, see Cornelia Hughes Dayton, *Women before the Bar: Gender, Law, and Society in Connecticut, 1639–1789* (Chapel Hill: University of North Carolina Press, 1995); N. E. H. Hull, *Female Felons: Women and Serious Crime in Colonial Massachusetts* (Urbana: University of Illinois Press, 1989); Lyle Koehler, *A Search for Power: The "Weaker Sex" in Seventeenth-Century New England* (Urbana: University of Illinois Press, 1980); Norton, *Founding Mothers and Fathers*; and Carolyn B. Ramsey, "Sex and Social Order: The Selective Enforcement of Colonial American Adultery Laws in the English Context," *Yale Journal of Law and the Humanities* 10 (1998): 191–228.

44 Oliver Wendell Holmes Jr., *The Common Law* (Cambridge: Belknap Press of Harvard University Press, 1963), 2.

45 Sir Henry Sumner Maine, *Ancient Law: Its Connection with the Early History of Society and Its Relation to Modern Ideas* (1861; reprint, New York: Dorset, 1986). See also Weinstein, "Adultery, Law, and the State."

46 Ramsey, "Sex and Social Order," 202–7.

47 Tony Tanner, *Adultery in the Novel: Contract and Transgression* (Baltimore: Johns Hopkins University Press, 1979), 98.

48 Michael Grossberg, *A Judgment for Solomon: The D'Hauteville Case and Legal Experience in Antebellum America* (New York: Cambridge University Press, 1996), 52.

49 See ibid.

50 Herbert, *Dearest Beloved*, 201, reads this scene as the triumph of the new model of the family. See also Michael J. Colacurcio's perceptive reading in "'Woman's Own Choice.'"

51 See Berlant's excellent discussion of how Hawthorne adjudicates "the differ-

ent claims for federal, state, local, and private identity that circulate through the American system" (*Anatomy of National Fantasy*, 203). On the importance of local connections for Hawthorne, see also Carey Wilson McWilliams, *The Idea of Fraternity in America* (Berkeley: University of California Press, 1973).

52 On expatriation, see I-Mien Tsiang, *The Question of Expatriation in America prior to 1907* (Baltimore: Johns Hopkins University Press, 1942), and Alan G. James, "Expatriation in the United States: Precept and Practice Today and Yesterday," *San Diego Law Review* 27 (1990): 853–905.

53 In a chapter illustrating James Kettner's claim that the concept of citizenship emerging from the Revolutionary War was based on the "idea of volitional allegiance," not on descent, Werner Sollors argues that *The Scarlet Letter* illustrates the great American myth of consent.

> What is Nathaniel Hawthorne's *Scarlet Letter* (1850) but the story of Hester Prynne, a woman who was separated from Chillingworth, the old-world embodiment with whom she had been connected in a marriage that was not based on love and that remained associated with paternal authority? Separated from the old world by the "road" which took her to America, a road she can visualize again from the scaffold, she takes up with Dimmesdale, the living spirit of the new world, love, and a higher law; and their consent relationship had a "consecration of its own."

Yes, but at the end of the book we also get an exodus—imagined or real—of characters for Europe. Just as Pearl abandons the "new" world, so, when Hester and Dimmesdale dream of starting anew, they plot an escape to the "old" world of Europe. Hawthorne is clearly playing with the myth of America as the land of opportunity for people seeking to escape an oppressive past. See Werner Sollors, *Beyond Ethnicity: Consent and Descent in American Culture* (New York: Oxford University Press, 1986), 166; James H. Kettner, *The Development of American Citizenship, 1608–1870* (Chapel Hill: University of North Carolina Press, 1978), 173.

54 In 1976 Nina Baym noted that Hester on her return helps to bring about "a modest social change" (*The Shape of Hawthorne's Career* [Ithaca: Cornell University Press, 1976], 130).

55 Michael Walzer, "Introduction," in *Toward a Global Civil Society*, ed. Michael Walzer (Providence: Berghahn Books, 1995), 1.

56 *Trustees of Dartmouth College v. Woodward*. See Mark D. MacGarvie, "The Dartmouth College Case and the Legal Design of Civil Society," in *Charity, Philanthropy, and Civility in American History*, ed. Lawrence J. Freedman and Mark D. MacGarvie (New York: Cambridge University Press, 2003), 91–105.

57 Kathleen D. McCarthy, *The American Creed: Philanthropy and the Rise of Civil Society, 1700–1865* (Chicago: University of Chicago Press, 2003). McCarthy claims that Jacksonian individualism led to a resistance to this form of communal giving. I would argue that it made activities like Hester's all that more important. I am indebted to Olivier Zunz's excellent review, "Philanthropy as Creed: The Encounter between Past and Present," *Reviews in American History* 32 (2004): 506–11.

58 For a major treatment of "civil religion," see Robert Bellah, *The Broken Covenant: American Civil Religion in Time of Trial* (Chicago: University of Chicago Press, 1975).

59 Describing how Hester turns from radical speculations in chapter 13 to willing submission to authority on her return, Bercovitch argues that in America citizens consent to their own subjection. Reading *The Scarlet Letter* as a book about Hester's individualism, he asserts that "the only plausible modes of American dissent are those that center on the self" (*Office of "The Scarlet Letter,"* 31). A liberal ideology of "dissensus," not consensus, "the American ideology" works by channeling dissent into a form of social cohesion, as Dimmesdale does in his Election Sermon when he projects into the future the image of an alternative, better world. This image of a not-yet-achieved America accommodates potentially conflicting and mutually exclusive individual visions by operating according to a logic of both/and, not the either/or logic of contradiction. As provocative as this reading is, Bercovitch's neglect of the rise of civil society causes him to minimize important developments in the eighteenth century, such as the structural transformation of the public sphere. (See Jürgen Habermas, *The Structural Transformation of the Public Sphere* [Cambridge: MIT Press, 1989]). It also contributes to his insistence that *The Scarlet Letter* is about individualism, so much so that, for him, the focus of the famous forest scene is on "the individual, not the couple" (Bercovitch, *Office of "The Scarlet Letter,"* 122). Working within a Lockean framework that opposes the individual to society, he does not consider how civil society opens up a space for interpersonal associations as opposed to individualistic self-fashioning.

60 Disputing the secularization thesis that sees the modern idea of progress as a secular version of the Judeo-Christian sense of temporality, Hans Blumenberg proposes instead a reoccupation thesis. Whereas modernity inherited from the medieval period a set of questions from Christian theology, some—if not all—of its answers to those questions are legitimately new, not simply secularized versions of old ones. Reoccupying the position of old answers, new ones may not generate the radical break with the past that champions of modernity assert, but they do bring about an important transformation. See Blumenberg, *The Legitimacy of the Modern Age,* trans. Robert Wallace (Cambridge: MIT Press, 1983).

An example of such reoccupation at work in American history is the replacement of a life-size portrait of George III in the Governor's Place in Williamsburg, Virginia, with one of George Washington in the same pose. Reoccupying the position of the king in a monarchy, Washington has, nonetheless, a different role to play in a republic. Similarly, in reoccupying the role of subjects in a monarchy, citizens in a republic help bring about a structural transformation in their relation to the state, just as Hester, in reoccupying her old cottage, has a different relation to the Puritan magistrates.

61 Berlant, *Anatomy of National Fantasy,* 98. Reading Hawthorne's portrayal of seventeenth-century Boston allegorically to solve the "problem of understanding national citizenship in early national America" (ibid., 6), Berlant, like Berco-

vitch, concentrates on the containment of Hester's antinomian radicalism, as expressed in chapter 13. Berlant and Bercovitch differ, however, in their interpretations of the significance of that containment. For Bercovitch the couple's adultery releases radical sympathies that are eventually subordinated to a higher sense of national justice prophesied in Dimmesdale's Election Sermon, whereas for Berlant the adultery unleashes a radical sense of justice that is eventually repressed in favor of Hester's sympathetic concern with the mutual happiness between men and women. In abandoning her radical anxieties about "the foundation for justice" for worries about domestic relations, Hester abandons the political implications of her initial rebellion. By the book's end, Berlant writes, "the tale of Hester and Dimmesdale, a political scandal, is reduced to a *mere* love plot" (ibid., 154; my emphasis). Hester is still focused on "love," but love now imagined in "the diminished, private 'region' often called Hester's 'feminism'" (ibid.). I have two important differences with Berlant. First, what she calls a "diminished, private 'region'" I see as the beginnings of a civil society. Second, Berlant, like Bercovitch, posits the continuities of the "Puritan/American project" (ibid., 158). Supplementing her narrative of secularization with Louis Althusser's account of the ideological interpellation of subjects, Berlant assumes that Winthrop's subjects have the same relation to the state as citizens in a nineteenth-century democracy. That is, I have tried to show, not the case. For more on the limits of Althusser for discussions of U.S. citizenship, see Chapter 1.

Pease, in *Visionary Compacts*, makes a number of interesting points about *The Scarlet Letter* in relation to civic duty, but he also neglects the crucial role of civil society and confines himself to a discussion of the "reciprocity between the public and private worlds" (82). His sense of community also depends upon Rousseau's "general will," which Pease equates with an American notion of a "public will" (24). But an independent civil society is important because it allows for associations that resist potentially tyrannical conformity enforced in the name of an abstract "general will," the most obvious example being the "reign of terror." Pease himself champions Hawthorne's Puritans, finding in them a positive "unrealized vision of community" (53).

62 See Laura Hanft Korobkin, "The Scarlet Letter of the Law," *Novel* 30 (1977): 193–217.

63 Walzer, "Introduction," 1.

64 Stephen Nissenbaum, "Introduction," in *The Scarlet Letter and Selected Writings of Nathaniel Hawthorne* (New York: Modern Library, 1984), vii–xlv.

65 Hutner, *Secrets and Sympathy*, 20.

66 Nathaniel Hawthorne, *Tales and Sketches* (New York: Library of America, 1996), 1078–79.

67 Michael Walzer, "The Concept of Civil Society," in Walzer, *Toward a Global Civil Society*, 7–27, quotation at 24.

68 Hawthorne, *Tales and Sketches*, 286.

69 For Hawthorne's views on slavery, see Chapter 7.

70 Arthur M. Schlesinger Jr., *The Vital Center: The Politics of Freedom* (Boston: Houghton Mifflin, 1949), 38, 165, 38, 161, 170.

71 In a sixteenth-century book on citizenship translated for 1845 publication in the United States, Ansaldo Ceba writes, "'Mercy,' Sopatus taught his brother, 'which transcends justice, cannot be called mercy;' otherwise, one virtue would come in collision with another, which is directly opposed to all principles of moral philosophy" (*The Citizen of a Republic: What Are His Rights, His Duties, and Privileges, and What Should Be His Education*, trans. C. Edwards Lester [New York: Paine and Burgess, 1845], 86). Civic myths, I am arguing, are a narrative response to such collisions.

Chapter 3

1 Thomas Wentworth Higginson, *The Complete Civil War Journals and Selected Letters of Thomas Wentworth Higginson*, ed. Christopher Looby (Chicago: University of Chicago Press, 2000), 334–45. Eight days later he wrote his mother that the story was "admirably done" (340).

2 Lida F. Baldwin, "Unbound Old Atlantics," *Atlantic Monthly* 100 (1907): 680.

3 Allan Nevins, *The War for the Union* (New York: Scribner, 1971), 3:227.

4 Edward Everett Hale, "The Man without a Country," *Atlantic Monthly* 7 (1863): 665–79, quotation at 666–67. Future references will be included parenthetically in the text.

5 His style owed much to his early work for his father's newspaper, where he learned the following rules for writing:

   1. Know what you want to say.

   2. Say it.

   3. Use your own words.

   4. A short word is better than a long one.

   5. Leave out fine passages.

   6. The fewer the words, other things being equal, the better.

See Norris H. Laughton, "Preface," in *The Man without a Country*, by Edward Everett Hale (Philadelphia: Artemus, 1908), viii.

6 Wayne Whipple, "Introduction," in ibid., xi.

7 Fred Lewis Pattee, "The Short Story," in *The Cambridge History of American Literature* (New York: G. P. Putnam's Sons, 1918), 2:374.

8 Carl Van Doren, "Introduction," in *The Man without a Country*, by Edward Everett Hale (New York: Limited Editions Club, 1936), x.

9 Clifton Fadiman, "Introduction," in *Masterpieces of World Literature*, ed. Frank H. Magill (New York: Harper and Row, 1949), x.

10 Jean Holloway, *Edward Everett Hale: A Biography* (Austin: University of Texas Press, 1956), 142.

11 Van Wyck Brooks, "Introduction," in *The Man without a Country*, by Edward Everett Hale (New York: Franklin Watts, 1960), ix, v.

12 Roy P. Basler, Marion Dolores Pratt, and Lloyd A. Dunlap, eds., *The Collected Works of Abraham Lincoln* (New Brunswick: Rutgers University Press, 1953), 3:547.

13 Ibid., 4:241.

14 Ibid., 268.

15 George P. Fletcher writes, "The literary monument of the Civil War was . . . 'The

Man Without a Country.' . . . [It] expresses the sense of organic nationhood that prevailed at the time." I argue that it also helped to create that sense of nationhood. Fletcher also claims that other scholars "overlook the consolidation of the United States as a nation in the mid-nineteenth century European sense of the term" (*Our Secret Constitution: How Lincoln Redefined American Democracy* [New York: Oxford University Press, 2001], 64, 12). But in 1946 Merle Curti gave a learned account of the move from "the older legalistic concept of the Union to the organic theory of the nation" (*The Roots of American Loyalty* [New York: Columbia University Press, 1946], 174). According to Curti, "The consciousness of treason, and its negation of patriotism, owed much to Edward Everett Hale's 'The Man without a Country'" (148). See also Hans Kohn, *American Nationalism: An Interpretive Essay* (New York: Macmillan, 1957), and, more recently, Melinda Lawson, *Patriotic Fires: Forging a New American Nationalism in the Civil War North* (Lawrence: University Press of Kansas, 2002).

16 Quoted in Paul C. Nagel, *One Nation Indivisible: The Union in American Thought, 1776–1861* (New York: Oxford University Press, 1964), 184.

17 Garry Wills, *Lincoln at Gettysburg: The Words That Remade America* (New York: Simon and Schuster, 1992), 175.

18 Edward Everett Hale, *The Man without a Country and Its History* (Boston: H. J. Stilman Smith & Co., 1897), iii. Carl Van Doren picks up on Hale's comment and writes, "In 1800 Americans said, as European still do, the United States *are* this or that. By 1860 many Americans, though not all, naturally said the United States *is*. A fanatical grammarian might argue that the Civil War was fought to decide which copula should be used" ("Introduction," ix).

19 Wm. Sloane Kennedy, "Edward Everett Hale," *Century* 29 (1885): 338–43, quotation at 341.

20 See Forrest McDonald, *States' Rights and the Union: Imperium in Imperio, 1776–1876* (Lawrence: University Press of Kansas, 2000).

21 Charles Sumner, "Are We a Nation?," in *Charles Sumner: His Complete Works*, ed. George Frisbie Hoar (New York: Lee and Shepard, 1900), 16:47–48.

22 Basler, Pratt, and Dunlap, *Collected Works*, 4:253.

23 Sumner, "Are We a Nation?," 16:42.

24 Basler, Pratt, and Dunlap, *Collected Works*, 4:252.

25 Daniel Webster, *The Papers of Daniel Webster: Speeches and Formal Writings*, ed. Charles M. Wiltse and Alan Berolzheimer (Dartmouth: New England University Press, 1986), 1:326.

26 Wills, *Lincoln at Gettysburg*, 129.

27 Joseph Addison, *Cato: A Tragedy* (Philadelphia, 1786), act 4, scene 4; Garry Wills, *Cincinnatus: George Washington and the Enlightenment* (Garden City, N.Y.: Doubleday, 1984).

28 William Bennett, *Our Sacred Honor: Words of Advice from the Founders in Stories, Letters, Poems, and Speeches* (New York: Simon and Schuster, 1997).

29 John Frost, *Lives of the Heroes of the American Revolution* (Boston: Phillips and Sampson, 1849), 177.

30 C. Edwards Lester, *The Artist, the Merchant, and the Statesman* (New York: Paine

and Burgess, 1845), 2:129. In the same year Lester published a translation of Ansaldo Ceba's sixteenth-century *The Citizen of a Republic: What Are His Rights, His Duties, and Privileges, and What Should Be His Education*, trans. C. Edwards Lester (New York: Paine and Burgess, 1845). The book was dedicated to John Quincy Adams. Upon Charles Sumner's death, Lester also published *Life and Public Service of Charles Sumner* (New York: United States Publishing Co., 1874).

31 David Potter, "Nathan Hale and the Ideal of American Union," *Connecticut Antiquarian* 6 (1954): 23, 25.

32 Wills, *Cincinnatus*, 12, 30n.

33 On the importance of Burr in Hale's story, see Robert A. Ferguson, "The Trial of Aaron Burr," in *The Trial in American Life* (Chicago: University of Chicago Press, 2007).

34 "The Man without a Country" was so popular that even though, as prose, it could not be included in Hazel Felleman, ed., *The Best-Loved Poems of the American People* (Garden City, N.Y.: Doubleday, 1936), this excerpt from Scott's poem is included in the section "Patriotism and War," appearing behind only "The Star-Spangled Banner" and "America the Beautiful." The excerpt from Scott's poem is also included in John M. Foote, ed., *Patriotic American Stories* (Philadelphia: John C. Winston Co., 1937).

35 In the German translation, "country" is consistently translated as "*Vaterland*." But in this passage involving Africans, it is translated as "*Heimat*," an indication that the translator did not think of Africans as having a country in the same sense as Americans or Europeans. Since Nolan compares a country with a mother, the use of "*Vaterland*" works against the gendered implications of the story. See Edward Everett Hale, *Der Mann ohne Vaterland*, trans. Margit Boesch-Frutiger (Aarau/Frankfurt a.M.: Sauerländer Verlag, 1958), 40.

36 Eva March Tappan, *American Hero Stories* (Boston: Houghton Mifflin, 1906), 48.

37 Robert J. Allison, *The Crescent Obscured: The United States and the Muslim World, 1776–1815* (New York: Oxford University Press, 1995), 190. The 1924 film *The Man without a Country* includes Decatur as a character.

38 Joseph Ellis, *American Sphinx: The Character of Thomas Jefferson* (New York: Knopf, 1997), 204.

39 Max Boot, *The Savage Wars of Peace: Small Wars and the Rise of American Power* (New York: Basic Books, 2002), 6.

40 Charles Lee Lewis, *The Romantic Decatur* (Philadelphia: University of Pennsylvania Press, 1937), 86–87.

41 Alexander Slidell Mackenzie, *The Life of Stephen Decatur* (Boston: Charles C. Little and James Brown, 1846), 324.

42 See Chapter 7 for a discussion of what Decatur actually said.

43 Whipple, "Introduction," iv.

44 On echoes to Milton's *Paradise Lost*, see Daniel Aaron, "'The Man without a Country' as a Civil War Document," in *Geschichte und Gesellschaft in der Amerikanischen Literatur*, ed. Karl Schubert and Ursula Müller-Richter (Heidelberg: Quelle and Meyer, 1975), 55–61.

45 Edward Everett Hale, "Northern Invasions," *Atlantic Monthly* 13 (1864): 247.

46 Whipple, "Introduction," iv.

47 Edward Everett Hale, "Philip Nolan and the 'Levant,'" *National Geographic Magazine* 16 (1905): 115.

48 Hale, *Man without a Country and Its History*, x.

49 Ibid., xviii.

50 Whipple, "Introduction," v–vi.

51 Thomas Wentworth Higginson, "Edward Everett Hale," in *Carlyle's Laugh and Other Surprises* (Boston: Houghton Mifflin, 1909), 166.

52 Holloway, *Edward Everett Hale*, 144.

53 George Winston Smith, "Broadsides for Freedom: Civil War Propaganda in New England," *New England Quarterly* 21 (1948): 291–312.

54 See Arthur H. Cash, *John Wilkes: The Scandalous Father of Civil Liberty* (New Haven: Yale University Press, 2006); Audrey Williamson, *Wilkes: A Friend of Liberty* (London: Allen and Unwin, 1974); and George F. E. Rudé, *Wilkes and Liberty: A Social Study of 1763–1774* (Oxford: Clarendon Press, 1962).

55 The issue seemed to be resolved March 3, 1863, when Congress authorized the president, during the rebellion, to suspend habeas corpus. But it also required the secretaries of state and war to furnish district and circuit judges lists of all citizens of loyal states held as political prisoners. If a grand jury had been adjourned without finding an indictment, the prisoner could be freed upon taking an oath of allegiance. This requirement was frequently ignored.

56 Benjamin R. Curtis, "Executive Power," in *Constitutional History of the United States*, by George Ticknor Curtis, ed. Joseph Culbertson Clayton (New York: Harper and Brothers, 1896), 2:668.

57 Ibid., 672.

58 Ibid., 682, 676, 678.

59 Herman Melville, *Billy Budd, Sailor (An Inside Narrative)* (Chicago: University of Chicago Press, 1962), 112; William E. Rappard, *The Crisis of Democracy* (Chicago: University of Chicago Press, 1938), 265.

60 Rutledge Wiley, in a foreword to "A Symposium on Constitutional Rights in Wartime," *Iowa Law Review* 29 (1944): 379.

61 J. G. Randall, *Constitutional Problems under Lincoln* (Gloucester, Mass.: Peter Smith, 1963), 80–81.

62 Curtis, "Executive Power," 672.

63 My account of Vallandigham relies heavily on Frank L. Klement, *The Limits of Dissent: Clement L. Vallandigham and the Civil War* (Lexington: University Press of Kentucky, 1970).

64 Ibid., 29.

65 John G. Nicolay and John Hay, *Abraham Lincoln: A History* (New York: Century, 1890), 7:328–29.

66 Klement, *Limits*, 153–54.

67 See Michael Kent Curtis, *Free Speech, "The People's Darling Privilege": Struggles for Freedom of Expression in American History* (Durham: Duke University Press, 2000).

68 Abraham Lincoln, "The Truth from an Honest Man. The Letter of the President.

President Lincoln's Views. An Important Letter on the Principles Involved in the Vallandigham Case. Correspondence in Relation to the Democratic Meeting, at Albany, N.Y. (Union League No. 31)," in *Union Pamphlets of the Civil War, 1861–1865,* ed. Frank Freidel (Cambridge: Belknap Press of Harvard University Press, 1967), 2:741. Future references to this work, cited as Corning, will be included parenthetically within the text.

69 This frequently quoted statement helped to produce and reinforced the popular image of Lincoln as a tenderhearted, compassionate man. Stories of him pardoning condemned soldiers were told and retold. According to Barry Schwartz, "Such stories could fill a volume; and, with their deep cultural significance, they were broadcast through short story, essay, poetry, and painting. And they fed the new movie industry" (*Abraham Lincoln and the Forge of National Memory* [Chicago: University of Chicago Press, 2000], 180). In fact, there were more military executions in the Civil War under Lincoln than in all other U.S. wars combined. See Robert I. Alotta, *Civil War Justice: Union Army Executions under Lincoln* (Shippensburg, Pa.: White Mane, 1989).

70 James Ford Rhodes, *History of the United States from the Compromise of 1850* (New York: Harper and Brothers, 1899), 4:251.

71 Allan Nevins, *The War for the Union* (New York: Scribner, 1960), 2:455.

72 Don E. Fehrenbacher, "Lincoln and the Constitution" and "The Paradoxes of Freedom," in *Lincoln in Text and Context: Collected Essays* (Stanford: Stanford University Press, 1987), 113–42.

73 Mark E. Neely Jr., *The Fate of Liberty: Abraham Lincoln and Civil Liberties* (New York: Oxford University Press, 1991), 199, 198. Paul Finkelman sums up the lesson of Neely's book as "War threatens individual liberties, even when the chief executive is sensitive to democracy and disinclined to be oppressive" ("Civil Liberties and the Civil War: The Great Emancipator as Civil Libertarian," *Michigan Law Review* 91 [1993]: 1353). Wills is more accurate when he says that Neely makes a case that "Lincoln's supposedly unconstitutional acts were fewer and less grave than supposed" (*Lincoln at Gettysburg,* 287 n. 33).

74 Frank J. Williams, *Judging Lincoln* (Carbondale: Southern Illinois University Press, 2002), 72, 77.

75 Daniel Farber, *Lincoln's Constitution* (Chicago: University of Chicago Press, 2003), 174.

76 Klement, *Limits,* 252.

77 Hale, *Man without a Country and Its History,* viii.

78 Francis Wayland Jr., "Letter to a Peace Democrat," *Atlantic Monthly* 12 (1863): 784.

79 Edward Everett Hale, "Introduction," in *A History of the Kansas Crusade,* by Eli Thayer (New York: Harper and Brothers, 1889), xii.

80 Ibid., xvii.

81 See Hale's April 13, 1862, sermon "The Future Civilization of the South," quoted in George M. Fredrickson, *The Inner Civil War: Northern Intellectuals and the Crisis of the Union* (1965; reprint, New York: Harper and Row, 1968), 117–18.

82 Hale, *Man without a Country and Its History*, xi.

83 Leonard W. Levy, *Jefferson and Civil Liberties* (Cambridge: Harvard University Press, 1963), 88.

84 Tattnall is frequently credited with coining this phrase, but it is listed as a proverb in F. P. Wilson, *The Oxford Dictionary of English Proverbs*, 3rd ed. (Oxford: Clarendon Press, 1970), 69. Tattnall probably encountered the phrase in Sir Walter Scott's *Guy Mannering* (1815, chap. 38). On Tattnall's actions in Chinese waters, see Robert Erwin Johnson, *Far China Station: The U.S. Navy in Asian Waters, 1800–1898* (Annapolis: Naval Institute Press, 1979), 98–106. Observing the action, Edward Trenchard wrote in a journal that Tattnall added, "And he'd be damned if he'd stand by and see white men butchered before his eyes. No, sir. Old Tattnall isn't that kind, sir. This is the cause of humanity" (Edgar Stanton Maclay, *Reminiscences of the Old Navy* [New York: G. P. Putnam's Sons, 1898], 83).

85 Hale, *Man without a Country and Its History*, iv. Hale repeats this description in other introductions.

86 Norris H. Laughton, "Notes," in *Man without a Country* (1908), 93.

87 Russell A. Sharp, "Introduction," in *The Man without a Country*, by Edward Everett Hale (Cambridge: Houghton Mifflin, 1923), xi.

88 Robert D. Madison, "Introduction," in *The Man without a Country and Other Naval Writings*, by Edward Everett Hale (Annapolis: Naval Institute Press, 2002), viii–ix.

89 George Washington, *Writings*, ed. John Rhodelhamel (New York: Library of America, 1997), 965.

90 Benjamin Franklin, *The Papers of Benjamin Franklin*, ed. William Willcox (New Haven: Yale University Press, 1975), 19:410.

91 Van Doren, "Introduction," ix.

92 The 1924 film *The Man without a Country* remedies that situation. Concerned that Hale's written account "tells the tortures Lieutenant Nolan suffered in being separated from all he had ever loved" without giving "an inkling of how they reacted to the endless years of sorrow," it portrays the agony of his loving mother and gives him a wife, who, never losing hope for his return, devotes her life to getting him pardoned. See Walter F. Eberhardt, "The Woman's Side of the Man without a Country," in *The Man without a Country: Illustrated with Scenes from the William Fox Screen Glorification of This Immortal Classic, a Roland V. Lee Production* (New York: Grosset and Dunlap, 1925), 29–30.

93 Basler, Pratt, and Dunlap, *Collected Works*, 4:259. Elsewhere he says, "A nation may be said to consist of its territory, its people, and its laws. The territory is the only part which is of certain durability. One generation passeth away, and another generation cometh, but the earth abideth forever" (5:527). Lincoln thus shares Francis Lieber's view that a "Country . . . is the dwelling-place of a Nation." Lieber also makes a distinction between "nation" and "people" in terms of "organic unity." See "Nationalism" in *Hamilton's Republic: Readings in the American Nationalist Tradition*, ed. Michael Lind (New York: Free Press, 1997), 117. For more on the definition of a nation, see the discussion on Sumner's "Are We a Nation?" in the next chapter.

94 Basler, Pratt, and Dunlap, *Collected Works*, 4:260.

95 Ibid., 23.

96 Those deeds are not limited to the creation of political institutions. In the First Inaugural, Lincoln also notes how the people turn the land into battlefields, patriot graves, and hearthstones. In his December 1, 1862, message to Congress, he describes how "steam, telegraphs, and intelligence" have made the nation's territory suited for "one united people" (ibid., 5:527).

97 Benedict Anderson, *Imagined Communities: Reflections on the Origin and Spread of Nationalism*, rev. ed. (London: Verso, 1991).

98 Edward Everett Hale, "Introduction," in *The Man without a Country* (Boston: Little, Brown, 1911), vii. Hale first used the quotation by Kingsley without the claim for universality in an introduction he wrote during the Spanish-American War in 1898.

99 For details on some of these translations, see Chapter 7.

100 As Hale might have known, Nolan's knowledge that new stars stand for new states is another possible anachronism. That practice was not made official until an 1817 law.

101 Edward Everett Hale, "Introduction, May 5, 1898," *Outlook* 59 (1898): 117. Hale cut a number of passages for this wartime version of the story, such as the section on Porter taking possession of the Nukahiwa Islands and Madison and the Virginians flinging away that opportunity. This particular cut may have been an attempt to minimize the imperial designs of the United States in the Spanish-American War. It could also have been motivated by an effort to minimize criticism of the South in order to unite North and South in the campaign against a common enemy. For instance, a section about Texas is also cut, as is an early one about the strict secrecy about Nolan maintained since the Madison administration ended in 1817.

102 Edward Everett Hale, "Author's Note to Edition of 1897," in *The Man without a Country and Other Stories* (New York: Thomas Nelson and Sons, 1906), 18.

103 Higginson, "Edward Everett Hale," 165.

104 *Nation*, April 17, 1902, 307.

105 See Sandra Stotsky, *Connecting Civic Education and Language Education: The Contemporary Challenge* (New York: Teachers College, 1991).

106 Whittier's "Barbara Frietchie" was published in the same volume of the *Atlantic* as "The Man without a Country."

107 Foote, *Patriotic American Stories*, xi–xii, xv, 245, xv.

108 Gary Nash, "The Great Multicultural Debate," *Contention* 1 (1992): 83.

109 Jürgen Habermas, "Citizenship and National Identity: Some Reflections on the Future of Europe," *Praxis International* 12 (1992): 1–19, esp. 8.

110 In fact, the difference has less to do with affect—any close reading of Lincoln reveals how much he relies on affect—and more with principles and ideals. Nonetheless, in the wake of 9/11, Hale's story has experienced a minor revival, with publication of new editions for the first time in quite a while and with an American citizen known as "the American Taliban" referred to in the press as "a man without a country." If this revival pales in contrast to those in the past, it is

not surprising, given the patriotic fervor that arises with threats to the national security.

111 Vallandigham's denunciation of Lincoln as a despot and a tyrant has been kept alive by a small minority of critics. For instance, Edmund Wilson called him a dictator and compared him to Bismarck and Lenin. Wilson's criticism inspired fictional accounts by Gore Vidal and William Safire. See Edmund Wilson, *Patriotic Gore: Studies in the Literature of the American Civil War* (New York: Oxford University Press, 1962). For a summary of the dictatorship debate up to 1984, see Herman Belz, *Lincoln and the Constitution: The Dictatorship Question Reconsidered* (Fort Wayne, Ind.: Louis A. Warren, 1984). See also Fehrenbacher, "The Anti-Lincoln Tradition," in *Lincoln in Text and Context*, 197–213. More recently, libertarians have taken up the banner and criticized Lincoln as a despot who created an authoritarian, centralized state. See Jeffrey Rogers Hummel, *Emancipating Slaves, Enslaving Free Men: A History of the American Civil War* (Chicago: Open Court, 1996); Charles Adams, *When in the Course of Human Events: Arguing the Case for Southern Secession* (Lanham, Md.: Rowman and Littlefield, 2000); and Thomas J. Dilorenzo, *The Real Lincoln: A New Look at Abraham Lincoln, His Agenda, and an Unnecessary War* (Roseville, Calif.: Prima, 2002).

Some of Lincoln's defenders helped to create the image of him as a tyrant. Horace Bushnell, for instance, revived the Puritan view articulated by John Winthrop that "civil liberty" requires submission to the will of the chief magistrate, who in turn is responsible to God. Dismissing the "sovereignty of the people," he claimed that "the magistrate is sovereign over the people, not they over him, having even a divine right to bind their conscience by his rule" (qtd. in Fredrickson, *Inner Civil War*, 137).

112 As John Stuart Mill makes clear in *On Liberty*, published just before the Civil War in 1859, making the people sovereign does not eliminate the threat to civil liberties.

113 Basler, Pratt, and Dunlap, *Collected Works*, 4:438, 426.

114 Henry W. Bellows made precisely this argument in support of Lincoln. "To rally round the President," Bellows preached, "—without question or dispute—is the first and most sacred duty of loyal citizens, when he announces, not that the Constitution merely, but the National life and existence are in peril. He is the official judge of this—and if we do not accept his testimony, we have nothing to trust. . . . [He] speaks as the Government, and for the Government, with all the wisdom and capacity the Government has" (Henry Whitney Bellows, "Unconditional Loyalty," in Freidel, *Union Pamphlets of the Civil War*, 1:514).

115 Basler, Pratt, and Dunlap, *Collected Works*, 4:429.

116 Quoted in Edward S. Corwin, *The President: Office and Powers, 1787–1948* (New York: New York University Press, 1948), 282.

117 Numerous people have detailed how Lincoln increased presidential power. See, for example, Arthur M. Schlesinger Jr., *The Imperial Presidency* (Boston: Houghton Mifflin, 1973).

118 Basler, Pratt, and Dunlap, *Collected Works*, 4:215–16.

119 On the importance of the ship-of-state metaphor in the antebellum period, see

Nagel, *One Nation Indivisible*, 215–19. On Longfellow's poem, see Hans-Joachim Lang and Fritz Fleischman, "'All This Beauty, All This Grace': Longfellow's 'The Building of the Ship' and Alexander Mackenzie's 'Ship,'" *New England Quarterly* 54 (1981): 104–18. George Bancroft wrote, "The position of Abraham Lincoln on the day of his inauguration was apparently one of helpless debility. A bark canoe in a tempest on mid-ocean seemed hardly less safe" ("The Place of Abraham Lincoln in History," *Atlantic Monthly* 15 [1865]: 757–64, quotation at 762).

120 Frank Freidel, *Francis Lieber: Nineteenth-Century Liberal* (Baton Rouge: Louisiana State University Press, 1947), 318, 335, 336.

121 Mackenzie, *Life*, 295.

122 Charles Sumner, "The Mutiny on the Somers," *North American Review* 107 (1843): 228.

123 Basler, Pratt, and Dunlap, *Collected Works*, 4:281. In his *American Commonwealth*, James Bryce repeats a widely quoted story in which Lincoln, early in the war, told Secretary of Treasury Salmon Chase, "These rebels are violating the Constitution to destroy the Union. I will violate the Constitution if necessary to save the Union; I suspect, Chase, that your Constitution is going to have a rough time of it before we get done with this row." Without clear documentation, this story has been dismissed by historians as a likely fabrication. Nonetheless, the fact that it was once widely told is in itself revealing. Quoted in Clinton Rossiter, *Constitutional Dictatorship: Crisis Government in the Modern Democracies* (Princeton: Princeton University Press, 1948), 229 n. 12.

124 James M. McPherson, "How Lincoln Won the War with Metaphors," in *Abraham Lincoln and the Second American Revolution* (New York: Oxford University Press, 1990), 93–112. Historian Michael P. Johnson calls Lincoln a "wordsmith" in "Introduction: Abraham Lincoln, Wordsmith," in his *Abraham Lincoln, Slavery, and the Civil War: Selected Writings and Speeches* (Boston: Bedford/St. Martins, 2001), 1–12. Johnson includes Lincoln's letter to Corning in response to the Vallandigham affair but sides with Lincoln by implying that the protest was about the military draft. See also Ronald C. White Jr., *The Eloquent President: A Portrait of Lincoln through His Words* (New York: Random House, 2005).

125 Dilorenzo, *Real Lincoln*, 163.

126 Wills, *Lincoln at Gettysburg*, 147.

127 1 U.S. 337 (1949) at 37.

128 Robert H. Jackson, *The Supreme Court in the American System of Government* (Cambridge: Harvard University Press, 1955), 75. His comment comes directly after a description of the difficulty of the decision to declare constitutional the internment of Japanese Americans in World War II. In *Korematsu v. U.S.* 323 U.S. 214 (1945) at 244, Justice Jackson had argued, "The armed services must protect a society, not merely its Constitution." That argument was, however, part of a courageous dissent.

129 *Ex parte Milligan*, 4 Wallace 2 (1866) at 81. For more on this case, see the next chapter.

130 372 U.S. 144 (1963) at 159–60.

131 *Ex parte Milligan*, 4 Wallace 2 (1866) at 30.

132 The government's constant control over Nolan's life undercuts Linda Kerber's use of him to illustrate the condition of statelessness. Far from stateless, Nolan never escapes the surveillance of the state. Kerber also has Hale responding to *Ex parte Milligan*, which was decided three years after Hale's story was published. See Kerber, "Toward a History of Statelessness in America," *American Quarterly* 57 (2005): 727–49, esp. 742.

133 In 1867 Hale was highly critical of Washington bureaucracy. "Now, in the best of times," he wrote, "Washington is the point in the United States most ignorant of the real spirit of the American people" ("The United States Sanitary Commission," *Atlantic Monthly* 19 [1867]: 419). When he became chaplain of the Senate in 1903, someone asked him, "Do you pray for the Senators, Dr. Hale?" His supposed response was "No, I look at the Senators and pray for the country" (Brooks, "Introduction," x).

134 See the arguments of Peter Karsten and Barry Schwartz discussed in Chapter 1. Karsten, *Patriot Heroes in England and America* (Madison: University of Wisconsin Press, 1978), and Schwartz, *Abraham Lincoln and the Forge of National Memory*.

135 Eberhardt, "Woman's Side of the Man without a Country," 54–60.

136 Russell A. Sharp, "Questions for Study," in *Man without a Country* (1923), 67–68.

137 *Kennedy v. Mendoza-Martinez*, 372 U.S. 144 (1963) at 177.

138 John R. Adams, *Edward Everett Hale* (Boston: Twayne, 1977), 37.

139 *Kennedy v. Mendoza-Martinez* 372 U.S. 144 (1963) at 179.

140 Holloway, *Edward Everett Hale*, 123. Holloway cites Edward Everett Hale, "Introduction, May 5, 1898," 116. Holloway also mistakenly reports that Vallandigham was banished to the Confederacy *after* losing the October election.

141 Holloway, *Edward Everett Hale*, 135. To accept Hale's pronouncement that Vallandigham had been completely forgotten is especially neglectful, since Hale himself was forced to alter his comment. Far from being forgotten after the Ohio election, Vallandigham made his way back to the United States and influenced the Democratic platform in the 1864 election. Although he remained a thorn in the administration's side, no one bothered him, since it was clear that his arrest had served mainly to publicize his cause. After the war, he entered a lucrative legal practice until his bizarre death in 1871. Demonstrating how he would defend a client accused of murder by showing the impossibility of him holding a pistol a certain way, Vallandigham killed himself when he pulled the trigger of a mistakenly loaded gun. Hale's readers, it seems, called this death to his attention. For an 1897 edition, Hale wrote, "Perhaps he is living still. The general reader of to-day would not know his name, but that in some address he said that he did not want to live in a country which did something or other which the National Administration, under Lincoln, had done . . . forgotten, till now, as long" (*Man without a Country and Its History*, iii–iv). Hale's comments for this edition were used for a number of subsequent editions. Then for one in 1906, making no other changes to it and without acknowledgment, Hale substituted, "I am afraid that men who remember him now, remember him most often from the tragic circumstances of his sudden death . . . forgotten till now, as long, except for his tragic death in 1871" ("Author's Note to Edition of 1897,"

4–5). Unable to ignore the notoriety of Vallandigham's death, Hale still denies the importance of the constitutional issues he raised.

142 Foote, *Patriotic American Stories*, 129, 3.

143 Basler, Pratt, and Dunlap, *Collected Works*, 4:263.

144 Wills, *Lincoln at Gettysburg*, 147. Judge Williams writes, "What made Lincoln a successful commander in chief was his constitutional flexibility, which allowed him to bend the Constitution within the framework of its intent without breaking it" (*Judging Lincoln*, 77).

Chapter 4

1 See Fredric Jameson, *The Political Unconscious: Narrative as Socially Symbolic Act* (Ithaca: Cornell University Press, 1981), 236, 249, 286–97.

2 Clinton Rossiter, *Constitutional Dictatorship: Crisis Government in the Modern Democracies* (Princeton: Princeton University Press, 1948), 5. Rossiter's argument draws on the work of Carl Schmidt, whose claim that sovereignty is defined by the "exception" has become so popular today, filtered through the work of Giorgio Agamben. Rossiter's assessment of Schmidt suggests limits to the empirical applicability of Schmidt and Agamben.

A trail-blazing, if somewhat occasional work defining the distinction between constitutional and non-constitutional dictatorship was Carl Schmidt: *Die Diktatur*. . . . Schmidt, who was at the time advocating a broad interpretation of the emergency powers of the German President, separated all extraordinary public offices into two categories: the commissioned dictatorship (*kommissarische Diktatur*) and the sovereign dictatorship (*souveräne Diktatur*), but he lumped so many heterogeneous offices under the former category (The Roman dictator, Wallenstein, the "commissioners" of the Middle Ages, Lincoln) that he failed in the end to draw a sufficiently precise distinction between constitutional dictatorship and opportunistic Caesarism. (14 n. 10).

3 Ibid., 7, 223, 7.

4 Charles Sumner, "Are We a Nation?," in *Charles Sumner: His Complete Works*, ed. George Frisbie Hoar (Boston: Lee and Shepard, 1900), 16:62. Future references to this work, cited as Nation, will be included parenthetically in the text.

5 Bruce Miroff, Raymond Seidelman, and Todd Swanstrom, *The Democratic Debate: An Introduction to American Politics* (Boston: Houghton Mifflin, 1998), 433.

6 Thomas Paine, *The Rights of Man*, ed. Eric Foner (1791–92; reprint, New York: Penguin, 1984).

7 John Dickson, "Civil Rights," in *Encyclopedia of the Social Sciences*, ed. Edwin R. A. Seligman (New York: Macmillan, 1930), 513.

8 Ibid.

9 Milton R. Konvitz, "Civil Rights," in *International Encyclopedia of the Social Sciences*, ed. David L. Sills (New York: Macmillan, 1968), 312.

10 For a somewhat different, but very important, discussion of the concept of liberty, see Robert A. Ferguson, "The Dialectic of Liberty," in *Reading the Early Republic* (Cambridge: Harvard University Press, 2004), 51–83.

11 John A. Marshall, *American Bastille* (Philadelphia: Thomas W. Hartley and Co., 1883), xxx.

12 Ibid., xxxi, xiii.

13 Duncan Andrew Campbell, *English Public Opinion and the American Civil War* (Woodbridge, Suffolk: Boydell Press, 2003), 106.

14 Daun Van Ee, *David Dudley Field and the Reconstruction of the Law* (New York: Garland, 1986), 162.

15 *Ex parte Milligan*, 71 U.S. 2 (1866) at 56. Future references to this case will be included parenthetically in the text and notes.

16 Charles Sumner, "The Mutiny on the Somers," *North American Review* 107 (1843): 231. For precedents Sumner cites the trial excusing British soldiers for firing on people during the Boston Massacre prior to the Revolutionary War and the 1806 *Selfridge* case. The latter was suggested to him by Justice Story.

17 Abraham Lincoln, "The Truth from an Honest Man. The Letter of the President. President Lincoln's Views. An Important Letter on the Principles Involved in the Vallandigham Case. Correspondence in Relation to the Democratic Meeting, at Albany, N.Y. (Union League No. 31)," in *Union Pamphlets of the Civil War, 1861–1865*, ed. Frank Freidel (Cambridge: Belknap Press of Harvard University Press, 1967), 2:747.

18 Justice Davis was fully aware of the argument of self-defense. Arguing for Milligan, Field brought it up by quoting the maxim *Necessitas quod cogit defendit.* "Private persons," he admits, "may lawfully tear down a house, if necessary to prevent the spread of a fire. . . . A mutiny, breaking out in a garrison, may make necessary for its suppression, and therefore justify, acts which would otherwise be unjustifiable" (36). But for neither Field nor Davis did the circumstances of Milligan's case reach the threshold of necessity.

19 Charles Warren, *The Supreme Court in United States History* (1922; rev ed., Boston: Little, Brown, 1926), 2:427.

20 Alan Nevins, "The Case of the Copperhead Conspirator," in *Quarrels That Have Shaped the Constitution*, rev. ed., ed. John A. Garraty (New York: Harper and Row, 1987), 118. See also Frank L. Klement, "The Indianapolis Treason Trials and *Ex parte Milligan*," in *American Political Trials*, rev. ed., ed. Michal R. Belknap (Westport, Conn.: Greenwood Press, 1994), 97–118.

21 Theodore Clark Smith, *The Life and Letters of James Abram Garfield* (New Haven: Yale University Press, 1925), 1:395, 2:825–26.

22 Warren, *Supreme Court*, 2:438, 433–34.

23 John W. Burgess, *Political Science and Comparative Constitutional Law* (Boston: Ginn, 1890), 1:250.

24 Warren, *Supreme Court*, 2:440.

25 Mark E. Neely Jr., *The Fate of Liberty: Abraham Lincoln and Civil Liberties* (New York: Oxford University Press, 1991), 184.

26 Neely uses the same quotation from Burgess that I do, but he eliminates Burgess's contrast between the minority and majority opinions to make it look as if Burgess supports him. To be sure, in a footnote he quotes another passage from Burgess that comes closer to his position. "The practices of the Administration

are," Burgess wrote, "to be considered as the precedents of the Constitution in civil war rather than the opinion of the Court." Neely then adds, "The precision of the term 'civil war' rather than 'war' in Burgess's statement here, of course, made his prediction entirely irrelevant to the future course of American history" (ibid., 260–61 n. 61). But Burgess's statement was made in 1901, as the United States was putting down an "insurrection" in the Philippines. Since the United States claimed the Philippines as its own, it would have considered its military effort as part of a "civil war," just as the British considered the Revolutionary War a civil war. Burgess was not making an abstract judgment. He was providing justification for the government to ignore *Milligan* in its war in the Philippines, something it did with a terrible cost to the liberties of Filipinos. Neely's only quotation from *Milligan* is a frequently cited passage, lacking a page reference (ibid., 260 n. 44). When he does reference *Milligan*, he does so incorrectly (ibid., 244 n. 11).

27 In fact, *Milligan* saved a man from imprisonment, whereas Lincoln's famous speech had no such immediate effect.

28 Roy P. Basler, Marion Dolores Pratt, and Lloyd A. Dunlap, eds., *The Collected Works of Abraham Lincoln* (New Brunswick: Rutgers University Press, 1953), 4:271.

29 Ibid., 7:23.

30 Rossiter, *Constitutional Dictatorship*, 238–39.

31 Edward S. Corwin, *The President: Office and Powers: History and Analysis of Practice and Opinion* (New York: New York University Press, 1940), 166.

32 Neely, *Fate of Liberty*, 184; Rossiter, *Constitutional Dictatorship*, 238.

33 Rossiter, *Constitutional Dictatorship*, 239. Rossiter's own "realism" turns out to be somewhat different from his mentor's. Harshly critical of the Court's refusal to declare unconstitutional the relocation of Japanese Americans during World War II, Rossiter quotes from Justice Jackson's "coldly realistic" dissent in *Korematsu v. U.S.*: "If the people ever let command of the war powers fall into irresponsible hands, the courts yield no power equal to its restraint. The chief restraint upon those who command the physical forces of the country, in the future as the past, must be their responsibility to the political judgments of their contemporaries and the moral judgments of history" (ibid., 284).

34 Writing thirty years after the decision, Henry M. Field, David's brother, asserted that Justice Davis, who, better than anyone, knew the "natural sympathy, even to tenderness, of the late President," must have tried to write a decision that "would have been the first prompting of a great heart that had ceased to beat." Field mistakenly reports that four justices "voted to sustain the decision of the court martial" (*The Life of David Dudley Field* [New York: Scribner, 1898], 190).

35 Charles Fairman, *Reconstruction and Reunion, 1864–88*, pt. 1, in *History of the Supreme Court of the United States* (New York: Macmillan, 1971), 6:201.

36 Nevins, "Case of the Copperhead Conspirator," 118.

37 Fairman notes that in fact one could argue that "*Dred Scott* asserted a Fifth Amendment liberty, whereas *Milligan* was read throughout the Southern States as a new affirmation that Congress would not be allowed to interfere with their own peculiar institution" (*Reconstruction and Reunion*, 236). Fairman also reports

that, when attacked, Justice Davis pleaded for public help from former justice
Curtis, the dissenter in *Dred Scott* and the articulate author of "Executive Power"
(ibid., 234–46).

38 Ibid., 266 n. 102.

39 Warren, *Supreme Court*, 2:428, 448, 447.

40 David Dudley Field along with William Cullen Bryant did support President
Johnson's veto of the Freedman's Bureau bill. Even though the veto was not
sustained, Bryant's *New York Evening Post* expressed grave concern that the bill's
authorization of "military protection" and "military jurisdiction over all cases
and questions" concerning freedmen's rights would be a pernicious "danger to
the liberties of the country" (Fairman, *Reconstruction and Reunion*, 344).

41 Ibid., 60.

42 See Aviam Soifer, *Law and the Company We Keep* (Cambridge: Harvard University
Press, 1995), 121–25.

43 *United States v. Cruikshank*, 92 U.S. 542 (1876) at 542.

44 Ibid., 544.

45 Van Ee, *David Dudley Field*, 208.

46 Fairman, *Reconstruction and Reunion*, 188.

47 Eric Foner, *Reconstruction: America's Unfinished Revolution, 1863–1877* (New York:
Harper and Row, 1988), 456.

48 Charles Sumner, "Supplemental Civil Rights Bill," in Hoar, *Charles Sumner*,
19:223, 226, 260, 262.

49 A sense of this resistance can be found in Sidney Lanier's poem called "Civil
Rights" (1874). John D. Kerkering discusses it in *The Poetics of National and Racial
Identity in Nineteenth-Century American Literature* (New York: Cambridge University
Press, 2003), 128–29. Kerkering mistakenly calls the bill that eventually passed
the Civil Rights Bill of 1874, and he misreads the poem by attributing the views
of its uneducated, "cracker" narrator to Lanier. The poem is a protest against
the proposed bill, but Lanier delivers the protest indirectly by dramatizing the
effect it had on a certain class of Southerners. Lanier dismissed comparisons
between his poem and Bret Harte's "The Heathen Chinee." For details about the
incidents that brought the act before the Supreme Court, see Mark S. Weiner,
Black Trials: Citizenship from the Beginnings of Slavery to the End of Caste (New York:
Knopf, 2004). On congressional debates, see Alfred H. Kelly, "The Congressional Controversy over School Segregation, 1867–1875," *American Historical Review*
64 (1959): 537–63, and William P. Vaughn, "Separate and Unequal: The Civil
Rights Act of 1875 and Defeat of the School Integration Clause," *Southwestern
Social Science Quarterly* 48 (1967): 146–54.

50 Frederick Douglass, "The Supreme Court Decision," in *Life and Times of Frederick
Douglass: Written by Himself*, rev. ed. (Boston: DeWolfe Friske and Co., 1892), 539–
54. Douglass countered charges that African Americans desired social equality
by stressing how whites in the South violated cherished values of American liberty. See, for instance, "Liberty of Speech South" and the section "Decadence of
the Spirit of Liberty" in "Why Is the Negro Lynched?," in *The Life and Writings of
Frederick Douglass*, vol. 4, *Reconstruction and After*, ed. Philip S. Foner (New York:

International Publishers, 1955), 245–46, 511–12. As Douglass well knew, one of the major free-speech issues in the antebellum period grew out of the effort to censor abolitionist literature, an effort brought to national attention by the mob assassination of Elijah Lovejoy. See Michael Kent Curtis, *Free Speech, "The People's Darling Privilege": Struggles for Freedom of Expression in American History* (Durham: Duke University Press, 2000).

51 *Civil Rights Cases,* 109 U.S. 3 (1883) at 25.

52 Ibid., 13. In *Bell v. Maryland* Justice Goldberg uses Bradley's correspondence to argue that, because the Civil Rights Cases were decided before the passage of Jim Crow legislation, they do not rule out the possibility of appealing to the Fourteenth Amendment to pass federal civil legislation banning racial discrimination in public accommodations. But he failed to win over a majority of the Court; thus Congress had to rely on a loophole in the 1883 decision and base its 1964 Civil Rights Act on the commerce clause. See 378 U.S. 226 (1964) at 309–10.

53 Loren P. Beth, *John Marshall Harlan* (Lexington: University of Kentucky Press, 1992), 229.

54 *Civil Rights Cases,* 109 U.S. 3 (1883) at 26.

Chapter 5

1 William Dean Howells, *My Mark Twain* (New York: Harper, 1910), 101. Carl F. Wieck, in *Refiguring "Huckleberry Finn"* (Athens: University of Georgia Press, 2000), makes the most sustained effort to link *Huckleberry Finn* to Lincoln. Wieck is also the author of *Lincoln's Quest for Equality: The Road to Gettysburg* (DeKalb: Northern Illinois University Press, 2002).

2 See, for example, Sara de Saussure Davis and Philip D. Beidler, eds., *The Mythologization of Mark Twain* (Tuscaloosa: University of Alabama Press, 1984); Guy Cardwell, *The Man Who Was Mark Twain: Images and Ideologies* (New Haven: Yale University Press, 1991); and Louis J. Budd, "Mark Twain as an American Icon," in *The Cambridge Companion to Mark Twain,* ed. Forrest G. Robinson (New York: Cambridge University Press, 1995), 1–26.

3 Quoted in "TV Times," *Los Angeles Times,* January 13, 2002.

4 Charles Flint Kellogg, *NAACP: A History of the National Association for the Advancement of Colored People* (Baltimore: Johns Hopkins University Press, 1967), 206.

5 Richard Hill, "Government," in *The Mark Twain Encyclopedia,* ed. J. R. LeMaster and James D. Wilson (New York: Garland, 1993), 334–46, quotation at 336.

6 Arthur M. Schlesinger Jr., "The Opening of the American Mind," *New York Times Book Review,* July 23, 1989, 1, 26–27.

7 For a selection of the debate, see James S. Leonard, Thomas A. Tenney, and Thadious M. Davis, eds., *Satire or Evasion? Black Perspectives on "Huckleberry Finn"* (Durham: Duke University Press, 1992).

8 Jonathan Arac, *Huckleberry Finn as Idol and Target: The Functions of Criticism in Our Time* (Madison: University of Wisconsin Press, 1997).

9 Robert Penn Warren, "Mark Twain," in *New and Selected Essays* (New York: Random House, 1989), 114.

10 Lionel Trilling, *The Liberal Imagination: Essays on Literature and Society* (New York: Viking, 1950), 9.

11 Myra Jehlen, "Banned in Concord: *Adventures of Huckleberry Finn* and Classic American Literature," in Robinson, *Cambridge Companion to Mark Twain*, 113, 96, 114. See also Sacvan Bercovitch's argument that this book, whose portrayal of Huck and Jim on the river has been taken as the emblem of the ideal society, "makes for a savagely funny obituary to the American dream" ("Deadpan Huck," *Kenyon Review* 24 [2002]: 90–134, quotation at 134).

12 Jehlen, "Banned in Concord," 113.

13 David Hollinger, "National Culture and Communities of Descent," *Reviews in American History* 26 (1998): 323.

14 Michael Schudson, *The Good Citizen: A History of American Civic Life* (New York: Free Press, 1998).

15 Quoted in Louis J. Budd, *Mark Twain: Social Philosopher* (Bloomington: Indiana University Press, 1962), 107. See also Roy Blount Jr., "Mark Twain's Reconstruction," *Atlantic Monthly* 288 (2001): 67–81, quotation at 80. On Twain's mugwumpery, see James S. Leonard, "Mark Twain and Politics," in *A Companion to Mark Twain*, ed. Peter Messent and Louis J. Budd (Oxford: Blackwell, 2005), 94–108.

16 *Mark Twain's Autobiography*, ed. Albert Bigelow Paine (New York: Harper and Brothers, 1924), 2:15.

17 Ibid., 8.

18 An example of classical republican thought is Ansaldo Ceba's sixteenth-century *The Citizen of a Republic*, which was translated in an 1845 U.S. edition dedicated to John Quincy Adams. Mugwumpian in having a chapter titled "The Citizen Must Have No Party But Country, and Strive to Reconcile All Enmities," it also insists that independence depends upon "advantages of fortune," such as "nobility, wealth, pure fame, honor, children, and political influence" (*The Citizen of a Republic: What Are His Rights, His Duties, and Privileges, and What Should Be His Education*, trans. C. Edwards Lester [New York: Paine and Burgess, 1845], 154, 28).

19 Charles W. Eliot, "What Is a Liberal Education?," *Century* 28 (1884): 203–12, quotation at 207.

20 Gerald W. McFarland, *Mugwumps, Morals, and Politics, 1884–1920* (Amherst: University of Massachusetts Press, 1975), 129.

21 Samuel Warren and Louis Brandeis, "The Right to Privacy," *Harvard Law Review* 4 (1890): 193–220.

22 L. E. Fredman, *The Australian Ballot: The Story of an American Reform* (East Lansing: Michigan State University Press, 1968).

23 Schudson, *Good Citizen*, 170.

24 Jehlen, "Banned in Concord," 95.

25 Frederick Anderson, William M. Gibson, and Henry Nash Smith, eds., *Selected Mark Twain–Howells Letters, 1872–1910* (Cambridge: Belknap Press of Harvard University Press, 1967), 235, 237.

26 Ibid., 236, 239, 240.

27 Trilling, *Liberal Imagination*, ix.

28 "What Is Liberalism?," *Life*, January 7, 1946, 26.

29 Trilling, *Liberal Imagination*, x, xiv, xv.

30 Ibid., 101.

31 Ibid., 112–13, 108.

32 Jeremy Larner, "Politics and the Novel," a special edition of *Los Angeles Times Book Review*, August 13, 2000, 17. Larner illustrates Arac's claim that many champions of *Huckleberry Finn* show little evidence of reading the book with any care. Moralistically demanding that every literate American know who spoke Huck's famous line about going to hell, he locates the line in the wrong chapter; he has Aunt Sally, not Miss Watson, set Jim free; and he speaks of "Nigger Jim" although the phrase never appears in *Huckleberry Finn* itself.

33 The still-unsurpassed reading of the ending is Henry Nash Smith, "Introduction," in *Adventures of Huckleberry Finn* (Boston: Houghton Mifflin, 1958), v–xxix.

34 Raymond Williams, *Marxism and Literature* (Oxford: Oxford University Press, 1977), 128–35.

35 Bernard DeVoto, *Mark Twain's America* (Moscow: University of Idaho Press, 1932), 320.

36 *Mark Twain's Autobiography*, 2:21.

37 Anderson, Gibson, and Smith, *Selected Letters*, 241.

38 Budd, *Mark Twain*, 63–85, 86–110.

39 Howells, *My Mark Twain*, 35.

40 On the book's composition, see Walter Blair, "When Was *Huckleberry Finn* Written?," *American Literature* 30 (1958): 1–25, and Victor A. Doyno, *Writing "Huck Finn": Mark Twain's Creative Process* (Philadelphia: University of Pennsylvania Press, 1991).

41 Evan Carton, "Speech Acts and Social Action: Mark Twain and the Politics of Literary Performance," in Robinson, *Cambridge Companion to Mark Twain*, 167.

42 James M. Cox, *Mark Twain: The Fate of Humor* (Princeton: Princeton University Press, 1966), 175.

43 Lynn Altenbernd, "Huck Finn, Emancipator," *Criticism* 1 (1959): 298–307, quotation at 299.

44 See Aviam Soifer, "Reviewing Legal Fictions," *Georgia Law Review* 20 (1986): 871–915, esp. 886–87.

45 Mark Twain, *Adventures of Huckleberry Finn*, ed. Walter Blair and Victor Fischer (Berkeley: University of California Press, 1984), 165. Future references will be included parenthetically in the text.

46 Louis J. Budd, "The Southern Currents under Huck Finn's Raft," *Mississippi Valley Historical Review* 46 (1959): 222–37, quotation at 227.

47 Shirley Fisher Fishkin is the most vocal advocate of reading *Huckleberry Finn* allegorically in this way. She also provides a comprehensive summary of the best of these readings. See *Was Huck Black? Mark Twain and African-American Voices* (New York: Oxford University Press, 1993), 68–76.

48 Mark Wahlgren Summers, *Rum, Romanism, and Rebellion: The Making of a President, 1884* (Chapel Hill: University of North Carolina Press, 2000).

49 Francis Lieber, *On Civil Liberty and Self-Government: Enlarged Edition in One Volume* (Philadelphia: Lippincott, 1859), 267.

50 Fishkin, *Was Huck Black?*, 73–75. Wieck, *Refiguring "Huckleberry Finn,"* offers an extensive analysis, but, rather than seeing how the Supreme Court's decision alters the book's racial politics from its moment of composition to its moment of production, Wieck attributes almost prophetic power to Twain, arguing that the national climate that helped to produce the Court's decision "aided Twain to clarify and resolve the difficulty he had been having finishing a novel in which the interrelated humanity and rights of a black man and a white boy were of central importance" (63). See also Harold Beaver, "Introduction," in *Adventures of Huckleberry Finn* (London: Allen and Unwin, 1987), esp. 38.

51 Frederick Douglass, *Life and Times of Frederick Douglass: Written by Himself* (1892; reprint, New York: Collier Books, 1962), 501. After Garfield won the 1880 election, Twain urged him to reappoint Douglass marshal of the District of Columbia. Calling Douglass a "personal friend," Twain praised his "brave, long crusade for the liberties and elevation of his race" (*The Life and Writings of Frederick Douglass*, ed. Philip S. Foner [New York: International Publishers, 1955], 4:114).

52 Mark Twain, *Life on the Mississippi* (New York: Limited Editions Club, 1944), 415.

53 Ibid., 412.

54 Budd, *Mark Twain*, 99.

55 Jay B. Hubbell, *The South in American Literature* (Durham: Duke University Press, 1954), 822.

56 Quoted in Blount, "Twain's Reconstruction," 80.

57 Mark Twain, "Consistency," in *The Complete Essays of Mark Twain*, ed. Charles Neider (Garden City, N.Y.: Doubleday, 1963), 576–83, quotations at 580, 580, 577, 582–83.

58 Even debunkers assume that the book celebrates what Arac calls its "imaginative construction of the autonomous individual" (*Idol and Target*, 153). Criticizing what others champion, they overlook Jehlen's insight that the book questions individualism while also celebrating it.

59 Warren, "Mark Twain," 121.

60 Trilling, *Liberal Imagination*, 109.

61 Ibid.

62 Steven Mailloux, *Rhetorical Power* (Ithaca: Cornell University Press, 1989), 78, 79.

63 William Dean Howells, "Mark Twain," reprinted in *My Mark Twain*, 141. The essay first appeared September 1882 in *Century*.

64 See Soifer, "Reviewing Legal Fictions," 886–87.

65 Morton G. White, *Social Thought in America* (New York: Viking, 1949).

66 Stacey Margolis, "Huckleberry Finn; or, Consequences," *PMLA* 116 (2001): 333, 332, 333.

67 Tom Quirk, "Life Imitating Art: Huckleberry Finn and Twain's Autobiographical Writings," in *One Hundred Years of Huckleberry Finn: The Boy, His Book, and American Culture*, ed. Robert Sattelmeyer and J. Donald Crowley (Columbia: University of Missouri Press, 1984), 41–55, quotation at 53. See also Neil Schmitz, "Mark Twain's Civil War: Humor's Reconstructive Writing," in Robinson, *Cambridge Companion to Mark Twain*, 74–92.

68 Mark Twain, "The Private History of a Campaign that Failed," *Century* 31 (1885): 193–204, quotations at 203.

69 John Gerber, "Mark Twain's 'Private Campaign,'" *Civil War History* 37 (1955): 37–60, quotation at 42.

70 Mailloux, *Rhetorical Power*, 72.

71 Ibid., 64. Blaine quotations are from "Smarting under Defeat / Mr. Blaine Makes a very Foolish Speech. / He Waves the Bloody Shirt Vigorously, and Plays upon the Prejudices of the Ignorant," *New York Times*, November 19, 1884, 1.

72 James Bryce, "Thoughts on the Negro Problem," *North American Review* 153 (1891): 641–60, quotation at 650.

73 See Hugh J. Dawson, "The Ethnicity of Huck Finn—and the Difference It Makes," *American Literary Realism* 30 (1998): 1–16. Arac ignores Pap's Irish background when he accuses Twain of simplifying the country's ethnic complexity by giving us an "America of WASPs and slaves" (*Idol and Target*, 107). On Twain's ethnic caricatures, see Henry B. Wonham, *Playing the Races: Ethnic Caricature and American Literary Realism* (New York: Oxford University Press, 2004) and "'I Want a Real Coon': Mark Twain and Late-Nineteenth-Century Ethnic Caricature," *American Literature* 72 (2000): 117–52.

74 Thomas Nast, "The Ignorant Vote—Honors Are Easy," *Harper's Weekly*, December 9, 1876.

75 "The Curious Republic of Gondour," *Atlantic Monthly* 36 (1875): 461–63, quotations at 461.

76 Mailloux, *Rhetorical Power*, 64 n. 13.

77 Arac mistakenly claims that Pap is the "only person in the book to use the language of 'rights'" (*Idol and Target*, 55).

78 "A Grave Responsibility," *Century* 29 (1885): 462.

79 "Definition of the Term 'Mugwump,'" *Cleveland Gazette*, December 5, 1885, 1.

80 Summers, *Rum, Romanism, and Rebellion*, 309.

81 Quoted in Ray Ginger, *The Age of Excess* (New York: Macmillan, 1965), 74.

82 David Donald, "Introduction," in *Essays on the Civil War and Reconstruction*, by William Archibald Dunning (1897; reprint, New York: Harper and Row, 1965), viii.

83 General James S. Brisbin and William Ralston Balch, *The Life and Public Career of James A. Garfield* (Philadelphia: Hubbard Brothers, 1881), 561.

84 Arac, *Idol and Target*, 92–98; Jane Smiley, "Say It Ain't So, Huck: Second Thoughts on Mark Twain's 'Masterpiece,'" *Harper's*, January 1996, 61–66. Tourgée politely waited until after Stowe died to utter criticism, but when he did, he noted the inaccuracy of her treatment of slaves, who are "in intellectual and moral qualities simply 'blacked Yankees'" ("The Literary Quality of *Uncle Tom's Cabin*," *Independent*, August 20, 1896, 3–4, quotation at 3).

85 Albion W. Tourgée, *Bricks without Straw* (New York: Fords, Howard, and Hulbert, 1880).

86 Alan Gribben, *Mark Twain's Library: A Reconstruction* (Boston: G. K. Hall, 1980), 2:707. Twain bought the book on October 6, 1880. It is also possible that he bought Tourgée's *A Fool's Errand* in an 1880 edition that also included Tourgée's account of the Ku Klux Klan, *The Invisible Empire*.

87 Albion W. Tourgée, *Letters to a King* (New York: Phillips and Hunt, 1888), 235, 237.

88 Albion W. Tourgée, *An Appeal to Caesar* (New York: Fords, Howard, and Hulbert, 1884), 72.

89 Albion W. Tourgée, "Aaron's Rod in Politics," *North American Review* 132 (1881): 139–62, quotation at 145.

90 Tourgée, *Appeal*, 378.

91 Ibid.

92 Tourgée, *Letters*, 5, 7, 6, 133, 134, 198.

93 Ibid., 233, 135, 6.

94 Tourgée, *Appeal*, 379.

95 Another exception is Huck's alliance with Mary in the Wilks episode.

96 Richard Adams provides a stimulating comparison of Twain and Tourgée in an unpublished manuscript, "The Genuine Article: Albion Winegar Tourgée, Mark Twain, and the Logic of the Genuine."

97 Tourgée, *Letters*, 205, 7–8, 202–3, 201.

98 Ibid., 201.

99 Charlie Reilly, "An Interview with John Barth," *Contemporary Literature* 22 (1981): 1–23, quotation at 4.

100 Lieber, *On Civil Liberty and Self-Government*, 271.

101 Richard Poirier, *A World Elsewhere: The Place of Style in American Literature* (New York: Oxford University Press, 1966).

102 Martin Green, *Re-Appraisals: Some Commonsense Readings in American Literature* (New York: Norton, 1965), 136. See also Julius Lester, "Morality and *Adventures of Huckleberry Finn*," *Mark Twain Journal* 22 (1984): 43–46. Lester writes, "Twain's notion of freedom is the simplistic one of freedom from restraint and responsibility" (46).

103 Tourgée, *Letters*, 201.

104 T. S. Eliot, "The Boy and the River: Without Beginning or End," introduction to *Adventures of Huckleberry Finn* (New York: Chanticleer, 1950), xiii.

105 See Schmitz, "Mark Twain's Civil War," and "Mark Twain in the Twenty-First Century," *American Literary History* 16 (2004): 117–26.

106 Tourgée, *Letters*, 6.

107 Quoted in Louis B. Rubin, *George Washington Cable* (New York: Pegasus, 1969), 218–19.

108 Albion Winegar Tourgée, "The South as a Field for Fiction," *Forum* 6 (1888): 404–13.

109 For accounts of the tour, see Guy A. Cardwell, *Twins of Genius* (East Lansing: Michigan State University Press, 1953); Arlin Turner, *Mark Twain and George W. Cable: The Record of a Literary Friendship* (East Lansing: Michigan State University Press, 1960); and Stephen Railton, "The Twain–Cable Combination," in Messent and Budd, *Companion to Mark Twain*, 172–85.

110 George Washington Cable, "The Freedman's Case in Equity," *Century* 29 (1885): 418.

111 Henry W. Grady, "In Plain Black and White," *Century* 29 (1885): 910.

112 Arthur G. Pettit, *Mark Twain and the South* (Lexington: University of Kentucky Press, 1974), 131.

113 Grady, "In Plain Black and White," 910; Summers, *Rum, Romanism, and Rebellion,* 188.

114 For a different account of the delayed publication, see L. Terry Oggel, "Speaking Out about Race: 'The United States of Lyncherdom' Clemens Really Wrote," *Prospects* 25 (2000): 115–58.

115 Willis Wager, "Note," in Twain, *Life on the Mississippi,* 385.

116 The best studies of the book's reception are Winfried Fluck, *Ästhetische Theorie und Literaturwissenschaftliche Methode: Eine Untersuchung Ihres Zusammenhangs am Beispiel der Amerikanischen Huck Finn-Kritik* (Stuttgart: Metzler, 1975); Victor Fischer, "Huckleberry Finn Reviewed: The Reception of *Huckleberry Finn* in the United States, 1885–1897," *American Literary Realism* 16 (1983): 1–57; Mailloux, *Rhetorical Power*; and Arac, *Idol and Target.*

117 W. S. Scarborough, "The Negro in Fiction as Portrayer and Portrayed," *Southern Workman and Hampton School Record* 28 (1899): 358–61.

118 Charles W. Chesnutt, "The Negro in Books," in *Essays and Speeches,* ed. Joseph R. McElrath Jr., Robert C. Leitz III, and Jesse S. Crisler (Stanford: Stanford University Press, 1999), 426–40. Chesnutt knew Twain well enough to be invited to the famous dinner for him at Delmonicos in 1905.

119 Jay B. Hubbell, *Who Are the Major American Writers?* (Durham: Duke University Press 1972), 138.

120 In "Deadpan Huck" Sacvan Bercovitch provides a brilliant rejoinder to this tradition of criticism with his analysis of the book's use of humor.

121 B. T. Washington, "Mark Twain," *North American Review* 191 (1910): 828–30, quotation at 829.

122 Sterling Brown, *The Negro in American Fiction* (Washington, D.C.: Howard University Press, 1937), 68.

123 Ralph Ellison, "The Seer and the Seen" (1946) and "Change the Joke and Slip the Yoke" (1958), both reprinted in *Shadow and Act* (New York: Random House, 1964), 24–44, 45–59.

124 Peter J. Kellogg, "Civil Rights Consciousness in the 1940s," *Historian* 42 (1979): 18–41, quotation at 25.

125 Arthur M. Schlesinger Jr., *The Vital Center: The Politics of Freedom* (Boston: Houghton Mifflin, 1949), 190.

126 Schudson, *Good Citizen,* 8.

127 Arac, *Idol and Target,* 9.

128 See Peaches Henry, "The Struggle for Tolerance: Race and Censorship in *Huckleberry Finn*," in Leonard, Tenney, and Davis, eds., *Satire or Evasion?*, 25–55.

129 Howells, "Mark Twain," 57.

130 Howells, "Mark Twain: An Inquiry," in *My Mark Twain,* 169–70. The essay appeared originally in 1901 in *North American Review.*

131 Ernest Hemingway, *Green Hills of Africa* (New York: Scribner, 1935), 20–21.

132 Howells, "Mark Twain: An Inquiry," 169.

133 Ibid., 170.

134 Thomas Dixon also wrote a novel and a play celebrating Lincoln. See *The Southerner: A Romance of the Real Lincoln* (New York: Grosset and Dunlap, 1913) and *A Man of the People: A Drama of Abraham Lincoln* (New York: Appleton, 1920).

135 Henry W. Grady, "The New South," in *The Life of Henry W. Grady, Including His Writings and Speeches*, ed. Joel Chandler Harris (1890; reprint, New York: Haskell House, 1972), 85.

136 Mark Twain, "Lincoln's Birthday," in *Plymouth Rock and the Pilgrims and Other Salutary Platform Performances*, ed. Charles Neider (New York: Harper and Row, 1985), 198–200, quotations at 200.

137 Justice Brown writes, "'The great principle,' said Chief Justice Shaw, p. 206, 'advanced by the learned and eloquent advocate for the plaintiff,' (Mr. Charles Sumner,) 'is, that by the constitution and laws of Massachusetts, all persons without distinction of age or sex, birth or color, origin or condition, are equal before the law'" (*Plessy v. Ferguson*, 163 U.S. 537 [1896] at 544).

138 James Bryce, *The American Commonwealth* (1888; reprint, Indianapolis: Liberty Fund, 1995), 2:1186 n. 19, 1181.

139 James Bryce, *The Hindrances to Good Citizenship* (New Haven: Yale University Press, 1909), 7, 127. The introduction, the chapter on indolence, and the conclusion were published for teaching purposes in a Riverside series edited by Ada L. F. Snell, an English professor at Mount Holyoke College: James Bryce, *Promoting Good Citizenship* (Boston: Houghton Mifflin, 1909).

140 Charles W. Chesnutt, "Abraham Lincoln: An Appreciation," in McElrath, Leitz, and Crisler, *Essays and Speeches*, 349–52, quotation at 350.

141 Garry Wills, *Lincoln at Gettysburg: The Words That Remade America* (New York: Simon and Schuster, 1992), 148, 52, 99.

Chapter 6

1 On issues of gender in *China Men*, see Donald C. Goellnicht, "Tang Ao in America: Male Subject Positions in *China Men*," in *Reading the Literatures of Asian Americans*, ed. Shirley Geok-lin Lim and Amy Ling (Philadelphia: Temple University Press, 1992), and Leilana Nishime, "Engendering Genre: Gender and Nationalism in *China Men* and *The Woman Warrior*," *MELUS: The Journal of the Society for the Study of Multi-Ethnic Literatures of the United States* 20 (1995): 67–82.

2 Maxine Hong Kingston, *China Men* (New York: Random House, 1980), 155. Future references will be included parenthetically within the text. Kingston's legal history is not always accurate. For instance, she lists the victory of *Yick Wo v. Hopkins* as 1896 instead of 1886, and her account of this case and the 1879 constitution is a bit misleading.

3 Gary J. Jacobsohn, *Apple of Gold: Constitutionalism in Israel and the United States* (Princeton: Princeton University Press, 1993), 89.

4 Thomas Bailey Aldrich, *The Poems* (Boston: Houghton Mifflin, 1897), 275–76.

5 Erika Lee, *At America's Gates: Chinese Immigration during the Exclusion Era, 1882–1943* (Chapel Hill: University of North Carolina Press, 2003); Mae M. Ngai, *Impossible Subjects: Illegal Aliens and the Making of Modern America* (Princeton: Princeton Uni-

versity Press, 2004). Previous work by Lucy E. Salyer documents how cases involving Chinese created judicial authority for that development; see *Laws Harsh as Tigers: Chinese Immigrants and the Shaping of Modern Immigration Law* (Chapel Hill: University of North Carolina Press, 1995). In addition, Charles McClain, *In Search of Equality: The Chinese Struggle against Discrimination in Nineteenth-Century America* (Berkeley: University of California Press, 1994), gives an excellent general account of the legal battles as well as the agency of the Chinese in appropriating the U.S. legal system to protect their rights.

6 In re Ah Lung, the Chinese-Laborer from Hawing Kong, 18 F. 28 (C.C.D. Cal. 1883). See McClain, *In Search of Equality*, 155–56.

7 Act of March 26, 1790, ch. 3, #1, 1 Stat. 103 (repealed 1795).

8 Act of July 14, 1870, ch. 254, #7, 16 Stat. 256.

9 19 How. 393 (1857) at 404.

10 19 How. 393 (1857) at 416.

11 Prior to the Fourteenth Amendment U.S. citizenship itself was somewhat limited, since the division of powers between federal and state governments often made state citizenship more important in terms of protecting rights than U.S. citizenship. The Fourteenth Amendment changed that situation, and even though, as we saw in Chapter 4, the Supreme Court reasserted various powers of state citizenship in *Cruikshank*, the Civil Rights Cases, and others, the scope of U.S. citizenship has come to dominate.

12 See *The Statutes at Large of the United States of America from December, 1891, to March 1893, and Recent Treaties, Conventions, and Executive Proclamations* (Washington, D.C.: Government Printing Office, 1893), 27:25–26.

13 McClain, *In Search of Equality*, 202–23; Salyer, *Laws Harsh as Tigers*, 46–52; Anna Pegler-Gordon, "Chinese Exclusion, Photography, and the Development of U.S. Immigration Policy," *American Quarterly* 58 (2006): 51–77.

14 T. J. Geary, "Should the Chinese Be Excluded?," *North American Review* (1892): 58–67.

15 Ibid., 63. On this widespread belief, see Andrew Gyory, *Closing the Gate: Race, Politics, and the Chinese Exclusion Act* (Chapel Hill: University of North Carolina Press, 1998).

16 Geary, "Should the Chinese Be Excluded?," 62.

17 Ibid., 64–65. For a discussion of the duties that we owe to people beyond our borders, see "Symposium on Duties beyond Borders," *Ethics* 98 (1988): 647–756.

18 Geary, "Should the Chinese Be Excluded?," 65–66.

19 *Fong Yue Ting v. United States*, 149 U.S. 698 (1893) at 724, 723.

20 Salyer, *Laws Harsh as Tigers*, 54.

21 On the exclusion of Chinese women, see Sucheng Chan, "The Exclusion of Chinese Women," in *Entry Denied: Exclusion and the Chinese Community in America, 1882–1943*, ed. Sucheng Chan (Philadelphia: Temple University Press, 1991), 109–23, and Eithne Luibhéid, *Entry Denied: Controlling Sexuality at the Border* (Minneapolis: University of Minnesota Press, 2002), 41–54.

22 "Brief on Behalf of the U.S.," November 19, 1895, 6, folder 11198, box 594, Admiralty Case Files, Records of the U.S. District Court, RG 21, National Archives, Pacific Region, San Bruno, Calif.

23 "Opinion of Judge Morrow," January 3, 1896, 14, ibid.

24 Brief on Behalf of the Appellant, *United States v. Wong Kim Ark*, 169 U.S. 649 (1898) (No. 904), 34.

25 See, for instance, George D. Collins, "Are Persons Born within the United States Ipso Facto Citizens Thereof?," *American Law Review* 18 (1884): 831–38, and "Citizenship by Birth," *American Law Review* 29 (1895): 385–95; Henry C. Ide, "Citizenship by Birth—Another View," *American Law Review* 30 (1896): 241–52, and "Citizenship," *American Law Journal* 2 (1885): 3–6; John A. Hayward, "Who Are Citizens?," *American Law Journal* 2 (1885): 315–19; Marshall B. Woodworth, "Citizenship of the United States under the Fourteenth Amendment," *American Law Review* 30 (1896): 535–55, and "Who Are Citizens of the United States? Wong Kim Ark Case—Interpretation of Citizenship Clause of Fourteenth Amendment," *American Law Review* 32 (1898): 554–61; Boyd Winchester, "Citizenship in Its International Relation," *American Law Review* (1897): 504–13; Simeon E. Baldwin, "The Citizen of the United States," *Yale Law Journal* 2 (1893): 85–94, and "The People of the United States," *Yale Law Journal* 8 (1899): 159–67; "Comment," *Yale Law Journal* 7 (1898): 366–67; "Citizenship of Children of Alien Parents," *Harvard Law Review* 12 (1898): 55–56 (reprinted in *Central Law Review*, 46 [1898]: 498); and "Comment," *Central Law Review* 42 (1896): 299–300.

Discussions were influenced by two treatises on citizenship published in the late nineteenth century: Alexander Porter Morse, *A Treatise on Citizenship by Birth and Naturalization, with Reference to the Law of Nations, Roman and Civil Law, Law of the United States of America, and the Law of France* (Boston: Little, Brown, 1881), and Prentiss Webster, *A Treatise on the Law of Citizenship in the United States Treated Historically* (Albany: Matthew Bender, 1891).

For more recent analysis of *Wong Kim Ark*, see Owen M. Fiss, *Troubled Beginnings of the Modern State, 1888–1910* (New York: Macmillan, 1993), 313–15, and Charles J. McClain, "Tortuous Path, Elusive Goal: The Asian Quest for American Citizenship," *Asian Law Journal* 2 (1995): 33–60.

26 On *Calvin's Case* and its influence on the United States, see Polly J. Price, "Natural Law and Birthright Citizenship in *Calvin's Case* (1608)," *Yale Journal of Law and the Humanities* 9 (1997): 73–145.

27 169 U.S. 649 (1898) at 655. Future references will be included parenthetically within the text. Not on the Court when the case was argued, Justice Joseph McKenna did not take part in the decision.

28 112 U.S. 94 (1884) at 102.

29 Partially in response to *Elk*, the Dawes Act of 1887 allowed Native Americans who showed themselves competent in managing land allotments to become citizens. The 1924 Citizenship Act then extended citizenship to all Native Americans, making the jurisdictional issue in terms of citizenship irrelevant.

30 Quoted in Rogers Smith, *Civic Ideals: Conflicting Visions of Citizenship in U.S. History* (New Haven: Yale University Press, 1997), 313.

31 Collins, "Citizenship by Birth," 386–87. Collins makes a similar argument in his 1884 essay "Are Persons Born within the United States Ipso Facto Citizens Thereof?," 832.

32 19 How. 393 (1857) at 418.

33 The majority could, of course, respond that the change in language from the 1866 Civil Rights Act to the Fourteenth Amendment indicated a significant change in intention.

34 Collins, "Citizenship by Birth," 389–90.

35 112 U.S. 94 (1884) at 102.

36 Smith, *Civic Ideals*, 3.

37 Étienne Balibar, "Subjection and Subjectivation," in *Supposing the Subject*, ed. Joan Copjec (New York: Verso, 1994), 11. Balibar argues that Heidegger irreversibly challenged this way of thinking and then turns to citizenship to challenge Heidegger's revision. The more accurate explanation, according to Balibar, is that "the men of 1776 and 1789" began "to think of themselves as free subjects, and thus to identify liberty and subjectivity" because in "conquering and constituting their political citizenship" they "had abolished the principle of their subjection" (11–12).

38 J. G. A. Pocock, *The Machiavellian Moment: Florentine Political Thought and the Atlantic Republican Tradition* (Princeton: Princeton University Press, 1975).

39 *Downes v. Bidwell*, 182 U.S. 244 (1901) at 280.

40 Ibid., 381.

41 112 U.S. 94 (1884) at 121.

42 163 U.S. 537 (1896) at 561. Harlan would prove to be wrong about how southern Jim Crow laws would apply to persons of Chinese ancestry. In *Gong Lum v. Rice* (1927) the Supreme Court upheld Mississippi's ruling that Chinese Americans were members of the "colored races" and could not attend white schools.

43 See McClain, *In Search of Equality*, and Gabriel J. Chin, "The *Plessy* Myth: Justice Harlan and the Chinese Cases," *Iowa Law Review* 82 (1996): 151–82.

44 *Chae Chan Ping v. United States*, 130 U.S. 581 (1889) at 595.

45 *Fong Yue Ting v. United States*, 149 U.S. 698 (1893).

46 *Lem Moon Sing v. United States*, 158 U.S. 538 (1895).

47 163 U.S. 537 at 559.

48 Drawing on Harlan's unpublished law school lectures, Linda Przybyszewski, *The Republic According to John Marshall Harlan* (Chapel Hill: University of North Carolina Press, 1999), 121, shows that he "did not come to proclaim a commitment to the equality of all men before the law because of some abstract Enlightenment ideal of a universal human identity." But even she fails to note that his commitment was to the equality of all citizens before the law, not all men.

49 Quoted in Chin, "*Plessy* Myth," 160.

50 Quoted in Przybyszewski, *Republic According to John Marshall Harlan*, 122.

51 Smith, *Civic Ideals*, 441. Smith supports his interpretation of *Wong Kim Ark* by pointing out that members of the majority as well as the minority had strong anti-Chinese biases. Indeed, at the time the Court, which was essentially the

Plessy Court, had few, if any, cosmopolitan humanists. Only Justice Brewer ruled fairly consistently in favor of the Chinese, and he was frequently a dissenter.

Influenced by Smith, T. Alexander Aleinikoff adds in a footnote that *Wong Kim Ark* "arguably provides a counterexample" to his claim that "cases considering federal authority over immigrants, Indian tribes, and territories reached essentially the same result: that Congress had plenary power to construct the American state and its membership largely immune from judicial review," a power it used to advance its "conception of the United States as a white, Anglo-Saxon nation-state" (*Semblances of Sovereignty: The Constitution, the State, and American Citizenship* [Cambridge: Harvard University Press, 2002], 213 n. 127, 11). Aleinikoff does not mention that *Plessy* dissenter Harlan also dissents in this case.

52 Smith, *Civic Ideals*, 629 n. 89.

53 Peter H. Schuck and Rogers M. Smith, *Citizenship without Consent: Illegal Aliens in the American Polity* (New Haven: Yale University Press, 1985), 79.

54 457 U.S., 202 (1982).

55 Schuck and Smith, *Citizenship without Consent*, 99.

56 Smith, *Civic Ideals*, 441.

57 *Chae Chan Ping v. U.S.*, 130 U.S. 581 at 606.

58 Jacobsohn, *Apple of Gold*, 92. Not everyone affirms such a vision. If Kingston considers *Wong Kim Ark* a "victory," Lisa Lowe, while not discussing the case itself, condemns a "formally equivalent" definition of citizens because it masks persistent racial inequalities from "the racial and ethnic immigrant populations to whom that notion holds out the promise of membership" (*Immigrant Acts: On Asian American Cultural Politics* [Durham: Duke University Press, 1996], 144). But advocacy of formal legal equality in determining eligibility for citizenship should not be confused with arguments for a "color-blind Constitution." Refusal to take race into account in determining who can become a citizen is not necessarily a denial that race can affect the opportunities of citizens living within the polis. For a different attack on the "decorporealizing" abstraction of "formally equivalent" citizenship, see Michael Warner, "The Mass Public and the Mass Subject," in *Habermas and the Public Sphere*, ed. Craig Calhoun (Cambridge: MIT Press, 1992), 377–401. In contrast, see Chantal Mouffe's endorsement of Hannah Arendt's view that "one's identity as a citizen should not be made dependent on one's ethnic, religious or racial identity" (*Dimensions of Radical Democracy: Pluralism, Citizenship, Community* [London: Verso, 1992], 9).

59 *Wong Kim Ark* also affected U.S. imperialism. Since Hawai'i and the insular territories acquired later in 1898 from Spain were clearly under U.S. jurisdiction, those intent on excluding their dark-skinned inhabitants from U.S. citizenship had to find a way to get around *Wong Kim Ark*. In the Insular Cases the majority of the Court found a way to do so by declaring these territories under U.S. jurisdiction but not fully incorporated into the nation. Thus, the citizenship clause of the Fourteenth Amendment did not apply to those born in the insular territories.

60 Robert Post, "Introduction: After Bakke," *Representations* 55 (1996): 8. See also Jürgen Habermas's claim in "Multiculturalism and the Liberal State," *Stan-*

ford Law Review 47 (1995): 849–54, that people should have a right to group membership but also the right to abandon it if it limits their possibilities for development.

61 In a footnote legal historian Salyer urges her readers to turn to *China Men* for "a compelling story of the immigration experience from the Chinese perspective" (*Laws Harsh as Tigers*, 270 n. 129).

62 Josiah Strong, *Our Country: Its Possible Future and Its Present Crisis* (New York: American Home Missionary Society, 1885), 43.

63 Lee, *At America's Gates*, 105.

64 W. E. B. Du Bois, "Strivings of the Negro People," *Atlantic Monthly* 80 (1897): 194–98, quotation at 195.

65 See Werner Sollors, "A Critique of Pure Pluralism," in *Reconstructing American Literary History*, ed. Sacvan Bercovitch (Cambridge: Harvard University Press, 1986), 250–79, and *Beyond Ethnicity: Consent and Descent in American Culture* (New York: Oxford University Press, 1986). See also David Hollinger, *Postethnic America: Beyond Multiculturalism* (New York: Basic Books, 1995).

66 Frederick Jackson Turner, "The Significance of the Frontier in American History," in *The Frontier in American History* (New York: Henry Holt, 1920), 23. For more on the melting pot, see Sollors's unsurpassed chapter, "Melting Pots," in *Beyond Ethnicity*, 66–101.

67 Geary, "Should the Chinese Be Excluded?," 61.

68 *Regents of the University of California v. Bakke*, 438 U.S. 265 (1977) at 400–401.

69 Horace M. Kallen, *Culture and Democracy in the United States: Studies in the Group Psychology of the American Peoples* (New York: Boni and Liveright, 1924). The best critical account of Kallen remains Sollors, "Critique of Pure Pluralism."

70 Mary Antin, *The Promised Land* (1912; reprint, New York: Penguin, 1997), 179. On reactions to Antin calling the Pilgrim fathers "our forefathers," see Sollors, "Critique of Pure Pluralism," 261 n. 15.

71 Roy P. Basler, Marion Dolores Pratt, and Lloyd A. Dunlap, eds., *The Collected Works of Abraham Lincoln* (New Brunswick: Rutgers University Press, 1953), 5:527.

72 Ibid., 4:271.

73 Ibid., 7:23.

74 See David Leiwei Li, "*China Men*: Maxine Hong Kingston and the American Canon," *American Literary History* 2 (1990): 482–502.

75 Basler, Pratt, and Dunlap, *Collected Works*, 5:527.

76 Patricia Linton, "'What Stories the Wind Would Tell': Representation and Appropriation in Maxine Hong Kingston's *China Men*," *MELUS: The Journal of the Society for the Study of Multi-Ethnic Literatures of the United States* 19 (1994): 37–48.

77 Przybyszewski, *Republic According to John Marshall Harlan*, 120.

78 Kenneth L. Karst, *Belonging to America: Equal Citizenship and the Constitution* (New Haven: Yale University Press, 1989).

79 In simultaneously suggesting a diasporic identity and a sense of belonging, Kau Goong's statement supports King-Kok Cheung's argument that a focus on diasporic identity can work in conjunction with Asian American efforts to "claim"

America rather than be in tension with them. Indeed, interaction between dia-sporic and American identities allows both to be continually reconstructed. See King-Kok Cheung, "Re-viewing Asian American Literary Studies," in *An Inter-ethnic Companion to Asian American Literature*, ed. King-Kok Cheung (New York: Cambridge University Press, 1997), 1–36.

80 See my discussion of postnational, transnational, and global citizenships in Chapter 7. See also the special issue "Cities and Citizenship," in *Public Culture 8* (1996). In contrast, see Frederick Buell's argument in *National Culture and the New Global System* (Baltimore: Johns Hopkins University Press, 1994), which is one of many, pointing out that globalization does not abolish national culture; it alters it. Hollinger, *Postethnic America*, 151–52, argues that today's diasporic situation is not as historically unique as someone like Arjun Appadurai claims.

81 "Children of Alien Parents," 56.

82 The original title was *Gold Mountain Man*. See Maxine Hong Kingston, "On Un-derstanding Men," *Hawaii Review* 7 (1977): 43–44.

83 Working within an Althusserian framework, Lowe faults Althusser, nonethe-less, for failing to recognize that sites of interpellation are "not only multiple but also hybrid, unclosed, and uneven" (*Immigrant Acts*, 146). Lowe champions diasporic identities for their capacity to challenge hegemonic state rule that is enforced through rituals of citizenship. But there is no guarantee that such hy-brid subjects will be resistant subjects. In fact, people interpellated as national citizens might have more potential to resist a global capitalist economy than transnational ones. Furthermore, rituals of citizenship are not always in service of the state. A long tradition sees virtuous citizens as those with the courage to question state authority.

84 Shu-mei Shih, "Exile and Intertextuality in Maxine Hong Kingston's *China Men*," in *The Literature of Emigration and Exile*, ed. James Whitlark and Wendell Aycock (Lubbock: Texas Tech University Press, 1992), 65–77.

85 George Bancroft, "The Place of Abraham Lincoln in History," *Atlantic Monthly* 15 [1865]: 757–64, quotation at 764.

86 For Kingston's engagement with Whitman, see *Tripmaster Monkey* (New York: Random House, 1990). See also Xilao Li, "Walt Whitman and Asian American Writers," *Walt Whitman Review* 11 (1993): 179–94.

87 On silences in Kingston's work, see King-Kok Cheung, *Articulate Silences* (Ithaca: Cornell University Press, 1993).

88 On dialogue in other works of "minority" fiction, see Paulla Ebron and Anna Lowenhaupt Tsing, "From Allegories of Identity to Sites of Dialogue," *Diaspora* 4 (1995): 125–51.

Chapter 7

1 Julia Lupton, *Citizen-Saints: Shakespeare and Political Theology* (Chicago: University of Chicago Press, 2005), 215–16.

2 Roy P. Basler, Marion Dolores Pratt, and Lloyd A. Dunlap, eds., *The Collected Works of Abraham Lincoln* (New Brunswick: Rutgers University Press, 1953), 1:112.

3 Hester, Nolan, and Huck all have affinities with Lupton's "citizen-saint." Both a

messenger from a divine world and a civil servant, the citizen-saint inspires new possibilities for citizenship by dramatizing the sacrifices entailed by initiation into civil society. We have already seen how Trilling calls Huck and Jim a community of saints. Hester's saintly aspects are indicated by the religious iconography associated with her; Nolan's, by Danforth calling him "this dear, sainted old man" as well as by the passage he marks in the Bible linking his country to the heavenly city. See Lupton, *Citizen-Saints*, and Edward Everett Hale, "The Man without a Country," *Atlantic Monthly* 7 (1863): 678.

4 Henry Nash Smith, *Virgin Land: The American West as Symbol and Myth* (Cambridge: Harvard University Press, 1950), v.

5 Richard Slotkin, *The Fatal Environment: The Myth of the Frontier in the Age of Industrialization, 1800–1890* (New York: Atheneum, 1985), 16.

6 Robert Penn Warren, "Mark Twain," in *New and Selected Essays* (New York: Random House, 1989), 103–36, quotation at 128.

7 Jay B. Hubbell, *Who Are the Major American Writers?* (Durham: Duke University Press, 1972), 138.

8 E. W. Barrett, "Lessons on American Authors, Nathaniel Hawthorne," *Education* 14 (1894): 417–20.

9 Twain complained to Howells, "I can't stand George Eliot, & Hawthorne & those people; I see what they are at, a hundred years before they get to it, & they just tire me to death" (Frederick Anderson, William M. Gibson, and Henry Nash Smith, eds., *Selected Mark Twain–Howells Letters, 1872–1910* [Cambridge: Belknap Press of Harvard University Press, 1967], 250).

10 Robert Penn Warren, "Hawthorne Revisited: Some Remarks on Hell-Firedness," in *New and Selected Essays*, 69–102, quotation at 88.

11 Nathaniel Hawthorne, *The Letters, 1857–1864*, centenary ed., vol. 18 (Columbus: Ohio State University Press, 1987), 381.

12 *Dred Scott v. Sandford*, 19 Howard 393 (1857) at 416.

13 See Brook Thomas, "Stigmas, Badges, and Brands: Discriminating Marks in Legal History," in *History, Memory, and the Law*, ed. Austin Sarat and Thomas R. Kearns (Ann Arbor: University of Michigan Press, 1999), 249–82.

14 Nathaniel Hawthorne, *The Scarlet Letter*, centenary ed., vol. 1 (Columbus: Ohio State University Press, 1962), 161, 263.

15 Michael Walzer, "The Concept of Civil Society," in *Toward a Global Civil Society*, ed. Michael Walzer (Providence: Berghahn Books, 1995), 7–27, quotation at 7.

16 Reinhold Niebuhr, *Moral Man and Immoral Society: A Study in Ethics and Politics* (New York: Scribner, 1932), xxii–xxiii.

17 From today's perspective Hawthorne clearly committed a major error in discrimination when he wrote a friend in July 1851, "I have not, as you suggest, the slightest sympathy for the slaves; or, at least, not half so much as for the laboring whites, who, I believe, as a general thing, are ten times worse off than the southern negros" (Nathaniel Hawthorne, *The Letters, 1843–1853*, centenary ed., vol. 16 (Columbus: Ohio State University Press, 1985), 456. Despite that alignment of sympathies, I disagree with Eric Cheyfitz's argument that Hawthorne's attitude on slavery should make us stop reading his works—and not simply

because in the same letter Hawthorne indicates that he signed a Free-Soil document on the new Fugitive Slave Law. See Eric Cheyfitz, "The Irresistibleness of Great Literature: Reconstructing Hawthorne's Politics," *American Literary History* 6 (1994): 539–58. Jonathan Arac also uses Hawthorne's position on slavery to determine the book's politics; see Jonathan Arac, "The Politics of *The Scarlet Letter*," in *Ideology and Classic American Literature*, ed. Sacvan Bercovitch and Myra Jehlen (New York: Cambridge University Press, 1986), 247–66. In addition, see Jennifer Fleischner, "Hawthorne and the Politics of Slavery," *Studies in the Novel* 23 (1991): 96–106; Deborah L. Madsen, "'A' Is for Abolition: Hawthorne's Bond Servant and the Shadow of Slavery," *Journal of American Studies* 25 (1991): 255–59; Jay Grossman, "'A' Is for Abolition? Race, Authorship, and *The Scarlet Letter*," *Textual Practice* 7 (1993): 13–30; Laura Hanft Korobkin, "The Scarlet Letter of the Law: Hawthorne and Criminal Justice," *Novel* 30 (1997): 193–217; and Jean Fagan Yellin, "Hawthorne and the Slavery Question," in *A Historical Guide to Nathaniel Hawthorne*, ed. Larry J. Reynolds (New York: Oxford University Press, 2001), 135–64.

18 Harold M. Hyman and William M. Wiecek, *Equal Justice under Law* (New York: Harper and Row, 1982), 505.

19 *Hodges v. United States*, 203 U.S. 1 (1906) at 19.

20 Nathaniel Hawthorne, "Chiefly about War Matters by a Peaceable Man," *Atlantic Monthly* 10 (1862): 43–61, quotation at 48.

21 Roy P. Basler, Marion Dolores Pratt, and Lloyd A. Dunlap, eds., *The Collected Works of Abraham Lincoln* (New Brunswick: Rutgers University Press, 1953), 4:271.

22 Robert Rantoul Jr., "Report on the Abolition of Capital Punishment," in *Memoirs, Speeches, and Writings of Robert Rantoul, Jr.*, ed. Luther Hamilton (Boston: J. P. Jewett, 1854), 439.

23 The best discussion of the move toward the organic, corporate model remains Merle Curti, *The Roots of American Loyalty* (New York: Columbia University Press, 1946), esp. "The Reconstruction of Loyalty," 173–99.

24 Benedict Anderson, *Imagined Communities: Reflections on the Origin and Spread of Nationalism*, rev. ed. (London: Verso, 1991).

25 The distinction is Ferdinand Tönnies's.

26 J. M. Barbalet, *Citizenship* (Minneapolis: University of Minnesota Press, 1988), 2. See also the passage quoted from Berlant in Chapter 1.

27 Quoted in Paul C. Nagel, *One Nation Indivisible: The Union in American Thought, 1776–1861* (New York: Oxford University Press, 1964), 218.

28 Maxine Hong Kingston, *China Men* (New York: Random House, 1980), 171.

29 Louis J. Budd, *Mark Twain: Social Philosopher* (Bloomington: Indiana University Press, 1962), 104.

30 Mark Twain, *Plymouth Rock and the Pilgrims and Other Salutary Platform Performances* (New York: Harper and Row, 1984), 94–98.

31 Hawthorne, "Chiefly about War Matters," 50.

32 Werner Sollors, "Americans All: 'Of Plymouth Rock and Jamestown and Ellis Island': or, Ethnic Literature and Some Redefinitions of 'America,'" <http://www.nyupress.org/americansall/>.

33 Mary Antin, *They Who Knock at Our Gates: A Complete Gospel of Immigration* (Boston: Houghton Mifflin, 1914), 26, 98.

34 Nathaniel Hawthorne, *The Scarlet Letter*, centenary ed., vol. 1 (Columbus: Ohio State University Press, 1962), 11–12.

35 Mary Antin, *The Promised Land* (1912; reprint, New York: Penguin, 1997), 269, 178. Antin once considered "My Country" for the title of her book, noting its echo of Hale's "The Man without a Country." Instead, she uses the title for one of her chapters. In that chapter she quotes Hale's maxim "Personal presence moves the world" (183). I am indebted to Werner Sollors for pointing out these connections. See his "Introduction" and "Explanatory Notes" in ibid., xxvi, 304–5.

36 Virginia McLaughlin Yans, "Mary Antin," in *Dictionary of American Biography*, sup. 4, 1946–1950, ed. John A. Garraty and Edward T. James (New York: Scribner's, 1974), 23.

37 Jim Zwick, ed., *Mark Twain's Weapons of Satire: Anti-Imperialist Writings on the Philippine-American War* (Syracuse: Syracuse University Press, 1992), 186–89, quotations at 188–89.

38 Twain himself did not associate "My country, right or wrong" with Hale's story. In his *Autobiography* he explicitly mentions "The Man without a Country," only to use it against his enemy Bret Harte, whom, he felt, lacked moral convictions. "Harte, in a mild and colorless way, was that kind of man — that is to say, he was a man without a country; no, not a man — man is too strong a term; he was an invertebrate without a country" (Mark Twain, *The Autobiography of Mark Twain: Including Chapters Now Published for the First Time*, ed. Charles Neider [New York: Harper and Brothers, 1959], 303). Twain mistakenly remembers Hale writing his story as the Civil War was about to break out.

39 Zwick, *Mark Twain's Weapons of Satire*, 135, 190–91, 186–88.

40 Zechariah Chafee Jr., *Freedom of Speech* (New York: Harcourt, Brace and Howe, 1920), 366, 371.

41 Charles Lee Lewis, *The Romantic Decatur* (Philadelphia: University of Pennsylvania Press, 1937), 185, and Alexander Slidell Mackenzie, *The Life of Stephen Decatur* (Boston: Charles C. Little and James Brown, 1846), 295.

42 Mackenzie, *Life of Stephen Decatur*, 352–53.

43 Wai Chee Dimock makes a similar point in "Scales of Aggregation: Prenational, Subnational, Transnational," *American Literary History* 18 (2006): 219–28.

44 Linda Bosniak, "Citizenship," in *The Oxford Handbook of Legal Studies*, ed. Peter Crane and Mark Tushnet (New York: Oxford University Press, 2003), 183–201, quotations at 191.

45 Mark Van Doren, *Nathaniel Hawthorne* (New York: Viking, 1949), 201–32.

46 Bosniak, "Citizenship," 191.

47 Edward Everett Hale, *The Man without a Country* (New York: H. M. Caldwell, 1897), xx.

48 Walter F. Eberhardt, "The Man without a Country: The High Peak of Cinema Art," in *The Man without a Country: Illustrated with Scenes from the William Fox Screen Glorification of This Immortal Classic, a Roland V. Lee Production* (New York: Grossett and Dunlap, 1925), 13.

49 David Miller, *Citizenship and National Identity* (Cambridge: Polity Press, 2000), 96.

50 Henry Shue, "Mediating Duties," *Ethics* 98 (1988): 687–704, quotation at 691.

51 Veit Bader, "Fairly Open Borders," in *Citizenship and Exclusion*, ed. Veit Bader (New York: St. Martin's Press, 1997), 28–60, quotation at 57 n. 46.

52 David Hollinger, *Postethnic America: Beyond Multiculturalism* (New York: Basic Books, 1995), 138. Kenneth L. Karst speaks of citizenship's "expanding . . . circle of belonging" (*Belonging to America: Equal Citizenship and the Constitution* [New Haven: Yale University Press, 1989], 3).

53 Hollinger, *Postethnic America*, 141; David Hollinger, "National Culture and Communities of Descent," *Reviews in American History* 26 (1998): 325.

54 One of the first advocates of transnational citizenship was Randolph Bourne in his 1916 essay "Trans-National America." But as Sollors has pointed out, "In order to construct a dynamic pluralistic transnationalism Bourne needed monistic stable ethnic identities based on fixed national origins (that he questioned elsewhere)" ("Americans All").

55 Bosniak, "Citizenship," 191.

56 Judith N. Shklar, *American Citizenship: The Quest for Inclusion* (Cambridge: Harvard University Press, 1991), 4.

57 Hannah Arendt, *Men in Dark Times* (New York: Harcourt, Brace, and World, 1968), 81.

58 Hannah Arendt, *Eichmann in Jerusalem: A Report on the Banality of Evil* (New York: Random House, 1965), 240.

59 Gertrude Himmelfarb, "The Illusions of Cosmopolitanism," in *For Love of Country*, ed. Joshua Cohen (Boston: Beacon Press, 1996), 72–77.

60 Shklar, *American Citizenship*, 1.

Index

16, 218–21; compared to Kingston, 20, 216–17, 225–26; *The House of the Seven Gables*, 33; and sympathy, 33–39, 42, 44–45, 48, 52–54, 144, 249 (n. 25); *The Blithedale Romance*, 35; *The Marble Faun*, 36, 218; as civil servant, 50–51; "The Great Stone Face," 51; "Young Goodman Brown," 52; and view of history, 53; and slavery, 53, 220–22, 227–28; compared to Hale, 54, 223–25, 229; and Lincoln, 223; and treason, 223, 229; "Chiefly about War Matters," 223–24, 227; and view of nation, 223–25, 248–49 (n. 18); and immigration, 229

Hawthorne, Sophia, 35

Hayes, Rutherford, 122, 139

Haywood, John A., 18

Hegel, Georg Wilhelm Friedrich, 46, 248 (n. 12)

Heidegger, Martin, 279 (n. 37)

Hemingway, Ernest, 168, 175

Hendler, Glenn, 3

Henry, Patrick, 58–59, 61–62, 89

Herbert, T. Walter, 34, 36

Higginson, Thomas Wentworth, 55, 69, 84, 255 (n. 1)

Hill, Richard, 126

Himmelfarb, Gertrude, 237

Hobbes, Thomas, 243 (n. 49), 247 (n. 4)

Hodges v. United States, 222

Hofstadter, Richard, 16

Hollinger, David, 7–8, 127, 235, 282 (n. 80)

Holloway, Jean, 56–57, 99

Holmes, Oliver Wendell, 125

Holmes, Oliver Wendell, Jr., 39

Howe, Julia Ward, 99

Howells, William Dean, 20, 23, 32, 125–26, 132–33, 136–37, 146, 148, 167–68, 170–75, 283 (n. 9)

Hubbell, Jay B., 142, 167–68

Hutchinson, Ann, 31

Hutner, Gordon, 50

Ignatieff, Michael, 5, 7

Immigration, xi, 1, 21, 153, 156, 177–215, 222, 226, 228–30, 233, 280 (n. 51); legal/illegal, xi, 202–6, 215, 228; assimilation v. appropriation, 198–202, 218; paper sons, 203, 206. *See also* Antin, Mary; Kingston, Maxine Hong: *China Men*

Immigration and Naturalization Service, 179

Imperialism, 82, 87–89, 105, 109, 120, 230–32, 261 (n. 101), 280 (n. 59)

In re Look Tin Sing, 184

Insular Cases and *United States v. Wong Kim Ark*, 280 (n. 59). *See also Downes v. Bidwell*

Irish, 153–54, 179, 186, 273 (n. 73)

Jackson, Andrew, 16, 33, 45, 47, 53, 83, 128, 130, 224, 254 (n. 57)

Jackson, Robert H., 94–95, 263 (n. 128), 267 (n. 33)

Jacobsohn, Gary, 179, 195

James, Henry, 148, 171–72, 218

James, William, 144

Japanese American internment, 71, 263 (n. 128), 267 (n. 33)

Jay, John, 118

Jefferson, Thomas, 17–18, 20, 73, 81–82; Apostle of Liberty, 17, 83

Jehlen, Myra, 126–27, 132, 272 (n. 58)

Johnson, Andrew, 107, 119

Johnson, Michael P., 263 (n. 124)

Johnson, Reverdy, 121

Johnson, Samuel, 231

Johnson-Reed Act, 179, 278 (n. 29)

Jus sanguinis, 185, 188–89, 194–95, 208

Jus soli, 185, 186–89, 194–95, 208

Kafka, Franz, 97

Karst, Kenneth, 5, 286 (n. 52); *Belonging to America*, 208

Karsten, Peter, 17, 264 (n. 134)

Kellogg, Charles Flint, 125

Kelly, George Armstrong, 16